FOUCAULT AND LITERATURE

FOUCAULT AND LITERATURE

Towards a Genealogy of Writing

Simon During

London and New York

First published 1992
by Routledge
11 New Fetter Lane, London EC4P 4EE

Simultaneously published in the USA and Canada
by Routledge
a division of Routledge, Chapman and Hall Inc.
29 West 35th Street, New York, NY 10001

Typeset in 10/12pt Baskerville by
Intype, London
Printed in Great Britain by
TJ Press (Padstow) Ltd, Padstow, Cornwall

British Library Cataloguing in Publication Data
During, Simon
Foucault and literature : towards a genealogy of writing.
1. Literature. Criticism. Foucault, Michel
I. Title
801.95

Library of Congress Cataloging in Publication Data
During, Simon
Foucault and literature : towards a genealogy of writing / Simon
During.
p.   cm.
Includes bibliographical references (p.   ) and index.
1. English literature—History and criticism—Theory, etc.
2. American literature—History and criticism—Theory, etc.
3. Foucault, Michel—Contributions in criticism.   4. Foucault,
Michel—Views on literature.   5. Foucault, Michel—Influence.
I. Title.
PR21.D87   1992
820.9—dc20   91–17468

ISBN 0–415–01241–4
0–415–01242–2 (pbk)

For Nicholas and Lisa

CONTENTS

ACKNOWLEDGEMENTS

During this book's rather prolonged period of gestation, I have drawn heavily on other people's kindness and tolerance. Professionally, I should like to thank, in particular, Ken Ruthven, Terence Hawkes, Catherine Gallagher, Lisa O'Connell and Anne Maxwell, all of whom responded to earlier drafts – and helped, in various ways, the process of completion.

My original editor, Jane Armstrong, was exceptionally encouraging. The goodwill of my colleagues at the University of Melbourne has sustained me. But it was Lisa and Lisabeth who have really paid the price for this book. May this book provide, somehow, some recompense.

INTRODUCTION
Before reading Foucault

Michel Foucault was a different kind of intellectual from his predecessors, one whose work articulated a new relation both to the institutions in which he worked and to a wider public. By the end of his life, he held a prestigious chair at the Collège de France and his work was leaving its traces, more or less directly, on an extraordinarily wide range of academic research. As Didier Eribon's recent biography makes apparent, it was not a position that he would have achieved, despite the power of his work, had he not become an active member of the French academic system and its patronage networks; had he not, for instance, been involved in the Gaullist reform of higher education in the early sixties (Eribon 1989, 158–61). But, as Eribon also makes clear, his personal history included a suicide attempt, a nervous breakdown, a short period of institutionalization, a police file, accusations of theft as a student and so on. To the end (he was, tragically, to die of complications following his infection with HIV), his gayness remained a source of potential scandal within conservative educational institutions. It might be thought that there is nothing unusual in this: such divisions between the public and the private are common enough, after all. What is remarkable in Foucault's career, though, is the way in which he brought the two sides of his life together. His academic skills, resources and prestige worked in the interest of his personal life and all those who share such lives – the institutionalized, prisoners, the "mad," those whose enjoy sexual acts outside of the so-called "normal," and other victims of socially sanctioned violence.

Foucault's reconciliation of the academic and the marginal or transgressive did not come easily. He kept his own private life private, never publicly reflecting upon the shift of institutional relations that his career represented. Yet, since his death, the conditions that made his work possible are becoming less obscure. It is important, I think, to take note of them in approaching his achievements. Most obviously, during his lifetime, opportunities for serious analysis and publication outside the academy diminished. This meant that, even in France, old "free-floating" intellectuals like Jean-Paul Sartre and Maurice Blanchot were being succeeded by professional teachers and researchers like Foucault. Second, the expansion of student numbers after the Second World War, a world-wide phenomenon, offered academic work a larger constituency than ever before. Writing aimed at readers with a tertiary education and an interest in academic or quasi-academic trends, could become widely recognized, fashionable even – all the more so if it breached traditional disciplinary divisions. Last, and most importantly, during the fifties and sixties established political parties, including the PCF (the French Communist Party), became less and less connected to the actual needs, desires, and interests of individuals. Individual and group identities could be organized around categories, such as age, gender and sexual preference, that a political system based on representative democracy did not in fact represent. It became possible for intellectuals-as-academics to articulate these interests through their scholarly work. And when that opportunity was seized, the present's relation to the past began to change. In particular, an extraordinary new account of modern society sprang to view – one which Foucault expressed most lucidly and freshly. This account also changed perceptions of literature's function and status.

My book offers an interpretation of Foucault's analysis of modern society and culture for students of literature. That is the purpose of its first seven chapters, which introduce his work in roughly chronological order. I have wanted to help disseminate the exciting shifts that his work embodies as widely as possible, presupposing no prior acquaintance with his work. Not that I have felt constrained to repeat his own themes and research: in the second half of my third chapter, for instance, I offer an account of the development of British state power and welfarism in relation both to a particular kind of writing and to literary criticism. And, in my last two chapters, I have tried to move past his work by showing how it has allowed us to re-formulate the terms and methods of literary history. For, in developing his contribution, one also, I think, keeps it alive.

There is a problem with a book which claims, at least in part, to offer an interpretation of Foucault. For he himself often complained about interpretation or what he called "commentary." When he criticized commentary he was dissociating himself from a procedure close to the heart of the modern humanities, falling as they do between the interpretative methodologies that we can call, on the one hand, historicism and, on the other, hermeneutics. Hermeneutics regards interpretation as necessary because it assumes that texts or events lose their original meaning both as time goes by and in the process of communication. Historicism engages in interpretation because it supposes that texts or events conceal, and are ordered by, an absent structure (a "context" or a political "unconscious") that a good reader can bring to light – if not necessarily as a "meaning" then as a condition of possibility. Foucault's argument against interpretation goes like this: to set up textual analysis as a play between origins and texts leads to infinite regression. It is not just that each interpretation, being a text itself, requires further commentary; no text can ever have a moment when it is present to itself. As he bluntly put it: "If interpretation can never be achieved it is simply because there is nothing to interpret" (Foucault 1971b, 187). It is always too late to uncover an "original meaning," a stable "context," so that, as Foucault also wrote, "everything is already interpretation" (ibid.). And the search for textual origins and true meanings has institutional consequences: it allows "good readers" to be grouped together in professions or schools that develop approved procedures and exclude others. Under the domination of interpretative paradigms, literary and cultural pedagogy and research have tended to reconstitute the truth of past moments and writings so as to establish a cultural heritage, rather than, for instance, circulating information, uncovering forgotten voices, debating and working through difficult methodological or theoretical problems.

Through the vicissitudes of his career, Foucault tried not to interpret. Yet few contemporaries have themselves attracted so much commentary. Books and articles about him continue to flow from the presses, sometimes repeating his thought in a tabulated, clear form, sometimes explaining his own influences and place in the contemporary context, sometimes – to take just two instances – arguing that he is really connected to the new right or that, at the very heart of his work, we find an avant-garde literary theorist. His own remarks help explain why: commentary makes its objects attractive in a process which obscures them as it explains them. It generates itself. Of course the widespread fascination with Foucault cannot be explained merely as a product of interpretation's internal and formal law of accumulation. His work is important and fascinating just because, in resisting the disciplinary boundaries and interpretative procedures, it acquired an extraordinary variety. To read it well one must know about, say, biology before Linnaeus (history of science), the theory of social control (sociology), Heidegger's "destruction of metaphysics" (phenomenology), Greek sexual practices (the classics), the experiments of the French new new novel (literary theory/history), the history of punishment in the eighteenth century (social history) and so on. The reason for this richness of subject-matter is not simply that Foucault, working to offer the unrepresented a voice, is no respecter of disciplinary specialization. Rather, he no longer operates in an intellectual context for which it goes without saying that *this* approach is proper to *that* topic, or that *this* topic connects with *that* one – just because that is the way it has traditionally been in academic research. The unproblematic parcelling out of modes of thought to specific topics being no longer possible, Foucault turns to history. Not, however, traditional academic history but one which will help us act in the present, either politically or, as he puts it in his last works, ethically.

3

For him, to write history requires constant, theoretical attention to method-ologies, purposes and effects in the lived-in world. So the diversity of Foucault's work can also be read as a moment in the contemporary crisis of knowledge's reflection on itself. One might say that for Foucault there never are any absolutely good reasons for deciding what counts as know-ledge and what does not. That is why he is drawn to treat of the history of theory – as he does in what perhaps remain his most powerful works, *The Order of Things*, and *The Archaeology of Knowledge*.

Why has this method in the humanities become unyoked from content, why do scholarship and critique find it so difficult to avoid a theoretical self-reflection which is, however, clearly inadequate and, indeed, in decon-struction, articulates its own lack of grounds? The most seductive answer – which Foucault himself broached, and which requires large generalization – again points to the shift in relations between the political and academic work. It is becoming a truism that today we live in a post-revolutionary, post-enlightened age; that the grand ideals of progress, justice, equality, collectivity and universal freedom are no longer fully legitimated. Even the political division between left and right seems to be dissolving along with the belief that an active, enlightened and future-directed spirit can guide, however fitfully, the onward flow of events. Traditionally, the left, from within party politics, guarded and urged on the state's role in fulfilling the promise of the revolutionary epoch – to make society more equal and just; while the right protected individual liberty, especially in the market. Within the marxist tradition, intellectual work was supposed to support and facili-tate the proletariat's coming to power against both the market and its ally, the nation-state. But where enlightened and progressivist discourse, based on a sense that the majority is oppressed and, more importantly, can come to know itself as oppressed, falls silent, who can tell the difference between left and right? With the increasing marginality of the traditional political oppositions and struggles, the conceptual divisions that structured political analysis have also come increasingly to seem peripheral. Terms like "the state," "civil society," "class," "capital" and "the family" no longer pro-vide the categories in which the important political stories need to be told.

All this begs the question of *why* the ideals of the left have lost their legitimation. Foucault offers two, connected answers: first, because the enlightened categories of "justice" and "equality" fail to come into close enough contact with the specific needs and wants of individuals and groups; and second, more originally, because technologies of social administration have become detached from that political apparatus established in the age of revolutions, whose developed form is modern representative democracy.[1] Almost invisibly, power and politics have become disjunct.[2] This is the line of thought that has made Foucault, in Jürgen Habermas's words, "the philosopher of my generation" who "has most lastingly influenced the *Zeitgeist*": and, we might add, a writer whose work leaves traces even

4

where it provokes no commentary (Habermas 1986b, 107). As the ideals of the Left become problematic, so do those of the humanities – not because they belonged to the Left but because they have traditionally been marked as non-political. To the degree that the field of the political is no longer considered to be contained within the state apparatus – within the machinery of elections, legislation and the political parties and so on – but to work on all areas of life, then the humanities lose their legitimacy and confidence. Their task (as they traditionally knew it) was to produce "civilized," civil, impartial selves who might appreciate, understand, critique and preserve the history, tendencies and treasures of their culture outside of any partisanship or self-interest. Such aims are now generally interpreted as idealist and exclusionary. Just as left/right divisions no longer organize political groupings, the humanities no longer transcend power. Increasingly, they have become (seen as) merely another form of training, or a means of transmitting cultural capital. And this shift has profound consequences for the study of literature.

It is because Foucault is the writer who has most carefully thought through these shifts that I have wished to examine and introduce his work. Yet the claim that he provides a new account of modern society and culture ignores certain difficulties. Surprisingly enough, the favourable reception given to Foucault's work in literary studies owes less to its break with the past than to the way that many of its values and protocols are shared with traditional literary criticism.[3] At least since the emergence of criticism as an autonomous discipline, literary studies have never moved very far from a particular account of modernity. Let us remember that F. R. Leavis assiduously attacks that very Jeremy Bentham who turns out to be the promulgator of the "Panopticon" which Foucault will use as an image of modern power in *Discipline and Punish*. Leavis's hatred of what he called "the technologico-Benthamite" is just one instance of a discourse of "counter-modernity" which is as old as the idea of "the modern" itself (Leavis 1972, 122). Another is to be found in the pastoralism and nostalgia of the founding fathers of American "new criticism" – as several recent studies have shown.[4] Foucault may be no pastoralist, nevertheless literary criticism's general orientation towards counter-modernity has predisposed it to receiving his work easily and well. One topic in particular is central to this shared counter-modernity, and that is subjectivity. Critiques of subjectivity have a long history: they were mounted by Hegel and Goethe both of whom scorned the "inwardness" of Hellenized Christianity, and both of whom believed that romanticism, with its privileging of personal experience, its interest in the self's depths, intensified the interiority of modern selves. Modernist writers like T. S. Eliot and Joseph Conrad, for instance (who are certainly not simply champions of modernity), also recognized that inwardness was an effect of bourgeois "interiority," of a middle-class fetishizing of the cosy private sphere. Among intellectuals, disquiet with the notion and value of subjectivity is maintained by Matthew Arnold (in his critique of Wordsworth), the young Marx, the Frankfurt school, Heidegger (who finds the origins of the modern subject in Plato), Leavis and Raymond Williams. Thus, to take some important recent examples influenced by Foucault's work, when Catherine Belsey finds the origins of the "liberal bourgeois subject" in the mid-seventeenth-century revolutionary period; when Francis Barker argues that a new social domain of "depoliticized privacy" appears in England as the "old sovereignty of the Elizabethan period was disassembled," or when Nancy Armstrong argues that modern subjectivity is first articulated in conduct books aimed at domesticating bourgeois women, whatever their disagreements over origins, they are operating absolutely in the mainstream of counter-modern literary studies (Belsey 1985, 33–5; Barker 1984, 10; Armstrong 1987). Within this broad frame of agreement, however, Foucault – and those influenced by him – drag the notion of the subject away from the philosophers and sociologists who deal with abstract categories such as "interiority" or "capitalism." They examine, historically, the technologies of "subjection" by which individuals are formed as individuals. Foucault himself goes on to explore the ways in which individuals can construct and shape their own lives. Whereas his peers, and many of his followers, want to demonstrate and abjure the abstraction to which modern subjectivity is condemned, Foucault wants to analyze the production of individuation, the uses to which it has been put, and, indeed, its benefits. This is another of his contributions to recent thought.

I do not mean to write as if "Foucault" were a name with a single referent. How can it be, covering as it does such an array of topics? And the question of whether this corpus has any unifying thread remains open. Foucault himself set out the nature of the problem when he confessed: "To write a book is a certain way of abolishing the preceding one. Finally one notices – to one's comfort and disappointment – that what one has done is quite close to what one has already written" (1984a, 23). Indeed, he seems to regard the version of himself he produced at each stage of his career as a father-figure to be rejected and destroyed. In a fit of enthusiasm, he even once wished that his works could "self-destruct after use, like fireworks" (1975a, 3). This is disconcerting not just because each period in his consistently adventurous work could rewardingly be further developed, but because he often writes in a tone of unimpeachable authority. However, sons who disown their fathers often also follow in their footsteps, and his work which shifts, rejects and consumes itself does also return again and again to the same topics.

Even if we can account for Foucault's work as a series of histories which question and describe the formation of subjectivity and (with the exception of the last books on Greek ethics) of modernity, it is necessary to remember

6

that it also undergoes profound internal shifts of direction. His most influential commentators in America, Hubert Dreyfus and Paul Rabinow, have
divided his career into four stages:[5]

1. early Heideggerian stage
2. proto-structuralist or archaeological stage
3. genealogical stage
4. ethical stage.

According to this scheme, the first moment in Foucault's career, from
which he later took pains to distance himself, is to be found in his introduction to the translation of Ludwig Binswanger's *Dream and Existence* (1954b),
and is maintained in *Madness and Civilization* (1965; 1st edn, 1961). The
second is ushered in with *The Birth of the Clinic* (1963), and continues to
dominate his work up until *The Archaeology of Knowledge* (1969), its central
expression being *The Order of Things* (1966). The third stage, in which
Foucault, rereading Friedrich Nietzsche, turns to an analysis of power, is
signalled in the essay "Discourse on Language" (1971), and developed
both in *Discipline and Punish* (1975) and the first volume of *The History of
Sexuality* called (except in the English translation) *The Will to Knowledge*
(1976). The final moment in Foucault's career belongs to the last two
volumes of *The History of Sexuality* in which he turns his back on the analysis
both of the modern world and power, to attend to "techniques of self" –
to manners and sexual ethics in the classical and early Christian world.

These divisions ignore two crucial factors. The first is the role that
thinking about literature itself plays in Foucault's thought. It divides his
career in two. In the first period – which finishes in the early seventies –
his work repeatedly praises and analyzes the kind of avant-garde writing
he associates, for instance, with Sade, Artaud, Raymond Roussel and the
French "new new novelists" of the sixties. These writers are not just
important on the sidelines of his work – as if Foucault were only a literary
critic when he was not getting on with the real business of writing history
or theory. On the contrary, he then believed that such writing revealed
something profound and limiting about the relation between language and
the modern world, and thus about knowledge and all cultural practices
whatsoever. For him, at this stage of his career, a certain mode of avant-
garde writing replaces traditional ethics in the modern world. It marks
and transgresses a limit which frames two influential theories of language
– first, the theory that language can be adequately analyzed as a set of
representations which mirror the world (the so-called "correspondence
theory"), and, second, that language forms an internally consistent system
that can unambiguously hook on to the world (the so-called "coherence
theory"). In disrupting these notions of language, transgressive writing (as
it is often called) also aims to clear an ideological space: a space for action,
experimentation, chance, freedom, mobility. It also breaks with the notion

that writing is the product of a single and simple self. The self may be dispersed by transgressive writing because such writing provides its readers with no stable and "realist" linguistic codes by which to position themselves, no author or characters to be identified with. Despite large differences, this belief in the epistemological and political role of advanced writing links Foucault with 1960s contemporaries such as Derrida and Philippe Sollers – who are also heirs to the programme of older novelists and theorists such as Maurice Blanchot and Georges Bataille.

Just before 1970 Foucault turned his back on what he was to call the "theorization of writing" (1980b, 127). It is far too simple to say that the events which caused this turn were the upheavals of May 1968. Later, he refused to locate himself in this way – insisting that at that moment he was in North Africa, writing a (never-to-be-published) book on the painter Manet. Nevertheless, ripples of that moment and its preconditions were not easy to escape. He too is a "soixant huitard." "Without the political opening of those years," he said in a 1977 interview, "I would perhaps not have had the courage . . . to pursue my inquiry in the direction of punishment, prisons, and discipline" (quoted in Ferry and Renaut 1990, xix). And it is then that he turns away from the de-subjectivizing, only tenuously political values and effects buried in *écriture* (writing), to considerations of the roles played by those who write – that is, he begins to think about authors and, more crucially, intellectuals. He does so in part because the Leninist question of who the effective agents of social change *are* dominates 1968 political debate. Avant-garde writing now appears to be bound up with the old aura surrounding the "great writer" – its swansong, in fact. (Obviously, the question is complicated by the fact that avant-garde writing itself is avowedly *not* simply determined by conscious intention or authorial self-expression.) Around 1968, even Sartre, the "great writer" *par excellence*, declared that he would follow rather than lead the demands of those most directly touched by injustice and suffering, and gave up his authority under the banner of that suddenly foregrounded political category, "solidarity." At a crucial moment, Sartre's rather Foucauldian advice to the students was merely "reinvent your own tradition" (Cohen-Solal 1988, 463).

On another plane, Foucault began to believe that the grand theorization of writing and the mythology of the intellectual as the prophetic and privileged voice of large collectivities failed to take into account the way in which quite specific knowledges and techniques have proliferated. Some of these – nuclear science especially – now have effects of life and death, that is universal effects, though whose who have mastered and control them represent no sector of the public, have no clear ethical or political responsibilities or constraints, and may receive little or no fame. The father of the A-bomb, Robert Oppenheimer, was for Foucault the first "specific intellectual." Foucault's perception of the end of the "universal intellectual," who *wrote* and who appealed to a public sphere characterized by the free exchange of writings, led him to concentrate not on experimental writing or the history of knowledge but on the mechanisms of social control and production. After 1968, he would almost always choose his topics not out of an academic interest, or simply as a writer, but as a specific intellectual whose historical techniques could help to change the formations whose genealogies he traces. This did not mean that he stopped being interested in writing or discourse in order to ground his politics on history. Rather, he turned to the production, circulation and intersection of discourses *as* events. Such a project was certainly not quiescent, for specific intellectuals work in "a struggle that concerns their own interests. . . . Such struggles are actually involved in the revolutionary movement to the degree that they are radical, uncompromising and nonreformist, and refuse any attempt at arriving at a new disposition of the same power with, at best, a change of masters" as he wrote at the time (Foucault 1977a, 216). This is, as he also said, they are "revolutionary" in that they wish to change both institutions and consciousness (ibid., 228). Or, as he put it in a much less combative statement in 1983, the specific intellectual must "disengage" those familiar systems of thought which underpin, or form "one body with" our "perceptions, attitudes, behaviour." Here, fifteen years after 1968, the task of defamiliarization requires not just an alliance with the other groups of the disadvantaged and silenced but with those who are closest to – indeed, inside – the practices of our current institutions.[6]

As we have begun to see, Foucault's insistence on taking into account the social role from which he writes must be thought about not just in terms of his own work but in the light of the relations between academics and the French establishment. In an article of unusual interest to anyone thinking about the intellectual community in which Foucault's work appeared, Pierre Bourdieu and Jean-Claude Passeron argue that connection between French sociologists and bureaucrats increased during the sixties. Sociology, and the human sciences in general, had not been intellectually dominant in France, at least since the turn of the century when Émile Durkheim had reigned over the "New Sorbonne." In the sixties, however, in the interests of economic and governmental efficiency, that began to change. A so-called "Commission of Eighteen" was established in 1963 to propose new policy for "literary and scientific instruction," and this led to reforms by the Minister of Education, Christian Fouchet, in 1965.[7] Simultaneously, the education system began to move away from teaching traditional philosophy towards a sociology concerned to be at once modern, to bring about modernization and to question the nature of modernity. The policy advisors articulated views that emerge against a background of journals, clubs, debates in which a select number of figures were expected to generalize across a wide variety of subjects: history, philosophy, literature, sociology, psychology – a more recent figure of this kind would

9

be Alain Minc, whose writings are almost unknown in the anglophone world. As tertiary education increasingly became joined to the apparatuses of modernization and economic productivity, relations between the élite Grands Écoles and the universities directed to a mass clientele became tense. The universities were seen to be providing a perfunctory service to individual students. For Bourdieu and Passeron, Foucault – who was a member of the Commission of Eighteen – is to be positioned at the intersection of two needs: the state's need for activist intellectuals to provide information and expertise, and the students' need for intellectuals who might articulate their dissatisfaction. Foucault's reputation among his peers, they write dismissively,

> derives from the polyphonic talent which accompanies his playing in the long discordant registers of the history of philosophy, the philosophy of history, the history of the sciences and the philosophy of the sciences to compose a philosophy of the history of the sciences which is simultaneously a history of the philosophy of the sciences.
>
> (206)

This "talent," they imply, appealed to the half-educated graduates of the devalued universities.

But, far from accepting the role of the intellectual as a social technician at the service of the administration and modernity, far from playing seer across the various half-mastered registers, Foucault's work after 1968 was fundamentally aimed at disrupting the connections between the establishment and intellectuals. It was directed towards bringing state institutions, like the universities and prisons, into closer contact with their clients, such as prisoners. Even if at the end of his life he wished for alliances with administrators, they remained subversive alliances. Certainly, his work's residual or manifest aestheticism works against the technocratic imperative. It is less orientated towards offering policy analysis within established administrative and governmental frameworks than to reconceptualizing the structures of state administration from the outside – from the distance available to the academy and, even, the media. Indeed, one of the ways he described the project of the latter part of his career was as a critical analysis of that form of political rationality for which the state, its preservation and security, comes first. In particular, he wished to explore the relations of "governmentality" between such states and the individual. And this work on a historical formation in which "people's happiness becomes an element of state strength" (1988c, 158) was implicitly carried out in order to promote forms of happiness that cannot be bound to the state's will to power.

In this light, we can say that Dreyfus and Rabinow's fourfold division ignores not only the importance of literature for Foucault's work, but also its political motives. They read him as if he were simply an academic, a philosopher or a philosophic sociologist rather than also an activist intellectual. This becomes even more distorting in the very last phase of his career – which is, on the surface at any rate, the least political of all, and which has puzzled many of his admirers. Edward Said, for instance, deplores it; he sees it, in a thinly veiled reference to Foucault's personal sexuality, as connected to the private exploration of "different kinds of pleasure" (Said 1984, 9). In the second and third volumes of *The History of Sexuality* and in a series of related essays, Foucault turned to the ways in which individuals form themselves. There he began to investigate the space of private liberty in which the individual has room to work on him or herself rather than be worked on by others (or is passively driven by "psychological" forces). Many reasons have been adduced for this shift – the impact of the time he spent at Berkeley, California and Stephen Greenblatt's work on "Renaissance Self-fashioning" (itself influenced by anthropological approaches to culture and self-formation); the late-seventies political shift of attention away from collective politics towards the politics of personal style, and his disillusion with Shi'ite fundamentalism. (He had originally supported the opposition to the Shah.) Probably more important than any of these was the coming to power of the French Socialist government in 1981. In an interview given at the time, Foucault pointed out, approvingly, how the government rejected popular opinion on its policies on immigration, nuclear weapons and the death sentence, relying instead on a "left-wing logic," but the subsequent path of Mitterand's administration into an amalgam of rationalizing economic management and populism clearly unsettled him.[8] Late in 1983 he was already complaining that the socialists had not thought in sufficient depth about the prison problem, and that he himself, to his regret, had not had any contact with magistrates, politicians or the legal profession (Foucault 1984e, 37). In this situation, his old sensitivity to the difficulties which beset the intellectual in regard to political action gave way to a sense of futility and a new surge of aestheticism, not quite, this time, connected to the hopes of "transgressive writing," but rather to the possibilities of individual "self-governmentality."

The move towards examining the techniques in which individuals fashion themselves is certainly not without precedent in his earlier work. It is true that there the word "ethics" had always carried a negative charge. At the height of his interest in transgression, Foucault had written: "it must be detached from its questionable association to ethics if we want to understand it and to begin thinking from it and in the space that it denotes" (Foucault 1977a, 35). Here he is clearly thinking of ethics, as he does in *History of Madness*, as a "choice against unreason": in that book he was even able to write: "In the classical age, reason is born (*prend naissance*) in the space of the ethical" (Foucault 1961a, 174). However, when Foucault comes to concede that the space of contestation in our culture is not

11

primarily linguistic, then transgression and the ethical may – to some degree – reconcile themselves. He can accept, what had in fact always been true for him, that a way of writing is also a manner of living, as he said about the clumsy style of the hermaphrodite Herculine Barbin (Foucault 1980d, xii). Thus, in an important instance of his drawing together ethics, history writing and transgressive values, he can call the confessions of the nineteenth-century peasant and parricide, Pierre Rivière, "beautiful." For Foucault, Rivière's crime was, in the last instance, expressive: Rivière's purpose in committing murder was precisely to write up the act and its history – which he finally did in jail. It was an attempt to invent a coherent self, to drag his voice out of the reach of the discourses of the authorities and to grab some fame – in which he was, belatedly, successful enough. Thus the aesthetic turn in Foucault's later thought is not quite the immense shift of direction it may appear. The ability to create one's own lifestyle (a word which still leaves a bad taste in the mouth of many intellectuals), to shape an aesthetics of existence, turns out to be a space where liberty is still available to individuals in a society which, as Foucault's genealogical investigations help show, has become increasingly dominated by the concept of "normality" as defined against the "pathological." Of course, this "liberty" stands against the classic, and opposing, formulations of liberalism and social democracy – on the one hand, freedom as formal protection from social intervention and, on the other, freedom as adherence to just and rational laws embodied in the state.

If Foucault's *oeuvre* is difficult in part because it is traversed by a series of unstable breaks and continuities, and because it seems both so near to, and so far from, the traditional biases of the "humanities," it also remains strange for an Anglo-American readership, just because it is French. This, as we have already seen in considering the role of the intellectual, generates more than linguistic difficulties. It has often been noted that one of Foucault's own limits lies in his not taking national differences seriously enough. I suspect that this is a heritage both of his own period as a young man in the French Communist Party and of the intense value given to French nationalism by the (quasi-fascist) right especially from the period of the Dreyfus affair up until the Second World War. Anyway, it is worth drawing attention to the more obvious ways in which the difference between French and Anglo-American histories and societies condition our reading of his work. We should note that he has been enormously successful in the United States and the United Kingdom as much because of, as in spite of, these differences. Generalizations based on French conditions stimulate and provide challenges to general claims based on Anglo-American conditions, and Foucault, unlike most traditional historians, does make such general claims about, for instance, the disciplinary archipelago and modern power. That remains one of his inheritances from a French academic and intellectual scene whose élite, at least until very recently, and

despite Foucault's own declaration of the end of the "universal intellectual," remained confident and glamorous.

To begin with history, France became bourgeois later and more violently
than did Britain and only through a revolution that involves a takeover of
the state apparatus. French state power, both under the Bourbons and
Napoleon, controlled pedagogical, medical, and civil institutions to a much
greater degree than in Britain. It also has a past dominated by Catholicism
rather than Protestantism which perhaps explains why, except for a few
fleeting gestures, Foucault does not take up the Weberian connections
between Protestantism and the emergence of the modern order. He works
against a firmer background of absolutism and statism. France is still in
many ways a more repressive as well as a more centralized or *dirigiste*
society than Britain or America. For instance, there is for us a moment of
shock when we learn that there, as late as the 1970s, only guards, lawyers
and prisoners could enter a prison. Foucault, probably the most influential
thinker about penal institutions in our era, had never been inside one until
he visited Attica in the United States. And, for France, unlike Britain, the
nineteenth century really was a century of revolutions. This means that
the sense that the proletariat's day might come survived right up until the
seventies and perhaps still survives: as late as 1970, Louis Althusser could
declare: "Revolution is now on the agenda" (quoted in Elliot 1987, 225).
In particular, memories of the great Revolution and the 1871 Commune
remain alive – if hidden – in Foucault's work. At least until the 1980s,
the possibility of profound social change occasioned by mass protest and
disruption pervades it, though in the Anglo-American tradition *that* expectation is almost impossible. This is true even if Foucault's work is implicitly
targeted against that kind of leftist thought which considers the Revolution
to be the ground – or the seed – of modern political justice. It is directed
against that thought (at the same time as it absorbs certain of its hopes)
just because the PCF retained its prestige right up until 1968, largely
because of its important and courageous, if sometimes over-glorified role
during the Second World War in resisting the Nazi occupiers and their
collaborators. Foucault's dual resistance to statism and marxism also
means that neither pre-absolutist forms of republicanism and the theories
attached to them (the "civic humanism" that J. G. A. Pocock has examined
so rewardingly) nor economism (the insistence that economic determinants
ultimately ground social events and transformations) have much presence
in his thought.[9] Also, perhaps surprisingly, Foucault never examined the
history of political thought and institutions, at least in his writing as
against his teaching. He places to one side the whole question of the
emergence of the political in the modern era, conceived of either as a
discursive field dominated by the discourse of "natural rights," or (to use
the language of the eighteenth century) as the expression of mercantile
"commerce's" will to consolidate its connections to the state, or, finally,

as an institutional space, based on representation, in which interests may be negotiated and legislation passed. Of course, one reason for this omission is that he emphasizes the neglected question of how power works outside the arena of the political. But another is that France, having the late eighteenth and nineteenth rather than the seventeenth century as its revolutionary era, was in fact slow to shape an autonomous and truly effective arena for political debates and decision-making, preferring varieties of "Caesarism," as Marx pointed out in *The Eighteenth Brumaire*.

Quite apart from politics, historiography, philosophy and literary criticism all had and have a very different shape in France than in the English-speaking world. There, academic history and philosophy, despite the encroachments of sociology, a series of "reforms" in higher education and much restiveness, have retained official and cultural prestige. Perhaps, in part, this is because in France, with its centralized administration, education confers power and career opportunities in a way that more narrow class markers have done in Britain, and, also, because there the market has offered less opportunity for "upward" mobility than it has for Americans. Entry into a Grand École continues to guarantee opportunities for a good career. In France philosophical texts are still taught in secondary schools, Jacques Derrida having helped resist recent technocratic onslaughts on this late gift of the Enlightenment. But literary criticism, as we know it, does not really exist there: that is very much an English discursive formation. In a work on Foucault and *literature*, it is important to give brief notice of some reasons for this, though it is a topic I will return to from a different direction and in more depth at the beginning of chapter 8.

Anglo-American criticism begins in the modern mercantile public sphere, with the eighteenth-century essayists, as part of a civilizing mission. It gains its strength in the stirrings of mass pedagogy in the early nineteenth century and the "cultural hygiene" movement later that century – to be transformed by Arnold, Eliot, Leavis and the New Critics into an enemy of, variously, technocratism, revolution, popular culture, the domination of science, provinciality, introspection and individual or "crackpot" religious enthusiasm. In the first instance, it aims to produce a particular kind of individual – not just literate and rational but confident, sensitive, sympathetic and imaginative individuals who could be administered by a minimum of state and juridical intervention. It produces persons who govern themselves. In the second instance, it produces a notion of pure or essential literariness which cannot be reduced to, or explained by, other forms of knowledge. In France, however, things were different: for instance, Charles-Augustin Sainte-Beuve, the French literary journalist, upon whom Arnold modelled himself, remained more impressionistic, less "cultural political" than his admirer. He worked in the week-by-week literary scene and retained state prestige outside the teaching profession as a member of the

Academy and, for a while, as a Senator. The French state officially offered culture an aura that the British public sphere, dominated by the needs of capital, did not. French culture was more a signifier of national identity than a traditional bulwark against democratic and technocratic drives and wants. And Hippolyte Taine, the other great French literary figure contemporary with Arnold, produces a *science* of literature based on psychology, racist biology and positivistic historiographical principles. In his work, *good* literary texts are not thought of in ethical terms: ultimately they offer modes of knowledge which may drive (admittedly, non-revolutionary) national progress. So nothing in France prepares the way for modern Anglo-American literary criticism which in its purest forms, in T. S. Eliot, I. A. Richards and in Leavis's earlier works, cannot be turned into a tool for morality or even for explicating the *meaning* of texts – whatever forms of individuality it can help mould. For modern literary criticism, texts are untranslatable into beliefs or propositions: it analyzes "the life in language," and produces selves, at least in principle, turned against mere administration, though its pupils usually became teachers or imperialist public servants. This discursive practice (to use a middle-period Foucauldian term) barely existed in France even as a programme. In the United Kingdom and the United States, where "culture" lacked state sanction, criticism can, paradoxically, enter the university system retaining traces of its early anti-institutionalism.

Literary criticism's denial that literary texts are primarily propositional is shared by post-structuralism, which has, thus, been absorbed by literature departments quite rapidly despite debates between "theory" and its enemies. Yet when one thinks of post-structuralism as connected to older literary criticism in a shared suspicion of literature as a set of propositions or interpretable "themes," then the bulk of Foucault's work – his histories for instance – does not seem to belong to post-structuralism at all. It might be easiest to say that though Foucault's targets are also the targets of post-structuralism thought of as a general field, his methods and interests differ from those of writers like Derrida, Roland Barthes, Paul de Man and Jean-François Lyotard. He remains a historian whose work is designed to undo the conceptual bases and cultural-historical purposes of conventional historiography. Now that post-structuralism itself is becoming more a memory, or a series of repetitions, than an expanding and developing field, this, along with its diversity and range, represents the continuing attraction (and risk) of Foucault's work.

To think of Foucault in this context, one needs a concrete sense of what constituted post-structuralism as a general movement. We should note at once that the name "post-structuralism" is not only vague but seriously misleading. The movement did *not* simply move beyond structuralism: its deepest roots lay quite elsewhere – in the French reception of phenomenology, and Edmund Husserl and Heidegger's work in particular. To take up the first of these assertions: it is now widely accepted that post-structuralism was less a development from, and a break with, structuralism than a moment or a potential that exists within it. At the very beginning of his essay "Force and Signification" (1963), arguably the first post-structuralist essay, Derrida noted that "structuralist consciousness is a catastrophic consciousness, simultaneously destroyed and destructive, *destructuring*" (Derrida 1978, 5–6: italics his). This "destructuring" does not refer to structuralism's turn away from the analysis of what texts – or cultural formations – *mean* towards analysis of the mechanisms by which effects of meaning are achieved, but the way in which structuralism is "in the register of method, a solicitude and solicitation of Being, a historico-metaphysical threatening of the foundations" (6). This is the difficult language of Heideggerian phenomenology. For the young Derrida, structuralism must be understood in primal and ontological terms, in its relation to Being. As such, surprisingly, it comes to be regarded as a mode of responding to, and safeguarding oneself from, the menace of the world. For him, structuralism returns the threat of the world back onto the world, breaking its objects out of familiar ties ("destructuring" them) at the same moment as it discovers their totality and autonomy. It works with ideal forms, finished, spatialized, and totalized objects, objects that exist without an origin. It also works in the clear light of the objective gaze. Thus, as Derrida notes, literary structuralism, in particular, cannot account for the *force* (the effects) of texts, though he concedes that to take this force into account is not to discover, once and for all, what a text means. Structuralism also neglects history and the way in which the "history of the work is not only its *past*, the eve or the sleep in which it precedes itself in an author's intentions, but is also the impossibility of its ever being *present*, of its ever being summarized by some absolute simultaneity or instantaneousness" (14). Like non-Heideggerian phenomenology (Derrida remarks explicitly that "modern structuralism has grown and developed with a more or less covert dependence on phenomenology" (27)), structuralism solicits its objects in a double sense. It shakes them, as it were, off the world ("solicitation" having a root meaning of "shaking"), and seeks to comprehend and to care for them in order to ward off the danger of their unfixability. In *The Order of Things*, Foucault also analyzes the "common ground" between structuralism and phenomenology: he sees them both as attempting to find discursive regularities in experience, the first by finding the forms which order "experience," the second by "raising the lived horizon of all our knowledge to the level of our discourse" (Foucault 1970a, 299).

Post-structuralism differs from a structuralism already conceived of as a kind of phenomenology both in its affirmation of the riskiness, the unsettledness, the play and history of things beneath their ideal and totalized forms, and an acceptance of and attention to, the gaps and connections between what is knowable and what is not. Very schematically, one can put it like this: structuralism carves the world up into large units – texts, genres, language, kin-systems, etc. – each complete, discrete, formally knowable and thus perfect. In this move it formalizes and abstracts the relations that exist *between* structures, failing to account for them as transactions. It does so in the interests of truth. Post-structuralism points out that this breaking of the world's continuities, exchanges and flows is an effect of the desire to know, and, believing this a limit rather than an end, reworks structuralism in three directions. It uses structuralism to continue the work of destructuring in an ethico-political spirit, so as to undo the barriers to thought and action implicit in familiar labels, perceptions and purposes. It attempts to undo the formal and bounded categories of structural and functionalist analysis so as to permit a more concrete – less mystified – sense of the messy interactions and misfirings between events. And it also hearkens philosophically and, at its best with formidable technical skill, to the conditions of possibility of its own activities. These conditions of possibility turn out to be impossible to recuperate in any fully ordered manner. In noting this impossibility, post-structuralism returns, especially in Derrida's and de Man's work – and despite their assertions to the contrary – to something like an ontological concern for what happens not socially, politically, psychologically and so on, but (to use the conventional metaphor) at the "deeper" level of existence itself. (This is already far too simple: for instance, Derrida and de Man both provide critiques of metaphors like that of "depth," "basis," "fundament" or "profundity" that have traditionally been used to construct and describe ontology.) On the other hand, Foucault interrogates the past and constantly encounters the difficulty of writing histories which have ethico-political purposes but make no transcendental truth claims. His early *History of Madness* is a Heideggerian history of how an affirmative connection with the ontological unfixability of things is lost in modernity; his *The Order of Things* is a history of knowledge's disruption by a primal absence of order, and his later genealogies are stories of how knowledge, by virtue of the way it affects the world, can be analyzed in social and political terms as a mode of power finally irreducible to particular social interests or functions. To cite Edward Said's useful term, the young Foucault attempted to secularize, to *world*, post-structuralist ontology by writing histories of those institutions that permit the forgetting of chancy, "meaningless" Being.

In general terms, we can now begin to see how Foucault's work, like post-structuralism as a whole, is pivoted on its refusal of three schools of thought: humanism and the privileging of subjectivity; hermeneutics/ historicism and the privileging of understanding; dialectics and the privileging of teleology, to which we can add psychoanalysis and its privileging

17

of a primal lack, especially in its theme of "castration" as the mechanics by which the subject gains autonomy. As we shall see in the last chapters of this book, both humanism and hermeneutics appeal to a wider category still, and one that is harder to escape – representation or mimesis. But the critique of humanism is especially important in this list because it joins two phases of Foucault's work together. It is only after having described modernity as the age of *man* that his earlier historical (or archaeological) analysis of knowledge could be transformed into his later critical (or genea-logical) account of modern government. In placing modernity firmly under the sign of humanism Foucault is developing Heidegger's thought – it is this orientation that allowed him, near the end of his life, flatly to declare: "For me Heidegger has always been the essential philosopher," even if he went on to remark that Nietzsche had had a more powerful impact still (Foucault 1988b, 250). But French anti-humanism in the early 1960s also develops both from the critique of cultural imperialism implicit in Claude Lévi-Strauss's structuralist anthropology and from Louis Althusser's work. Lévi-Strauss is the formulator of the notion that we are embarking on an era for which "man is dead"; while for Althusser history is "a process without a subject" which promises no fulfilment of repressed or "alienated" human potentialities.[10] In this confluence of structuralism, marxism and phenomenology "humanism" comes not so much to refer to the rejection of God and the progressivist atheism of "Humanist Societies" (the kind of humanism professed by the Autodidact in Sartre's *Nausea* for example) as to the belief that there exists a human nature and human needs that remain constant across different cultures, classes and genders.[11] It also carries the thesis that a particular kind of psychology is essentially human. For humanism, human beings have a unified self in which consciousness determines behavior and in which thought and feeling can, at least poten-tially, mesh into a harmonious whole. It is within humanism that important notions like alienation have meaning, for alienation – and, to some degree, oppression – depend on the possibility that human beings may not fill the potential of what Ludwig Feuerbach (a so-called "young Hegelian" and a crucial influence on the young Marx) called their "species being," their *humanness*. Where consciousness fails to control action, and emotions fail to connect with reason, there humanists find alienation. They invest immense cultural value in *Bildung*, a term which refers not only to the development that harmonious intermeshing of all human faculties within the individual, but also to the analogous development and harmonious intermeshing of all individuals within an (organic) society. Thus humanism carries with it not only an analytic presupposition – that there are features essential to *all* human beings, but a morality – life-stories and history ought to tend towards completion as an interlocking of related but separate parts. Implicitly, humanism also carries an administrative protocol: society is to produce individuals who fulfil their human potential. This is the moral politics (as one might call it) that Nietzsche recognized in George Eliot for whom a faith in the perfection of God has been transformed into a faith in the perfection of Humanity.

Anti-humanism is more than a side-show to twentieth-century thought, not least because it is inseparable from literary modernism. In that context T. E. Hulmes's *Speculations* is its most celebrated statement, but in fact anti-humanism pervades advanced writing of the period around the First World War, not just in its themes but in its structures. To give one example – we may recall Birkin's desire that man be wiped off the face of the earth in Lawrence's *Women in Love* (1920), and, in the same novel, the savage portrait of Gerald's father, Mr Crich, who worships the "highest, the great, sympathetic, mindless Godhead of humanity" (Lawrence 1974, 242). As soon as the novel sets itself against the old humanist order, it cannot return to those narrative techniques of resolution and rich characterization which depend on the particular set of over-arching relations already noted: a coherent individual completing his or her potential in a coherent and consensual society which, in turn, is to be regarded as having a specific place in a generalized, non-conflictual, and ultimately transhistorical, Humanity. But modernist anti-humanism is also important for our purposes because it is through his reading of the movement's major monuments during the early 1950s (especially works by Heidegger and Nietzsche) that Foucault found his project.[12] An account of Heidegger's work, in particular, is required to describe the background of Foucault's writings. He was, after all, Foucault's "essential philosopher."

Heidegger was not concerned with what he, like Foucault, thought of as "anthropology," but with ontology. In his early work, he developed what he called an "existential analytic" which analyzes the basic structures of Being-in-the-world (*Dasein*) as against a human essence already expressed in, or signified by, human history; independently, that is, of any social and cultural determinations. Most particularly, the existential analytic is not an analysis of the life-conditions of the post-Cartesian man of reason; indeed, it is intended to describe what reason itself presupposes. In Heidegger's terms, *Dasein* is the structure within which Being manifests itself among beings.[13] *Dasein* cannot structure a being that is an end in itself, because the question of understanding Being is itself essential or, rather, "constitutive" of *Dasein*. Thus *Dasein* is also a form of fundamental "transcendence" – just because no fixed or limited project or object can satisfy the questioning of Being. "Authentic" thought cannot base itself on any naive notion of experience in which the world is simply given. Beings are directed towards what Gilles Deleuze, in his commentary on Foucault, calls "the fold of being. Being as fold" (Deleuze 1986a, 117). And yet for Heidegger, especially the later Heidegger, "Being" was not itself a given, rather it was revealed in *Dasein*'s engagement with the world; it requires what he would come to think of as the "opening" or "clearing" created in the practices by which societies and lives are constructed. This aspect of Heidegger's thought broaches what might be called an ontology of ethics, where "ethics" has the sense that Foucault gives it in his last phase, that is, a practice that produces an individual's way of life or selfhood.

It would be wrong, however, to think of Heidegger as a secular thinker. *Dasein* is thrown into the world, into time and finitude; in this sense it is ontologically contingent. And this is why it cannot be properly expressed in any subject-object relations for which the subject operates in terms of a-temporal, masterful, principles, the clear light of reason for instance. This is why, too, it continually and restlessly transcends limits and origins. *Dasein* is constituted by anxiety at the instability and chanciness of its own being, by an experience of nullity and meaninglessness most intensely expressed in death's simultaneous necessity and arbitrariness. This anxiety separates *Dasein* from other beings in the world: it is individualized, as Heidegger put it, in its anticipation of death. With anxiety comes a care (*Sorge*) for the otherness of things which in turn is linked to a learning in the process of doing rather than doing in line with what has been learnt. In his later work, after what is called the "turn" (*Kehre*), Heidegger reads the history of the West after Socrates as the history of the forgetting of the question concerning the truth of Being, or, in another formulation, as the story of the "withdrawal of Being." The forgetting of Being occurs within a historical process ordered by a will to power, and the primacy of rationality and use-value. This was Heidegger's appeal – one that is often disowned – to the "Western Marxists" who see the story of modern society as one of increasing domination of human beings over both nature and one another. For them, the emphasis on rationality in the West helps such domination. Foucault's work, in some very broad way, belongs to this way of thinking, as he confesses in his remarks on his teacher, the historian of science, Georges Canguilhem.[14] Yet, for Heidegger, paradoxically, the forgetting of Being *belongs* to Being – which, indeed, discloses itself by withdrawal. (This notion of the retreat of Being, along with a certain reading of Nietzsche, will lead to those later French theories of transgression described in chapter 4.) In the first instance, then, Heidegger avoids humanism because the object of his own concern and analytic, *Dasein*, is not man or consciousness but is describable only in terms of the basic presuppositions for Being-in-the-world – a so called "transcendental structure." Furthermore, Heidegger suggests that thought is not primarily concerned with the human – for him, to believe that man exists at the centre of things is to forget the question concerning the truth of Being and the simultaneously close and distant relation that the human race has both with Being and with the ready-at-hand world. Humanism is a metaphysics in that it replaces concern for Being with an interest in man and the whole apparatus – representations, most of all – that permit man to frame the world as what Heidegger calls a "standing reserve" – there for humanity's control and use.[15] Since this forgetting is characteristic of metaphysics in general, and therefore of all Western conceptual dealings with the world after Socrates and Plato, Heidegger argues that it is only in his own thought that the death of humanism can be glimpsed. In intellectual historical terms, Heidegger (rather than Levi-Strauss) opens the way for Foucault's claim that he, in turn, foresees the "death of man," as well as for his concentration on the ways in which the humanist subject "man" is, in fact, the effect of adminstrative and governmental agencies (a connection I develop in chapter 5.)

This may seem to take us some distance from poststructuralism. Yet in his astute reading of *The Letter on Humanism*, published as "The Ends of Man," Derrida points out that what Heidegger says about *Dasein* and what he says about the potential of man or "we"/"us" cannot be rigorously distinguished. Which carries the implication, characteristic of Derrida, that so long as we do philosophy in the language that we inherit from the philosophic tradition, then we can never finally eradicate a residual humanism. But it is also in that lecture on the ends of man (written in the exciting months of April/May 1968) that Derrida feels the necessity to define the contemporary field of French thought. Predictably enough, he sees that field as ordered by the attempts to break with metaphysics and humanism, and sketches what he calls the "trembling" of French thought at this epoch under three headings – each of which is worth briefly attending to because they too clarify the cultural field in which Foucault's work was produced and received.

The first of Derrida's categories is the "reduction of meaning": the structuralist endeavour to determine "the possibility of *meaning* on the basis of a 'formal' organization which in itself has no meaning" (Derrida 1982c, 134; italics his). This is a negative description of Foucault's archaeology, which demonstrates how the conditions for "meaning" or truth change throughout modern history; a history, for Foucault, without linear direction. And Derrida also declares that this project is a "critique of phenomenology" because phenomenology attempts to reveal and understand the basic structures of existence through what lies ready-to-hand. Yet, as Derrida notes, the critique of phenomenology – the refusal of the drive to come closer to an understanding of how things are – requires a radical break from *all* forms of Western "meaning" or "thought." This break is itself motivated by a sense of progress, that is, of progressing beyond the limits within which the order of things is conceived of as having, or grounding, meaning. Thus the "critique of phenomenology" "has all the characteristics" (as Derrida puts it) of the progressive humanism that it rejects. The second of the moves considered by Derrida is "the strategic bet": the attempt to locate oneself outside the conceptual frame that one inhabits, an outside which must exist at least in so far as Western thought is (as it seemed in 1968) "trembling" under new pressures. Such a strategy

21

can either try to work *towards* the outside from within current procedures and the languages that we inherit – and, of course, there is no other language available. But this runs the risk of consolidating what we already have just because it claims the aura of the different, the outside, for the same, the inside. On the other hand, it may try something totally "discontinuous" and new – and run the risk of blindly treating the already known as if it were that something. For Derrida, at this point of his career, deconstruction must "weave and interlace these two motifs . . . which amounts to saying that it must speak several languages and produce several texts at once" (135). In the heady days of the late sixties it looked as if those who embraced the "strategic bet" could embark on a long and radical project of *fröhlich* (joyful) self-undoing and a refusal to live or think in terms which give primary value either to nostalgic categories like the "forgetting of Being" or proleptic and existential ones like the "inevitability of death." The last – Utopian – move considered by Derrida turns towards Nietzsche. It insists on the difference between human perfection as conceived by humanism and those who do not believe that a questioning directed towards Being will permit anything "fundamental" to be engaged. The latter is the lesson of Nietzsche's Superman, and it falls outside of anything academic labour can provide. It requires a form of language not in the service of technology, power, will or self-discovery – a kind of poetry in fact. And, at crucial moments, both Heidegger and the young Foucault write or "think" through such language. As Foucault remarked at the presentation of his thesis (*Madness and Civilization*) to the Sorbonne in 1961, "To speak of madness, it is necessary to have the talent of a poet." To which an examiner, Georges Canguilhem, replied, "Mais vous l'avez, monsieur" (Eribon 1989, 133).

If we allow that the field of French thought around 1968 is organized by these three possibilities: (1) structuralism or the "reduction of meaning"; (2) the "strategic bet" or deconstruction as the continuation of phenomenology by a mode of analysis which attempts neither to repeat nor to invert Western thought but to place "it under erasure" by showing that all insides are always also outsides and vice-versa, all identities are constituted by differences and vice versa; (3) the leap beyond man into a writing that undoes origins and ends, then Foucault ultimately goes another way altogether. These possibilities may have helped ordered his *oeuvre* up until 1970 but his final response to the end of man will not be to dissolve the "subject" into texts, to reduce meaning, or to place a stake on the total defamiliarization of our conceptual web. He follows Nietzsche, and a certain side of Heidegger, in insisting that the thinker's task is to show how knowledge is used to shape individuals, their lives and bodies. For him the large questions and large claims can only be articulated following careful attention to documents both well known and forgotten, and after deliberation on analytic methods. In the archives, traditional concepts and debates take on a different appearance: they become discourses – sets of sentences with their own materiality. In particular, the grand ontological questions concerning Being, the humanist emphasis on "lack" and "completion" lose their seduction. So do grandiose claims for the intellectual – who now becomes what might be called a discursive technician. Foucault works towards a world that carries less aura for political reasons – he believes that the glamour of concepts such as "Humanity" or "Art" have been obstacles which obscure the relations between the individual and the apparatuses that administer modern society. They have reduced liberty, beauty and risk. Liberty, beauty and risk may be reclaimed, if at all, in the techniques that people are able to apply to the shaping of their own existence. This, then, is Foucault's way of becoming not an anti-humanist but a post-humanist, not a writer on the left but a post-revolutionary writer. As we shall see, within academic literary studies, Foucault's shift has been absorbed into that "new historicism" which rejects what the late Foucault rejected but, generally speaking, without maintaining the concrete ethical and political interests that drove his work. Today, the notion that humanist institutions and discourses have consolidated new forms of "governmentality" and administration has almost become an academic commonplace. It lacks political tension or energy. How could it be otherwise when the methods and analyzes of a great scholar who was also an outsider, a public figure, and a transgressor, and whose work depended on his being these things, have been taken up by a more or less self-enclosed and professional academy? Obviously those who take Foucault's contribution as seriously as it deserves will feel the demand to elaborate and move past it, but perhaps its real challenge lies in the question: "can it continue to be used to break down the limits of academic professionalism?" – and that requires real changes in our methods and topics of study.

23

1

MADNESS

EARLY WORK

Foucault's career has its roots in his years as a student at the École Normale Supérieure. There he studied philosophy under Jean Hyppolite and also came under the influence of the historian and philosopher of science Gaston Bachelard. In Hyppolite he encountered a thinker who, with Alexander Kojève, draws Hegel's thought into the French philosophic tradition. Hyppolite's Hegel is not an enlightened philosopher who can affirm the identity of the rational and the real, and the "cunning" with which reason makes use of negativity, closure and death. On the contrary, he is the forerunner of those recent philosophic schools for whom desire and negativity provide history's *continuing* and inescapable motor force. As Foucault was to put it in a commemoration address given after his teacher's death: for Hyppolite, philosophical thought sketches out a field it can never cover (1969a, 132). An ambitious claim lies implicit in this – once we are permitted to think of a Hegel for whom reason and history can never merge, or, rather, for whom this merging (known as "totality") is utopian rather than realizable, and for whom "reason" itself works not to resolution but as an ongoing process, then much European philosophy since Hegel's time might exist as footnotes to the master. The anxiety of this influence was especially intense as, by the 1950s, Hyppolite, under the spell of Heidegger, was already able to articulate his position explicitly against both historicism and humanism.[1] It is scarcely an exaggeration to say that Foucault is haunted by this dark and non-totalizing dialect throughout his career though he comes to draw it into his own writing fully only when he conceives of his work as a "history of problematizations."

In Bachelard, Foucault comes into contact with a body of work difficult to read as Hegelian on any terms. Bachelard argues that justifications for the rationality of science cannot be considered independently of the history of scientific thought and practices. Georges Canguilhem will flesh out this thesis into the "Foucauldian" argument that the human sciences are developed on the highly administered subjects of the modern state. For

Bachelard, however, each scientific theory involves a finite "epistemology"; that is, a set of assumptions about what counts as true knowledge. Science, which continuously breaks with common sense, creates its own objects. It deals not with things as they really are but with theoretical constructs: developing not as an orderly continuum, not as a gradual unfolding of increasingly rational theories, but in leaps and discontinuities. As old sciences are sedimented into new modes of common sense, new sciences break from common sense again. Thus each past theory, each past epistemological frame, must be understood in its own terms and not, in the Hegelian manner, as anticipating the present and opening into the future. Yet the philosopher of science must account for past scientific theories from the standpoint of the present. In particular, the Newtonian order must be regarded not as "natural" or "true" but in the defamiliarizing light of post-Newtonian physics. Even from these summary remarks we can see that Hyppolite and Bachelard (who work in quite different philosophic registers) are both concerned with the question of the *limit* of science or philosophy and, indeed, the history not so much of knowledge itself as of its limits. Foucault takes from his teachers the notion that careful historical research reveals stories about the continual interplay between "truth" and its objects – "continual" because no theory can bridge the separation between truth and its objects once and for all.

On finishing his degree, instead of continuing with philosophy or history – the traditional paths for entry into teaching or public administration – Foucault turned to psychology. What was still more unorthodox, he turned towards so-called existential psychology, which decisively rejects the dominant French psychological tradition founded by Freud's rival, Pierre Janet. Resisting claims to scientificity, existential psychology applies (often rather trivialized) versions of Heidegger's analytic of *Dasein* to actual non-"normal" mental phenomena. Bachelard, Hyppolite and the existential psychoanalysts do not – *cannot* – merge as a seamless web in Foucault's work. His very first book *Maladie mentale et personnalité* (1954a) is dramatically split in two. The first half consists of a critique of both evolutionary psychology and Freudianism from the post-Heideggerian point of view. He argues that neither psychoanalysis, which is based on the individual's life history, nor any psychology which regards mental events as effects or aspects of physical lesions or regressions, can account for the fact that mental illness is experienced as, for instance, anxiety. This means that, whatever causes it, the illness as lived remains connected to a deeper and fundamental reality, an "a-priori" as he calls it, which constitutes Being-in-the-world and shapes human moods and responses. So mental pathology is not simply to be regarded as a deviation from normalcy, it involves a flight from the world towards a radical solitude, an abandonment of meaning for incoherence. Such a flight is "morbid," yet it is also a movement towards the profoundly unstable structures of human existence, upon which the same order of cause and effect is built. In its second part, however, the book has a different tone. It urges a marxian analysis of the ways that the symptoms of mental pathology are determined by social contradictions. (Foucault had not long left the Party at this time). Mental illness is here understood as a strategy for coping with social alienation; indeed it depends quite closely on the Russian psychology of the time. These two approaches, which barely seem to belong in a single book, can never unite, because of what I want to call the historico-ontological gap. This gap exists because, from the side of existential psychology, actual social contradictions must themselves be reducible to the fundamental conditions of Being-in-the-world; whereas from the side of historicism, "anxiety," "boredom" and so on do not belong to the way things are but are characteristics of individuals formed by specific historical circumstances – or historical and cultural discourse about such individuals. Foucault tries to sidestep this discrepancy by differentiating mental illness from madness. Madness (*la folie*) becomes the name for a condition which expresses a basic, not to say cosmic, lack, while mental illness is the term used to describe how society conceives of, and controls, madness. It is important to grasp this move because it, and increasingly subtle versions of it, remain basic to his work right up until the work on power.

In the same year as *Maladie mentale et personnalité* appeared, Foucault also published a long "Preface" to Ludwig Binswanger's *Dream and Existence* (itself first published in Germany in 1930), although the "Preface" was actually written the year before. Thus Foucault's work begins, like Derrida's, when he introduces a German phenomenological work. (Derrida translates Edmund Husserl's late work *The Origins of Geometry*.) In his preface, Foucault does not summarize Binswanger's thesis, or produce a commentary on it, rather – in an approach which will become characteristic – he defines its "problematic" (to use a word that he borrowed from Bachelard). This problematic is the confrontation between Freud and phenomenology, and the topic which highlights this confrontation most clearly is the dream. Binswanger rejects psychology's title as the founding science of man. For him there is an ontological condition of possibility within which "man" operates. As Foucault puts it in directly Heideggerian terms: "Let us say . . . that being man (*Menschsein*) is after all only the effective and concrete content of what ontology analyzes as the transcendental structure of *Dasein*" (1954b, 11). Binswanger's task is to show how this transcendental structure is to be traced in psychoanalysis. Foucault suggests that the transcendental structure of *Dasein* can be connected to the concrete contents of that structure – that is, human existence (*Menschsein*) – by analyzing the conditions in which meaning is possible. The logic goes like this: being man means living in a world which had meaning or significance, so the conditions of possibility of being-man are also the preconditions of meaning. But the grounds of meaning are *things* which can never be fully explained purely in terms of their communicative function or in a grid that already contains a semantic (or "meaningful") aspect. Thus meaning is already embedded in a primordial world of space and time. And Binswanger, as a phenomenologist, also wants to give a fundamental account of these primordial experiences (or forms) embedded in space and time.

On the other hand, meaning itself must already *express*: "In order to mean something, the word implies a world of expression which precedes it" (1986a, 41). Foucault argues that what underlies all its structures is an act of expression: "word and image are conjugated in the first person at the very moment that they achieve objective form" (1986a, 41). Here "expression" differs from signification: it belongs neither to the social world of communication, not to the structuring processes that semiotics brings to light, nor to the psychological world of interpretation and therapy. Rather, it describes the way that the meaning of the image itself is shaped and constructed by experiences – as if signs must carry the traces of experiences (of pleasures and pains) in order for them, ultimately, to have meaning. (In Husserl's *Logical Investigations*, to which Foucault and Binswanger are deeply indebted here, "meaning" is the product of the resistance that the materiality of the signifier presents to the act of expression.) Thus, in existential psychology, dreams express or (in this sense) "mean" more than they apparently signify – and what they express are not symptoms, phantasies, simple desires or traumas but primordial, ontological forces. Indeed, the dream's first person, its subject, connects to the way that things fundamentally are just because dreams are not in the ordinary sense of the term meaningful, saturated by signification: "they are rich by reason of the poverty of their objective content" (44). This category of "poverty" that permits the (paradoxical) passage from being to meaning can be analyzed. Foucault argues that to do so one must move, at least provisionally, from Husserl and Heidegger to Freud. Phenomenology has a deeper understanding of the processes of, structures of, and lacks in meaning than psychoanalysis, but it needs psychoanalysis to fill out these meanings, to show what they indicate. Thus the formula which determines the "Preface": "Phenomenology has succeeded in making images speak; but it has given no one the possibility of understanding their language." That is existential psychology's task, borrowing as is does from psychoanalysis the interpretative techniques spelled out in Freud's *The Interpretation of Dreams*. Where does psychoanalysis fail? Freud believes that the symbol fully connects the interior world of meaning to the exterior world of matter and sensation just because it is what it means (and what it means is, ultimately, always *desire*) – rather than how it feels or what it looks like. According to Foucault in the "Preface," psychoanalysis has ignored the materiality of the image, the stuff of the imaginary, at the same time as it tells us that signification can never divest itself of a certain materiality. In short, Freud turned expression into signification too easily, and so came to believe that stories about familial and inter-generational conflict could ultimately explain the shaping of subjectivity and the "meaning" of cultural forms. (One should remember that another interpretation of Freud's work is possible: for instance, in their work Nicolas Abraham and Maria Torok have insisted on the importance of "word-things," words *as* things, in the mental processes that Freud brings to light.) This is the beginning of Foucault's long critique of Freud as remaining too close to the human sciences, as believing that the conditions which make consciousness possible can be drawn into the domain of science, that the opaque thisness of things can be make to speak. (As I have already indicated, later in Foucault's career this critique will broaden out into an attack on the analytic power of the category of "lack" – or "castration" – itself. We can put it like this: Foucault will come to envisage a poverty that is not a lack.)

This play between the materiality of signs and their "expression" is focused on by much of the philosophic work done in France between Merleau-Ponty and Derrida. (Such work will reach its fullest development during the 1960s in Jean-François Lyotard's *Discours, figure* and Gilles Deleuze's *Logique du sens*). It also lies behind Derrida's use of words like "trace" and "spacing" which gestures to a spatio-temporal object (more apparent in writing than in the voice) which is the precondition of the effect we call "meaning"; but which cannot either ever ground meaning or be fully accounted for within it. As we began to see in the "Preface," an insistence that sheer, meaningless, chancy materiality enables the order of sense is characteristic of post-phenomenological thought, though Derrida and Paul de Man remind us that we cannot permit our sense of the irreducible materiality of the sign to reassure us that language might function *outside* the paradoxes of signification, that language can be accounted for in terms of the play of the matter which is its vehicle.

In second generation phenomenologists like Binswanger, the basic, onto-logical conditions of existence are layered or broken: Being is folded in the Heideggerian sense. At one level, these conditions take the form of simple polar oppositions. The play of light and shade, the movement from large close spaces to distant ones, rising and falling – these become the contents of experience embedded in *Dasein*. For this kind of thinking, phrases like "falling in love" are not just metaphors. As Binswanger writes: "The nature of poetic similes lies in the deepest roots of our existence where the vital forms and contents of our mind are still bound together. When, in a bitter disappointment, 'we fall from the clouds,' then we fall – we *actually* fall. Such falling is neither purely of the body nor something metaphorically derived from physical falling" (1963, 223). Here language is the immediate expression of the shape of our responses (so to speak) at the deepest "anthropological" level. Yet for Binswanger, phenomena like "rising" or "falling" in turn become what can only still be described as "metaphors" for increasingly abstract conditions: the play of authenticity and inauthenticity, of risk and stasis and so on in the human condition. Or rather, deep experiential content is structured as the play of oppositions between dark and light, here and there, rise and fall and so on. At the most "profound" level, human experience consists, in fact, of the play of opposition itself – a thesis which begins to dissolve phenomenology into structuralism. Nevertheless, in the early introduction to Binswanger, Foucault, not yet a "post-structuralist" or a "post-phenomenologist," can still champion a "philosophy of expression," expression, as we have seen, standing for something beyond meaning already embedded in the meaning given to the world by man. The phrase "expression," and its synonym "experience," do not pull the whole problem far enough away from notions of intention and subjectivity; they permit Foucault to place his work in what he thinks of in the "Preface" as the passage between "anthropology" and "ontology." It is only in his archaeological studies that he turns away from any attempt to *understand* and appropriate the so-called "deep" and experiential conditions of the lived world.

The strongest moment of the "Preface" occurs when Foucault embarks on a summary history of dream. He traces the story of dream-commentaries and the use of dreams for literature from Aristotle to the Romantics. But he also argues, "what has changed from one epoch to another has not been . . . the reading of destiny in dreams, nor even the deciphering procedures, but rather the justification of this relation of dream to world, and the way of conceiving how the truth of the world can anticipate itself and gather together its future in an image capable only of reconstituting it in a murky form" (1986a, 47). Foucault sets out a narrative of the connection between the dream as primordial form and what is held to be the truth of the dream at particular epochs. This presupposes, in the manner of Bachelard, that the "truth of the world," or what is true in the world, is not an absolute but varies in time and place. Truth about dreams becomes belief about what is true in dreams. Much more radically, it also presupposes that truth is *more* relative than the dream. For the young Foucault, dreams are an "anthropological index of transcendence" (49). It is there that the central structures and polarities of existence reveal themselves, just because they are indices of solitude (not "subjectivity") and of the irreducible thisness of existence. And Foucualt differs from Binswanger in his account of what dreams indicate. Space is especially important (as is so often the case in Foucault's writing): the dream "deploys itself" in the "original spatiality of the scene," where that "scene" is radically to be distinguished from geographical space. The dream scene is not divided into "near" and "far," rather motion is a perpetual series of sudden encounters ("nothing but displacements"); it is not bounded but is "paradoxically closed by the infinite openness of the horizon; it is not secure or the "sign of my power" (*signe de ma puissance*) in that it is fundamentally porous – in dreams a train can travel into a room via the window, journey right through one's head and then crash out through castle gates without even being derailed (60–1). (As such it is not cinematic, for instance.) Furthermore, dreams in their universality, solitude and sheer materiality are always closer to death than life. "Death is the absolute meaning of the dream" (55), it is the "open horizon" in relation to which dreams occur. More generally still, at the level that Foucault is concerned with, what one dreams is always the same, because the "first person" who dreams is not a socially constructed individual but (somehow) an expression of experience itself before the split into subjectivity and objectivity. This is why the dream is not so much constructed in and by images as trapped or weighed down by them. Images clog the sheerness or freedom of fundamental experience, thus, paradoxically, it is in them that the "first person" begins to be individualized. And psychotherapists are to the dream-work, what poets are to the tropes that language throws at them: both are limited by the finitude of their material. The poet "consumes and destroys" images in collecting and signing them; the therapist, who locates the movement of a particular "imagination" toward existence and death *beneath* images, achieves the "transcendental reduction of the imaginary" (72).

Foucault is not merely introducing Binswanger in his "Preface," he is developing his own line of thought, his own style. Intriguingly for our purposes, Foucault's major departure from Binswanger lies in the way that, unlike his master, he deals not with dreams as such but with the *literary* or discursive account of dreams. His history, necessarily, relies on texts which deal with dreams from Heraclitus to Novalis, via, amongst others, Shakespeare and Racine. This has one important consequence: what Foucault finds in dreams is literature, not just in the sense that the task of the therapists has more in common with the practice of poets than it does, for instance, with that of medical practitioners, or in the sense that literary writing often attempts to appropriate the content and forms of dreams. He finds literature in his own writing. How else to read lyrical passages such as this?

> The subject of the dream, the first person of the dream, is the dream itself, the whole dream. . . The dream is an existence carving itself out in barren space, shattering chaotically, exploding noisily, netting itself, a scarcely breathing animal, in the webs of death. It is the world at the dawn of its first explosion when the world is still existence itself and is not yet the universe of objectivity. To dream is not another way of experiencing another world, it is for the dreaming subject the radical way of experiencing its own world.
>
> (1986a, 59)

The dream is the moment of absolute creativity and (existential) freedom in which the "lessons of the tragic poets," learnt before the fall into truth and objectivity, still enact their message – as they do in that metaphor of the dream as a "scarcely breathing animal." Again, Foucault never escaped this interaction between the literary and the phenomenological, the poet and the theorist. Increasingly, though, it existed merely in his demand that his work express his life (as in, say, a political commitment or in experiments with sexual or narcotic pleasures and intensities). But, of course, this interaction moves in two directions: Foucault's life also expresses his work. And that cannot be true of the dream (or of madness): they can only refer to work, they cannot be ordered by it.

HISTORY OF MADNESS

In 1961, seven years after his first book, and after a great deal of difficulty in finding a publisher, the intended first volume of a long history of madness appeared under the title *Folie et déraison: Histoire de la folie à l'âge classique* (*Madness and Unreason: The History of Madness in the Classical Age*). Almost immediately Foucault became a star – at least in the literary world which, somewhat to his chagrin, hailed the book first. A year later a revised version of his first book was published renamed *Maladie mentale et psychologie*. The second half of this little work (which replaces the material on Soviet psychology) remains the best summary of Foucault's new story of madness. The shift involved is perhaps best glimpsed in the question that Foucault asked himself when he altered the last sentence of the first part of *Maladie mentale et personnalité*:[2] "If this subjectivity of the insane is both a call to and an abandonment of the world, is it not of the world itself that we should ask the secret of its enigmatic status? Is there not in mental illness a whole nucleus of significations that belongs to the domain in which it appeared – and to begin with, the simple fact that it is circumscribed *as* an illness?" (1976a, 56.) Here the emphasis turns firmly from phenomenological understanding or ontology towards the world, that is, towards the history of the fate of madness. There are hints here that history will not be the history of thought but of practices: it is easy to see that madness is called an illness not just in a theory, but within a practice – the building of hospitals, the accreditation of doctors, a system of observation and so on. The historico-ontological gap is still apparent, however, in the disjunction between madness as a "call to and abandonment of" the world and its "significations," that is, the signs by which it is recognized in history. Thus Foucault's history of madness is again a history both of the way madness is defined and produced within society and of madness itself as an "experience" which precedes its "significations." Yet there is a difference between this approach and that of his first book. Although at the very beginning of *Madness and Civilization*, in a preface which was omitted from later editions, Foucault claims that he wants to write from

31

the position of madness in and for itself: "the zero point in the course of madness at which madness is an undifferentiated experience" (1965a, ix), in fact the voice of madness itself changes both as "madness" is defined in different ways and as different social practices are applied to the "insane." *Each* side of the division between madness and sanity are historicized which makes a crucial departure from the programme sketched in his treatment of dreams in the Binswanger preface. One reason for this is that madness, unlike dreaming, has a public face.

Foucault's narrative tells of a huge division acted out in the modern history of Western culture – the split between reason and its other, madness. In its own broadest terms, this is a narrative of the loss of the tragic sense of madness within the secularization of the culture (or, in the Nietzschean terms that Foucault repeats, the tragedy of the loss of tragedy). Of course such a story is familiar and thus comforting; not only does the sweet and sour task of telling the tale of secularization define and validate sociology after Max Weber, the loss of "the tragic sense of life" is a commonplace of romanticism as it flows into conservative modernism. Similarly, and more concretely, attacks on psychiatry as a reduction of the power and meaning of madness were almost *de rigueur* in surrealistic circles. But what is remarkable about Foucault's book is not his tolerance for the "experience" of that madness which cannot belong to the calm, Apollonian world of sociology and psychiatry but the way such sympathies are harnessed to tell a stunningly detailed story of modernity. *Madness and Civilization* is one of the most important books of the period because of the way in which the romantic and sociological theses and modes are turned onto and into a concrete history of an unprecedently wide range of events – concerning, to take examples at random, the shift in cures for the insane, the changing characteristics of the population of the asylum, art history, the cycles of accumulation and over-accumulation in an expanding capitalist economy, the state's attitude to its subjects, and the changing conceptions of work itself. This complex history is organized under an array of abstract headings interrupted by readings of specific paintings and texts chosen to instantiate particular eras or formations within eras. Foucault has learned from phenomenology – the phenomenology of the early Hegel meditated through Hyppolite – to freeze historical moments within constellations consisting of both abstract categories and concrete examples which are presented without interpretation, without reference to any tradition of scholarship and dispute. (It is interesting to note that Canguilhem thought the book Hegelian (Eribon 1989, 129)). Foucault has also learnt to stress almost indistinct, seemingly minute differences in quite specific areas – in the history of "passion" for example – and to set these minute differences into the scaffolding of his larger historical moments. No doubt this method involves a series of simplifications and forgettings: the forgetting of the channels of erudition and dispute by which the past, in part, retains a place in the future; the forgetting of the partial or figurative nature of the relation between example and wider formation; the forgetting of continuities between eras; the forgetting of the historical position and limited point of view of the writer; a forgetting, even, of the effects and "madness" of the text itself (the way it cannot account for its own structure) but this systematic amnesia enables the book's insights, its energy and ambitiousness.

Madness and Civilization pivots around two dates. In 1657 in Paris the destitute and insane were taken off the streets and placed in the Hôpital Générale, founded the previous year. For Foucault this event, which was preceded by other similar moves, is the sign of the inauguration of the "great confinement" and the classical age of madness. Then, for the first time, the state took responsibility for the insane; an early move in that trajectory by which it will later take responsibility for the unemployed, the sick, the old, the sexually abused. During this period the mad were incarcerated in large institutions often along with criminals and the destitute. No "cures" were attempted as their condition was not viewed as a medical one and their fates were of little public concern. Almost 150 years later, at Bicêtre in 1794, Pinel unchained the inmates of his asylum, ushering in the era of modern and humanitarian mental sciences. Thus, as will also be the case for *The Order of Things*, the story divides into three epochs: the pre-classical, the classical (the work's centre) and the modern. In *Madness and Civilization*, the pre-classical era is born in the late fifteenth century as the medieval ravages of death – famine, plague and war disappear from the foreground of history. In a certain failure of historical tact and grasp, Foucault takes the model of the "dark ages" very seriously indeed, that is to say, *literally*. The period before the fifteenth century functions as a negative plenitude, the epoch of death, from which modernity can emerge in an Oedipal act of which the book itself, by constructing an image of the pre-Renaissance period as a black monolith, is partly guilty. The work is able to begin only by radically simplifying the epoch which predates its narrative: it is as if the complexities of its story and method would have no hold there. Foucault argues that as society and culture return to life and regain their confidence in the early modern period, the constant presence of death is replaced by an ever-present madness. Madness mediates between life and death; to be mad is to be in the presence of death in life. It circulates through Renaissance society, not just figuratively, but in those actual Ships of Fools which sailed, quite haphazardly, from place to place.

Madness has a meaning in the Renaissance; then contact with madness had value because it spoke of certain universal truths lacking in the everyday world. Like the dreams of Binswanger's "Preface," for Foucault, Renaissance madness, at least sometimes, could talk of the void, of a crucial but energetic absence at the heart of things. In painting it could

33

work through the imagination, appearing in the superbly conceived gar-
goyles, monsters and dream figures of Bosch, Breughel and Dürer. In their
vigour, they displayed the courage to confront, face to face, a meaningful
evil and disorder. But, as in Erasmus' *The Praise of Folly*, madness also
existed as folly. Here madness is used by, or, as Foucault puts it, is "in
dialogue with," rationality. It is the mask of satire-as-critique. Most darkly,
madness is the mind dominated by illusion, especially the illusion of autonomy and modernity. In the Renaissance, ambition or overweeningness are
not far from madness, because they were not simply moral errors or
psychological problems but refusals of human mortality. Both as folly and
as a sign of the void, madness represented a chink in human experience
through which Being – the ontological – became socially accessible. Madness, thus, had its own reality and universality. Yet what was in question
here, of course, is not madness as it essentially is, but certain Renaissance
articulations or "significations" of madness both as an idea and in relation
to social practices, that is, the "ensemble" of madness.

After the Renaissance comes the classical period – Foucault's schema of
historical periodization remains quite conventional, if drawn with unusual
broadness. He picks out Cervantes and Shakespeare as conserving the pre-
classical in the classical period, for "they testify more to a tragic experience
of madness opening in the fifteenth century, than to a critical and moral
experience of Unreason developing in their own epoch" (1965a, 31). In
them madness lies "beyond appeal"; for their characters it leads straight
to death, being connected still to a realm which, though social, transcends
the human. And in their works madness's truths are "eternal" in the sense
that the confusion between appearance and reality is not stopped by a
character's death or the fiction's end. Yet this very inability to fix the
border which distinguishes the real from the feigned points to a safer, more
modern, madness than that in which death, cosmic disorder, the devil, can
prowl. In Shakespeare and Cervantes, madness can become a mask – like
Hamlet one can pretend to be mad. Perhaps madly: here a secular economy
of madness begins. Madness functions no longer as punishment or fate,
but is tied to what we might call an imperialism of seeming, a social habit
of using deceit for real ends – a kind of hypocrisy. This habit is connected
to a certain shift in subjectivity, for the hypocrite no longer belongs to a
cosmic order in which what seems true to mere humanity may always be
false in God's eyes. Not even God can judge whether Hamlet or Don
Quixote are mad or not.

Foucault argues that only with Descartes does writing enter the classical
age and fall into step with the great confinement. Cartesian rationalism
requires at its base a moment at which nothing is open to doubt thus all
belief must be tested, soaked in scepticism by being reflected upon. That
process leads to the cogito, the famous foundation sentence: "I think
therefore I am" which itself cannot be doubted. For Descartes the greatest

threat to the certainty of reason still lies in the ever present possibility of madness as illusion, in the question: "how can I be sure that I am not mad?" To this he has no rational answer since scepticism loses its efficacy at this point. Madness is not like other "errors" – dreams and hallucinations say – from which the subject wakes into communal existence and once again can ask the question ("What can't I doubt?") that establishes metaphysical foundations. That one has to be sane to ask this foundational question does not stop Descartes short – even though his demand for epistemic security now presupposes a division between madness and sanity that no act of pure reason can account for. Madness is simply excluded by fiat: I, me, am not mad, least of all when I ask: "what can't I doubt?" To interrogate one's grounds is to be sane. This exclusion of madness is made in the name of what Foucault calls the "sovereignty of the subject," that "I" who is reasonable and knows himself – without any absolutely certain reason – not to be mad (1961a, 58). The important consequence of this, for Foucault, is that the sovereign subject of reason can no longer communicate or empathise with madness. *La folie* (madness) becomes *la déraison* (non-reason). And after Descartes the oppositional hierarchy by which the rational is placed against the non-rational or the "mad" tends to replace the older moral and religious oppositions, good versus evil or the sacred versus the profane. (It is worth noting that Derrida's famous review of *Madness and Civilization* contains, amongst much else, a counter-interpretation of Descartes' passage on madness. Derrida argues that Descartes never does "set aside," once and for all, the possibility of "total error for *all* knowledge gained from the senses or imaginary construction" (Derrida 1978, 48; italics his), ultimately because, for Descartes, the philosophic *topos* – the rational or intelligible structure of being – cannot be grounded on the senses.)

The discursive transformation of *la folie* into *la déraison* occurs more or less concurrently with the great confinement. And certainly the social event, the locking up of the mad, is *like* the philosophical event – the break between madness and the sovereign subject in Cartesian rationalism. But Foucault argues that the great confinement is basically a result of economic circumstances: the seventeenth century contained long periods of economic severity so that herding people off the streets into institutions was a means of dealing with that long depression, both by constraining them and by attempting to inculcate them with economically productive habits. Given that Foucault does not wish to establish a base/superstructure model to account for attitudes and practices towards the mad, the relation between the emergence of *déraison* and confinement, at least at their moment of emergence, can never be more than one of resemblance. Indeed Foucault offers no conspectus within which the split between reason and madness and the emergence of the new institutions and apparatuses of control can be finally tied together. This tolerance of emptiness, of explanatory gaps, makes his book difficult but it also keeps it out of the marxian and sociological mainstream. *Madness and Civilization* is not interested in providing totalizing explanations of the phenomena it deals with. We might even say that, in circulating such fissures, in helping them become acceptable for academic knowledge, the text itself absorbs some of what lies outside reason's empire (and, thus too, perhaps, begins to manage the "madness" of history itself).

Since the seventeenth century madness has taken the form of *déraison* in the West. This is true even of Foucault's great tradition of writers who keep some memory of the tragic meaning of madness alive: Nietzsche, Nerval, Sade, Hölderlin, Roussel, Artaud. Thus without attempting to follow Foucault's account of the relations between reason and madness in detail, it is necessary to have some grasp of the constitution of *déraison*. Once madness loses all value and sense, all connection with order, then reason itself enters into a new crisis. For reason is no longer madness's rival on a plane both share – which Foucault calls, in a Heideggerian spirit, the plane of *Being*. When reason cannot distinguish itself from madness, it can only banish madness into non-being so that it becomes possible to view reason itself from the side of non-being, as itself a huge, crazy, negative structure; as, in fact, *déraison*'s ghostly double. For Foucault, *déraison* takes two main forms in the classical age: passion and delirium. Passion is a state which covers and connects the body and the mind, it is caused by love, shock and so on, these causes becoming more specific and proximate as the eighteenth century proceeds. On the other hand, delirium is a state solely of mind, and, as we shall see, is more pertinent to the cultural space occupied by literature. Delirium is reason working not in its own light, but in darkness; reason seen under the sign of negation. Delirium is not (like dreams or "error") illogical, for it has its own consistency. As the *Encyclopédie*, that great tome of the French Enlightenment, puts it: in delirium the mind works "blindly" (1965a, 106); it is "reason dazzled." That last phrase, with which Foucault makes much play, is intended to imply that delirium is a reason which is so blinded by its own light that it loses that light at the very moment that it retains reason's structure. It is a simulacrum of reason. We might note in support of Foucault's reading of delirium that passage in Burton's *The Anatomy of Melancholy* (an English work which Foucault does not cite) where the author cheerfully confesses: "I am as foolish, as mad as anyone" (Burton 1932, 120). It is mad to be learned and lucid even about madness.

In a much more famous passage Locke (another Englishman whom Foucault does not quote) writes that the mad: "do not appear to me to have lost the Faculty of Reasoning: but having joined together some *Ideas* very wrongly, they mistake them for Truths; and they err as Men do, that argue right from wrong Principles" (Locke 1975, 161). Indeed for Locke, Descartes is, in effect, *mad* in that he establishes his whole chain of reasoning on exactly such "wrong principles." Empiricism resists *déraison* by refusing deduction, the basis of reason. But Locke also knows that if rhetoric replaces reason we are not better off – then he can ask this Hamlet-like question: "if the strength of persuasion be the light that must guide us, I ask how shall anyone distinguish between the delusions of Satan and the inspiration of the Holy Ghost?" (703–4.) More particularly, under delirium the sovereign subject loses that power to doubt which, as we have seen, is the guarantee of Cartesian reason. Madness becomes then an intense susceptibility to discourse: a surrender to language's power to present the false as true. Delirium, as right reason disconnected from being, remains everywhere present at hand even if there can be no exchange between it and the world of light. Rousseau in his *Discourse on the Origin of Inequality* will take delirium quite literally to be the condition of the "human soul" in a modernity deserted by God: "Instead of being, acting constantly from fixed and invariable principles, instead of that celestial and majestic simplicity, impressed on it by its divine Author, we find in it only the frightful contrast of passion mistaking itself for reason, and of understanding grown delirious" (Rousseau 1973, 38). Thus – for Foucault – the obsessive interest in the play of light and darkness in the Enlightenment, the work of the (often forged) painter Georges de la Tour, with its dramatic images of the power of shadow, being his favoured example in *Madness and Civilization*.

Foucault does not use Rousseau's remarks, or the plain speaking of the English empiricists, as sources for eighteenth-century thought. Instead, he turns to Diderot's *Jacques the Fatalist*, a work which, he says, teaches us a "lesson much more anticartesian than all Locke, all Voltaire, or all Hume" (1972a: 368). In Diderot, delirium acquires a new sense: it is not reason's mimic other, not an element of a madness which can be excluded by fiat, rather it indicates and embodies the composition of the real and subjectivity. Unreason finds its way back into the reason which excluded it. On the one hand, dreams, slips, madness itself, begin to mean something for reason, once again they carry information about the structures of man's relation to the world, so that reason is contaminated by its use of its opposite. But, on the other hand, and more profoundly, in Diderot, Being (now as against reason) is delirious because its internal mediations can collapse and the partially autonomous levels and formations as well as the oppositions by which being-in-the-world is constituted (in particular that which separates the subject from the object) can coalesce and fail. During the late eighteenth century the several possibilities of utter solitude, sheer appearance, and absolute plenitude are invoked under the sign of delirium – and not just by Diderot. Is the world nothing but what we perceive (Bishop Berkeley)? Or, on the contrary, is it merely the motion of masses of atoms (Holbach's materialism)? Or – another alternative – is it the material emanation of a Universal Spirit (pantheism)? Yet where Being, now conceivable as utterly full *or* utterly empty, is thus torn from reason, the play of mediations themselves (for instance, the structures which connect subjects to one another, which tie knowledge to the world, which permit appearances to correspond to reality) themselves appear delirious. For they may express – ontologically – nothing, that is to say, mere chance. For Foucault, this essential chanciness is the meaning of Rameau's nephew's laughter, which "prefigures in advance and reduces the total movement of nineteenth-century anthropology." Here too the most difficult question that modernity asks of itself is first posed: "why is not possible to maintain oneself in the difference of *déraison?*" in "the non-being of the real" (1972a, 368). But this "experience of *déraison,*" as Foucault calls it, will remain hidden in the shadows until Artaud and Roussel begin to write.

CONFINING TOLERANCE

For Foucault, the age of confinement ends when madness regains connection with the world of reason and sanity. In the Renaissance it did so as a negative bearer of value; at the end of the eighteenth century madness is exposed to the clear light of order as curable at first by morality, then, at the beginning of the nineteenth century, by medicine. Pinel unchains the inmates of Bicêtre in the name of morality. The cessation of harsh physical restraint is possible because his patients are supposed to be open to moral persuasion and development. As Foucault is quick to note, this permits the entry of "cures" which are punishments, old "symbolic" methods now becoming coercive. ("Symbolic" cures were those which imitated the symptoms they were directed against.) The moral cure produces guilt in patients through coercion and invigilation (1965a, 265). In a radical rejection of the Whiggish thesis that this represents an advance in civilized, humanitarian values, Foucault regards this new technique as working on new areas of subjectivity, the soul and mind of the patients. In this move the authorities' power is increased. The insane are no longer hidden from view: to use Foucault's terms, they move from confinement to the asylum. In England, where the mad had previously been placed in public institutions or in private "madhouses," the important dates are the founding of the Quaker retreat in 1792, and a series of legislative measures between 1807 and 1845 which enshrined the new principles of non-restraint and "moral treatment."

Asylums look different from the old houses of confinement: they are smaller, designed to have the appearance of private dwellings. They are placed in the countryside partly as a protection against contagious diseases but also to signify freedom and health. Nor are they filled by quite the same population as in the classical age: paupers and the insane are nowhere likely to find themselves in the same institutions – not even in the workhouse, for instance. The mad are less likely to be found in ordinary prisons too. Yet gradually the asylums acquire their own modes of discipline. Just after the Revolution, Cabinas develops what Foucault calls the first "objective gaze" directed towards madness (1972a, 460). For the first time, weekly, sometimes daily, records of each patient are kept: inmates are often forbidden to communicate with one another; soon after the technology is invented, photographs are taken of them; they are under constant surveillance often in the name of "attendance." (See also Donnelly 1983, Part 1, for this history.) Under this objective gaze, which begins to replace locks and bars, the mad take their place in the "positivity of known things" and, in these specific terms, "madness begins to speak again" (ibid., 463). The mad also become the object of individual attention (in that process which Foucault will later call "individuation") as part of the effort to order their lives – which is also the effort to use their lives to develop scientific truth. As their numbers increase, the new asylums cannot hold all those directed towards them. The great debate of the middle period of Victoria's reign concerned the question: why the increase? Was it the pressure of modern life? Did it merely indicate that the institutionalized and shiftless population were being ejected from the workhouse to the asylum? The most plausible reason for the rise in the inmate population according to recent research is that the working class in particular became increasingly willing to institutionalize family members (see Scull 1979, 221–53).

It is clear that such changes are not simply humanitarian, whatever the rhetoric under which they were inaugurated. And Foucault argues that the causes of the move from confinement to the asylum must be looked for more in the history of the institutions and their contexts than in the ideals of the reformers. For a long time confinement in the horrific, fever-ridden classical institutions had been seen as a cause of, as much as a solution for, madness. But more importantly, views about work and productivity change during the eighteenth century. Idleness, which under the older Christian dispensation had been conceived of as a sin, is now seen as a failure to produce and contribute to the wider national prosperity. The need to turn individuals into producers leads the mad back to the fold, the ability to work becomes more important than the absence of right reason. This in part orders the shape of their institutions, some of which now, vainly, aim for economic self-sufficiency. However, the mad, unlike the poor or criminals cannot be drawn into the new modes of production, and thus they require different institutions, indeed, they become the very type of the institutionalized subject.

Even though Pinel, unlike Tuke the British "reformer" of the asylums, was medically qualified, the reformers had no essential need for doctors in their asylums. After all the mad were to be dealt with morally rather than medically. (Actually Foucault makes less of this point than do later historians. See Ingleby 1983.) The medicalization of the insane is the last step in the gradual loss of otherness available to madness in dominant Western articulations, and lies outside Foucault's work proper, which is, of course, a history of *classical* madness. The madman becomes fully an object for doctors not because medicine was especially effective in dealing with such disorders, but because, first, doctors were already in the houses of confinement, and, second, they had a specific kind of authority. Doctors had always fought against fever in the classical asylums, so they were *in situ*; but they also now gain particular prestige, they become signs of disinterested authority and social concern who can control and order the mad for their own good. In a savage twist, the doctor deprives madness of all significance; it is looked at only in terms of the individual life and organism, "anthropologically" as Foucault puts it (he now intends the word negatively), and not, as it was still in the classical age, in terms of some general structure. As an "illness" (though the analogy with physical sickness begs many questions) it becomes a phenomenon without meaning. According to Foucault, the mad become not so much senseless (*insensé*) as alienated: they relate to truth only in so far as they provide examples for the doctor's scientific truth; that is, for medical discourse. Even so, in the richness and fullness of the doctors' descriptions of the causes of madness (such as social and historical progress) and in the closeness of their contact with the mad, the doctor too may encounter what Foucault can romantically call the "freedom" of the mad "experience" (1961a, 614).

Once madness is constructed as a *health* problem, the old question of the mad's responsibility for their acts becomes more urgent. Are their acts mere symptoms? But what if such acts are illegal? In such questions, the competency and authority of two professions is in question: doctors and lawyers. In the face of the legal profession's and the media's intense protest, doctors begin to be called into court rooms to make insanity defences (see Smith 1981). Of course, the precondition for this entry is madness's medicalization: once given names like "moral insanity," diagnosis extends into previously untouched areas. Most radically, insanity is not just recognized in its spectacle, in hallucinations and delirium but in symptoms of an underlying condition which may only occur irregularly – in a single act of murder even. Such a condition was called monomania and, early in the nineteenth century, was diagnosed whenever an act could not be ascribed a motive. Confronted with monomania, the forensic question could be posed dramatically: is this person insane and thus not responsible, not open to punishment, or a criminal deserving the full rigour of the law? Thus in the courts two opposing discursive practices contended for management of trials, sentencing and custodial practices: one borrowed from the old discourse of man as determined, the other from that of man as free. Torn between these points of view a whole new species came into existence: the criminal insane. What is in question, here, is not merely an intensification of the old "free-will" debate (which asks: how can human beings be free if their behaviour belongs to a network of cause and effect?) but a dispute about what kind of technology and discourse ought to be brought to bear on certain kinds of law-breaker. In the early years of this dispute, syndromes, whole diseases, had short histories: monomania quickly became "disaggregation of the ego" for instance. But despite this discursive insta-bility the doctors who used these words had immense authority, at least in regard to their patients.

The doctors' authority was much greater than that of the lawyers, police or asylum keepers because they possessed the ability to "cure" – the truth about their patients was in their hands. This doctor/patient relationship was unsymmetrical. From the patients' point of view the doctor became what Foucault calls a "thaumaturge" – a figure who may, or may not, perform "magical" cures across a distance which permits no true exchange, and in which "the authority which he has borrowed from order, morality, and the family now seems to derive from himself" (1965a, 275). From the side of the doctor, the patients' behaviour underwent shifts, "cures" even, which could not be accounted for by medical techniques. Patients who cured themselves may have been faking their original condition; these "true cures of false illnesses" (276) repeat the older formation in which madness and simulation of madness were never far apart. Only with Freud does the patient–doctor couple itself become the object of therapeutic interest, mainly through the concepts of transference and counter-transference, by which the doctor–patient relationship repeats – or, better, re-enacts – (a version of) the events that caused the patient's trauma. Freud inherits and intensifies Pinel and Tuke's works: he completed the long task of taking madness out of confinement, but he did so only by exploiting to its maximum the image of therapist as thaumaturge. The psychoanalyst who listens silently becomes "the mirror in which madness, in an almost motionless movement clings to and casts off itself" (278). But the psycho-analyst cannot "liberate" or "explain" what is essential to *déraison*. For Foucault, *it* "flashes forth" only in the literary counter-canon, in Hölderlin, Nerval, Nietzsche, Artaud.

It should be clear that this long story of madness is deeply embedded in the history of literature. The shape and style of the connections that Foucault draws between the two spheres is set forth in a series of moving, if somewhat purple, passages in the "Conclusion" of his book (in the French, titled "The Anthropological Circle"). Here, where he invokes Goya's *Disparates*, Foucault's work undergoes a change of mode: it becomes poetic in the sense that it apostrophizes its object: endowing madness with much of the force and aura it claims to derive from it. A will to valorize the others of reason is apparent. (We can note echoes of the description of dreams in the Binswanger "Preface" cited above.)

Madness has become man's possibility of abolishing both man and the world – and even those images that challenge the world and deform man. It is, far beyond dreams, beyond the nightmare of bestiality, the last recourse: the end and the beginning of everything. Not because it is a promise, as in German lyricism, but because it is the ambiguity of chaos and apocalypse. . . .

And this madness that links and divides time, that twists the world into the ring of a single night, this madness so foreign to the experience which is contemporary to it, does it not transmit – to those able to receive it, to Nietzsche and to Artaud – those barely audible voices of classical unreason, in which it was always a question of nothingness and night, but amplifying them now to shrieks and frenzy? But giving them for the first time an expression, a *droit de cité*, and a hold on Western culture which makes possible all contestants, as well as *total* contestation?

(1965a, 281, translation modified)

As literary *déraison*, madness contests humanism; it drags the human away from the centre of the world picture. As the power of the night, it is an adversary of the Enlightenment. *Déraison* stays inside and outside of history, remaining in the shadows of that light of classical Reason which illuminates the development of mankind and turns chronicle into history. Yet that night itself "links and divides time." Like death, it is a periodic irruption into the order of temporality, one which organizes temporality itself. We may think about this in terms of the following question: if there were no death what meaning would time have? Conceived of as death's younger sibling, madness ultimately works against the possibility of literature itself. If, as art comes closer to madness, the modern world is "arraigned by the work of art," (288) madness itself remains too disruptive, too other, to be framed within art: "where there is a work of art, there is no madness" (288–9).

Nietzsche's, Artaud's and Sade's personal madnesses swallow their lives, coming from nowhere as it were, compelling them to write and threatening the "sense" of their writings but also disappearing in their writing. Nonetheless, as the constant threat of their moment of collapse, madness grants those works their force of contestation and prestige (though Foucault would soon cease to believe in any notion of "total contestation"). So, unlike a certain deconstruction, Foucault's book does not permit us to think of texts as mad in their "undecidability" – or, to take one instance of many, in the way they may depend on repetitions that they can only disavow. That is, he is not interested in what Shoshana Felman calls "the vanishing point of the uninterpretable toward which the effort of interpretation heads, but where it falls apart . . . [where] the rhetoric of madness meets, and merges with, the very madness of rhetoric as such" (Felman 1985, 32). He refuses to analyze "mad" literary works as if they belong to an *institution* of literature which, today, belongs mainly to the professionalized academy that exposes such works to (the failures of) "interpretation" and pedagogy. If he insists on the importance of the writers' lives and the disappearance of lived madness in its written expression, he also traces that historical construction and control of "madness" as a signifier and as a way of acting and thinking. These can never be grasped through the metaphor of the "madness" of the text. Yet, though in general Foucault wishes to make it as difficult as possible to treat of madness as a literary *topos* rather than as an event, no doubt *Madness and Civilization* has accelerated what it would prevent, and in part that is because the book did, sometimes, gesture towards an essential madness, which, as Foucault also recognized, could never be recuperated for communication. Also – as we shall see – the abstract and rejected "madness" of writing or rhetoric returns under another guise in the "transgressive" theory that Foucault will elaborate in his literary essays throughout the sixties.

2

MEDICINE, DEATH, REALISM

In 1963, two years after *Folie et déraison* appeared, Foucault published two monographs on very different topics. One, *Death and the Labyrinth*, was a critical study of Raymond Roussel, a French poet, dramatist and novelist whose experimental works, written around the time of the First World War, were much admired both by the surrealists and by French new novelists of the sixties. The other, *The Birth of the Clinic*, was a history of medicine during the period of the French Revolution.[1] These works, so apparently dissimilar, have a single impulse: they both explore the history and signification of death in modernity, and, by virtue of this alone, share something with the earlier works on dreams and madness. *The Birth of the Clinic* offers a detailed description of the medical management of life and death at the end of the eighteenth century, while the monograph on Roussel is a critical examination of an extraordinary moment in what Foucault thinks of as life's colonization of Being, inaugurated in the Revolutionary era. It is as if the two sides of *Madness and Civilization*, its literary or existential and its historical aspects, can no longer cohere in a single book when Foucault comes to focus on life and death rather than reason and madness. In this chapter I outline Foucault's work on medicine, dealing with the Roussel book in the next chapter. Because that work forms the basis for his later account of power in modern society, I have elaborated it a little by connecting it to the history of public health in Britain during the nineteenth century. And I bring some medical history into connection with literature by offering a brief reading of three canonical, nineteenth-century, realist novels.

THE BIRTH OF THE CLINIC

At an empirical level, *The Birth of the Clinic* recounts the pre-history of the moment in which medicine becomes a fully fledged clinical science. According to Foucault, it does so with the publication of Broussais's *Examen de la doctrine généralement admise* in 1816. This history is not conceived of as a progressive heaping-up of discoveries, but as a series of shifts or breaks.

44

The proposition that intellectual history is essentially discontinuous is stated much more boldly here than it was in *Madness and Civilization*, both because *The Birth of the Clinic* deals specifically with the emergence of a science, and because its narrative no longer presupposes that any essential experience has been displaced or forgotten like *la folie* in the earlier book. *The Birth of the Clinic* is not telling the story of a subject – medical science – whose identity transcends the history being recounted or whose formation is the *telos* of the narrative.

Like *Madness and Civilization*, *The Birth of the Clinic* is concerned with the interrelation between institutions, here, hospitals and clinics, and the theories and practices which emerge in them. To focus coherently on this set of relations and the breaks they undergo, Foucault presents the "medical gaze" as his narrative's protagonist: in French the book is subtitled "une archéologie du régard medical." Foucault's usage of this term develops from the way he treated the relations between doctors and patients in an untranslated section of the "Birth of the Asylum" chapter of *History of Madness*:

> The madman of the classical internment was offered to the gaze; but this gaze basically did not fasten on him himself, it fastened on his monstrous surface, his visible animality. At least it comprised a form of reciprocity since a healthy man was able to read in it, as in a mirror, the imminent movement of his own fall. The gaze that Tuke now inaugurates as one of the major elements of existence in the asylum, is at once deeper and less reciprocal.
>
> (Foucault 1972a, 506)

Here the gaze is not just an experience but a relationship between doctor and patient, a relationship which takes place in a space which is both real and discursive. It is a real space in the obvious sense that, at various historical moments, doctors examine patients using particular methods and tools, in different kinds of rooms, in different institutions. The space is discursive in that the medical gaze is organized in terms of how relations between doctors and patients were conceived. But in history the real and discursive do not belong to two disconnected orders: more specifically, the medical gaze is preconditioned by what Foucault calls, in a phrase which will remain important to him, its "concrete a-priori." In this context, the term refers to the conditions of possibility of any particular organization of what Foucault calls the "medical experience" – where this "medical experience" is the effect of a complex constellation, a conglomerate of discourses, social pressures and so on, rather than a set of rules or a Bachelardian "epistemology." For instance, it does not just consist of (implicit) criteria for deciding what counts and what does not count as a fact for medicine, at what stage of the illness the essence of the disease is thought to be found and so on. It also includes the political and economic

45

forces which operate on the construction of hospitals. The metaphor "medical gaze" spatializes relations between doctor and patient and allows the complexity of those relations to acquire a coherent, narrativisible form. It permits Foucault loosely to tie the disparate phenomena of medical history – its "discoveries," the architectural spaces built by the profession, their tools and so on – to discursive and material conditions without needing to draw on concepts like cause and effect, intention, and function. It permits him to see that an "ensemble" of practices may come together in what he will later call a "strategy."

What, in brief, does Foucault have to say about the medicine during the period? It undergoes three quite distinct stages: moving from "classificatory", to the "clinical" and finally to the "anatomo-clinical." In the classificatory period, doctors regarded diseases as ideal types, each with its own natural history, each connected to one another by an elaborate system of resemblances. Patients were contingent to their disease: their bodies merely provided an opportunity for the disease to appear, and did not demand close examination. It was the disease that was studied, not its concrete manifestation. The "proto-clinics," that had existed since the seventeenth century, were institutions in which the total field of diseases could be seen. In them, the patient was not a case, but an example of a condition. Because diseases had their natural course, the doctor's role was to let that course run, under the age-old adage *primum non nocere* – "above all do no harm." This course could be perverted by artificial environments, of which the hospital (itself a major cause of disease) was by far the most threatening. According to Foucault, the classificatory approach comes to an end not because it was proved wrong or because of new discoveries, but through the impact of social and political events. In 1776 the Royal Society of Medicine (in France) decided to attempt to prevent outbreaks of epidemics, by collecting data on their occurrence and controlling the environments in which they happened. Hence the medical gaze moves outside the "circle of knowledge" of the ideal types and natural history of diseases, onto the world (Foucault 1973a, 29). In this move, the clinic proper forms.

Doctors begin to work within a political and social "space" – that of the nation's health. This shift reaches its climax during the Revolution:

This medical field, restored to its pristine truth, pervaded wholly by the gaze, without obstacle and without alteration, is strangely similar, in its implicit geometry, to the social space dreamt of by the revolution, at least in its original conception; a form homogeneous in each of its regions, constituting a set of equivalent items capable of maintaining constant relations with their entirety, a space of free communication in which the relationship of the parts to the whole was always transposable and reversible.

(ibid., 38)

The free medical gaze was considered to be obstructed by the unreformed institutions – the old universities and hospitals in which old lore and fevers dominated. When they were dismantled under the pressure of the Revolution and its uprooting of old institutions, the classificatory system which typified diseases began to disappear as well. In the proto-clinics, where the actual manifestation of a disease was never identical to its pure form or "morbid essence," there existed an inevitable gap between the visible and the real. Disease was manifested both in symptoms which permit "the invariable form of the disease to show through" (90) and signs which indicate the stage that the disease has reached in its course. This gap between the visible and the real closes in the post-Revolutionary clinic, as the disease is examined less as an abstraction or an essence made concrete than as an event working on the patient's body. There, as Foucault elegantly phrases it, "a language which did not owe its truths to speech but to the gaze alone" would be spoken. Of course the new clinics are themselves institutions, and teachable skills are required in order to *see* the disease. So when such clinics emerge a new split appears, this time between doctors trained in clinics and medical officers whose training largely consisted of mere curative practice, and whose domain was the working of disease in society, but who were forbidden, for instance, to perform complex surgical operations. (Charles Bovary is the most famous literary example of this grade of the profession.)

In the first edition of his book at least, Foucault uses structuralist notions to describe the doctor's gaze in clinical medicine:

> The formation of the clinical method was bound up with the emergence of the doctor's gaze into the field of signs and symptoms . . . [it] involved the effacement of their absolute distinction and the postulate that henceforth the signifier (sign and symptom) would be entirely transparent for the signified, which would appear, without concealment or residue, in its most pristine reality, and that the essence of the signified – the heart of the disease – would be entirely exhausted in the intelligible syntax of the signifier.
>
> (ibid., 91)

To state it more simply, diseases will not acquire, in theory at least, the status of "natural signs" – readable from what lies present to hand. Foucault turns from natural history to philosophy in order to attack the epistemological grounds of "natural signs." He uses arguments which have become familiar in post-structuralism but which are, in fact, traditional enough. Claiming that "clinical thought merely transposes . . . a conceptual configuration whose discursive form was available to Condillac" (92), Foucault shows that, in order to posit a "language of action" as the "origin of speech," Condillac must assume that "action (in medical terms, "sign" and "symptom") must already be structured as language. (In his *Essay on*

47

the Origin of Language, first published in 1772, Herder, already following Rousseau, had made the same point against Condillac: "Either he supposes the whole thing called language to have been invented prior to the first page of his book, or I find things on every page that could not possibly have occurred in the orderly continuity of a language in formation" (Herder 1966, 99)). For Foucault, Condillac can remain blind to this sleight of hand (or metalepsis – a mistaking of effect for cause) because he oscillates between two positions. On the one hand, he regards knowledge and language as continuous with reality and history in an uninterrupted line that leads from the elemental to the complex. On the other, he regards the structure of knowledge as a mirror of the structure of the world: a mirror whose accuracy can be gauged by "calculation." In a very Hegelian move, Foucault argues that this contradiction had its analogues in clinical medicine, and it is this which led to clinical medicine's collapse. Doctors begin to intrude into the bodies of their patients in order to prise out their secrets. They begin, after Bichat, to work on the physical surface of the body and not on the body as a set of abstract, *readable*, phenomena. Their gaze penetrates, it becomes active. In this period the stethoscope is invented, the medical thermometer, percussion and ausculation comes into wide use and Bichat, in particular, gains an international reputation as a virtuoso of the knife.

As doctors open up bodies, both dead and alive, conceptions of its workings and disease change. Attention moves from organs (or what Foucault calls "organic volume") to the very substance of the body itself – tissue:

> In anatomo-clinical experience, the medical eye must see the illness spread before it, horizontally and vertically in graded depth, as it penetrates into the body, as it advances into its bulk, as it circumvents or lifts its masses, as it descends into its depths. Disease is no longer . . . a pathological species inserting itself into the body wherever possible; it is the body itself that has become ill.

(136)

And "where the body itself has become ill," clinical signs refer not to diseases but to lesions, to local, if diffuse, pathological events. Physiology separates itself from classical anatomy. Each disease exists at a precise locality: it *is* a particular lesion, tumour, whatever secondary effects may exist. Thus, for instance: a pulse rate is not first read as the sign of an already hypothesized general condition, but taken to ascertain whether further investigation is needed. And, more importantly, medical research begins to be radically distinguished from therapy: knowledge is not measured solely by its capacity to effect "cures" or curative regimes.

In this shift from organs to tissue, from interpretation to intervention, from therapy to research, the relation between life and death changes for medicine. Whereas in classical medicine the table of diseases existed on the backdrop of *nature*, for pathological anatomy, they are present against the background of *life*. The content of diseases become the "vital processes," they themselves are viewed as "the pathological form of life." But life leads to one end – death, and each pathological event or form belongs to, as much as it indicates, the end that it anticipates:

> Bichat relativised the concept of death, bringing it down from that absolute in which it appeared as an indivisible, decisive, irrecoverable event; he volatilized it, distributed it throughout life in the form of separate, partial, progressive deaths, deaths that are so slow in occurring that they extend even beyond death itself. But from this fact he formed an essential structure of medical thought and perception: that to which life is *opposed* and to which it is *exposed*; that in relation to which it is living *opposition*, and therefore *life*; that in relation to which it is analytically *exposed*, and therefore *true*.
>
> (144–5)

Foucault regards the emergence of Bichat's medicine as a profound occasion for Western culture. The absorption of death into life means that each patient will for the first time become an individual for medicine. Now, each case has its own pattern of pathology; for instance, each organ dies at its own time rather than death occurring at a stroke. And now everyone has their own way of dying.

This is all the more true for "anatomo-clinical" medicine, in which disease becomes an exaggeration or excess of the normal life-processes, and needs to be controlled by anti-stimulant procedures. (In it, leeches and bleeding, particularly recommended by Broussais, make a marked return to fashion.) At the deep level of tissue, each disease belongs to a single process of disorganization and morbidity. The attention to the surfaces of the individual body's depths (a clumsy but unavoidable formulation) has aesthetic consequences. As Foucault notes in a passage which anticipates the famous last sentences of *The Order of Things*: "To *discover* . . . will no longer be to *read* an essential coherence beneath a state of disorder, but to push a little farther back the foamy line of language, to make it encroach upon that sandy region that is still open to the clarity of perception but is already no longer so to everyday speech – to introduce language into that penumbra where the gaze is bereft of words" (169). Medical language acquires "extraordinary formal beauty" in its effort to exceed the passive and external gaze. Foucault gives as an example a passage from Laënnec's first, and very figurative, description of cirrhosis of the liver:

> The liver, reduced to a third of its volume, was, as it were, hidden

49

in the region that it occupies; its external surface, slightly mammillated and emptied, was a yellowish grey in colour; when cut, it seemed to be made up entirely of a mass of small seeds, round or oval in shape, varying in size from a millet seed to a hemp seed.

(ibid.)

But the anatomo-clinician is also, Foucault observes, Sade's contemporary.[2] That is to say, at some level of great abstraction, medicine joins hands with the literary anatomizers of death or decay in life from Goya to Baudelaire, sharing with them a "gaze that envelops, caresses, details, atomizes the most individual flesh and enumerates its secret bits . . . that fixed, attentive, rather dilated gaze which, from the height of death, has already condemned life" (171).

ENGLISH DEATH

For Foucault, it is in medicine after the French Revolution that "Western man constitutes himself in his own eyes as an object of science." It is there that the relation of life and death takes a form in which it becomes meaningful to say that "the experience of individuality in modern culture is bound up with that of death" – a move which in fact historicizes Heidegger's claim that death individuates *Dasein*, that authentic existence is directed towards death, nothingness. In the clinics where corpses were dissected, where living bodies were increasingly carefully inspected, notions of salvation and progress overlap with a discourse on health, and the doctor (and Bichat in particular) acquires the power and prestige proper to a representative of historical emancipation. Before the eighteenth century, Western medicine had had little sense that it was in control of bodies and diseases. On the contrary, the advantage had then belonged to disease often conceived of as part of a man's fallen state and a punishment for sin. As we have seen, medicine, shuttling between tradition and faddishness, constituted at best a passive resistance to disease's inevitability. With Bichat this relation begins to be reversed. Medicine becomes an active force; diseases await their conquest, just as in the political arena old authoritarian institutions await their democratization.

Only later, once he had begun to develop a theoretical account of modern power, did Foucault fully spell out the interrelations of this shift in medicine's role and that of social organization in general. These interrelations can only be sketched out briefly here, though they will be placed in a wider frame in chapters 6 and 7 below. In the essay "The Politics of Health in the Eighteenth Century," Foucault argues that during the eighteenth century a "noso-politics" emerges, whose sweep is larger than any more visible division between public and private medicine. Its object is the "social body" – that is, the population considered as a biological entity.

Noso-political administrative strategies are not imposed from "above," but are defined as being in the *general* interest – even if these strategies cover a number of different targets and involve a variety of procedures (from child-rearing to dealing with "fevers" for instance). The basic aim of the new politics of health is (as in *Madness and Civilization*) the transformation of the "people," or the "mob" into a labour force, the management of whose productivity gradually becomes a primary interest of the state (1980b, 173). Now medicine and hygiene become "instances of social control" (ibid.); the sharp spatial differentiation between sickness and health is dissolved as questions of health move out of those "curing machines" (180), the hospitals, onto the urban conglomerations in general. This move is all the more powerful because statisticians had shown that the anti-stumulant techniques championed by Broussais were not more successful than any other regime in curing the epidemic fevers that swept Europe in the first half of the nineteenth century.[3] Research and clinical practice become even more removed from one another, and the need to reconcile them becomes intense. So, the sick are increasingly cared for at home (by doctors with "rounds") and also in what we would call out-patient units, while statisticians, journalists and bureaucrats roam the street gauging the fitness of the social body and researchers open up the bodies of corpses and animals.

To enable this shift, a new rhetoric is called upon. We find it in the English reformer Southwood Smith's famous essay "The Uses of the Dead for the Living": "An Enlightened physician and a skilful surgeon are in the daily habit of administering to their fellow men more real and unquestionable good, than is communicated, or communicable, by any other class of human beings to another. Ignorant physicians and surgeons are the most deadly enemies of the community: the plague itself is not so destructive" (Smith 1824, 59). Clinical medicine gains its authority by its ability to renounce verbal tradition, the old lore of medical knowledge. Memory is replaced by a "patient and minute research" which, in Southwood Smith's words, gazes through the "thick veil" of the body to reveal the "most curious and wonderful operations of animal economy" – life itself. Looking past the veil of the flesh sorts the saviours from the quacks.

The apotheosis of medicine occurred with different rhythms, and in rather different domains, in France and England. In particular, the English gaze emerges triumphant from two separate battlegrounds. The first is that of anatomy and the fight against ancient burial practices and attitudes to the dead; the second that of epidemiology and especially the fight against cholera. In each case, but especially the latter, medicine becomes a central strut in the foundations of modern statism (and will later find a new sub-discipline "state medicine"). Here what is combated is a death linked not just to disease but to unproductivity and social disorder. Let us begin with the less familiar of these two struggles, that of the anatomists.

51

In *Hugh Trevor*, a Jacobin novel by Thomas Holcroft, the enlightened hero, fleeing at night from his enemies with his servant, finds himself in an outhouse and promptly falls alseep. Then:

> I was awakened from wild slumbers . . . Again and again I asked "What have you heard? What ails you?"
>
> It was long before he could utter an articulate sound. At last, shaking more violently as he spoke, and with inexpressible horror in his voice, he gasping said – "A dead hand" –
>
> "Where?" –
>
> "I felt it! – I had hold of it! It is now at my neck."
>
> For a moment I paused; not daring to stretch out my arm, and examine. I trembled in sympathy with him. At length I ventured.
>
> Never shall I forget the sensation I experienced, when, to my full conviction, I actually felt a cold, dead, hand, between my fingers!
>
> I was suffocated with horror! I struggled to overcome it; again it seized me; and I sunk half entranced!
>
> (Holcroft 1978, 289–90)

It gets worse: some very shady characters throw another body into the room which turns out to be piled with dead organs. It is a moment at which heroes may fitly be invoked: "Alexander and Caesar themselves would have shook, lying as we lay, hearing what we heard, and seeing what we saw" (292). But daylight changes everything. "In the relation of this adventure, I have given a picture not of things as they were afterwards discovered to be, but as they appeared to us at the time, reflected through the medium of consternation and terror" (296). The gory outhouse is revealed to be a dissecting room; and the murderers are "resurrectionist men" – whose work it was to supply doctors with corpses. The narrator continues: "These things ought not to be terrible; but to persons of little reflection, and not familiarized to them, they always are" (297). This curiously clumsy manipulation of time attempts to harness Gothic terror to quasi-revolutionary preaching. Melodrama is used in an attempt to familiarize horror – a rhetorical move to become characteristic of the anatomist's case.

Medicine as an enlightened profession, Foucault's clinical medicine, required corpses. Hopes were expressed that all medical students would dissect five subjects in order to become qualified. In this climate, writers make huge claims for anatomy: "perhaps it is impossible to name any one subject which it is of more importance that the community should understand" (Smith, 1824, 60). And everyday life becomes invaded by strange cadavers:

> A young lady having been afflicted with the toothache, had the careous tooth extracted; but subsequently a disease arose in the lower

jaw, from whence the tooth had been removed; the whole of the lower jaw became enlarged and continuing in magnitude for several years, until at length she seemed to have, as it were, a double head, formed by an immense secretion of osseous and cartilaginous substance, the rictus of the mouth intervening. In this state I saw her about three months previous to her death and after that catastrophe occurred, the cemetery and grave being pointed out to one of the resurrection-men, a party went in the course of a few nights, and disinterred the body; which they decapitated, bringing away the head only, but leaving the bleeding corpse exposed on the ground, the coffin lid and shroud being also left in different places, forming, with the empty coffin, a horrible exhibition to the public gaze.

(132)

It is hard not to read this incident except as symptomatically: a woman with two heads, decapitated – after Medusa, Salome, Judith, what can this be except an image of terror? An image, perhaps, which once again demonstrates how the knife, unable to dissociate itself from the castrating stroke, fails to settle the threat of the phallic woman? (That, of course, is a very un-Foucauldian sentence to write.) Certainly, to decapitate a woman has always presaged destruction: it is as if, if we let the body-snatchers get away with this, then ours will be Herod's fate – as if what happened to those who saw Medusa might happen to us too. The same doctor recalls another, less overdetermined, incident in which, having refused to pay the body-snatchers five guineas at the "commencement of [an] anatomical season," they dumped two corpses in "a high state of decomposition" in the middle of the West End. This piece of spontaneous industrial action caused a riot, and a recently established instrument for social control was called upon: "I suppose I should have been immolated, but for my contiguity to the police officer Sir Robert Baker who came forward with his police establishment by which means I was protected" (134). Gruesome descriptions such as these, veering between technical language and mythical sensationalism, were essential to the doctors who had to overturn traditional attitudes towards the sanctity of the dead. Not only did they reveal that monstrous bodies were already massively out of place, neither consecrated nor hidden, exposed to the public eye and threats to the fragile public (and perhaps psychic) order; they also steered a shift away from the vulgar horror they induced towards an inspection of corpses by a science whose full legitimation they could only anticipate.

The task of the reformers was not just to argue that the use of the dead to the living overcame the older inviolacy of the dead in their graves, nor to overturn laws which in fact date back to interdictions on the use of cadavers by witches, but to organize a mechanism by which available bodies could be transported invisibly from the place of death to the clinic.

Thus reformers concentrated, first, on arguing that the use of unclaimed paupers' corpses for purposes of dissection did not constitute another form of exploitation by the rich of the poor and, second, on proscribing the times and means by which corpses should be conveyed through the streets without scandal. They were successful – in 1832 an Anatomy Act was passed by which the old witchcraft laws were superseded and bodies could legally be used by students. In a connected move five years later a General Registry was established in which all births, marriages and deaths were recorded, though it was only in 1874 (1855 in Scotland) that civil registrations of births and deaths were made compulsory (Wohl 1983, 11). This store of statistical information was to provide the basis for a fully developed "state medicine" in which doctors would have control not just over their individual patients but over the population as a whole, conceived of as a social body.

Yet the scandal of corpses in the public sphere and the related question of their use-value did not completely die away until later in the century. It is true that after 1832 body-snatchers disappeared. But the urban cemeteries remained hygiene problems which, as the reformers argued, required centralized state intervention. Cemeteries smelt to high heaven, corpses were often piled on top of one another, sometimes with a mere couple of inches of dirt as cover. In his *Report on the Internment in Towns*, an appendix to his earlier sanitation report, Edwin Chadwick, the reformer's leader, argued against the view that a cycle of over-population and thus poverty and death was inevitable, a view derived from the so-called "pessimistic" interpretation of Malthus. Disease was caused by bad sanitation – particularly in drains, housing and cemeteries; a concept known as the "sanitation idea." To control disease a central agency was required because the parishes or unions, even had they the will, were unable to link local effects to the larger causal pattern or to finance engineering works unconfinable to local boundaries. The programme of the new, progressive and directive statism was succinctly summed up in the slogan "centralisation not representation" – "not representation" because the individuals whose lives the reformers ordered were not themselves to be represented in the processes of central planning. Thus, also, the "sanitation idea" opposed the New Poor Law's attempts to connect welfare administration to the parish. This programme of centralization and inspection became linked in the political domain with the wider implications of Benthamite reform, and evoked strong opposition from those whose politics, like Foucault's much later, were based on the local. To counter such resistances, Chadwick (who began as a crusading journalist) used melodrama and sensationalism just like Smith. One of his opponents on the Poor Law Commission wrote to him "your Report reads like one of Ainsworth's novels, and I will think furnish some good hints for deepening the horrors of his next Jack Sheppard production" (quoted in Lewis 1952, 68). But the discourse spread –

even *The Times* published a story of a gravedigger digging through "severed heads, arms, legs or whatever came [his] way with a crowbar, pick-axe, chopper or saw" in a ghastly parody of medical surgery.[4]

After 1831 death is seen unnecessarily to spill into life most of all because of cholera. Historians have argued that revolutions followed outbreaks of the disease in Europe; in England there were riots against the doctors fuelled by the fear that cholera was being spread especially in order to provide the dissectionists with more corpses (see Linebaugh 1975). Such fears were not confined to Europe: rumours about the techniques of inoculation against cholera and resistance to public health officials became an important, displaced form of colonial resistance in India (Arnold 1988). Two aspects of the centralizers' approach to cholera need to be stressed. First, it provided an impetus for an extremely detailed surveillance of proletarian conditions – a drawing of new social data into an information network. The gathering of statistics (which were, as M. J. Cullen points out, often analyzed crudely and falsely) provided part of the impetus of reform because they presented a picture of immense social differences and, in particular, of the deprivations of the urban poor (Cullen 1975). At the same time, they helped organize social existence into structures more capable of being ordered and known by the state. As is well known, this data was used directly by the "condition of England" novelists of the 1840s, and is certainly part of the discursive inheritance and narratological techniques of later realist writers. Second, of the two hypotheses of cholera's causes, the wrong one was long preferred by eminent state doctors. Was cholera "contagious," the mysterious product of contact, or was it caused by local miasma? The reason why the miasma theory was preferred seems to be linked to its sanctioning a *need* for surveillance and control as well as a rhetoric of horror firmly fixed to place. If cholera's genesis was perceptible then it could be described in the sensationalism of the reports, and at last eradicated. Thus we find the strange hyperbole of the reformers being directed at this topic too: "We do not speak without weighing the import of the words we use, when we affirm that, in the whole range of physical and moral agencies, there is not one capable of producing in human beings, feelings and actions of such gross selfishness, and therefore capable of rendering human beings so utterly base, as the belief of the common doctrine of contagion" (Smith 1825, 521). It was only in the 1880s that the water-borne cholera bacteria was isolated, though statistical studies had long connected outbreaks to water. But a "virus" (as Southwood Smith called the bearer of contagion) which spread invisibly according to probabilities in a deadly inversion of the power of sympathy could not provide the impetus to re-order the material basis of proletarian lives. The bacterial hypothesis destroyed the strange hopes of Chadwick's report: which are to be found not so much in the idea that cleanliness, new housing and hidden corpses would make the social body more productive (and lessen Poor Law Relief costs), nor the metaleptic notion that a moral revolution would follow the triumph of hygiene, but in the amazing anticipation of medicine's total victory – the expectation that, after the eradication of miasmas, death would only occur as "euthanasia" – not really death at all (Chadwick 1965, 410).[5] Though we must be cautious here, for "euthanasia" changes its meanings in the middle decades of the nineteenth century: it moves from the sense "death without pain" to its modern sense "inducing death." In the ambiguity which underpins this lexical shift, the dream of an end of pain merges with the dream of a medical control of life itself.

Death, and the practices that surround it, were crucial for Chadwick's programme of bureaucratic centralization. In his report on the urban cemeteries, he suggests that intramural burials (that is, burial inside churches) be banned, coffins sealed, cemeteries shifted from the inner urban localities. He also proposes the creation of a "medical police" to supervise burials and record causes of death. This last was essential because it provided information on exactly how effective local authorities were in implementing the sanitation idea. A doctor peering into a corpse formed the keystone of state medicine. In his notorious article "Preventative Police," Chadwick – the journalist – had argued that Britain should possess a centralized system of "preventative police," borrowing the idea from the European absolutist states (though he also argued that France, for instance, its reputation notwithstanding, did not have such a police). But in his earlier work, his suggestions for a bureaucracy had been relatively vague. Even here his image of a "magistrate" who would preside over the police derives from medicine:

> By the imposition of a real responsibility on the magistrate, he would feel an interest in his official duties, similar to that experienced by professional men with regard to the advancement of the science to which they have devoted themselves. Under such circumstances investigations of such kind [surveillance of criminal hang-outs], would be as attractive not only to the moralist and legislator, but to the magistrate, on account of the curious psychological facts elicited, as are the dissections of subjects to anatomists in cases presenting new and unexpected physical phenomena.
>
> (Chadwick 1830, 303)

Despite immense social and political resistance to centralization following the hated New Poor Laws, Medical Officers were appointed by certain municipalities in the late 1840s and in 1855 Sir John Simon became the first "Central Medical Officer," based in London – though it was only in a series of Acts passed in the 1870s that the state took full control over the health of the social body. Thus it is over the corpses of the poor, that absolute site of non-resistance but a mine of information, in a rhetoric often borrowed from the popular fiction of the time, with the image of the doctor as enlightened conqueror of death in the background, that we find the English welfare state stirring.

The end of this stage in the story of mutilation, corpses out of place and the struggle of medicine against sacred death, seems to have come with invention of a new technology: mechanical cremation in the 1870s. In an article published in 1874, Sir Henry Thompson, an eminent medical researcher, argued that the problem of over-population and endangering the living world by the dead could now be solved. Not only was burial no longer simply a sanitation or space problem – corpses themselves could be used productively. Of course, defences of the tomb, those places of "peculiar sanctity for those whose dear ones sleep in them" were at once mounted (Holland 1873, 477). But the cremationists replied in different terms than those used by the dissectionists: for the latter the dead were primarily objects of knowledge, for the former they were economically valuable. Now the corpse becomes, as it were, a site of inorganic vitality: "Never [is] there greater activity than at this moment exists in that still corpse," Thompson writes of the point of death (Thompson 1873, 319). The activity is *chemical* – so that the cremationists argued that the ashes of the dead could be substituted for bone imported into England as fertilizer. The dead could cut the nation's import bill. They also pointed to bodies left on the streets – especially those of infants (often victims of that common crime of the time, infanticide, and the New Poor Law bastardy regulations), and, apparently, treated by local authorities like the corpses of cats and dogs because of the cost of burial. Cremation could be used on these bodies too. It could also form part of an apparatus of further hygiene and information processing, its cheapness making it easier to establish medical certificates for each and every death. Cremation could, thus, work towards further control of the social body.

The rhetoric of the cremationists was less melodramatic than anthropological; they applied a strategy of pseudo-scientific educational de- and re-familiarization to introduce their technology. Current burial practices could be described as just another rite: "the ordinary method of inhumation in this country is to leave the body exposed more or less to the air for a few days in a room or mortuary, to enclose it in a wooden box – this in the rich a leaden shell – and then to bury it in the ground" (Blyth 1884, 264). From a demystified point of view like this, Indian funeral habits (which included burning) could be preferred to English ones. Foreign customs are harnessed to sanction the utility of a radical break from local cultural values and practices. Thus it comes as no surprise to find that many of those involved in lobbying for cremation also belonged to the newly founded Anthropological Society. Turning Britain into the object of relativist ethnographical knowledge did not of itself loosen old traditions. What we can call a technology of "reculturation" was required – a secular and bureaucratic apparatus to acculturate British subjects in ways which reduce the presence both of old religious beliefs (which made of graves sacred places) and of values tied to the local memories (to which graveyards were central), and replace such beliefs and memories with a sense of belonging to, and working for, an abstract Humanity. It was clear to the cremationists that the teaching and promotion of literature and language could form a basis for this project of reculturation. And so we are not surprised to find that Sir Henry Thompson was not only the prime mover of cremation as a form of disposal of the dead but also the founder of the "English Society," one of the earlier groups which placed "English" at the very centre of the educational institutions.

I have begun to trace the order of things within which nineteenth-century realist novels revert again and again to doctors and medicine. The earlier promise of medicine, with its championing of the health of the social and individual body, and its intimate knowledge of how death flows through life, is achieved and problematized most profoundly in what have become for literary history two canonical novels of the time: Flaubert's *Madame Bovary* and George Eliot's *Middlemarch*. It is powerful testimony to Foucault's claim for the special place both of medicine in nineteenth-century society and culture, and of shifting interrelations between life and death (which, let me repeat, operate rather differently in England than in France), that these texts in particular are concerned at their very heart with the question of interventionist medicine. But the relations between literature and humanist, welfarist reculturation were not as simple as reformers like Thompson believed: literature, and the novel in particular, begins to develop an autonomous high cultural space in a complex series of resistances to, as well as appropriations of, the central supports of statism. Even a brief reading of those novels demonstrates this, though it becomes clearer still in a slightly later text like Henry James's *The Wings of the Dove* to which I will also address myself.[6] For me, the novel that most clearly signals the end of medicine's grand claims is Scott Fitzgerald's *Tender is the Night*, in which Dr Diver, a psychiatrist educated at Yale and Vienna, learns that he shares the "pathologies" of his patients: indeed, amazingly, so does the text's narrative voice as it fails to avoid the racist and homophobic slurs it knows to be a sign of a failure of clarity and "health." But a fuller discussion of *Tender is the Night* in which the noso-political and the literary do not interact, falls outside my purpose here.

MADAME BOVARY

It is no exaggeration to say that *Madame Bovary* represents French society metonymically through French medicine. The novel contains characters carefully chosen from each rung of the medical hierarchy. At the apex is

Larivière, the great surgeon who comes to provincial Yonville in time to witness Emma's death. Next is Canivet, a doctor from the provincial centre: when Charles, Emma's husband, botches an operation on Hippolyte's tendon, Canivet arrives to amputate the leg. It is he whose post-mortem on Charles's body finds "nothing." Then there is Charles himself, who is not a doctor proper, but a "medical officer of health" – that obsolete classification which allowed him only to practise within fixed localities and prevented him from performing major surgery without a doctor being present. Finally, there is the pharmacist Homais. This mapping of medical hierarchy in the novel means that Yonville's provinciality is measured not just by its distance from Paris as a centre of fashion – one of Emma's obsessions – but by its distance from Paris as the centre of medical knowledge. And, because the novel's implied readers are placed at the centre of things, that is, are not provincial, the text's "irony," which is an effect of that difference, also depends on the medical hierarchy. Yet *Madame Bovary* is very far from reproducing medicine's official discourses. It is Homais, standing at the bottom of the hierarchy, who utters the standard enlightened line: he sees medical intervention on the social and individual body as typifying progress as against superstition and religion. In him, enlightened phrases, the official – statist – view of doctors as heroes of civil society have become utterly debased, the stuff of pompous newspaper editorials. And he champions surveillance: at the novel's end he has a cripple removed from the streets into a state institution. On the other hand, Larivière, belonging to "the great school of surgeons created by Bichat," is "disdainful of honors, of titles and of academies" (Flaubert 1965, 234). The official medical hierarchy is placed against medicine's legitimating discourse in a chiasmic (or cross-shaped) structure. This chiasmus breaks continuities and exchanges: Larivière can hardly even talk to Homais; he can only communicate via a complex pun on "sens" (*sense*) and "sang" (*blood*) that Homais cannot hear. Speaking of Homais' supposed troubles with the thickness of his blood, Larivière mutters: "Ce n'est pas le sens qui le gêne" ('it isn't sense which gets in his way"). Charles and Canivet live and work in the zone that separates Larivière from Homais, across which they cannot connect. In this, the zone of the ordinary, practice and ideology merge and cancel each other. It tends towards "nothingness."

With Larivière medicine is a matter of sight: "his gaze [*son regard*], sharper than a lancet, penetrated straight into your soul and would disarticulate [*disarticulait*] a lie from all pretence and modesty" (Flaubert 1971, 327; translation mine). The metaphors in this passage offer Larivière's eyes a precisely surgical incisiveness. (*Disarticuler* in particular has a technical sense, to which translators have generally been less than just.) His eyes are lancets which, like Bichat's, work in the name of truth by cutting through tissues of preconceptions and lies. They vivisect. But he reaches a psychological truth rather than a medical or moral one. Truth and action here stand absolutely isolated from belief, including, it seems, a belief in science. Larivière "practises goodness without believing in it" (Flaubert 1965, 331). Even here death is crucial, because it is only on Emma's death that *all* the medical gazes are focused. Larivière watches Emma die without emotion, without a therapeutic move. At this moment, however, a crucial textual transaction does occur. In its ideological emptiness and unflinchingness, Larivière's death-scene gaze is borrowed by, or at least mimics, that of the narrator. Here the great doctor comes to embody the peculiar emptiness of the Flaubertian narrative voice and its refusal to offer any commentary based on belief. In traditional literary historical terms, we might say that the analytic exactitude of what Larivière sees becomes the text's realism, while his failure to believe stands for the text's proto-modernism. Flaubert's language has an exactness which at the novel's end we are invited to consider as clinical. Emma dies like this: "She soon began vomiting blood. Her lips became drawn. Her limbs were convulsed, her whole body covered with brown spots, and her pulse slipped between the fingers like a stretched thread, like a harp-string about to break" (233). To catch death's invasion of life as accurately as possible these tropes modulate into metaphor as does Laënnec's descriptions of the sick liver. But their clinical literariness shares nothing with the overdetermined melodrama to which surveillance is allied in early reformist discourse – and that, I think, is its point.

Emma's death scene, around which all the medical characters are grouped, has a fullness of detail intended to burst through the play of subjectivity and socio-political truisms so as to return readers to a *facticity*, a limit, that grounds neither a progressive theory of science or history, nor a virtue which believes itself. By contrast, the novel's other important medical scene occurs off-stage. Charles was encouraged by Homais and Emma to try to cure Hippolyte, the village cripple. As far as Homais at least is concerned this is an operation not just on the individual but on the social body: he reports it to the newspapers as an act in a national narrative of progress. When the operation fails Canivet is called in. He is of the old school: "it does not matter to me whether I carve up a Christian or the first fowl that comes my way," he declares airily (132). Again the scene describes intense pain but this time it is mediated through a conversation between Emma and Charles, itself determined by absence:

> Charles gazed at her with the dim look of a drunk man, while he listened motionless to the last cries of the amputé, following each other in drawn-out modulations, broken by sharp spasms like the far-off howling of some beast being slaughtered. Emma bit her wan lips, and . . . fixed on Charles the burning glance of her eyes like two arrows of fire about to be released. Everything in him irritated her now; . . . She revelled in all the evil ironies of triumphant adultery.

The memory of her lover came back to her soul towards this image, . . . and Charles seemed to her as removed from her life, as eternally absent, as impossible and annihilated, as if he were dying under her very eyes.

(133–4; translation modified)

Here Hippolyte's off-stage screams determine everything. In them, medicine relapses into its pre-enlightened past, into butchery. And, they trigger in the couple the opposite of Larivière's lucid gaze. Charles's sight withdraws from the world, becoming "dim"; Emma's, by contrast, in a clichéd "burning gaze . . . like two arrows of fire," sees what is not present, her lover – in a double irony because, for Emma, Charles is most absent when the medical gaze is most attentive: at the moment of death. For her, Charles is transformed into Hippolyte, "impossible, annihilated, as if he were dying." It is as if, strangely, absence permits that identification, that merging of difference within subjectivity and desire that presence, as marked by the clinical gaze, forestalls. Charles's failure to diagnose accurately, his surgical clumsiness, are at one with his failure to watch his patient now; a failure that the narrator and reader will not imitate when it is Emma's time to die. Pure medicine and high art will draw into themselves the privilege of what Foucault called the "pure gaze" in his introduction to *Rousseau juge de Jean-Jacques: Dialogues* – there setting it against that "gaze of surveillance" of which Homais is a master.

Yet Flaubert's novel cannot mimic the pure gaze, surgical incisiveness. A certain impurity is constitutive of writing, especially fiction, which, like this scene, turns readers' attention from reality towards words. The linguisticity of Emma's death-bed scene is foregrounded in that metaphor in which her pulse becomes, of all things, "like a harp-string about to break." Similarly, as Hippolyte screams in agony, Charles becomes for Emma "eternally absent" – it is then that she remembers her adulterous lover, re-narrating her life in the clichés of romantic fiction. At moments of greatest intensity, Emma lives in writing's diffusion of intensity, in narrative's – as against the gaze's – impurity, or, to put it more theoretically, in its focus on a presence that is also a nothing. It is in these terms that the "nothing" – the utter absence – that Canivet finds in Charles's corpse at the novel's end is supremely ambiguous. "Nothing" represents Charles's nullity of course – his place at the muddled centre of the text's chiasmic character structure. But it also represents the absence upon which medical gaze falls when it is directed towards desire, *bêtise* and finally textuality itself – all that which orders, or disorders, Charles and Emma's life, and of which the fiction is ultimately constituted. That "nothing" unsettles the complicity between surgeon hero Larivière and the empty proto-modernist narrative voice. Where the doctor sees nothing, the text finds its content. Not to pursue this track any further, what should be clear

61

enough by now is that Foucault's own scepticism as to the underpinnings of modern medicine and statism is anticipated by Flaubert. Furthermore, Flaubert works in a problematic at which the clinical gaze impossibly attempts to ally itself with language in a process of self-emptying – a process in which it reaches out to "nothing." This structure will be developed in Foucault's writings on literature where language turns back on itself as it broaches finitude, death. At least up until the early seventies, he belongs to a tradition of anti-statist cultural critique which is essentially literary.

MIDDLEMARCH

In *Middlemarch* (published in 1871, set in the provinces around the time of the 1832 Reform Bill), post-Bichatian medicine is already intertwined with state medicine. Lydgate, a young doctor who has embraced the new clinical medicine, is looking for the "fundamental knowledge of structure" in the body, because of his special interest in fevers and because of his sense "of the brief and glorious career of Bichat, who died when he was only one-and-twenty, but, like another Alexander, left a realm large enough for many heirs" (Eliot 1965, 118). Dorothea, who belongs to the landed gentry, breaks with both her class and gender by taking an active interest in pauper housing and the problem of drainage. The novel turns towards anatomy and the sanitation idea within a language heavily marked by vitalism. The titles of its main sub-divisions hint at this – "Waiting for Death," 'The Dead Hand," even "Old and Young" and "Sunset and Sunrise." To repeat Foucault's arresting phrase, in the novel, death is "volatized . . . distributed throughout life in the form of separate, partial, progressive deaths." Whereas in *Madame Bovary* death represents a limit, a finitude; here it is everywhere in the form of decay and invididual and social pathology. Whereas *Madame Bovary* presents its readers with a detailed, clinical description of death that has no utilitarian or ethical function, in *Middlemarch* the pure gaze has been replaced by a surveillance of the living which can only treat of things and events that have a capacity for exchange, or tend towards the status of information. In *Middlemarch*, characters are, to various degrees, either on the side of life (and energy) or approaching death (and repetition/stasis): it is placed in a province that its readers also inhabit. Nowhere is the text's vitalism more obvious than in the imagery which establishes the opposition between Ladislaw and Dorothea against Casaubon. The description of Dorothea's state of mind while she is honeymooning in Rome must suffice as an example: "What was fresh to her mind was worn out to his [Casaubon's] and such capacity of thought and feeling as had ever been stimulated by the general life of mankind had long since shrunk to a sort of dried preparation, a lifeless enhancement of knowledge" (228–9). Casaubon is living but lifeless, dead in every sense except technically. The biological focus of his lexicon, around which his characterization moves, is explicit enough ("preparation" is an anatomical word in this context).

If *Middlemarch*'s narrator marks the relation of life to death in the world, he is not, like the clinician, *institutionalized*. This difference is foregrounded by the fact that Lydgate's own medical career is described precisely in institutional terms. How should hospitals be managed? Should doctors sell (as well as prescribe) drugs? Should coroners be lawyers or doctors? What are the requisites of a medical education? The story of Lydgate's career, entwined in a long series of secrets and coincidences, and demanding considerable narratological complexity and skill, unfolds within struggles that such problems produced. In fact, the central event of that career, his compromised success in gaining a position in Bulstrode's new Hospital, echoes a famous medical scandal of the 1830s. Thomas Hodgkins, a so-called "curator of the dead" who named Hodgkins disease, failed to obtain a prestigious teaching and research job at Guy's Hospital for political reasons. He was a well-known anti-slavery activist and a supporter of "aborigines" ' rights while the hospital was controlled by the Clapham Sect – which meant that its directors had very close links to imperialist mercantile companies. Lydgate's career, like Hodgkins', is political, though it is one of his "spots of commonness" that his research and ambition cannot confront inevitable questions of power and institutionality head-on. Lydgate's attempts to set up a local fever hospital, to agitate for the medical profession to take over drug dispensing, to argue for a medical coroner, etc., like Dorothea's attempts to rehouse the poor, fail. By 1870 such failures could be read as local set-backs in the journey to triumph of the sanitation idea and state medicine. Indeed such a story is hinted at when Dorothea gives up her private charity work and marries a public man, an MP. This act of renunciation fits neatly into a sequence of "progressive" legislative measures, whose landmark was the 1866 Sanitation Act under which for the first time local authorities could be compelled to act against what were called health "nuisances" and which, in turn, was to lead to Disraeli's unifying 1875 Public Health Act. The confidence and authority of *Middlemarch*'s narrative voice, its ability to effect a closure that establishes justice, and grounds hope (and which, unlike Flaubert's is not self-emptying), is connected to this history. It finds its sanction in the final emergence of the centralized state over the lapses, dead ends and discords of the history of the sanitation idea, themselves expressed narratologically in the plot's non-realist windings.

Nowhere is the formation by which this triumph is conceived more clear that in Sir John Simon's *English Sanitary Institutions: Reviewed in their Course of Development in Some of their Political and Social Relations*. The book culminated an extraordinary career: Simon, who had been influenced by the French Saint-Simonians, was the first British Public Health Officer. Like

Sir Henry Thompson, he was a friend of the Lewes's. *English Sanitary Institutions* tells the tale of the struggle against fevers and is structured as a historical teleology, like most accounts of public health, and like *Middlemarch* itself. But it tells the story from a position in which political and administrative success has been achieved, so that the emphasis on the heroism of medicine is no longer central. Simon regards doctors as just one of "several sorts of special workmen" who must "ardently wish God-speed to those who are specialists in later divisions" (Simon 1890, 478). The modesty is false: in the book, the pathologies visible in "clinics and dead-houses" continue to form the essential basis of a set of partial social and cultural pathologies. Thus, for instance, "the Prevention of Crime is more than an affair of the police" for "over great territories of social evil, adjacent to the field of merely medical work, we seem to see on all sides, just as in our own province, the common pervasion of one deep want: the want of riper national education" (479). In this typical passage, the social body is transformed into a social psyche, formed by lacks and needs that the pun on want defines. Now that the state can order "solicitude and surveillance" (as Chadwick's report had put it fifty years before), it all the more requires a meta-sanitary idea, to which no gaze is adequate, best expressed by the term "education." This education is not simply pedagogical, it is not at all a matter of returning to memory. It belongs to a process of "fructification" and is grounded in a sympathy by which we can see "that deadness in one branch of growth tends to delay progress in other branches" (ibid.). Of such deadnesses two stand out: the first, in the private sphere, is charity, which prevents self-help and, in bequests able to transmit the will of the dead, is the old enemy of the Enlightenment; the second, in the political sphere, is democracy which Simon considers a politics of envy and, under the rubric "representation," is the old enemy of the centralizers.

Simon's book is important because it shows how the emergence of a certain brand of statism, after the melodrama of the early Benthamite reformers, is legitimized by a discourse coterminous with that of *Middlemarch*'s narrator. One also sees this discursive formation at work in the proceedings of an organization like the "National Association for the Promotion of Social Science" which was simultaneously concerned with, for instance, savings banks (anti-charity); life insurance figures (statistical accounting of the social body), cholera and infanticide (pathologies of the social body) and the institutional study of English (remedy for the social psyche). Here one encounters a shift from the earlier sense that, to increase productivity, society should be open to administrative control towards a stronger emphasis on non-regulatory techniques of social ordering and the production of "reculturated" individuals, that is, towards education and sympathy as the motors of what might be called cultural hygiene. This shift still inscribes those of us who work in the state's English Departments, though we are moving beyond its horizon. (The first section of chapter 8 extends this topic.)

THE WINGS OF THE DOVE

Perhaps medicine has its most complex entry into literature at the very end of the era of the realist novel, in Henry James's *The Wings of the Dove* (a text whose subtleties my remarks will barely touch). There, "after much interrogation, ausculation, exploration, much noting of his own sequences and neglecting of hers," Sir Luke Strett, a great "surgeon," tells Milly, the novel's very rich and virginal heroine, that she must "live" (James 1965, 159). Which we are to take to mean that she is dying. Sir Luke is given extraordinary aura in the story: his authority is simultaneously social, medical and psychological (if not, indeed, "spiritual"): he is, we are told, "half like a bishop, half like a general" (151). As a "great master of the knife" (312), he is also an heir to Bichat's glamour. But James, unlike Eliot and Flaubert, does not invoke Bichat's name. Sir Luke's aura is a product of a professional status connected to fees, to a network of verbal recommendations travelling through the upper-class community. To establish it, the Jamesian narrator is not required to describe his research or education. It requires no teleological history. Sir Luke's simple and non-interventionist advice is neither medical nor moral. It directs Milly towards a virtue which believes in no virtue in the sense that it valorizes without appealing to any moral discourse. Again the advice is vitalist. In fact, despite James's worry about this interpretation in his *Notebooks*, it has the specifically *sexual* overtones of the sentences James there regarded as "sufficiently second-rate." "Oh, she's dying without having had it? Give it to her and let her die" (James 1947b, 170). For Sir Luke, life and sex are inseparable.

Milly, like Emma when Larivière arrives, is dying but her death takes so long that medical advice can operate in areas previously the domain of morality and politics. The post-Bichatian view of the body as a site in which life struggles with death in a losing battle is pulled out of the clinic, turning away from the social body and the social psyche, towards individual psycho-sexual development. Yet the new reach of medical aura leads to a new set of ambivalences. Until its last book, a shadow of a doubt controls the text. Is Milly dying of a physical disease, or is she gripped by a will to die? To which of these possibilities is Sir Luke's injunction addressed? This is an ambiguity in which medicine itself is engaged, for as medicine gained power over the soul, it disentangled the mind from the body with increasing difficulty. Is Milly, the unimaginably rich American heiress, dying because for her there is no possibility of a world which does not commodify under her gaze, or because her death is so much in the interests of almost all of those who surround her, or because

65

she cannot form her own private self, being as she is, the object of such solicitude, the possessor of such means . . . ? And if to "live" is an ethical and psychological as well as a medical and sexual imperative then can one "die" from causes which are not somatic? In order to maintain this ambiguity, around which the plot turns, the narrator and the implied reader must know less than the doctor. Sir Luke may be uncertain about Milly's death, but the reader remains uncertain as to whether he is uncertain or not. Paradoxically, this possibility requires the immense prestige of medicine – for Sir Luke remains the still point of omniscience even if he does not (perhaps cannot) make a firm diagnosis. It is the veil that the novel draws over his judgement which creates a readerly distance from certainty about uncertainty.

At the novel's end it finally becomes clear that Milly is physically dying and a reproach is levelled at the reader's (and the other characters') *aesthetic* tolerance of ambiguity and, more broadly, the cultural longing for euthanasia. Merton Densher who is falling in love with Milly meditates:

> He had not only never been near the facts of her condition – which had been such a blessing for him; he had not only, with all the world, hovered outside an impenetrable ring fence, within which there reigned a kind of expensive vagueness, made up of smiles and silences and beautiful fictions and priceless arrangements, all strained to breaking; but he had also, with everyone else, as he now felt, actively fostered suppressions which were in the direct interest of everyone's good manner, everyone's pity, everyone's really quite generous ideal. It was a conspiracy of silence, as the *cliché* went, to which no one had made an exception, the great smudge of mortality across the picture, the shadow of pain and horror, finding in no quarter a surface of spirit or of speech that consented to reflect it. "The mere aesthetic instinct of mankind – " our youngman had more than once, in the connexion, said to himself; letting the rest of the proposition drop, but touching again thus sufficiently on the outrage even to taste involved in one's having to *see*.

(388)

This shares the value that *Madame Bovary* gives to a clear, clean look directed at corpses. However, the gaze averted from suffering and death, there recognized as philistinely anti-medical and anti-aesthetic, is now named merely aesthetic. It is against the fact that Milly's pain and death has *not* been seen, has not been open to an unflinching gaze, that Densher judges her circle as condemned to mere "taste." Yet again the text itself has inevitably entered into this "conspiracy of silence," the shared avoidance of death. It is no longer clear that what causes suffering can simply be *seen* and certainly Milly's painful death, unlike Emma's, remains undescribed. "Soul," energy, vitality, desire – they are not visible: Flaubert's attempt to connect the clinical gaze to aesthetic representation, and thus privilege the latter, is no longer possible.

The veiling of Sir Luke's gaze, the displacement of the Flaubertian body, has immense formal consequences. The urge to vision – or, better, correspondence to a visible reality – no longer grounds literary value in any simple manner. Rather it is as if the pure glance, the sight of things as they *are* and not as surveillance or aestheticism sees them, it is as if *that* gaze is the look that the *dying* direct at the living. It's a look that only a great doctor, who is also a bishop and a general, may recognize. Milly sees the true world – but only, incommunicably, from the side of death. It is as if what Blanchot thought true of Rilke is already at work in James: "to see properly is essentially to die" (Blanchot 1983, 151) so that, in James, writing that mimes the pure gaze is writing which comes from a reality that exists outside of exchange, representation and life. This kind of writing, unconnected to a recognizable social point of view or identity, permits language and narrative to turn in on itself, to become its own object. The prefaces that James wrote for his novels towards the end of his life urge a style of reading primarily interested in tone and the strategies by which anecdotes may be transformed into sustained fictions, into art. Yet, as we shall see in chapter 8, these formalist values and methods may themselves be taken up by a state pedagogy, not unconnected to the cultural hygiene programme.

Nonetheless, *The Wings of the Dove* signals a certain disarticulation of enlightened ideology from high-cultural novel writing. James is as much a precursor of transgressive writers like Blanchot as he is of I. A. Richards and F. R. Leavis. And it is no accident that, in his writing, we retreat from progressive humanism as our vision is withdrawn not just – in protest – from a cadaver over which a doctor, helplessly, knowingly, hovers; not just from the doctor's diagnosis, but from the point of view of the purest character. In James, the novel allows readerly identification with a rep-resented "real" world to trickle away as extraordinary linguistic and narra-tological techniques are foregrounded *because* it longs to see the world through the eyes of a corpse balanced between life and death – a corpse like those upon, or within, which the doctors legitimized themselves first by dissecting in their clinics and then by burying deep and burning in order to cleanse the world.

3

LITERATURE AND LITERARY THEORY

It was *Madness and Civilization* that drew the attention of literary critics to Foucault's work. At the end of an interview published in April 1964, Roland Barthes was able to point to "the spirit of 'vertigo' " with which "Michel Foucault has begun to speak of the Reason/Unreason couple" as "ultimately the essential subject of all theoretical work on literature" (Barthes 1981, 33). Of course, the literary dimension of Foucault's work was maintained even in the seemingly very non-literary field of his history of medicine. The introduction to *The Birth of the Clinic* has even become a classic of literary theory: it is there that Foucault distinguishes his methodology from "commentary" which (as "exegesis") was one of the mainstays of French criticism. When, however, Foucault comes to deal with literature head-on, as he does between 1962 and 1964 especially, he works within a paradigm rather different from, though connected to, that of his early work. The central moment of this literary phase of his career appears in his book on Raymond Roussel, in French plainly entitled *Raymond Roussel* – but translated into English as *Death and the Labyrinth*.

As we have already begun to see, Foucault's account of Roussel shifts. In *Madness and Civilization* Roussel (along with Artaud) was one of those who "arraigns the world" by showing that the world's fundamental structures cannot be colonized by reason; in *Death and the Labyrinth* Roussel writes within a problematic fundamentally defined by the "finitude of language." Between the two books, Foucault had become caught up in the intense debates about criticism and writing that characterized French intellectual life in the first half of the sixties. In particular, he became both a champion and theorist of the so-called "new new novel" associated with the programme of the journal *Tel Quel* and its editor Philippe Sollers. He, like others associated with *Tel Quel*, discussed and promoted the work of Georges Bataille, Maurice Blanchot and Pierre Klossowski, who had long remained somewhat at the margins of French literary life. (During the thirties and forties Bataille had refused to join the Surrealists; Blanchot had been connected with the collaborators in the early war period, and after the war all had fallen somewhat out of view in an intellectual scene dominated by the existentialists and the marxian left.) As I shall argue below, Foucault's next works – the archaeological books *The Order of Things* and *Archaeology of Knowledge* – emerge out of these debates and bear their traces.

ROUSSEAU

It is in his, as yet untranslated, introduction to Rousseau's posthumous text *Rousseau juge de Jean-Jacques: Dialogues*, published in 1962, that Foucault gives brief notice of this further shift towards the literary. This rich, if short, text in fact not only inaugurates Foucault's own linguistic turn, it anticipates, far in advance, certain concerns of his later work on power. And in its closing section Foucault turns back to the vexed question of the relation between literature and madness. There he writes a short dialogue (the form of Rousseau's own work) in which an interlocutor enquires: "Aren't the *Dialogues* the work of a madman?" to which the reply is, "This question would matter if it had a meaning: but the work, by definition, is not-mad" (1962a, xxiii). In *Madness and Civilization*, Foucault had already insisted that the work, as work, cannot be simply "mad," but now he goes on to declare that it is through a work's "place" in language that it relates to madness. How? Works have a double relation to language: the language of a work constitutes what the work says, but it also constitutes "that through which it speaks" (ibid., xiv). At this second level, language is "pure transgression" (a term loosely associated with Georges Bataille), for, though it is not a psycho-pathological category like delirium, it is delirious in having an ungrounded and ungroundable structure. Language is delirium in that, in principle, it cannot account for itself. Foucault aims to historicize, and spell out in more detail, the forms of this transgressive language. In his essay on Hölderlin, for instance, he writes: "This void to which poetic speech is drawn as its self-destruction, is what authorizes the text of a language common to both [work and madness]," adding characteristically: "These are not abstractions, but historical relationships which our culture must eventually examine if it hopes to find itself" (1977a, 85). One moment in particular has especial importance for the contemporary study of language's "mad" dissolution. In "La Folie, l'absence d'oeuvre" (an essay written in 1964 and attached to the 1972 edition of *Madness and Civilization*) Foucault argues that madness designates the emptiness which language after Hölderlin and Mallarmé (that is, in the "modernist" moment) locates in itself. Paradoxically, poetry gestures at, and enacts, this emptiness as it begins to situate itself in what Foucault calls, after Heidegger, *Being* (1964a, 19). How does poetry institute itself in Being? When it is written, first, so as to become a thing as much as a set of signs and, second, so as to connect to conditions of existence which are not limited by, or confined to, social, political or historical formations. In texts written towards these ends, language's strange existence on the margins of matter – not quite thing, not wholly "meaning" – passes itself off as constitutive of Being. The groundlessness of Being in the world can only be conceived of as itself linguistic: the "strange existence" of signs provides a sense of the strangeness of existence rather than vice versa. It follows that to analyze this strangeness or "madness" one must analyze linguistic structures, especially those of what Foucault calls "fiction."

This begins to make it clear why Rousseau in particular helped trigger Foucault's linguistic turn. (Rousseau will also form the focus for the later works of post-structuralism – especially in Derrida's *Of Grammatology* and Paul de Man's *Allegories of Reading*.) The reason is less that Rousseau is a major theoretical exponent of the priority of speech over writing than because he has a particular place in the history of the written word, one in which he articulates the modern problematic of literary production most forcefully. How to re-form the legitimations of society and its institutions through *writing*? How to be at once truthful, sincere, moral, transparent, natural and unique within texts which are written, circulate through in the market place and help produce an *image* of the author – the author as public persona, as star? Within this dilemma, Rousseau is driven to emphasise the first set of terms with special vehemence just because the second set bear on him so pressingly. According to Foucault, after writing his major autobiographical work, *The Confessions*, Rousseau attempted to solve this tension between transparency and its obstacles by restricting circulation of his text. *The Confessions* were never published in his lifetime, but Rousseau read the book aloud to his friends and admirers. This solution, however, founders on the silence that follows reading aloud, a silence which permits the uncirculated work and its author once again to become the subject of unsubstantiated gossip by those who were not present. In this uncontrollable circulation of language – rumours – the author again loses authenticity.

The *Dialogues*, on the other hand, are *written* – here his accusers' silence is given a voice: Rousseau, the public figure, judges Jean-Jacques, the private man. But now further problems enter: the text is again out of authorial control, its "paternity is put in question" because *anybody* may read it and the author cannot control the interpretations the work may elicit (1962a, viii). The solution to, or end of, these double binds could only occur at a point where writing and the voice merge together once and for all; this also being the point at which Jean-Jacques and Rousseau (and, as Foucault notes, still more complexly, Jean-Jacques-for-Rousseau and Rousseau-for-Jean-Jacques, etc.) might be unified. Within the structure of literary production, however, this moment is endlessly displaced and deferred. Indeed for Foucault it happens only as, and in, absence, death. Without the capacity for self-presence, Rousseau's self-presentation involves two systems, neither of which is controlled by him. In the first, the "surveillance-system," Rousseau is the object of surrounding but distant and silent gazes for which his actions are signs of his crimes and failures; in the second, the "system of judgement," his actions are not read as signs of hidden intentions, they are passively or "purely" observed and recorded. But this second system is linked to torture – in torture what is dragged out from the victim is true not by virtue of its correspondence to facts but by virtue of its relation to pain. At a certain point, the torturer accepts the tortured's word: what is the point of lying when one has reached the edge of death? In a radical and innovative reading that anticipates the argument of *Discipline and Punish*, Foucault argues that Rousseau would prefer the Judgement/Torture system to that of Surveillance/Signs. An historical agenda begins to appear here. It is as if, in privileging the Judgement/Torture system, he is preferring the pre-modern order to that of modernity.

Just as his book on madness owes much to his reading of a psychological phenomenologist like Ludwig Binswanger, Foucault's first important text on literature owes a great deal to phenomenological literary criticism – and, in particular, a school whose influence and vitality in France during the fifties and sixties has been massively underrated, especially in Britain and Australia. Specifically, the essay on Rousseau is indebted to Jean Starobinski's path-breaking *Jean-Jacques Rousseau: La Transparence et l'obstacle* (1957) as well as the Rousseau essays in Starobinski's *L'Oeil vivant* (1961). Not that Foucault repeats Starobinski's methods and findings – he is set on moving past them. To take two examples: first, for Starobinski, "feeling" in Rousseau is a natural "sign" – readable at least by Rousseau and unreadable only for others. For Foucault, on the other hand, feeling becomes a "sign" only under the effects of surveillance: Rousseau wants, impossibly, to utter words which are neither interpretable nor misinterpretable, but just *are*, as confession under torture, which is an *event*, escapes the fate of interpretation to the degree that it becomes a last word – uttered when the victim, on the threshold of death, has nothing left to lose. Second, whereas in his influential introduction to *L'Oeil vivant* Starobinski finds discourse situated in the gap between the "demanding gaze" with which we relate to the world and the passivity with which objects present themselves to our vision (that is, between desire and presence), Foucault finds in Rousseau a structure within which *signs* (the objects of surveillance and commentary) and *words* (the objects of judgement) can never coincide except in death or utopia.

Clearly Foucault is not commenting on Rousseau – he is not giving a true and clear account of the meanings of his text. Nor is he, like Starobinski, offering an account of what Paul de Man called Rousseau's "psychological ruses" (de Man 1983, 114). One might want to argue that Foucault is anticipating deconstruction as it emerges in debates over Rousseau between Paul de Man and Jacques Derrida (who define the movement partly *against* Starobinski). But this would be precipitate. For, unlike

Derrida, Foucault is not here concerned to argue that Rousseau's binds and tensions are the product of some basic structure whose effects (while not themselves merely linguistic) are coterminous with that of language itself. Nor does Foucault argue that Rousseau's work is an instance of some widespread but limiting formation – either cultural or metaphysical – like Derrida's notion of logocentrism which we may succinctly define as the privileging of presence. For Foucault, in Rousseau's work, language is connected to delirium in specific rather than universal ways. And, unlike de Man in his essay on Derrida's account of Rousseau, Foucault is certainly not interested in finding in Rousseau a writer as "clear-sighted as language lets him be" but who has been systematically reduced by his (logocentric) critics (139).

GOTHIC "MOTIFS"

In his essay on Rousseau, Foucault concentrates on what the phenomeno-logical critics called a writer's "mental universe." This is a slightly mislead-ing term because it refers not to a biographical state of mind, or to an extra-literary and psychological authorial intention, but rather to the object of the reader's (or critic's) act of reading. A "mental universe" is that structure or (to use a still vaguer term) tendency, which readers are in contact with when they read the works of a particular author. It cannot simply be identified with a text, or group of texts. As Jean-Pierre Richard put in his book on Mallarmé:

> To understand Mallarmé is not to find, behind the poem, a clear statement of a purpose which the poem disguises; quite to the con-trary, it is to unveil its *raison d'être*, the project of its obscurity. . . . We have wished to write a syntax, not a vocabulary of the Mallarméan imagination.
>
> (Richard 1961, 17–18)

And, at least in theory, the phenomenological "writing" of the "syntax" of an "imagination" involves not so much an emphatic grasp of the writer's obscure consciousness as mediated through the work, as the encounter of one self-reflection (the critic's) with another (the writer's). Yet in his review of Richard's book, Foucault strikes a rather different tone, one more familiar to Anglo-American criticism. For him, criticism does not examine the relation of

> a man to the world, not of an adult to his fantasies or to his child-hood, not of a *littérateur* to a language (*une langue*), but of a speaking subject to a being which is singular, difficult, complex, profoundly ambiguous (since its designates, and gives their being, to all other beings, itself included) and which is called language (*le langage*).
>
> (1964b, 1004)

Nonetheless, when Foucault writes most closely in the spirit of the phenomenologists, as, for instance, in his review-essay "So Cruel A Knowledge,"
language and subjectivity are not what is at stake. In that extraordinarily
subtle and careful piece, he compares the early eighteenth-century novelist
Claude Crébillon (and, specifically, *Les Égarements du cœur et de l'esprit*) with
J. A. Reveroni de Saint-Cyr (and, specifically, *Pauliska ou la perversité mod-
erne*). Foucault's analysis focuses on what the phenomenological critics
called "motifs" – privileged objects that crystallize and organize the dominant themes of a writer's imagination, or, as Foucault puts it, "figure an
experience" (1962b, 609). Both Crébillon and Reveroni belong, in a broad
sense, to the Enlightenment, and in each "transgression of the forbidden
emits light" (609). Crébillon's novel presents a world of veils, mirrors and
philtres: objects which facilitate communication, interrelations, disguise
and transformation. They work according to a logic by which the material
thickness of things decreases to the degree that they facilitate such relations.
It's a world of masquerade; one without essences. In the world that
Crébillon describes, to be initiated is to learn a language whose utterance,
part of a performance, increases social worth. His is a world, then, not
directed towards certainty and mastery, or, to use Foucault's terms, one
in which desire is never superimposed upon knowledge in an absolute
desire to know or towards an absolute knowledge of desire. A world,
instead, in which what counts is being an insider. Reveroni's novel, on the
other hand, figures its "experience" by appealing to the cage, the machine
and the "subterranean." In these motifs, the boundary between inside and
outside is firm, nowhere more so than in the contrast between the subterranean "virile bestiality" of the mob and the clear light of reason. To be
initiated into Reveroni's world is not to fit into social practices which,
using cunning and irony, confer prestige; it is to acquire the sovereignty
of knowledge. On the face of it, there exists an absolute difference between
the master of knowlege and his objects. Yet even in a world ordered by
cages, machines and a stark difference between reason's light and darkness's confusion, strange mutations and transactions can take place –
especially as light is emitted by the transgression of the merely conventional. Ultimately, in Reveroni's narratives, what is desired controls desire,
what is to be known – the secret, the hidden – orders knowledge just
because the purposes of knowledge – to understand and order nature and
society – coalesce with the desire for domination. This brief description of
Foucault's reading of the two novels is enough to show that, at least
implicitly, he is concerned with the historical shift from the pre-revolution-
ary into the post-revolutionary moment. The "mental universe" that he
presents is not that of an individual or an œuvre, but of a social event.
The motifs that he fastens upon belong less to private creative or readerly
imaginations than to history. Indeed Foucault goes so far as to argue that:
"the cage . . . opens the era of an instrumental knowledge which is no

longer connected to the somewhat shady ambiguity of consciousness, but to the meticulous order of technical persecution" (603). This way of thinking anticipates his later work on power, albeit a little crudely. And it is worth noting that in this essay Foucault seems to side not with an erotics of masquerade and transvestism but with Reveroni's heroine, Pauleski, and her "modern perversion." Her "strange initiation" takes place as she becomes part of the circuit of a torture-machine, designed to give a cruel man pleasure. In his subterranean chamber, she experiences the full force of the cage and the machine, but only – as Foucault reads Reveroni – in a mode for which her pain, her desire and her enlightenment become indistinguishable.

RAYMOND ROUSSEL

By contrast, in *Death and the Labyrinth* Foucault explores and stretches the phenomenological critical method so as to enable it to open out into his "archaeological" work.

Raymond Roussel, a contemporary of Proust's, was, like Proust, rich and gay. Unlike Proust, he was in his lifetime a failure – at least as a novelist, poet and dramatist. In particular, his repeated attempts to stage his plays became famous scandals (or jokes) supported, for reasons lost on him, mainly by the young Surrealists. More to the point, unlike Proust, Roussel was an anti-mimetic, experimental writer, though not a member of any avant-garde and apparently unaware of the radicalness of his methods. (The writer he admired most was Jules Verne and he seems not to have understood modernism and its cultural politics at all.) And, to use an outdated psychological term, he was not quite "sane." When he was nineteen he achieved a bizarre state of ecstasy or "glory." As he put it, in a statement we must take literally: "Everything I wrote was surrounded in rays of light; I would close the curtains for fear the shining rays that were emitting from my pen would escape through the slightest chink" (Janet 1987, 39). Later he became a patient of the famous psychologist Pierre Janet who wrote a brief case-study of him in *De l'angoisse à l'extase*. Before he died, Roussel wrote a short text, to be published posthumously, called "How I Wrote Certain of My Books." In it, he explains the procedure (*le procès*) of his prose (rather than his poetry) – a procedure which had hitherto been hidden and unrecognized. *Le procès* had three forms: in the first Roussel ended a narrative segment with a phrase which repeated the sounds but not the sense of the words with which it began – the text forming the bridge from one phase to the other. (Works written by this method were called "genesis-texts.") In the second, Roussel created passages by selecting two words, each with a double meaning, then placing the preposition "à" between them and again writing material connecting the first phrase to the second. (For example, "feuille à tremble," which first denotes an aspen leaf, at last refers to a leaflet headed "Tremble, people of France" via a little narrative.) In the third, he took a phrase at random (the address of his bootmaker, for instance) and transformed it into another phonetically similar phrase, around which a situation or event might be constructed.

Death and the Labyrinth is concerned neither with Roussel's life nor with his work but with those themes and motifs which are organized on what, gesturing towards J.-P. Richard on Mallarmé, Foucault calls his "tropological space." Foucault uses this phrase to refer to the way in which Roussel's process, his *hidden* use of repetition and the poverty of language (same sounds – different sense; fewer signifiers – more signification) is an analogy of the way in which "verbal signs" are hollow. What does this mean? Foucault argues that, by means of the process, Roussel says "two things with the same words" and it is this which "brings into play" "the fundamental freedom" of language: a freedom made possible by its poverty, by the fact that there exist fewer sentences than things to describe" (1986b, 16). If language were not poorer than the world, then linguistic narration could not conceal a mechanical procedure which generates it. Language's poverty and its attendant freedom, however, reveal a void: Roussel "felt there is, beyond the quasi-liberties of expression, an absolute emptiness of being that he must surround, dominate and overwhelm with pure invention" (ibid.). Roussel's "tropological space" has no origins despite that punning description of certain of his process texts as "genesis-texts" (genèse = jeunesse: genesis = youth). Between the work and the world, between one phrase and another, lie gaps, processes which themselves can never be fully fixed or filled. For, as Foucault notes, if Roussel reveals the secret of his work after his death, how can we be sure that that "secret" does not conceal a further secret, itself, formed by another "process"? The barrier between Roussel's tropological space and the critic or reader is Roussel's own death – that which separates the account of the texts from the texts themselves. Although recent research has shown that Foucault's version of Roussel's death is mistaken (by then an addict, he died of a barbiturate overdose in a room which Foucault believed wrongly to be locked from the inside), this does not affect the basic thrust of Foucault's claim that "the death, the lock and this closed door formed, at that moment and for all time, an enigmatic triangle where Roussel's work is both offered to and withheld from us" (4). (For an authoritative account of Roussel's last days, see Sciascia 1987.) On the one hand, the radical break that death imposes on the work forestalls attempts to provide full genealogical or causal accounts of his writing (explaining it fully in terms of, say, the author's biography – or any other context). On the other, that break draws the reader or critic into the work – we *share* the space in which words are interrupted by finitude, in which "language is a thin blade that slits the identity of things, showing them as hopelessly double and self-divided even as they are repeated" (23). The process – the hidden mechanical nature of Roussel's writing – anticipates or, as it were, incorporates death, by bracketing off life and pure expression.

It might be enough to say that in *Death and the Labyrinth* Foucault's "theme" has become language itself, its limits and its relation to the world. However, let us recall that Foucault is not thinking of "language" as the structuralists were to conceive of it – as a system able to produce effects of signification (a welding together of signified and signifier) by means of a network of repetitions, differences and substitutions. Rather language for Foucault here begins to take the form ascribed to it within post-structuralism: it is *not* an autonomous and bounded system but a fold within the world, another set of things, characterized by what Paul de Man called "spacing." It constitutes a condition delicately balanced between the ontological and the experiential: that is, a condition of Being as lived in an interval between a birth that cannot be remembered and a death that will never be experienced or concretely foreseen. In a manner very different from a certain "deconstruction" popularized (so to say) in the American academy, Foucault does not argue that Roussel's works reveal how it is impossible for "themes" or "representations" to struggle out of the trammels of linguisticity. Quite the opposite: in his early poems – written under the aura of his glory – Roussel attempts to "open up a universe without perspective" (107). There, language is used to clear an area, a "magical circle" in which "things appear in their insistent, autonomous existence, as if they were endowed with an ontological obstinacy which breaks with the most elementary rules of spatial relation" (106). It is as if Roussel demonstrates that language's failure to connect solidly to the world permits things to exist in a dazzling superficiality. And in Roussel's later poems, written after his failures (especially *Nouvelles Impressions* which consists of parentheses deeply layered within parentheses), language "measures the infinite distance between the eye and what is seen" (135); in these works, language hides "what it has to show, flowing at a dizzying speed towards an invisible void where things are beyond reach and where it disappears in its mad pursuit of them" (ibid.). In sum, Foucault is not simply concerned with language, he is also willing, indeed, driven, to talk about the gaze – *its* possibilities, effects and limits. This is the topic which *Birth of the Clinic* and *Death and the Labyrinth* share: in the first, Foucault had shown how modern medicine and the Enlightenment *tout court*, begin within a new "form of visibility" (1973a, 195) – that of the "absolute eye" (166) which aims to have contact with "visibilities" outside any limiting perspective. The dream that language might directly express the vision of an "absolute eye" is taken to its limits by Roussel (whose very pen is alight). But Roussel also experiences the failure of this dream; he goes on to connect language to that very different form of visibility whose centre is a hidden and distant obscurity in which Being withdraws from the world.

76

It is in these terms that one can say that these two books, published in the same year, and on matters which seem so far apart from one another, actually speak to one another very directly. *Death and the Labyrinth* demonstrates the failures and costs of the project whose first stirrings *Birth of the Clinic* recounts. (For more remarks on this topic I would recommend Deleuze's book on Foucault – see Deleuze 1986, 66ff.).

In Roussel's most widely translated and read works, the novels *Impressions of Africa* and *Locus Solus* (written during the middle of his career), relations between the visible and the sayable intersect and entwine one another in movements Foucault calls "the labyrinth" and "metamorphosis." (According to Foucault, similar relations, however, also organize his earlier and later work.) These "motifs" are not images: they structure the form and techniques of these books, as well as bearing some allegorical relation to the events described in them. And they do not belong simply to Roussel; his work represents one moment in their history, a history which seems to be that of the "tropological space" of the West itself. Foucault sees Roussel as "constructing and crisscrossing"

> the two great mythic spaces so often explored by Western imagination: space that is rigid and forbidden, surrounding the quest, the return and the treasure (that is the geography of the Argonauts and of the labyrinth); and the other space – communicating, polymorphous, continuous, and irreversible – of the metamorphosis, that is to say, of the visible transformation of instantly crossed distances, of strange affinities, of symbolic replacements.
>
> (80)

The "labyrinth" is the name for the quest for origins – a quest which does not so much fail in Roussel's books, as end with an "image of metamorphosis where chance and repetition are united" (93). The first part of *Impressions of Africa* minutely describes a series of bizarre performances, tricks and theatrical representations, performed under the orders of an African king by a motley collection of Europeans – a singer with four voices, a mechanical loom which reproduces pictures of its own accord, a bunch of grapes, ripened electrically, each of which has in its interior a tableau vivant, e.g. "The first pangs of love, experienced by Jean-Jacques Rousseau's *Émile*" (Roussel 1966, 120), etc. Its second half *explains* these performances: Roussel actually encouraged readers to read the second half of the book first. Similarly, in *Locus Solus*, which describes a tour around the great scientist Canterel's estate, Roussel, as Jean Cocteau put it, "reveals first [Canterel's] experiments and then the devices behind them" (Cocteau 1957, 97). Yet these explanations or stories of origins themselves end in legends and spectacles: "at the absolute beginning, when one is on the threshold of something else, the labyrinth suddenly offers the *same*" (1986b, 93–4). "The labyrinth" represents a journey of recovery, the

77

(linguistic) trek into obscurity whose purpose is to find a truth about origins or causes which, it turns out, do not differ fundamentally from that of which they are the "truth" or "cause." And "metamorphosis" represents the impulse to fill and enrich the interval between birth and death, and to transcend the latter. "In all ages, the aim of metamorphosis was to have life triumph by joining beings or cheating death by passing from one state of being to another" (87). Yet in Roussel, predictably, that aim also fails. In *Locus Solus*, Canterel revives corpses by using two substances "resurrectine" and "vitalium": under their influence the dead can repeat, endlessly, central events of their lives. Here metamorphosis, far from possessing an Ovidian richness, rests on something like the opposite. It becomes repetition, as if life were merely death injected with movement, reduced to the *appearance* or scenery of life.

How do these two large motifs – metamorphosis and the labyrinth – "crisscross"? Metamorphosis belongs, finally, to sight: in Roussel's performances things are *seen* to undergo transformation in a "sort of quasi-theatre" (95). But Rousselian theatre attempts to work as if the visible were as malleable and transformable as the narratable: as if a frog could turn into a prince not just in a story but in an image. From the other direction, the "labyrinth" is fundamentally verbal; it names the effort to use words to explain an event, to discover origins. And in attempting to merge the two orders, Roussel demonstrates the distance between them:

> it is the structure of the labyrinth which completely upholds Roussel's plays, as if it were a matter of eliminating everything that goes into its theatricality, to let appear as visible on stage only the shadow play of the secret. By contrast, never is it more a question of masks, disguises, scenes, actors, and spectacles than in the nontheatrical texts: the metamorphoses are only brought forth on stage through a narration, therefore changed and caught in the labyrinth of a discourse given second- or thirdhand.
>
> (96)

As we have seen, narrative and language *evacuate* the ground of the visible by providing a form of signification in which events are explained and essences created (the "tableness" of the table for instance), leaving sight to provide an image of surfaces. (We can never see "tableness" – only tables.) On the other hand, the "thereness" of the visible demonstrates the limit of language's ability to bind the world within a labyrinth of causal chains, histories and explanations. ("Thereness" because one can only see a thing in its presence though one can talk of it in its absence.) And these two strategies are played out within that "insufficiency of Being" which is also a plenitude of death: the "sun of language" is itself hollow (164). The sun of language? This strange and violent metaphor, which condenses the visible and the linguistic, is appropriate just because, in

Roussel's work, the visible (metamorphosis) and the linguistic (the labyrinth) fall away from one another in their coming together. The sun, the source of light, cannot be looked at; language, the source of sense, cannot be made sense of.

Finally, Foucault is interested in Roussel for reasons very similar to those which, at the end of his career, he would call *ethical*, that is to say, because he poses a particular way not just of writing but of living. In his account of *La Doublure* (an early verse novel written before the process texts for instance – during the experience of "glory" – and which mainly consists of descriptions of the Nice carnival), Foucault argues that Roussel's rituals, including his admission to Janet that "practising forbidden acts in private rooms, knowing that it is prohibited, risking punishment or at least the contempt of respectable people, that is perfection" (161), are not constitutively different from his writing. They too are structured by the space in which death and finitude restrict the system of language, and thus make of existence a mask that masks nothing, a "system which proliferates with rhymes, in which not only syllables are repeated but also words, the entire language, things, memory, the past, legends, life – each separated from and connected to itself by the fissure of death" (56). (As we can see from this passage, Foucault's description of that space which work and life share continues to owe something to his study of Binswanger – it may be worth noting that Roussel was intending to become a patient of Binswanger before he died (see Caburnet 1968, 103).) Roussel's "madness"; his repetitions and rituals (in food and clothing); his intense fear of death (he forbade the topic to be talked about in his presence); his obsessive privacy; his mimicry of the famous; his habit of travelling round the world without getting out of his cabin or his specially constructed touring vehicle; his love of work; his hidden sexuality; his ability to create his own environment – all this, together with the work produced, shows not just that "language alone forms the system of existence" (161), but that we live within structures ordered by language's relation to the world. What structures? Precisely, repetition, deferral, scarcity – in a word, finitude. Hollow language may be, like life itself, death's emissary in the world, but Foucault begins further to insist that this emptiness is the condition within which we are, as it were, imprinted onto our own lives – or, to use another metaphor, the condition in which we make texts of our lives' substance.

In *The Order of Things* and *The Archaeology of Knowledge* Foucault will concentrate this ontological account of language within the narrower field of the history of ideas in order to disrupt the calm world of academic and belletristic history. But the important "motifs" or assumptions of those works were developed in his study of Roussel. We can now, succinctly, enumerate them: first, that language, in contrast to the visible, is scarce – which determines the way that labyrinthine language "moves towards infinity," attempting to cover, explain, delve into everything but failing and doubling back on itself in its finiteness; second (and connectedly), that the relation between the sayable and the visible is, finally, one of exteriority – "things are perceived because words are lacking" (166); third, that language permits no origins; fourth, "discourse which describes" is that which "explains" (111) – that is, the hermeneutic project of deep understanding or grounded interpretation is misconceived because it finds interiors, resonances and analogies where there are only surfaces; fifth, events cannot be narrativized – history, like biography, is discontinuous, arbitrary, punctuated by words and death, linguistic; and last, notions of "death" and "the nothingness of existence" which had been the bogeys of enlightened thought and the catchcries of existentialism are now transformed into that "absence" and "poverty" which is at work in all discourse and to which less and less pathos attaches.

PROFESSING TRANSGRESSION

As we have seen, Foucault's book on Roussel remains technically and generically connected to the literary criticism of the so-called "phenomenologists," and Roussel himself was a writer of especial importance to those, like Robbe-Grillet, who were developing the "new novel" just because his texts play the sayable off against the visible. Yet in its articulation of crucial terms, and in its main concerns and direction, *Death and the Labyrinth* belongs to another tradition. Perhaps it is best to say that it is written within a triangle bounded on one side by a certain academic criticism (that of J.-P. Richard, Poulet and so on); on another, by the development of a programme to move past the "new novel," and, on the third, by the kind of writing associated with Blanchot, Bataille and Pierre Klossowski. In a series of essays written for the major avant-garde cultural and literary reviews between 1963 and 1966, Foucault became a theorist and champion of these latter writers. And because, unlike both the new new novel and the phenomenologists, they have not dropped out of Anglo-American view, it is as the author of these essays that Foucault the critic (rather than the historian), has had most impact on literary theory written in English. Yet the vagaries of Anglo-American reception cannot fully account for the way in which this side of Foucault's work has received a disproportionately large share of attention. He also turned towards Bataille and Blanchot in particular because of Derrida's criticism of his concept "the experience of madness" in *Madness and Civilization*. Derrida had argued both that madness as absolute other is not able to be known or historicized, and that one cannot speak for the absolute other as Foucault claimed to do in telling the story of the divide between reason and unreason. Discussing the new new novel with the *Tel Quel* group in 1964, Foucault mentions Derrida's critique in passing: "I'm not too sure about it, I was speaking about an experience which was simultaneously transgression and contestation" (1964e, 73). Certainly it is true that the word "contestation" at least appears in *Madness and Civilization* but the full problematic of "transgressive thought" is *not* there entered into. Consequently, it would be fair to say that Foucault engages this thought at least in part in order to counter Derrida's arguments.

Traces of Blanchot's, Bataille's and Klossowski's work are nowhere more apparent in *Death and the Labyrinth* than in its use of the term "labyrinth." Although that word was fashionable in the period (one of Robbe-Grillet's novels was called *In the Labyrinth*, for instance), it is Bataille who clears the way for Foucault's use of it. In an essay succinctly called "The Labyrinth" published twice in rather different forms, Bataille sets out a metaphysics that he claims to be capable of generating a theory of society. To state its argument very briefly: Bataille argues that in their solitude and mortality human beings are fundamentally insufficient, lacking. It is for this reason that their relations to one another and the world are labyrinthine or "entangled, unstable wholes," constructed to provide an illusion of substantiality. Being itself, Bataille writes, is "nowhere" (See Bataille 1988, 82ff., and 1985, 175). Human beings, in their isolation, connect to one another through language *at the same time* as they communicate their lack as anguish and in sacrifice to the Being that is nowhere. By now these ideas will be familiar enough. But when Foucault comes to write about Bataille directly, in his essay "Preface to Transgression," he develops both the historical and linguistic implications of such thought. Along with the "labyrinth" (and "sovereignty" and "sacrifice"), "transgression" is the word that most powerfully organizes Bataille's work. For Foucault, in its largest sense, this means "profanation in a world which no longer recognizes any positive meaning in the sacred" (1977a, 30) – or, in a particularly nice phrase, the death of a God who never existed. Yet transgression is an affirmative, a clean profanation: it "must be liberated from the scandalous or subversive, that is, from anything aroused by negative associations" (35). This is to begin to historicize the concept: transgression describes the manner of thought and being for those who take the death of God or the withdrawal of Being seriously but *well* (and thus it remains entwined with certain negative theological themes, where "negative theology" refers to a theology of the absent or absolutely distant God). Yet, more startlingly, the death of God according to Foucault, is also bound to the emergence of sexuality. With the Marquis de Sade, a sexuality which continually and violently crosses and recrosses the line into death becomes the site for an outpouring of discourse about life. At least until the early twentieth century, sexuality retains traces of the sacred. It is there that prohibitions continue to have force, coming into existence at the point at which they are broken. Sade's career marks the limits of the acceptable – the Same – in an enlightened world. And taking the death of God well, taking full advantage of it, means finding more objectivity in the world, more than can be found than when

81

the world is considered to be under God's guidance. This is especially true in Sadean sex, where the bodies of self and other become objects (rather than sensitive beings) at the threshold between life and death. For Sade, that is the border towards which sexuality, as the most powerful mode of transgression, always tends. After all, what poses a more powerful limit than death? (And what, in the light of this, is one to make of the fact that Foucault himself was to die of AIDS?)

Transgression, which proposes itself as the purest modern thought, differs radically from our older, more familiar conceptual habits. To begin with (and not unexpectedly), it replaces the dialectic for which the contradictions in, and limits of, social and conceptual formations are conceived of as propelling the progressive movement of history or the ever-widening grasp of knowledge. It also replaces reflection (and self-reflection), in which a "sovereign subject" remains outside the objects of its thought, able absolutely to master them (even when the subject is the object of its own thought); and finally it replaces "anthropological" thought for which work and finitude alienate man's essence or for which, in a twist, alienation itself may form the essential human experience. Transgression appeals to no grounds and origins. It *affirms* the "limitless reign of the limit" (44) "joyfully" (that, of course, is very much a Nietzschean term), though it has nothing positive or positivist to affirm. Transgressive thought dissolves the subject because it finds its finitude not where an "inside" is separated from, grounded on or reflects an "outside," but where the movement towards otherness begins to repeat what is not other – the Same. There are many ways of construing this relation. To take the least "metaphysical," strict divisions between texts, genres, thoughts, persons, for instance, break down because, for transgressive thought, what lies outside each unity or totality (and which defines it as a unity) also works within it (in order to delimit it). This is one sense, then, in which transgressive thought occupies the open rather than the closed border at which the Same and the Other interact with and repeat each other. Another is the way in which the labyrinthine explanations or interpretations of events and texts (literary criticism for instance) can only finally repeat that which they are designed to explain or interpret: here again an "outside" returns to an "inside," an Other to the Same. For Foucault, at least, even more than for Bataille, transgression is also linguistic, finding itself not in discourse about the world, or about the true, or even in discourse about discourse – rather finding itself just *as* discourse, *as* writing. It belongs to the "mad philosopher" who finds the "transgression of his philosophical being" not outside language but "at the inner core of its (language's) possibilities" (44). The "limitless play of the limit" or the breakdown of distinctions between "inside" and "outside" have force because any particular mode of analysis (such as dialectics) is itself linguistic and, thus, is not simply the tool of an originating subject of "thought." However, in emphasizing the connection between language and transgression within this theme of "desubjectiviz-ing," Foucault commits some violence on Bataille's thought. Bataille him-self can think of language as mere communication (Heideggerian *Rede* (gossip)) in which human beings trivially lose themselves, in contrast to serious communication which contains a continuity with, for instance, the rites of sacrifice. When Foucault finds transgression working with the language's formal conditions of possibility – this is very much a Bataille for *his* own time.

We can again ask that characteristically post-phenomenological question: what happens at the limits of language itself, when silence and the senses (especially vision) replace thought, talk, writing? In answer, Foucault finds in Bataille a specific motif – that of the upturned eye. The rich passage in which it is introduced is worth citing at some length:

> The eye, in a philosophy of reflection, derives from its capacity to observe the power of becoming always more interior to itself. Lying behind each eye that sees, there exists a more tenuous one, an eye so discreet and yet so agile that its all-powerful glance can be said to eat away at the flesh of its white globe; behind this particular eye, there exists another and, then, still others, each progressively more subtle until we arrive at an eye whose entire substance is nothing but the transparency of its vision. This inner movement is finally resolved in a center where the intangible forms of truth are created and combined, in this heart of things which is the sovereign subject. Bataille reverses this entire direction; sight, crossing the globular limit of the eye, constitutes the eye in its instantaneous being: sight carries it away in this luminous stream . . . hurls the eye outside of itself, conducts it to the limit where it bursts out in the immediately extinguished flash of its being. . . . In the distance created by this violence and uprooting, the eye is seen absolutely, but denied any possibility of sight; the philosophizing subject has been dispossessed and pursued to its limit: and this sovereignty of philosophical lan-guage can now be heard from the distance, in the measureless void left behind by the exorbitated subject.
>
> (46)

Bataille's "upturned eye" is opposed to the "philosophizing subject" whose thought is objective and who possesses what Rousseau called a "living eye": an eye within an eye within a eye.[1] It is also opposed to the panopt-ical vision – the point of view at the centre of the prison (or factory, or hospital) dreamed of by Jeremy Bentham, where, observed by none, each is observed. Bataille's eye flows into what it sees – it sees as an act in a field of acts, fluid in a fluid world. It does so via a dismemberment which reminds us of Rousseau's "Judgement/Torture" system. Where the "exorbitated" subject embraces the void and lets things be, the ceaseless murmur of language is all the clearer, the sayable is utterly detached from the visible. In the essay's final passages, this dismembered and "upturned eye" will view the world from the other side of the tomb, from death: it "crosses" the limit, and in doing so, it turns on itself, as if it, too, could see itself. But this is no "enlightened" gesture of self-reflection. Rather, the eye that has crossed the uncrossable limit sees surfaces rather than depths and layers and at last (crossing from one sense to another) seems to "touch absence" (52). Bataille's gruesome descriptions of orgasms reached as bodies are torn apart in his art-porn novel *Story of the Eye* are allegories of the way in which the sight of sight, reflection on oneself, connects the seeing subject either to nothing or to another surface – the eyeball itself. Again, the inward turn towards self-recognition made at the boundary of self (that is, at the point of death) finds not knowledge as light (or "enlightenment") but knowledge as discourse. For such knowledge, "life" is not a property of those beings in the world that have most value (who can see and feel, for instance). Bataille approaches Roussel's treatment of the world as if it were merely injected with vitalist substances. We might even say that both Bataille and Rousseau have a precursor in Henry James whose pure characters are only pure to the degree that they disappear from themselves. They ally themselves with a nothingness that holds no terrors, permitting the author all the more unrestrainedly to throw himself into the forms and pleasures of discourse.

THE NOVEL IN LITERATURE

"Preface to Transgression" is an essay about certain possibilities for thought in recent modernity, it is not especially directed at literature as such. Its interests are extended and focused in Foucault's roughly contemporaneous essays on Bataille's younger peers: Klossowski and Blanchot. In "Prose of Acteon" (on Klossowski) Foucault develops Nietzsche's account of the consequences of God's death. In *The Gay Science*, Nietszche famously asked how would one respond to a "demon" who said:

> "This life as you now live it and have lived it, you will have to live once more and innumerable times more. . . . The eternal hourglass of existence is turned upside down again and again, and you with it, speck of dust!" Would you not throw yourself down and gnash your teeth and curse the demon who spoke thus? Or have you experienced a tremendous moment when you could reply to him: "You are a *god*, and never have I heard anything more divine."
>
> (1988d, xxiv)

The passage asks a version of Locke's old question: how to tell the difference between a god and a devil? (Which in turn is a version of Descartes' struggle with the question of madness.) Now that neither God nor Satan manifest themselves immediately in the world, we find that their absence is also their "interlacement" (1964c, 448). This space in which gods may be devils and in which this world loses its uniqueness is that of simulacra. Foucault argues that simulacra are to be distinguished from *signs* whose significations are produced in a system of differences and are capable of fixing a distinction between the present and the absent, between the signifier and the signified. Simulacra point to an absence across an unbridgeable distance, they double each other across a limit marked and broken by the death of a God who never existed and whose (imaginary) disappearance forms a limit on whose far side the Other can always be a version of the Same. Simulacra make of presence a paradox, make of "reality" an "imaginary." At this point Foucault stakes a rather extraordinary claim: from the time of the Greeks, Western culture has in fact moved under the "experience" of simulacra rather than that of signification. That is most clearly seen both in the role that typology has played in organizing Occidental thought (for typology, a symbol refers back to its prefiguration rather than to a system of differences) and in the primacy of the concept of "fate" or Providence for which the "meaning" of events is finally unreadable. So Klossowski's work is one of "rediscovery" – Western history has always simulated itself as his characters do. Furthermore, in Klossowski, simulation orders not just the object world, "things and clues," but his writing itself. His writing is articulated in various voices which "trick" one another and cannot be distinguished from one another (xxivff.). Here analysis approaches its own collapse; past this point theorists themselves become writers of "fiction."

If "Prose of Acteon" affirms the analytic cogency of concepts such as repetition and simulacra (an affirmation already implicit in *Death and the Labyrinth*), Foucault's later essay on Blanchot, "Thought from Outside," explores the theme of exteriority. Here Foucault is more particularly concerned with language. He describes the way in which a particular utterance, "I speak," presupposes a system, a "supporting discourse," that provides it with an "object" (a referent), but is at the same time external to that discourse, because as an utterance it is also an act. Language unfolds as "pure exteriority" in this disjuncture between performance and "meaning" foregrounded in "I speak." Foucault maintains that that utterance causes modern "fiction" to tremble in the way that the paradox "I lie" had scandalized classical "truth" just because "I speak" is *always* true – even in a fiction. To say "I speak" is not to represent a piece of reality but to act, so that the fictionality of fiction disappears. In the "coincidence to itself" of the speech *act*, statements become "singularities," unable to find common ground in the system which enables them. In such acts, as they elude the distinction between truth and fiction, performance takes priority over, and becomes disjunct from, "meaning." According to Foucault, modern literature, therefore, is not characterized either by its self-reflexivity or by its use of mimesis or diegesis, but by its dispersion into a number of linguistic events (texts, utterances) each incommensurable to the other. *This* is the "being of language" in "contemporary Western fiction" (12). And, making familiar anti-psychological moves, Foucault goes on to argue that language in its exteriority to itself also disperses the humanist "subject." The subject of "I speak" is not to be found in the act of uttering, it disappears in the non-linguistic effect of the act itself. The subject of fiction is swallowed up into the silence that ceaselessly punctuates the equally ceaseless flow of utterances – as Foucault phrases it.

However, it is not in the essays on Bataille (and transgression), Klossowski (and the simulacra) and Blanchot (and exteriority) that Foucault addresses himself most clearly and effectively either to the historical emergence of literature, or to its contemporary forms. These topics are approached most fully in his more programmatic essays, especially the very dense "Language to Infinity," as well as in his reviews of, and discussions with, the "new new novelists." In "Language to Infinity," Foucault advances the unusual but intriguing thesis that "literature" as a discursive formation first appears with Sade and the Gothic novelists. (This ought to be considered against the more familiar and more sociological notion urged by Raymond Williams, that "literature" begins as the general category "polite letters" disappears, a shift concurrent with the decline of patronage and the entry of literary copyright.) What constitutes Foucault's Gothic or Sadean moment, the moment of literature's emergence? First, some texts then begin to attempt to move beyond language – either by producing intense sensation (terror), or, in Sade's case, by exhausting the possibilites of language in encyclopedic descriptions of the relations between bodies engaged in sex and violence, descriptions in which language begins to pass itself off as the manifestation of sheer desire (and, as we have seen, break down the vitalist distinction between "life" and "death"). Indeed, as Foucault notes in his 1964 essay on Flaubert's *The Temptation of St Anthony*: in the epoch of the library, the imaginary – the archive of fantasy images – exists less as opposition to the real than, positively, as the product of texts. Images are what the inner eye "sees" when readers read book after book after book (1977a, 89–90). (So when Roussel and Bataille set language against the visible they are attempting to cleanse the world of those "images" which exist as illustrations of words and narratives and which bind vision as much to language as to sight.) Second, the attempt to exceed language immediately moves back on itself: eighteenth-century sensational (or Gothic) novels (unintentionally) parody themselves in their necessity to engage their readers. To provide a scene for readerly identification, they must use realist and mimetic techniques. But in the slide from realism to the sensational and back again their attempt to move readers *immediately* (to frighten them for instance) produces distancing effects. Being in terror itself becomes indissociable from being represented as in terror. The real horor never happens – it is deferred from chapter to chapter and is finally explained away. This structure of deferral and slippage invites pastiche by other more completely realist texts: no doubt English speakers think of Jane Austen's *Northanger Abbey*. But Foucault refers to Bellin de Labordière's *Une nuit anglaise*. Third, Gothic writings engage a hidden *mise en abîme* (the so-called "Quaker box" effect in reference to the sides of a cereal packet which contains a picture of itself which contains a picture of itself which contains a picture of itself . . .). In trying to disengage themselves from the linguistic, using and evoking terror calmly, these works which attempt to exceed language, to pass themselves off as sensations become all the more linguistic. Language doubles itself as sensations become verbal, and "this wound of the double," as Foucault puts it, cannot be avoided (1977a, 109). This has institutional as well as metaphysical consequences. These texts' aim to move beyond their own linguisticity towards the non-linguistic *and* the non-visible produces folds and layers within language. Their moving "towards infinity" (towards what they cannot themselves represent or be), within increasingly "realist" modes of representation, together with an increasingly heavy weight of intertextuality, allows "literary" – as against rhetorical or journalistic – techniques to proliferate. It follows, notes Foucault, that "literature" (in the first instance, Gothic and Sadean literature) is *unreadable*, untranslatable because it is tied to the sensation it can never reach. Paradoxically, as Foucault suggests in his essay on Flaubert, those readers most addicted to literature, like Bouvard and Pécuchet (in Flaubert's novel of that name), are essentially passive, mere copyists or internalizers. They *become* the books in the library; their visions instantiate words; their indefinitely deferred sensations and desire for knowledge require the consumption of text after text after text.

Foucault also describes the emergence of literature as the shift from "rhetoric" to the "library" – these terms being, as it were, "motifs" in the text of history. In the epoch of rhetoric, writing is ordered by rules which permit an ideal but "mute" discourse to be turned into actual speech. Within the epoch of the Library, however, ideal speech ceases to exist, so that we have "the ranging to infinity of fragmentary languages" (67) – which we already know as the proliferation of singularities in the exteriority of one utterance to another. What is this "ideal speech"? Not just the original language that God spoke, but also the best way of talking, arguing, writing. As ideal speech slips away, writing is produced in a "self-conscious relationship to earlier texts" (92). The question that the essays on the contemporary avant-garde ask is: does *its* writing still belong to the Library? And Foucault seems to answer in a conditional affirmative: the new new novel – which he calls simply fiction – is a province of literature. It appears when literature accepts and enacts the impossibility of its own project – that of replacing language by experience, by sensation, from within language, of moving towards the real by a relay through other texts. Clearly modern fiction has been prepared for, and remains inseparable from, the transgressive and labyrinthine thought of Klossowski, Bataille and Blanchot. But – and here a new emphasis enters – it also forms part of that "network" (as Foucault calls it) established by Alain Robbe-Gril-let's work.

In a series of polemical essays, of which the most famous was "Nature, Humanism and Tragedy," (1958), Robbe-Grillet produced a programme and theory of his own writing based on his belief that humanism, the use of metaphor, and analogy all worked to one end. For Robbe-Grillet, metaphor connects things to one another within language in the interests of a human-ism that places human beings at the centre of the world. To take the point of a metaphor is to admit a "natural," a universal human ability to read the world in terms of analogies. In opposition to this, Robbe-Grillet wished to record the exteriority of things to one another. That is why he admired Roussel's work: there too language detaches itself from "pure" vision in its very attempt to produce visibilities; and explanation is inadequate to event (Robbe-Grillet 1965, 102). Robbe-Grillet does not work through a "point of view" – his novels describe events as if they are being seen through an apparatus which does not share the space or laws of perspective within which the events themselves occur. In a review essay, "Distance, aspect, origine" (1963), Foucault, however, is less concerned to examine Robbe-Grillet's attempt to "articulate the gaze" theoretically than to sug-gest that *distance* in the more recent writers involves something rather different than it does in Robbe-Grillet.[2] Thus, though the new new novel is "isomorphic" to its predecessor, existing on the same "table" as it and working to similar anti-metaphorical and anti-humanist ends, it differs in that it "is formed within language's relation to itself." The work of the *Tel Quel* group is based on "the verbal skeleton of what does not exist, just as it is" (1963a, 940), so that "there is not fiction because language is at a distance from things; but language is their distance, the light in which they exist and their inaccessibility, the simulacra in which alone they are permitted presence" (ibid.). At the far side of language, where it edges out to the world, what one finds is the murmur of language again – in obedience to what is becoming the familiar rule which states that the Other (to the degree to which it is *radically* Other) can only be encountered as a repetition of the Same. And if, in the new new novelist's work, distance is no longer spatial but discursive, that is also true of time. Time becomes "aspect" – which is the word grammarians use to describe how verbs signify temporality (as it is the concept that Heidegger appeals to in his account of the temporality of discourse, that is the way discourse is essen-tially placed in, rather than mimetic of, time (Heidegger 1962, 400)). In contemporary fiction, time is merely grammatical (Foucault does not say so, but this has been true ever since Flaubert, at least, according to Proust in his wonderful essay on that "grammatical genius" – as Flaubert is there called (Proust 1988, 89)). We can put it like this: the new new novelists treat the world in a profoundly non-Kantian manner, as if space and time were not the conditions of possibility for perception. In them, space and time become effects of meaning-processes, so that the world reveals itself as if it were sheer language – with no speaking subject prior to it and without reference to any fixed spatio-temporal world. And – to take the third term of the review essay – the *origins* of fiction are found in the act of writing itself. But of course this is not the kind of origin that is ever present, least of all in a unified subject behind a text. Foucault himself may not have stated it in this manner, but it is as if, again, the new new novelists find *their* "motif" for Being-in-the-world (what he called their "ontological indicator") in the paradox by which words bring their subject into existence by virtue of their own finitude, by virtue of their secondariness to the "reality" of which they are the trace and which they can signify only as it disappears.

HISTORY AND DISCOURSE

We have moved quite far from Foucault's praise for Artaud and Roussel as "mad" writers "arraigning the world" in *Madness and Civilization*. Indeed at the end of "Distance, aspect, origine" he again explicitly dismisses the idea that madness can help one think about modern literature (1963a, 942). As we have seen, in moving from madness to language as the site of contestation, Foucault was following a quite general trend whose most obvious manifestation was the review *Tel Quel*, though his own ability to work within a frame bounded by the literary phenomenologists on one side, the transgressive theorists on another and the writers who delivered themselves up to mechanics of the signifier on a third, remained unique. This quite general re-orientation of avant-garde French thought is finally more important in understanding the atmosphere in which Foucault wrote about literature than any specific incident such as Derrida's critique of *Madness and Civilization*. However, this is not to say that Foucault's work at this period is, in any simple sense at least, "deconstructive," a point which can be repeated and extended. For even at this moment in his career he remains willing to historicize. After all, it is in history that rhetoric turns into the Library and the Library folds into fiction, and it is there that the impossibility of presence, the reign of the simulacra and the limits of regarding the space/time couple as the foundations of the world's knowability all stand revealed. And it is in history that "literature" appears – as that form of writing which wishes to colonize experience for and by language.

Literature's history is not now so much allied to the story of madness as it is to that of death. It is tied, first, to the death of God and the consequent irruption of finitude ("the limitless reign of limits") and then to the death of the subject and the subsequent reign of writing. It is true that in "Language to Infinity," Foucault argues that the formations which collapse the division between the inside and outside, the here and the there collapse, do not require writing. The preconditions of such formations are found in those narrative structures which, since Homer, have used para- doxes of self-referentiality and self-repetition. Foucault's instance is modern however: the incident in Diderot's epistolary novel *The Nun* where a charac- ter complains of a letter going astray in the very letter being complained of:

> The reduplication of language, even if it is concealed, constitutes its being as a work, and the signs that might appear from this must be read as ontological indications. . . . These signs are often impercep- tible, bordering on the futile. They manage to present themselves as faults – slight imperfections at the surface of a work: we might say that they serve as involuntary opening to the inexhaustible depths from which they come to us.
>
> (1977a, 57)

Though the critical methodology here, in its attention to "slight imperfec- tions at the surface of a work," might seem to follow Derrida, Foucault is interested in the "virtual space of self-representation and reduplication" (1977a, 56) characteristic of a particular linguistic form – narrative – and most commonly carried by a particular technology – writing – rather than in language's "unrestricted economy" of difference and deferral. Split between history and "ontological indicators," he is working once more in the historico-ontological gap. If it can be argued from the side of decon- struction that the distinction between history and Being cannot be rigorously drawn, that language's "faults" belong to the conditions of signification as such, then it can also be argued, from the Foucauldian side, that it is important to attempt to historicize the unhistoricizable – if nothing else, in order to test and contest the power of the category "his- tory" itself. Or to put the argument in slightly different terms, "theory" charges "history" with simplifying, with requiring a certain conceptual carelessness and simplification in the categories by which it connects events to each other. History tells theory, in turn, that the play of simulacra, the clustering of singularities in discursive formations, the very hollowness of concepts like "influence" and "causality," are articulated in a history whose shape is ordered by the successive deaths of individuals.

Whatever the fallout of this debate, and whatever difficulties and con- fusions it may have led to in Foucault's work, his refusal to accept that historical shifts are controlled or limited by larger entities or structures such as "Being" or *écriture*, permitted him to remain at a distance from what he would call the "theorization of writing" – even at its period of greatest attraction. During this period he worked first on *The Birth of the Clinic* and then on *The Order of Things* – both *historical* works. But it is in "Distance, aspect, origine" that Foucault tries to break the impasse which follows the recognition that language is not quite historicizable. Writing of the relation between Robbe-Grillet and the newest novelists, as well as of the connections between those authors themselves, he notes: "It seems to me that the possibilities of language in a given epoch are not so numerous that one may not find isomorphisms" (932). That is to say, the relations between various discursive events at a particular historical moment involve patterns that no historical narrative can fully account for, but which exist within a particular poverty of discourse. Each historical moment contains a "network" and, as Foucault goes on to argue, if history sees the network in terms of "passages, intersections and nodes," criticism can regard it as a "reversible movement" (937). A grand claim is here staked. Criticism finds a language for what is "mute" in its objects: the reversibility of their ruptures and relations. For it, texts do not exist in time conceived of as a one-way street, as they do for traditional historians: after all, time punctuated by death has no final destination. In grasping this, criticism can be both secondary to the texts it reads *and* "fundamental," or original. It need not retrieve the past as if it were buried under a glacier of continuous and linear time. It can replay history. Time itself is merely an effect of "aspect," partly because "real" time – in which one was born and in which one will die – cannot be experienced; partly because temporal sequences cannot necessarily be reduced to causal sequences and vice versa. Little could be less Heideggerian or less marxian than this, but in "Distance, aspect, origine" Foucault comes to accept that his historical work is a criticism which, like transgressive fiction, breaks and breaks into, the fiction of history.

The refusal to regard history as a linear passage through time by appealing both to the clustering of discourse in its scarcity and to a more general ontological poverty, will characterize Foucault's next major work, *The Order of Things*. It is important to recognize that the methods and organization of that work belong partly to literary history, partly to a criticism anxious about its own secondariness to transgression, and partly to a polemics for a literary avant-garde which claimed that its writing represents the freshest, least mystified possibilities given to the epoch.

91

4

KNOWLEDGE

Foucault wrote two books during his "archaeological" phase. The first, *The Order of Things*, published in 1966, is a history of discourse since the Renaissance; the second, *The Archaeology of Knowledge*, published three years later, is a re-theorization of the first. "Re-theorization" is the appropriate word because *The Archaeology of Knowledge* does not provide a full and accurate account of *The Order of Things*' aims and achievements: it pushes them in a new direction. Both are self-consciously revolutionary works. Between them they posit a new "discipline," if not a "positive science" as Derrida described *his* rival to archaeology – grammatology – in 1967. Indeed, the word "archaeology" had long had a somewhat subversive and heightened sense in the French avant-garde. As far back as 1926, Georges Henri Rivière, a curator at the Trocadéro, had published what Rosalind Krauss calls a "panegyric" to an archaeology which he regarded as the "parricidal daughter of humanism" (Krauss 1985, 49). More immediately, the ambitiousness of both Derrida's and Foucault's claims belong to that "trembling" of French society during the sixties, mentioned at the end of my introduction.

These books are written as if the post-Renaissance period had come to an end. In them, the categories of mere modernity no longer cohere and can therefore begin to be broken with. Their project is one of defamiliarization: a turning of the Same into the Other as Foucault puts it at the beginning of *The Order of Things*. This is the point of the little story Foucault tells of that book's genesis. In one of his fictions Borges had described a "certain Chinese encyclopedia" in which

> animals are divided into (a) belonging to the Emperor, (b) embalmed, (c) tame, (d) sucking pigs, (e) sirens, (f) fabulous, (g) stray dogs, (h) included in the present classification, (i) frenzied, (j) innumerable, (k) drawn with a very fine camel-hair brush, (l) *et cetera*, (m) having just broken the water pitcher, (n) that from a long way off look like flies.
>
> (1970a, xv)

Apparently, the strangeness of this list, in which every item is an odd man out, helped Foucault see that the past classifications of Western knowledge are arbitrary, and undergo historical shifts in a series of not wholly ordered or "rational" breaks.

Foucault inherits a conviction that certain currents of modernity have lost their charge from his involvement in the "theorization of writing."[1] But, in embracing the end of modernity, he also indirectly draws upon the harder structuralism of Lévi-Strauss – however much he insisted he was not a structuralist. Lévi-Strauss's technical, anti-historicist arguments, first, that the "diachronic" (or history) cannot be called upon to explain the "synchronic" (or the social structures in existence at any particular moment) and, second, that the contents of cultural beliefs are independent of their function, heralded his grander claim that "man" was no longer at the centre of analysis or of history. To accept this meant a change of orientation in Foucault's historical work: in *Madness and Civilization* there is no sense that the structures and institutions which exclude and define madness are about to lose their power but *The Order of Things* is written as if poised on the brink of a new era. In its much quoted final sentence, Foucault anticipates, poetically if somewhat hesitantly, the moment when "man would be erased, like a face drawn in sand at the end of the sea" (1970a, 387).

On the other hand, *The Archaeology of Knowledge* moves away from both structuralism and the literary avant-garde. This is not merely a matter of tone and style, though in those terms this apparently grey, meticulous book, which starts and finishes in dialogues in some ways reminiscent of Hume and Rousseau, was certainly another departure for Foucault. It maintains the project of defamiliarization, but its programme for a radical re-description of the past owes (or seems to owe) less to Georges Bataille and Maurice Blanchot, than to Foucault's old teachers, the historians and philosophers of science, Bachelard and Canguilhem – and even to Louis Althusser. To use the book's own language, it presents the categories by which we can articulate the conditions of possibility for a discursive event to occur at any particular moment; or, to put it a little more simply, it systematically presents the various – historically various – categories and levels within which it is decided what statements are, or are not, true, meaningful and effective. It describes the rules which remove certain statements and groups of statements from the vernacular, or what Heidegger called *Gerede* (chatter). The notion of the rule is crucial here, for in *The Archaeology of Knowledge* Foucault supposes that knowledge is neither to be measured in terms of its correspondence to the world, nor to be thought of in terms of "codes" or "conventions," nor in terms of its internal coherence or "rationality." Knowledge consists simply of what is said and *its* internal divisions: though Foucault overlooks the ways in which the vernacular forms the background against which official knowledges emerge.

The analytic tone of the book is something of a mirage partly because, in declining to recount the history of knowledge in terms of its increasing rationality and truth, Foucault can still bring together an extraordinarily heterogeneous and fertile mix of themes. For instance, here we find Bachelard's "epistemological break"; Robbe-Grillet's connection between Sameness and humanism; a Roussellian gap between the visible and the sayable, and, not yet quite out of sight, a Tel Quelian acceptance of the textuality of Being. Thus the book's solemnity (which at least one critic has read as parodic) conceals an astonishing eclecticism, a synthetic approach, in which the various, very disparate strands of discourse of Foucault's earlier work come together, each displaced, indeed often almost unrecognizable.[2]

But the topos upon which these various approaches and notions rest remains the "end of man." Foucault means more by the phrase than did those who introduced it – like Nietzsche, the transgressive theorists, Levi-Strauss and the modernist anti-humanists (described in chapter 1). Yet what exactly? To answer this rather difficult question would lead us straight into the way that in *The Order of Things*, he divides the history of modernity into three distinct moments: that of the Renaissance, the "classical" and the "modern" itself. So let us say, provisionally, that "man" is the (deeply problematic) object on which modern knowledge is focused: "he" is the topic of the social sciences as they emerge throughout the nineteenth century; it is to counter "man's" dominance that *The Order of Things* offers a detailed history of the "soft sciences" – what we know as biology, linguistics, economics – as well as of the "human sciences," written as if those sciences have been exceeded. But "man" is also the horizon of "history" as it comes into being as a discipline of thought in the modern humanities. For Foucault, history, as a form of modern knowledge, projects, as its ultimate frame of reference, the continuous and teleological development of a subject of "consciousness," articulated through anthropological concepts like "progress," "alienation," "need," "want" and "liberation," all of which are implicit signs of a lack in "man" that history will complete. Technically, history relies on connective categories such as function or causality: it ties events together either by showing how they work to keep systems going or in a line of cause and effects. Although history is only one of a number of disciplines that promise, or have promised, to explain and order "man," it is privileged. For modern knowledge differs from its predecessors in that it regards its objects as primordially temporal, as thrown into time. And it is this backdrop – time, historicity, in front of which "man" lives – that is to be contested by archaeology. Perhaps the best way to begin to elucidate these difficult claims is to ask in a little detail "what *is* archaeology?" and that means that we must first treat of *The Archaeology of Knowledge* rather than the earlier and more historical *The Order of Things*.

ARCHAEOLOGY AS A METHOD

Archaeology is finally more defined against its enemies – humanism and "anthropology" – than in terms of a specifiable programme. At its very centre lies the notion of the *énoncé* or "statement," the basic element of knowledge. When strung together, ordered and framed, *énoncés* form "discourse" – and "discourse" is the second crucial term in the book, one destined to an amazing success especially in the American academy. Archaeology is primarily concerned with "regularities" and hierarchies of *énoncés*. *Énoncés* are not simply sentences because the same sentence may form different *énoncés* in different contexts: for example, "The Duke came to dine" in a fiction and in a biography. Also, some, perhaps all, sentences, may have (at least) two meanings, whereas *énoncés* cannot be punned. Nor are *énoncés* to be identified with those "meanings" themselves for *that* concept belongs to anthropology: "meanings" exist as those states of consciousness ('ideas") or intention which words are supposed to express or represent. (Obviously enough, *énoncés* are also neither to be identified as a proposition's denotation or reference or as its connotation or sense – the categories developed by Frege, which have long continued to support Anglo-American linguistic philosophy.) On the other hand, different sentences may form a single *énoncé*: synonymy does indeed exist, though, for Foucault, historians much over-emphasise it. *Énoncés* are not utterances (which Foucault calls enunciations) either – because each repetition of a sentence by a speaker constitutes a different utterance but not a different *énoncé*. Thus they are "neither visible nor hidden" (1970a, 109), and though, given all that they are *not*, this proposition has force, it is still difficult to understand how something "neither visible nor hidden" can be represented and analyzed.

Foucault meets this kind of objection by regarding *énoncés* as events. This is not to say that they are quite what, in a gesture to the work of J. L. Austin and his followers, he calls "speech acts" – because the performance of a single speech act (what Austin would call a "performative utterance"), unlike the *énoncé*, may require a string of statements (83–4). But analyzing *énoncés* as events helps Foucault to make two defamiliarizing moves. First, he can begin to see them as forming patterns not connected to the unities or frames in which they have previously been bundled, such as books, oeuvres, influences, disciplines or historical anticipations (regarding seventeenth-century puritanism as a forerunner of early nineteenth-century radicalism, to take a British instance.) He takes patterns of *énoncés* – discursive formations – out of the whole hermeneutic project with its double aim: to understand the present in terms of the past, and to read texts or utterances in terms of their "context" or "subtext." Second, when considered as an event, discourse can be placed in a set of "modalities," neglected while it was thought of in terms of "theories" or "concepts" or "ideas." To think in terms of discursive modalities is to enable us to ask questions like: what kind of thing counts as verification for a statement: reasoning by analogy or statistical quantification? – to take just two possibilities. Different discourses have different such criteria. *Énoncés* can also be thought of in terms of the strategies and institutions in which they are uttered. The same statement has more force coming from a professor than from an undergraduate; academies and disciplines define quite rigidly what kind of statements are or are not proper to them, and so on. Finally, *énoncés* exist in a network of choices, each of which is underdetermined, that is, cannot be known to be absolutely appropriate. Such choices are made (not necessarily consciously) to exclude, to control, to gain status and so on, and yet, being underdetermined, their intended effects may always misfire. It is Foucault's strategic and institutional conception of discourse – harking back not to his literary criticism but to his histories of madness and medicine – which also points forward to the work on power and sex to follow.

The Archaeology of Knowledge seems to be about discursive events and their regularities. The difficulty with a project conceived of in these terms is that analysis at the level of signification can never be reduced to analysis at the level of event, and vice versa. If statements are given force by their institutional setting or the authority of their utterer, it is also true that only certain statements can be uttered appropriately within a particular institutional setting *by virtue of* their sense. Foucault addresses this difficulty by distinguishing between a "system of enunciability" within which the *énoncé* is an event – and a "system of functioning" – within which it is a thing (129). This distinction organizes his book: he first discusses one, then the other. Yet the division is very problematic: utterances cannot be thought of simply either as events – like the scoring of a goal, or as representations – like a map. This, indeed is the question that Foucault's essay on Blanchot and "I speak" tackles. It might be argued (and Derrida often does argue) that one of the motors of history is the split within discourse between act and representation, the impossibility of deciding whether utterances are acts or representations. Why a "motor of history"? Just because a speech act may always be inappropriate: its sense may work against its performative force, so that discourse cannot be wholly socially managed. History moves forward, at least in part, in the impossible effort to bring the content of what is said, its truth-value, into line with the force of what is said, its impact on the world. By virtue of this discrepancy, new "meanings" may also always come into existence.

Let us leave this difficulty aside. Foucault calls "regularities in the dispersion of *énoncés*," "discursive formations" – and these, when considered in terms of their actual geographical or historical spread and limits, are called, in turn, "discursive practices." Discursive formations are not necessarily unified: they may include statements which contradict each other or point in different directions, and it is at these "points of incompatibility"

96

(65) that particular strategies form. The level of strategy is reached once there is a question of deciding which of the incompatible elements in a discursive formation is to be used in order to explain or legitimate a set of statements. The same is true at levels of greater regularity: for instance, as Foucault writes in *The Order of Things*, "at the archaeological level, the conditions of possibility of a non-verbal logic and a historical grammar are the same" (1970a, 297) – and so the choice of which discourse to use would be strategical rather than "natural" or imposed. Discursive formations pass over various thresholds, of which the most important is the clumsily named "threshold of epistemologization" (187), the point at which discursive formations begin to produce statements about their own "norms of verification," and thus, in Foucault's terms, begin to constitute a "science." He also posits two further thresholds – those of "scientificity" itself – at which laws for the construction of further propositions in the formation are articulated, and of "formalization" – at which a discourse begins to define its own conditions of possibility in formal axioms. For Foucault, scientific knowledge is not "truer" than non-scientific knowledge, nor is it formed in one discourse like another: it has just passed these particular thresholds. This constitutes its impotence as much as its strength. That a new "interpretation" of Galileo (whose work has been scientificized) would only be of importance to the history of science, whereas a new interpretation of Marx or Freud might change current marxism or psychoanalysis, is not in any simple way a sign of science's unique powers to "understand" or to produce truth, for instance. In general, for him, discursive formations exist as *the conditions of possibility* for the existence and repetition of particular sets of *énoncés*. The relation between *énoncés* and discursive formations is repeated in the relations between the archive (the most general category postulated by archaeology) and the discursive formation. The archive is the "general system of the formation and the transformation of the *énoncé*," so that it is at this level that Foucault finally defines archaeology – that which "describes discourses as practices specified in the element of the archive" (131). In one of the relatively few lyrical passages in the book, the archive is evoked as that which, "determines that all [the] things said do not accumulate endlessly in an amorphous mass . . . but are grouped together in distinct figures, composed together in accordance with multiple relations, maintained or blurred in accordance with specific regularities; that which determines that they do not withdraw at the same space in time" (129). Because it is the condition for the breaks between discourses, and because *all* statements and discourses belong to it (including, of course, *The Archaeology of Knowledge* itself), the archive is not itself able to be described. To say that the archive does not fold back on itself is also to say that the set of discourses which belong to it is necessarily fragmented and dispersed. If the archive could

view itself, a very grand meta-discourse would be possible. Here again language edges, impossibly, on infinity.

Foucault postulates another archaeological level – one that is wider than both the *énoncé* and the discursive formation, and narrower than the archive. He calls this the "positivity." It is the category at which the analyzes of *The Order of Things* are directed. "To analyze positivities is to show in accordance with which rules a discursive practice may form groups of objects, enunciations, concepts or theoretical choices" (181), or as he also puts it in a phrase which he had often used in his earlier work, "the positivity plays the role of what might be called a historical a-priori" (127). What is an example of a positivity? Foucault has in mind something like the discursive effect and reach of a term like "life" since the early nine-teenth century: it is part of what orders novels like those of D. H. Lawr-ence; literary criticism like that of F. R. Leavis, as well as biology after Cuvier and Bichat. The concept of a "historical a-priori," however, draws on formulations which exist at the very heart of metaphysics after Kant. Kant had argued that certain *Grundsätze* (fundamental principles such as causality) form the "conditions of possibility of experience" and are thus a-priori (prior to all experience) and "synthetic" – say something about the world in a way that merely "analytic" statements such as "all bachelors are unmarried" do not (Kant 1961, 194). Foucault is historicizing Kant: positivities are to particular historical discourses what the *Grundsätze* are to experience in general in Kant.

This rather unwieldy metaphysical relation permits Foucault a certain looseness because one positivity may order the shape of several discursive practices (novel writing, biology, criticism) – each of which may have passed over a different "threshold." Although he had described positivities in *The Order of Things*, Foucault had there identified the epochs of modern history each in terms of a particular "episteme." Now, in *The Archaeology of Knowledge*, epistemes are more or less eradicated. This represents an analytic opening out, for, if in the early book it often seemed as if there existed a single, inescapable mode of constructing knowledge for each period, now Foucault concedes that any specific historical moment consists of a "region of interpositivities" (159). This permits him to think about history not in terms of a succession of unified epochs, nor as a field upon which individual discursive formations operate, each within their own trajectory, each within their own institutions, but as a patterned space within which groups of discourses both share features with, and break away from, each other, pass through, or pass out of, the various thresholds available to the Western archive. Connected discursive formations each have their individual historical trajectory: thus, for instance, the emergence of history as a discipline in the eighteenth century precedes the sense that language has a history in the early nineteenth century (in what Foucault calls a "fragmented discursive shift" (176)). Yet it is worth noting that this account still does not contain room for a single discursive practice being conditioned within more than one positivity. Although it breaks with time as a continuum within which knowledge develops to perfection, Foucault's archaeology remains modelled on an image of history as forming sedimented – if fractured – layers. It is as if each archival moment, which belongs to a specific spatio-temporal point, may be conditioned only by *one* rule, one "positivity"; though, of course, any positivity can pattern a variety of discursive formations. This is a consequence of the fact that *énoncés* cannot be punned. And the notion of the positivity also makes it harder for Foucault to think of discourses as articulated within trans-actional and historical processes – particularly processes of exchange, incor-poration and negotiation. If we look at discursive formations as a result of such processes then, of course, they will always seem to be hybrids, rather than patterned by fixed conditions.

To define and present the notion of the "positivity," Foucault draws upon the ontology that he had begun to articulate in *Death and the Labyrinth*. For positivities are organized around the rarity and exteriority of *énoncés*. They are rare because what there is to be said is always limited, thus discourse is always formed in repetitions of *énoncés*; they are exterior because statements do not develop from, or connect to, each other *naturally* in terms of an immutable order. As we know, and as Foucault tirelessly repeats, the ultimate backdrop upon which *énoncés* are formed is not one in which concealed Being is the process unveiling itself; not the creation of a God who has handed his creatures a Holy Book and promised a return to his presence; not a history in which humanity (the Human Subject) progresses away from alienation and conflict towards liberty and harmony; not the tragedy of human insufficiency: it is rather – nothing, the "limitless reign of the limit," the absence, that Foucault considers to be (so to say) the page upon which Roussel and Blanchot write. This is the sense in which Foucault is a positivist and not an "anthropologist." (It is a sense peculiar to himself.) And as these rare and discontinuous utterances "accumulate" in material techniques (especially writing), history can be regarded as, in part, a succession of discourse wars, and also, in part, a domain within which ordered discursive formations emerge and disappear in shifts which have no absolute order. Discourse itself, however, is unhistorical: "it is immobilized in fragments, precarious splinters of eternity" (166) – where "eternity" must be understood quite outside its theological or humanist connotations (but rather in a sense that goes back – via Althusser – to Spinoza).

We can now grasp *The Archaeology of Knowledge*'s internal "points of incompatibility" more concretely. For, in addition to the problem of decid-ing whether an *énoncés* is an event or a proposition, there are three further (overlapping) difficulties. The first is that of fixing what Foucault himself called the "criteria of individualization" for specific *énoncés* or discourses;

the second concerns the fuzziness of the concept of those "conditions of possibility" which, as "historical a-priori," pattern each discursive formation, and the third relates to the old problem of the relation between words and things. Without providing a full theoretical critique of the idea of "archaeology," it is enough to say that it is hard to see how one could ever individuate, that is pick out, specific discursive formations from a set of statements without appealing to categories which are already in circulation. Even to name a discursive formation from current terminology (e.g. "natural history" or "biology") is to direct attention to limits already in place. Foucault claims that, for instance, statements belonging to "natural history" (a classical discursive practice) are not limited to works which those who worked as "natural historians" thought of as belonging to their discipline. That idea has immense appeal, but how is one to decide what statements do, or do not, belong to a particular discourse when they fall outside the boundaries within which they have been conventionally conceived? Only by regarding them as a "natural kind," as if each had its own unity which the archaeologist can grasp immediately. Foucault's rejoinder to this objection is to appeal to those "rules of formation" that constitute the conditions of possibility by which certain sets of *énoncés* emerge in discursive practices. (See Foucault 1978a for a rather more succinct use of the "rules of formation" concept.) But this does not solve the problem. Leaving aside the question of the origins and specificity of his own discourse, for which the notion of "rules" is privileged, any set of patterned phenomena can be described in terms of more than one law-like condition of possibility. To take two examples: on the one hand, we cannot articulate a single rule to describe the preconditions for our utterance of even a simple colour word like "blue." And on the other, moves like that of the knight in chess, which seem very rule-bound, can in fact be described according to an infinite set of laws. (These examples derive from Wittgenstein who remains – I believe – the least mystified theorist of the linked concepts of "rules," "conditions of possibility," and "laws.")

There exists a further difficulty with the notion of "conditions of possibility." They are recursive, moving into a *mise en abîme*. If, for instance, the archive is deemed to condition positivities, why stop there?[3] How do we know that there is only one archive? – and this question is not at all trivial. Might there not exist a set of conditions we could call, with a conscious sense of its limits, the *Western* archive? How do we know that the levels that Foucault posits are the only levels at which knowledge is articulated? Also, Foucault claims that "conditions of possibility" are not prescriptive, but descriptive, so that the archive backs out onto nothing. It is not constituted by a set of procedures followed – unconsciously – by any subject articulating *énoncés*. But this is, once again, to give away the power of individuation because a mere description of a field of statements cannot of itself determine the parameters of that field; it cannot fix where a particular "system of dispersion" begins and ends. Also, if Foucault's accounts of particular discourses and their strategies are descriptions, then the whole problem of commentary or hermeneutics re-enters, for just as there exists no single rule to describe patterned phenomena, descriptions are always articulated from a position of finitude, or to put it another way, from a particular point of view. (That "point of view" need not be simply that of an individual, of course.) As Dreyfus and Rabinow point out, such conceptual difficulties have one particularly damaging consequence – they reduce the role of the institutional aspect of discourse, its function in maintaining institutional structures. They also reduce the relations between the technologies of dissemination and *énoncés*. Finally, in aiming to offer a post-Kantian account of the historical formation of knowledge, archaeology may gesture at the network of practices by which individuals are formed and in which statements are uttered, but it cannot explain how such practices condition its own articulation.

The book's third difficulty is that it remains agnostic about the problem of the relation between words and things: to put it very simply it offers insufficient means of accounting for the way in which we know that, for instance, utterances about the circulation of gold are not helpful to describe the findings of the dissection of bodies. The appropriateness of a particular proposition (often) bears (some) relation to the *things* that the proposition is "about" – even if that referential relation cannot itself be pointed to. The criteria for the appropriateness of the utterance of a particular proposition within a particular context are not themselves merely, let alone necessarily, discursive; if they were, it would make no difference to our linguistic acts whether we were or were not, for instance, blind and without tactile sense. Thus, while we can never individuate a particular discourse merely by appeal to its propositions' referential force, it is also true that one can never individuate them totally without such appeal. This is not as crippling a difficulty for *The Order of Things* and *The Archaeology of Knowledge* as it may seem, for these books bracket off, rather than actively resist, the claims of reference. Indeed the epistemic shifts in *The Order of Things* are grounded on a continuity, granted by the (hidden) assumption that, for instance, natural history in the seventeenth century and biology in the nineteenth do indeed constitute different positivities but are aimed at the same kinds of things. Why, otherwise, would they be connected at all – especially as Foucault is certainly not interested in the ways in which they share or repeat a set of concepts? The problem is that Foucault's books of this period have been read as if they were, in the technical sense, idealist – as if they were saying "knowledge is just discourse" or "objects are only knowable through discourse" whereas what they are actually saying is that discourse has its own order, its own rules, enabled, not just by the mutual exteriority of different *énoncés* but by *énoncés'* deeply problematic exteriority to things.

KNOWLEDGE BEFORE MODERNITY: HEIDEGGER AND FOUCAULT

So much for the formal protocols and problems of archaeology. As we have seen, "archaeology" is presented much more tightly in *The Archaeology of Knowledge* than in *The Order of Things: an Archaeology of the Human Sciences* (to give the book its full title – in French it is called *Words and Things*).[4] Indeed, in the earlier book, the word "archaeology" is used to imply little more than that modes of thought at a particular epoch are not the product of a transcendent subject – whether the "spirit of the age" or the "rising bourgeoisie," for instance. It is as if discourse in *The Order of Things* means a (dispersed) mode of thought without a subject. Therefore, in archaeology, shifts from one epoch to another are relatively underdetermined or "discontinuous." Foucault does not pretend to account fully for the reasons or causes behind, say, the move from the Renaissance to the classical age, though, in fact, he does offer *some* such reasons, and these, surprisingly, often have a Hegelian structure, just as they had in *Madness and Civilization*. Where connections exist at all, it is within the contradictions or "points of incompatibility" of its predecessor that a new episteme emerges. By and large, however, following his transgressive literary criticism, history here is again exposed to chance and a certain reversibility. To take one important example: there are few reasons why the Renaissance episteme could not have followed rather than preceded that of the classical period.

In *The Order of Things*, what guides Foucault's archaeological excavations of the period before Mallarmé, Marx and Freud is Heidegger's reading of Nietzsche. In the late thirties, Heidegger gave a series of lectures on Nietzsche at the University of Freiburg at Breisgau which, though themselves only published in the 1970s, led to a number of formulations, most succinctly articulated in "The Age of the World Picture" ("Die Zeit des Weltbildes"). In these writings Heidegger sketches the history of thought after Plato in bold strokes. *The Order of Things* fills out, as well as distances itself from, Heidegger's graphic historiography. In particular, Heidegger characterizes the break between the "medieval" and the "modern" world as a shift from a privileging of both correspondence (*die Entsprechung*) and ranking in the "great chain of being," to a privileging of representation (*die Vorstellung*) and subjectivity. His argument, which works at a level of high generality, is too elaborate to sum up in a paragraph. But two points are worth drawing from it – one of which in fact derives from Derrida's rewarding response to it in his essay "Envoi" (translated – in part – as "Sending: on Representation"). For Heidegger, the origins of the way in which representation dominates modern analysis of the world lie buried in Plato's concept of *eidos* – which is often, problematically, translated as "view" (Heidegger 1977, 131). Thus Heidegger, unlike Foucault, works within a complex, conscious model of *long* historical continuity. In "Envoi,"

Derrida – again implicitly dissenting from Foucault – offers a commentary on the way in which Plato's *eidos* is "destined" (*geshickt*) to rule modernity in a relation which is not able to be represented (see Derrida 1982b, 313 and 1987a, 135). Derrida insists that there is a particular relation between the notion of the "epoch" and that of "representation." If history is conceived of as a succession of epochs along a temporal line then the self-containedness of each epoch already takes the form of a representation. In this sense the history is itself a moment in the (unrepresentable) transmission (*envoi*) or fate of representation. Also, the epoch of representation (in *The Order of Things* the classical era) is representative of the very model (the projection through history of a number of epochs) of which it is just an (in Foucault's case – unfavoured) example. That is to say, Derrida demonstrates that the work of both Foucault and Heidegger remains, despite themselves, embedded in representation – by their very attempt to describe representation as merely belonging to a particular historical moment.

It is within the relation that Heidegger posits between representation and subjectivity that archaeology can form itself as a socio-political anti-humanism. Representation as *Vorstellung* is relational, in it a represented object is available for observation and examination for a representing subject. The subject represents objects in order to gain some control over the world. In modernity, the representing subject also becomes a representative (*Repräsentant*) of a community. Heidegger regards this second mode of representation positively as part of the struggle against individualism within modern political structures, yet if one connects it to a *third* element of modernity, the politics of representation become vulnerable to a counter-reading. Within the representational paradigm, man becomes an object of knowledge and representation to himself, that is, simultaneously subject *and* object. As such, he may begin to order himself as a social being. Heidegger's word "*subiectum*" indicates this doubleness.[5] (It is necessary, here and throughout, to follow the sexism of Foucault's central term *l'homme*.) But further, man as *subiectum* is socio-politically formed in, and organized by, the institutions of representation through the imposition of norms and planning. For Heidegger, the "freedom" that follows when man becomes the subject of man (rather than God), requires and breeds a unique form of power – modern power. As he put it in his lectures on Nietzsche collected under the title Nihilism:

> Because such freedom implies man's developing mastery over his own definition of the essence of mankind, and because such being master needs power in an essential and explicit sense, the empowering of the essence of power as fundamental reality can therefore become possible only in and *as* the history of the modern age.
>
> (Heidegger 1982, 98)

All this, for Heidegger, is implied by anthropology – of which humanism is the "moral-aesthetic" instance. So once we accept that Heidegger's appropriation of Nietzsche provided the impetus for Foucault's account of pre-modernity, then we also accept that the attack on humanism is connected, from the very beginning, to a rejection of what will become, in *Discipline and Punish*, the "disciplinary" society. Heidegger's entwining of the history of knowledge and modern power provides the backdrop against which Foucault's archaeology and his genealogy merge into one another. This is true even though, in Heidegger's exposition of Nietzsche, modern power is not so much construed as "discipline" but as imperialism and the will to world domination.

RENAISSANCE AND CLASSICAL EPISTEMES

We can now discuss Foucault's history of knowledge since the Renaissance in a little more detail. Again following Heidegger (and others), Foucault argues that the Renaissance is dominated by a "mode of interpretation" which traces resemblances between things, in a way which makes of them "signatures" or "signs." The world exists as a "chain," a series of levels or "microcosms" which resemble each other. To take three examples of Renaissance signature-thinking: the land supports the same number of creatures as the sea, to each land creature is paired an analogous sea creature; the male genitals are the inverse of the primordial female genitals; in Francis Meres' popular *Palladis Tamia: Wits Treasury* (1598) each English author is compared to a classical equivalent. Such analogies, homologies and inversions are glued together by a "sympathy" which God breathes into the world. At the centre of this structure man exists as a "fulcrum of properties" (23) – which does not imply that a specific kind of analysis is required to produce knowledge about him. Man is not the topic around which Renaissance thought is centred. According to Foucault, the primary model of the world in the Renaissance period is, in fact, the book: it is then that knowledge takes the form of what he calls the "prose of the world." What this phrase expresses is the sense that, for the Renaissance, there is no difference between language and things – the latter are already "signatures" of God's creation, hieroglyphs to be decoded in commentaries which relate them to other microcosms in the chain of being. Thus, for instance, to tell the truth about a particular animal species is to describe what it looks like analogically *and* to transcribe the legends that have been told of it *and* to give an account of its properties – the way, when it enters contact with another being, a series of effects occur in which, once again, its shape and meaning are repeated. To use semiotic language: in the Renaissance, thought moves from signifier to signifier, unlike classical thought in which the signifier is, as it were, pushed out of sight under the weight of the signified.

104

In this sense, then, language exists at the limits of Renaissance thought: "the Renaissance came to a halt before the brute fact that language existed: in the density of the world, a graphism mingling with things or flowing beneath them, marks (*sigles*) made upon manuscripts or the pages of books" (79). It is revealing, therefore, to bring to mind a Renaissance text about language, one which Foucault himself does not mention – the first modern book on actual hieroglyphs, Pierius Valernaius's *The Hieroglyphs or a Commentary on the sacred letters of the Egyptians and other peoples* published in Basle in 1556. Valernaius regards hieroglyphs as icons of real objects and his analysis takes the form, not of an account of a hieroglyph's particular history or the system of relations between hieroglyphs, but rather as a description of the real objects of which the signs are supposed to be pictures and *their* import. Thus one hieroglyph "is" the bull and means "sharpness of hearing." To legitimate this interpretation, ancient legends and authorities as well as contemporary experiences are cited. There is, here, no sense of an *order* of fixed ideas or representations that enables hieroglyphs to stand in *for* such ideas or representations. In the eighteenth century, Bishop Warburton will regard hieroglyphs as a mid-point between the earliest languages that used mimetic image (icons) and the arbitrary sign of modern alphabets – a theory made possible because, for Warburton, an icon, a hieroglyph and an alphabetical sign are all representations of a single represented thing: that is, they are increasingly less primitive ways of pointing to, and substituting for, a reality which already has the structure of a set of representations. (For a rather different account of Valernaius's book, see Pope 1975.)

In the seventeenth century, the Renaissance sign begins to disappear, buried, Foucault suggests, under the mass of commentary and exegesis for which it began to seem that "the existence of language preceded . . . what one could read in it" (79). It also becomes impossible to sustain when, as those who followed Leibniz demonstrated, God does not watch over the world and "interfere providentially" – as Canguilhem put it.[6] Now, in a profoundly radical shift, the sign becomes a representation, an element which points towards an ordered set of identities and differences (mathesis) which does not materially or historically belong to the world, being instead the world's truth given "on its [i.e. truth's] own space" (78). To grasp the quite difficult concept of mathesis, it is necessary to understand that representations both "analyze" and "duplicate" the world's structure as it really is – outside of History or of God's will. Stated simply, it is as if, for the classical episteme, the world exists as what "ideas" reflect: each individual "idea" forms a natural unity – a self-enclosed identity – so that relations between particular ideas are external, their identity is not granted in terms of their interactions. What the "idea" and the part of the world reflected by an idea share is "nature": the idea belongs to human nature, the object to nature in general. This "nature" which "resembles itself"

(70), forms the ground which permits duplications and analysis to proliferate. Furthermore, one identity may be connected with another either in
terms of probability *or* in terms of a fixed structure of identity and difference. (Analyses of probability appear within the classical episteme.) To
locate an "idea" or "representation" on this large taxonomic grid is,
implicitly, to decompose the world into its constitutive elements. This also
means that duplication becomes the primary relation upon which thought
rests: if these atomistic representations reflect the real, the real also reflects
them – for knowledge of the real is gained through its decompositon into
ideas. Very importantly, the categories "duplication" and "analysis" did
not permit the recognition of two important limits and relations: first,
representations could not themselves be considered as material objects –
for classical thought, they did not carry traces of a matter irreducible to
representation; and, second, "representations" remained unframed by a
particular subject position or point of view.

It is as if the "world as idea" – the world as *nature* – is the world that
God sees. Where language duplicates reality, the question, "how can there
be such a thing as an untrue statement?" becomes crucial, and madness
is turned into "unreason" partly to answer it. Somewhat confusingly,
Foucault calls the new cultural space of representation or mathesis which
distinguishes the classical episteme, "discourse." And it is at this historical
moment that he finds specific and limited positivities at work: that of
"general grammar" (classical thought about language); "natural history"
(about plants and animals), "wealth" (about commodities and money).
He supposes that each of these positivities, in their own way, articulate
the epistemic shift from resemblance to representation, from the prose of
the world to mathesis. In "wealth," for instance, commodities, labour and
money enter a smooth, "natural" relation to one another, enabled by the
view that units of each of these categories can immediately substitute for,
or "represent," another. In the discourse of "wealth" there is little sense
that commodities, labour and money are formed in a system – the "economy" – that has its own laws and drives.

Of the three classical positivities that Foucault concerns himself with, I
wish to deal, briefly enough, with one: that of general grammar. (Excellent
accounts of the classical episteme in general are available in Sheridan 1980
and Cousins and Hussain 1984.) The task of "general grammar" is to
articulate the relation between natural language and the ideal order of the
table of representations. As one might expect, in it the sense of language's
materiality disappears: thought about language is an "analysis of thought."
the word "analysis" here is loaded: for in classical theory, language, of
course, simultaneously represents the world and breaks it down into its
elements. A word is regarded not just as an idea which represents a mental
idea, but as implicitly containing indexical indications, gestures which
point it toward the idea it represents. (This is necessary to the system,

because, without this capacity to point, how would one know what is to represent what?) For the classical era, different natural languages are to be analyzed, first, in terms of "kinship" – each is a *related* version of an ideal discourse; second, in terms of "designation" – in its relation to the primal sounds or verbal acts which first introduced nomination into the world (as expressions of feeling), and, third, in terms of "articulation" – the pattern which permits "words and the things they represent" to appear "without a hiatus between them" (336). The ontology of "general grammar," Foucault says, is to be encountered not at the level of nouns but of verbs. Language, as a version of the ideal mathesis just *is*; it is grounded in the *verbal* form "to be," whose "essential function" is "to relate all language to the representation that it designates" (95). Again this is a revealing concept: let us say that if language is, as it were, a painting of thought (which in turn is a painting of the world as we know it in and through representations), then the canvas of that painting or the ground of representation (which cannot itself be represented but which the paradigm demands) is an "isness" implicit in all propositions. To say "cat" is to say a "cat" *is* – even if it is only a fictional or mental cat as we moderns would say. (To test this assumption, Kant – at the beginning of the "modern" era – will ask the technical question "is existence a predicate?" That is, does uttering the word "is" of itself make an ontological commitment?) Foucault's formulation highlights the ontological thinness and instability of the classical episteme. In fact, his analysis tells the story of a Heideggerian gradual "retreat of Being." For classical thought, Being has been reduced to the canvas on which the grammar of ideas is sketched – the canvas whose back faces us, so oddly, so largely, in Velázquez' *Las Meninas*, the image which Foucault discusses in the introduction to *The Order of Things*.

THE ARCHAEOLOGY OF MODERNITY

In *The Order of Things*, modernity is, as one might expect, characterized by the "irruption of finitude." But the negative theological themes – the "tragedy of the death of tragedy" of *Madness and Civilization* or the "death of a God who never existed" of the literary essays, for example – have disappeared. Now modernity emerges, in two stages, at a concrete historical moment whose outer limits are 1775 and 1825, and whose period of most intense activity is 1785–1800. The break is conjured up in another of Foucault's purple passages:

> The space of Western knowledge is now about to topple: the *taxinomia*,
> whose great, universal expanse extended in correlation with the possi-
> bility of a mathesis, and which constituted the rhythm [*le temps fort*]
> of knowledge – at once its primary possibility and the end of its

107

perfection – is now about to order itself in accordance with an obscure verticality. . . . European culture is inventing for itself a depth in which what matters is no longer identities, distinctive characters, permanent tables with all their possible paths and routes, but great hidden forces developed on the basis of their primitive and inaccessible nucleus, origin, causality, and history. From now on things will be represented only from the depths of this density withdrawn into itself, perhaps blurred and darkened by its obscurity, but bound tightly to themselves, assembled or divided, inescapably grouped by the vigour that is hidden down below, in those depths.

(251, translation modified)

In the modern episteme, knowledge no longer duplicates and analyzes, now it confronts those limits and gaps which constitute things as they are, and throws those things, as it were, into their own space and time. For example, the economy is no longer seen as primarily formed within exchange – the exchange of discrete units (commodities each of which "represents" its market price, or the exchange of labour-hours for money); rather, as an autonomous system, it is considered to be controlled by its point of collapse, the point at which needs become unsatisfiable, the point at which increases of population overwhelm increases of production, or the point at which labour revolts against stored capital. That is the particular sense in which, for modern thought, the economy is determined by its finitude.

Strangely, the story of the irruption of finitude contains hints of the pressures of a social will – and that includes, though Foucault carefully avoids the term, revolutionary desire. The classical episteme is threatened by the will for freedom. "Representation . . . was to be paralleled, limited, circumscribed, mocked perhaps, but in any case regulated from the outside, by the enormous thrust of a freedom, a desire, or a will, posited as the metaphysical converse of consciousness" (209). Sade, the "divine Marquis," as the French still sometimes call him, expresses this "thrust" from the side of classicism. (Though in fact it is Thomas Hobbes whose work first announces this shift – from the side of reaction *against* the essential mobility of things.) In Sade, desire without limits, however dark and driven, still tends towards light and representation; it attaches itself to discourse. Kant expresses this desire from the side of the modern: as we have seen, he asks not how does knowledge duplicate the world, but, what are the conditions of possibility for knowledge/perception in the first place? This question throws two huge domains into a darkness which, however, modern thought cannot help but peer into: the domain of things as they are, outside of knowledge/perception, and the domain made up of other possible conditions for other possible knowledges.

Archaeology itself still works, just, within the modern episteme. Certainly faith in the transcendental and synthetic a-priori has been lost, but, as we have seen, in articulating a positivism of the historical a-priori, Foucault is still wrestling with those Kantian difficulties that elsewhere he dissects so neatly. The turn to history, which he is trying to overcome, dates back to the beginning of the modern era, for the thin ontological layer of representation-as-mathesis then dissolves, not just into desire, but into *time* and into *life*. To take time first: in the classical age, history was thought of in relation to the taxonomy of the world. For eighteenth-century specu- lation on language, for instance, there may have been a tongue – spoken by Adam and, presumably, by God – which represented and articulated the world perfectly in the past, and in the future man may invent such a language again. Here history is found in the distortions and catastrophes to which the world, in its fallibility, is prone; not so much *in* time as *outside* perfect duplication. But for modernity, history is an essence not an acci- dent; as the early Orientalists discovered, language itself is born and belongs to time. This does not mean that the *discipline* history becomes essential, but that each positivity has its own "historicity," its own tempo in which its elements are fated to change according to rules unique to itself (thus, for instance, "Bopp's Law" describes the phonetic drift of vowel sounds across languages over time independently of meaning). If the order of mathesis dissolves into autonomous temporal sequences, the thin being of representations also is swallowed up by an energy or force which lies "behind" it and which is neither itself representable nor tem- poral. In particular, Being becomes "life" – which can be something which stirs and directs the organic as against the inorganic, or, indeed, as in Fechner's panpsychism (and, in fact, the early Freud) is something *every- thing* "has" to some degree or other.

Foucault draws especial attention to three results of the dissolution of representation into historicity, life, desire, and will. First, and most simply, biology as the knowledge of "life" takes over from language the role of providing models for conceptualizations of the world in general. (This is to elaborate the thesis of *The Birth of the Clinic*.) Second, Foucault argues that modernity is incapable of "morality," for modern thought is *itself* a form of action, rather than a set of "ideas." Now discourse becomes a practice, thus incapable of the kind of theoretical self-reflection which moral imperatives require. The last thinker to attempt such reflection was Kant, whose "categorical imperative" is legitimated by Reason. (The categorical imperative is the ethical principle: "I ought never to act except in such a way that I can also will that my maxim should become a universal law.") But the rational and universalized subject (or "person- ality" as Kant would have said) demanded by the categorical imperative is still classical in that it does not face "the [modern] element of darkness that cuts man off from himself" (328). Surrounded by the darkness of these "limits without limit," thought and discourse become an event which

109

no other event can order. What replaces morality are judgements which decide what has, or does not have, (biological) life, use-value or intensity, or what belongs, or does not belong, to the vanguard of history. Life becomes a crucial term of evaluation: things have value to the degree that they have "life." Similarly, work, which has productive force within the discourse of political economy, can give value to economic elements of exchange – money and commodities. In the modern episteme, to work is not to live out the punishment for original sin, but to increase the vitality of the socius.

Foucault's remarks on modern morality are particularly important in the light of the role that "ethics" were to play in the final phase of his work. But the problematic that primarily interests him in his archaeology of the modern is metaphysical, and again follows from his literary essays. He argues that, once discourse finds its objects formed in conditions which themselves are not shaped discursively, a new and curious doubling appears. The duplication around which classical analysis revolved (the mirror relation between world and thought anchored in language) is no longer possible. Now, in "the analytic of finitude" the non-discursive exists both as other to knowledge *and* as that which enables and is absorbed by knowledge: just as for the Gothic novelists, for instance, the "sensational" – defined against mere words – was also the object that language was called upon to induce. (And the Gothic novelists wrote, of course, at the pivotal moment between the classic and the modern.) Somewhat similarly in Klossowski's thought, once the divide between God and man ceased, the "other" could always be the "same" – was or was not the old God "really" a devil? Or, to take another example, Ludwig Feuerbach argued that God was a reflection of human "species being" – an argument which placed the human species not just at the centre of the world but as the source of humanity's own horizon. God, the Other, *is* man, the Same. Here we come to the very heart of *The Order of Things*: this paradox works on and, more importantly, *shapes* that new formation – Man. Man is formed on *this* side of what Herbert Spencer called the Unknown, and he crosses into the Unknown to demonstrate how the Unknown provides the occasion for, and structures of, his own existence. "Man . . . is a strange empirico-transcendental doublet, since he is a being such that knowledge will be attained in him of what renders all knowledge possible" (318). This "doublet," "man," however, is explained in terms of the three dominant positivities: in terms of his biological emergence (the theory of evolution and the functions of the organism); in terms of that economic scarcity which constitutes species being after Malthus; or as a "speaking being," a function of the language that he utters and which divides him from nature. These various explanations can only fold "man" back into the facts or forces – biological, economic, linguistic – which cannot of themselves specify the human. This, then, is how the modern episteme articulates itself both as a "positivism" – in the gathering and recital of facts – and "eschatolog-ically" – in visions of a future moment at which history will overcome the split betwen the Known and the Unknown. It is in these terms that Foucault considers modern knowledge ultimately to take the form of an action that will allow man's essence or potential to be satisfied within the finitude that conditions him. Current lacks and divisions will give way to the completion of what we could call the human project. And, here, Foucault has in mind the thought of Marx, Hegel and Comte.

This division between the positive and the eschatological is the grandest version of a doubling which has three rather more local stages in the history of modern thought: (1) the empirical and the transcendental whereby the conditions for producing the truth about man (the transcendental) fail to overlap with the empirical truths about man that can be uttered at any actual historical moment; (2) the "cogito" and the "unthought" where the unconscious or *non dit* (whether psychological, historical or textual) remains "exterior" to the "thought" that it is summoned to account for – where thought and being are no longer connected by a "therefore" as in Descartes (again Foucault's formulation is influenced by the analysis of "I speak" in the essay on Blanchot); (3) the retreat and return of the origin, in which the attempt to find an origin for the human species fails – there being no simple moment at which language first appears or at which the human biological organism first emerges. (The reason for this is that the conditions which constitute "man," and which are grounded in the "human" must always have "already begun" before man appears.) Thus, in the logic of modern discourse, the origin of man tends to dissolve into preconditons for his emergence, and these *continue* to precondition his being. These preconditions belong to a temporal order which is not that of a human history. This permits Foucault to assert that, in the modern episteme, the "origin" "links man to that which does not have the same time as himself" (331) – language itself being a good instance of that which does not have the "same time" as man, even for those who consider the acquisition of language to be the difference between the human and other species. This concept of what Foucault calls "the retreat and return of the origin" may contain a subtle attack on Heidegger, whose roughly equivalent "retreat and return of Being" becomes now less a cosmic event than an expression of the modern humanism that Heidegger himself so despised.

At the archaeological level these doublings and discrepancies seem clear enough. If they have not been more widely recognized, that is because modern thought – where it is not transgressive – has fallen into a new dogma, what Foucault calls the "anthropological sleep." Nowhere is this sleep deeper than in the discipline "history" and what the French call the "human sciences." The human sciences (psychology, sociology, "history of ideas" and, at their margins, psychoanalysis, social anthropology, semiology) are primarily directed towards an appropriation of the

111

unrepresentable, that far side of the surface of things which is posited by modern knowledge or "anthropology" in its broadest sense. In appropriating the dark and vital ground for representation, the human sciences are strangely classical; they are what Foucault calls "hypo-epistemological" in their attempt to capture the unthought for thought. Yet, for them, the world is produced by man; representation is now simply a form of consciousness, as it was not for classicism. The specificity of the human remains ungraspable; "consciousness" or "ideology" or any other human product cannot provide a method and a domain proper to itself. Thus, on the one hand, each human science can claim priority (e.g. "There is nothing but psychology," "There is nothing but sociology," "Always historicize!"), and, on the other, each human science must appeal to models from elsewhere, in particular to the old positivities of "life, labour and language." This is a little simple, for, according to Foucault, the anthropological episteme forms in a triangular space, framed by (1) the mathematical/physical sciences, (2) biology, economics and linguistics and (3) a philosophical reflection whose sharpest moment is the archaeological "analytic of finitude." The human sciences lacerate themselves whenever they encounter the last as they do, most sharply, in *The Order of Things* itself.

The human sciences have developed through a sequence of models. Foucault notes that they were originally dominated by biological models – by the attempt, first, to conceive of society as an organic unity, ordered by its tendency towards equilibrium or to stable "norms," and second, to consider human activity as a function within this unity. The biological paradigm made place for an economic one for which society was modelled as conflictual – restrained by "rules which limit and are an effect of conflict" (357). And, more recently, language provides a paradigm in which human behaviour was itself "semiotic" – constructed within a cultural "system" whose final end was to form social differences, and thus a sense of meaningful activity. Yet the central problem of anthropology remains at work in the human sciences: when all the empirical data is in, when the method is formalized, when the paradigm is mastered, there is still something left over: the experienced, the human itself, the *telos* of the species, the rationale and being of life, its meaning, its satisfaction, topics which the human sciences endlessly discuss in one form or another, dreaming of a future in which the known and the experienced will be reconciled. History seems to offer a way out of the eschatological/positive gap. It promises that events and discourse can be explained simply in terms of a past context, a "partial totality" to which the present has access by virtue of some shared "humanity," some shared socio-political project, or to use the language of hermeneutics, some joint ontological horizon. But, of course, history cannot explain itself, it cannot catch its own tail because there "is always something still to think at the moment at which it thinks"

(372). The historian can always ask: what are the forces working on my history – as I write it?

In the final pages of *the Order of Things*, Foucault argues that this crucial incoherence, hidden by the dogma of anthropology, is broached most effectively by (Lacanian) psychoanalysis and social anthropology. For they do not attempt to colonize the unthought by the thought. Indeed, for Lacan, the Unconscious is language's hidden double: it exists as the unrecuperable trace of the processes by which the speaking and socialized subject is formed, as if that subject were one half and the Unconscious the other half of a torn-apart, already decentred, unity – the instinctive, demanding infant. (To put it very glibly, Lacan is already a transgressive thinker: for him, the Unconscious (the Other) is linguistic (the Same)). Social anthropology moves the central methodological categories of the human sciences (norms, systems and rules) back towards the unconscious. For it, these categories are no longer recuperable under the sign of the essentially human because, although they may produce signification and order, they no longer form a large sense or coherence that we can understand or treasure (in a base/superstructure theory or a "museum without walls" for instance). Thus psychoanalysis and social anthropology work as what Foucault calls "counter-sciences" which, with semiology (as it appeared in those heady days of the mid-sixties) might re-form "positivities exterior to man" and re-connect the world of learning to the dangerous and hidden double of modernity, that transgressive thought maintained by Artaud, Roussel, Blanchot, Bataille. . . . For Foucault, the counter sciences move away from the human sciences because, whereas the latter analyze systems in terms of "life" and "production," the latter find them working in terms of "death, desire, and the law." And the law, here, is not a principle of order and judgement, but a machinery whose most effective image or enactment perhaps remains Roussel's "process" – a principle by which production is ordered, but which cannot finally be identified, and which itself has no meaning. The second difference between the human sciences and the counter-sciences is that the latter do not read the present in anticipation of a future where the life-world will be ordered by the intervention of "scientific" knowledge which, in a circle, is itself legitimated by the accuracy of its descriptions of the world.

LITERATURE AND ARCHAEOLOGY

We are beginning to see how, by its own account, archaeology occupies a position adjacent, and subsequent, to that of the counter human sciences, psychoanalysis, semiology and social anthropology; a space bounded on the one side by modern positivism (and the replacement of the "synthetic a-priori" by the "historical a-priori") and on the other by transgressive thought. As a method which owes much to Blanchot, Bataille and Klossowski it belongs itself, if somewhat tenuously, to "literature"; while as a counter-science it poses a threat to the various modes of institutional literary studies which, in some forms at least, it sees as closely connected to the human sciences. And, of course by offering a new theoretical and positive account of the past it also, somewhat despite itself, becomes a resource for literary studies. How does *The Order of Things* itself treat of literary texts (and art objects)? What are the consequences of examining the study of literature as a human science?

For Foucault, writers like Cervantes, Sade, Hölderlin, Diderot and pain-ters like Goya and Velázquez operate within a slightly different logic to that which guides the discourses of "knowledge" proper. They escape the full force of the episteme which preconditions their moment (and thus they can fulfil a liberatory role) at the same time as they show those pressures at work most succinctly and clearly (and thus they have a exemplary role). To take *Don Quixote* as an instance: the novel's hero reads the world not in terms of representations but in terms of analogies. It is a sign of classicism's emergence that the Don is regarded as mad. More generally, Foucault argues that, after the seventeenth century, "poetry" as a category is characterized by its ability to "listen to the language of resemblance" (50) in a world where resemblances are connected to madness. Literature, here, is not just the domain in which old epistemes survive; it is what epistemic knowledge closes down upon. As fiction, as act, as connected to "madness," literature helps cause the anxiety that lies behind knowledge's demand for organization and exclusion – a demand which requires us to recognize an episteme as an episteme. Another less romantic account of the arts can be traced in *The Order of Things*. Aesthetic objects may also hinge epistemes to one another. Velázquez' *Las Meninas* shows clearly that classical knowledge takes the form of representations grounded on nature and grasped from an all knowing point of view, but it also contains a dark space, the pictured back of a canvas, upon which this knowledge will founder, and "man" will arise. Similarly, more or less contemporary writers in the counter-canon familiar from *Madness and Civilization* anticipate what has not yet happened – the "end of man." It is as if, in not having to pass through the thresholds which constitute knowledge as knowledge, or to be legitimated by the institutions that stamp knowledge as knowledge, aesthetic productions have a restricted slipperiness and freedom so that, potentially at least, it is in aesthetic objects that archaeological shifts first appear.

Literary studies themselves have no such slipperiness and freedom, they belong to epistemic knowledge. In *The Order of Things* we return to the rather familiar divison in which literature itself is regarded as more trans-gressive, closer to Being, than the criticism or literary history which cano-nize it. Archaeologically, this particular division occurs as literature quests for an autonomous space ultimately based, as we have seen, on the materiality and functionlessness of language. To define literature by a search for autonomy which breaks through representation is familiar enough; Foucault's review of J. P. Richard on Mallarmé tells just such a story. But its invocation in *The Order of Things* is worth citing at some length:

> Literature is the contestation of philology (of which it is nevertheless the twin figure): it leads language back from grammar to the naked power of speech, and there it encounters the untamed, imperious being of words. From the Romantic revolt against a discourse frozen in its own ritual pomp, to the Mallarmean discovery of the word in its impotent power, it becomes clear what the function of literature was, in the nineteenth century, in relation to the modern mode of being of language. Against the background of this essential inter-action, the rest is merely effect: literature becomes progressively more differentiated from the discourse of ideas, and encloses itself within a radical intransitivity; it becomes detached from all the values that were able to keep it in general circulation during the Classical age (taste, pleasure, naturalness, truth), and creates within its own space everything that will ensure a ludic denial of them (the scandalous, the ugly, the impossible); it breaks with the whole definition of *genres* as forms adapted to an order of representations, and becomes merely a manifestation of a language which has no other law than that of affirming – in opposition to all other forms of discourse – its own precipitous existence; and so there is nothing for it to do but to curve back in a perpetual return upon itself, as if its discourse could have no other content than the expression of its own form; it addresses itself to itself as a writing subjectivity, or seeks to re-apprehend the essence of all literature in the movement that brought it into being; and thus all its threads converge upon the finest of points – singular, instantaneous, and yet absolutely universal – upon the simple act of writing. At the moment when language, as spoken and scattered words, becomes an object of knowledge, we see it reappearing in a strictly opposite modality: a silent, cautious deposition of the word upon the whiteness of a piece of paper, where it can possess neither sound nor interlocutor, where it has nothing to say but itself, nothing to do but shine in the brightness of its being.

(330)

This is a different account than that of the literary or transgressive theory essays proper. As the double of "philology" (which begins to think about language in terms of language's own historicity), "literature" belongs to the modern episteme that it also escapes. Unlike modern knowledge, literature accepts that the "forces" behind representation, the dark, active dynamic of the world, cannot be appealed to in order to explain either itself or the

115

world. Thus it recoils from the aims and assumptions upon which the human sciences are based. Such a view implies that realism, as a form of representation, is not properly "literature." It also implies that "literature" in its essence remains unavailable to commentary, interpretation, explanation. In these terms, even the kind of quasi-phenomenological analysis carried out in *Death and the Labyrinth* would commit violence against its object. In showing that to write or talk is not necessarily to utter "discourse," literature is what escapes archaeology at the same time as it enables it. Thus archaeology would either demand of literary studies (which represent and *teach* literature) that they commit suicide – by the recognition of their own formation within historicism and the human sciences. Or that they undergo a profound transformation – that they too write about writing in the spirit of transgression, the post-Nietzschean spirit.

Yet, in Foucault's dismissal of commentary and criticism, another question for literary studies opens up: what would an archaeology of literary studies look like? It is strange that one does not actually exist and certainly it is now too late to begin to develop one – as any current Foucauldian account of the topic would have to lean not just on archaeology but on the analytics of modern power and of the formation of individual selves (as Ian Hunter's *Culture and Government*, which I discuss at the beginning of chapter 8, does). I think, however, that we can now sketch out the parameters of such a project. First, it would have to locate the point at which "literature" becomes a specific cultural form as do Foucault's literary essays – the point at which language chases the "sensational" in the Gothic novelists and when it turns inward with Hölderlin and, later, with Flaubert and Mallarmé, that is, when texts are produced within "literature" as an institution that has radically separated itself from discursive formations like history or philosophy. Then the history of discourse about literature would have to be written in the light of modern knowledge's rift between the positive and the eschatological. This is not especially difficult: for literary studies have long been divided between those old rivals and fraternal enemies, literary history and literary critcism. (The "new historicism" versus "deconstruction" debate, at least in its more banal forms, is the latest manifestation of this feud.) Literary history is based on the recovery and marshalling of facts about texts, genres and authors, facts which, if it is to be more than merely positivist, literary history can organize in terms of the dominant modes of modern knowledge – that is, in terms of evolution and biology (Hippolyte Taine), in terms of economics and class conflict (marxism) or linguistically (as in the various historicisms whose point of departure is Russian formalism: Bakhtin, Julia Kristeva, for instance) – or, of course, in combinations of each. Each particular form of knowledge provides the ground or context that conditions and explains the object of knowledge – literature itself.

The limits to literary history are encountered when its object retreats, when it becomes possible to say that "literature" escapes history. In this "retreat of the origin," no conditions for literature's emergence, no account of its context or ideological work, none of its structural features (even "defamiliarization" or "dialogicity") are able to grasp and fix it. Literary criticism makes of literature an unlocalizable (in Foucault's terms, "eschatological") object, which any formula or method can only reduce and destroy. The origin retreats most dramatically in reception theory, for which, at least in its most radical mode, there exists no "text in itself" – the text being wholly constituted through the readings given of it in particular interpretative communities. In the reader response paradigm, literary history rapidly transforms itself into the history of the readings given to texts as well as into the history of the uses to which texts have been put. Nonetheless, these "readings" (which are themselves texts) also disappear – driven by the same logic that destroys the "text-in-itself." But the origin does return, and it does so in many forms. For the mainstream of literary criticism, literature comes to consist of language that adequately expresses the unrepresentable forces that drive it. Thus, for criticism, perhaps since Dr Johnson and certainly since Coleridge and Sainte-Beuve, the literariness of literature exists in what Sainte-Beuve called its "mobility." The origin also returns in criticism's understanding of literary texts as the expression of the genius, the acute and extended subjectivity, of the writer, and then – by a process of internalization – that of the reader, all of which are based on, and repeat, the aura and "mobility" of literary language. Not that "genius" is the only transcendental category upon which criticism draws: one thinks of "life" (F. R. Leavis), "imagination" (the Romantics"), "emotive belief" (I. A. Richards) or even, much more complexly, "the mechanics of the signifier" of Paul de Man's so-called "rhetoric." As literary criticism continually retreats from, and returns to, making knowledge claims, it belongs to the epistemic frame for which "man" is the object of knowledge.

If literary studies do belong to the modern episteme, it follows that the challenge to push them outside the modern cannot take the form of obliterating either their positive content (here, literary history and "contextual" criticism) or their transcendental claims (here, those of pure criticism). A synthesis of these linked and opposed moments is not possible either, except in eschatological dreams of reconciliation. Indeed, by the time of *The Archaeology of Knowledge.* Foucault himself was ceasing to appeal to transgressive thought: his critique of modernity focused once again on the institutions of the modern era and their shaping of the social order and individual feeling and behaviour. Yet, by accepting that, in our time, language is conceived more as an act than as a map, and by retaining a sense that self-formation, as against the social or institutional formation of selves, is connected to the aesthetic – as the pleasurable, the beautiful, the rare, the carefully worked – Foucault will finally come to an affirmative understanding of literature which owes nothing to literary history or literary criticism. He will see literature as a mode of writing that contains and expresses styles of existence that – to some degree at least – resist the technologies of modern subjectification. The question that lingers in the face of this radical re-appraisal of literature is: what is lost when we give up on the attempt to treat writing as writing – the attempt that transgression itself pushes to a limit. Transgressive thought promises the dispersal of the subject through language, the singularity of the word and text, the blockage of that light of reason which searches out the shadows of being. At whatever remove, isn't what transgressive thought promises also what modern literary criticism promises – despite criticism's institutionality, despite the pedagogy in which (as we shall see) it forms sensibilities and despite its twinned and paradoxical relation to positive literary history?

5

GENEALOGY, AUTHORSHIP, POWER

In one sense, the final phase of Foucault's work on power or "govern-mentality" involves no violent shift of direction. The Nietzschean and Heideggerian heritage drawn upon in *Madness and Civilization*, the history of science of *The Birth of the Clinic*, the reading of the Gothic novelists and even *The Archaeology of Knowledge* were all directed at showing how certain discursive practices shape individuals and, indirectly, the institutions in which lives are led. In his early work, Foucault rarely shows signs of forgetting either that knowledge alters the world, thereby entering into relation with power or that, in reverse, the slow, often haphazard, construction of institutions, the articulation of styles of living, the techniques drawn upon to fashion selves, all not only require, but alter, knowledge. Yet although there is no *radical* break between the earlier and the later work, after Foucault had elaborated his archaeology, power did acquire a new relation to knowledge. In *The Order of Things* Foucault regards modern discourse as the dissolution of the a-temporal order of mathesis, as an attempt to appropriate the non-representable forces and conditions of his-toricity and life. When he moves the direct thrust of his analysis from modern discourse to modern power, he finds that, whereas in classical society, power was fixed, visible, mappable, in modern society it is uncontainable, untheorizable, productive – like modern discourse in fact. And he can now show that the central assumption of modern discourse – its *anthropological* sense that "man" is the subject of knowledge – rests upon, and is an effect of, massively complex power relations. To speak the language of theory: anthropomorphizing power must be both totalizing, so as to turn the Other into the Same, and dispersed, to work on and connect to the Other as Other. This means that what he had earlier formulated as the tendency of modern knowledge to splinter into singular *énoncés*, is now transformed into a vision of the social and historical field as a kind of disarticulated articulation, a field of power events, where the emphasis is simultaneously on "field" and on "events." This shift from knowledge to power, however, has profound consequences for his sense of his own social function. Politically, this field can only be contested in a "micro-

politics," a tactical response to particular situations, rather than in organizations that constitute representative democracy like the political party.
This, together with Foucault's archeological sense that "theoretical" (that
is, generalizing and self-reflective) statements have no special capacity to
direct action, allows him to argue that "universal intellectuals" will, in
our time, lose ground to "specific intellectuals."[1]

A second point must be made in broaching the later Foucault. It goes
without saying that he remains a critic of modernity, but after *The Archaeology of Knowledge*, his gaze past the modern no longer fixes on the future
– on the end of man and transgressive writing – but on the past, on a
history cleansed of historicism. As we have seen, almost indistinctly, with
deceptive modesty, he invites us to form ourselves as individuals as against
being formed by, and within, the social apparatus. How? By attending to
examples of a tradition of self-formation drawn from a historical panorama
that ranges from ancient Greece to the lives and works of modern aesthetes.
And yet, he insists (it seems a little sadly), today, such ethical self-fashioning must involve close attention to the most modern and most elusive of
all categories: the present itself – which we must take care not to consider
as a unity with clear and fixed boundaries. But because "ethics" and
"power/knowledge" belong to a single fold in Foucault's work I deal with
them together in chapters 7 and 8. In this chapter, I offer a theoretical
overview and summary of his account of modern power. But two prelimi-
nary matters need addressing. The first is concerned with the way that
Foucault thinks about his own activities: when he abandons the view that
avant-garde writing can break down the structures of subjectivity, one of
his first gestures is to re-theorize the role of the author. The second is
concerned with the way in which, when he interrogates the object of his
own researches, he re-encounters theoretical difficulties. What, finally, in
these books on "penality" and "sexuality" is he writing a history of? Is
there a connection between modern prisons, sex and education as they
emerge at the end of the eighteenth century, say? Why are his histories
not simply organized around periods? What is their relation to a positive
recital of facts, happenings and dates? After the early seventies, except in
one or two interviews, Foucault did not sustain such interrogations, but it
is important to take note of his most suggestive responses to them.

AUTHORSHIP

While he was finishing *The Archaeology of Knowledge*, Foucault gave a paper
at the Collège de France where he was soon to take up a chair. It was
called "What is an Author?" and along with the address he delivered on
taking up the new post – published as "The Order of Discourse" – it
provides a clear sense of how his shift away from archaeology was enabled
by the dismissal of his transgressive or literary heritage. "What is an

Author?" begins by obliquely distancing itself from those theories for which language "creates an opening where the writing subject endlessly disappears" (1977a, 116). Here he regards such a notion as "ethical," both in that it fails to fulfil its aims and enjoins practice rather than analysis. The "death of the author" is also a moment in the history of the relation between writing and death: once literature had had epic and heroic pretensions, it secured individual immortality, but in the modern world it "disperses" the author – it has even become a form of suicide. This last proposition refers back to Foucault's book on Roussel, who wrote to dissolve, or to de-individuate, himself. The modern author also aims to take on other voices – the voices of otherness. As he was to put it elsewhere, "literature's task is to say the most unsayable – the worst, the most secret, the most intolerable, the shameless" (1979a, 91). He goes on to insist that recent conceptions of *écriture* (and clearly he has Derrida in mind) have failed to understand this. The notion of *écriture* promised to help us grasp the conditions of possibility (or impossibility) for language as such rather than specific texts in particular. But, Foucault argues, the *écriture* theorists tend merely to transpose "the empirical characteristics of an author into a transcendental anonymity" (120). Even worse, for deconstruction (a word that Foucault himself does not use) there remains a hidden law behind language and texts, a machinery of "obscure contents," and "an aesthetic principle that proclaims the survival of the work as a kind of enigmatic supplement of the author beyond his own death" (ibid.). Deconstruction secures literature's immortality by its very erasure of authorial presence, by its undoing of the claim that literature represents the world or expresses subjectivities.

Foucault's argument is less than fair to Derrida, who could reply that he does not regard language either as having transcendental conditions peculiar to it *or* regard it as always already given in the form of *énoncés*. For Derrida, language is precisely where the transcendental enterprise fails – which is not to say that that enterprise could ever entirely disappear. Nor are the effects and preconditons of language able to be analyzed in archaeological terms, or through an account of power-relations. Language is, as it were, its own ground – a notion that points to a strange fold or doubling which limits any account of a discursive practice's preconditions. And Derrida could also object that, despite our usual sense of death, for him, it does not quite stay on the far side of life. It is not simply an end. Derrida is not interested in securing immortality but in breaking down the opposition between the mortal and the immortal – the most crucial opposition of all. For Derrida, there are many deaths – that of the body, of memory, of fame, indeed, absence as such carries death's traces. If that were not the case there would be no writing, as writing is to be regarded less a grand replacement for what is absent than the attempt to incorporate absence. Writing, for Derrida, is an act which, necessarily, though not

necessarily knowingly or welcomingly, shelters a little death. This incorporation of death is the obverse of writing's ability to live on, but it also
means that writing is always already a little empty, absent – dead. And,
of course, this description draws Derrida very close to Foucault's account
of Roussel and to transgressive theory in general.

Indeed Foucault's attack on Derrida seems to involve a hidden agenda
and some embarrassment *because* he is rejecting that "theorization of writing" which is still – just – necessary to his thought at this point of his
career. Necessary because, as we have seen, this theory kills the author as
the founding subject of "works" which express his or her meaning. Only
once the author is dead in this sense can writing be reduced to discourse,
so as to become available to an analytics of institutionality and power.
Oddly, the first paragraph of "The Order of Discourse" invokes non-
discursive language as the object of desire:

> I would have liked to slip surreptitiously into the talk [*discours*] that
> I am about to give today and into those that I will perhaps give
> here in years to come. Rather than launching into speech I would
> have wanted to be enveloped by it, and to be carried far beyond all
> possible beginnings. At the moment of speech, I would have liked to
> perceive that a nameless voice had long preceded me. It would then
> have been enough for me to connect to and pursue its phrasing, to
> lodge in its gaps without anyone noticing – as if, holding itself in
> suspense for an instant, it had made me a sign. There wouldn't have
> been a beginning: instead of being that from which discourse comes,
> I would have been at the mercy of [*au hasard de*] its unfolding, a tiny
> lacunae, the point of its possible disappearance.
>
> (1971a, 7: translation mine)[2]

This is subtly, if deeply, ironic: the controversial Michel Foucault, in his
inaugural address on taking up a chair at perhaps the most prestigious
institution of the French academic system, wanting to "slip surreptitiously"
into the lecture theatre. It is impossible. Which is the point. This impossible desire works to the same end as the implied attack on Derrida in
"What is an Author?": both lead towards accepting the irretrievably social
and institutional nature of language. Yet there remains a certain equivo-
cation. In these essays, it is still as if language, as formed by the rules of
discourse, commits a violence against, or even represses, writing as the
domain of materiality, chance and reversibility. It reduces "the great peril,
the great danger with which fiction threatens our world," as Foucault puts
it in "What is an Author?" If this is so, what then of the productivity,
the affirmative power of discursive formations? As we have seen, Foucault
can insist that discourse is produced in ordered patterns because *énoncés*
are discrete, rare, and drawn into existence only as they open out onto an
already patterned and visible (or, better, *sensible*) exterior or non-discursive

world. In "The Order of Discourse" the tension between the view that institutionally sanctioned knowledge reduces the power of writing, and the view that the rule-boundedness of such knowledge is a productive force, is resolved by dividing the task of discourse-analysis in two. On the one side, discourse analysis is to be "critical," examining the ways that discourse works to exclude, limit or appropriate. On the other, it is to be "genealogical," examining the shifting rules for the production of discourse. But, in the seventies, the critical side will often fall out of sight – as if the powers of discourse and the social apparatus do not work in modes that words such as "exclusion" or "constraint" properly describe, or as if there is no "real" to be left out of account, or contained, by social and discursive practices: as if, for instance, there is no "true sex" which is ignored or repressed by a failure, or refusal, to talk about or act on "sexuality." To put it another way, it is as if, in his work on power, discourse continues to have the effect of controlling, colonizing or constraining otherness – only there is no otherness. And this is different from saying that there is no way of recuperating or representing that otherness. By supposing that no reality exists against which we might test the social construction of meaning or the social ordering of individual lives, Foucault admits no "repressive hypothesis" at the level of ontology – to use the name he will give to the (false) belief that society has repressed sexuality. Criticism reappears as a Foucauldian programme in the early eighties however, as he becomes threatened once again by the power of the state to demand use-value of all knowledge, without providing a framework for marginal needs and wants to be expressed.

So when Foucault asks "what is an author?" in the early 1970s he tries strenuously not to answer in terms familiar from transgressive theory. An "author" exists in a particular field defined, first, against the actual person who writes (and who may write in many discourses even within a particular text); second against the linguistic "subject of enunciation" who is denoted in words like "here" or "I" ("shifters," whose reference varies according to their context or the identity of their speaker); third, s/he is defined against the narrative persona who may, or may not, be represented in any particular piece of writing. Instead, the concept "author" is a means of grouping and valuing writing: "Homer" or "Hippocrates" are authors despite doubts as to their actual existence. The concept must be considered primarily in terms of its effect, it is not a historical constant. It is not as if all authors are, or have been, considered to have the same relations to their texts. But these relations do fall into patterns. There are, for instance, connections between particular genres and the particular "author-functions" – which is the name Foucault gives to the structure in which the notion of the "author" can be used differently in different kinds of writing. Some genres have authors whose name is (usually) that of the person who wrote them (high literary texts); some do not (much daily journalism, jokes etc.) and others have authors whose name is not that of their writer (Mills & Boon/Harlequin romances). Not very convincingly, Foucault argues that "authors" come into historical being only when writing is able to be censored, when an individual can, potentially at least, be punished for their writing. Also,the authority of an author differs across disciplines: science is defined in part by the fact that a scientific paper is not "true" or "false" by virtue of the name that signs it. This regime of truth, Foucault tells us, had its origins in Greece when Plato began to reach for a "truth" defined against Hesiod's "Theogeny," which Plato believed to be an inspired retelling of mythic origins. In modernity there has been a shift of author function: the authorial name has become a *property* – in a process we can trace by examining the history of copyright laws. Although Foucault does not spell it out, it is important to note that modern enforceable copyright begins in Britain with the 1709 English Copyright Act, and there are close connections to the construction of a literary canon of great authors, and the degree to which the copyright was, on the one hand, enforceable, and, on the other, limited. Before 1709, certain printers had had the right to print the works of their authors *in perpetua*, even if these rights were not enforceable. Jacob Tonson had such an interest in Milton's works, for example. After 1709, these rights could only be given for twenty-one years – and though this decision was legally contested throughout the eighteenth century, its principles were upheld. Once copyright lapses, an author is open to market forces, his or her name becomes a commodity, an advertisement. It is in this context that modern canonicity has its origins. This process is concurrent to another in which a network of differences began to organize the flow of subjectivity between text, genre and author. Novel writers in the eighteenth century were ascribed little wit or deep subjectivity while Romantic poets drew deeply on their subjectivity, ascribed to their "genius." Foucault argues that literary criticism is directed towards creating "authors" who mirror the profundity and uniqueness of their texts, then, in a reverse move, it places these "authors" as the text's origin (as I argued in my description of an archaeology of criticism). This particular tactic was anticipated in early Christian textual criticism by St Jerome for whom the personal saintliness of a text's (often putative) author formed the ultimate citeria for its entry into the canon, and who developed rules for deciding whether or not a particular work formed part of an authorial *oeuvre*, that is, was "authentic." At the apex of this process – though Foucault does not mention it – the author effect may conflate the life and the book: as in Proust's case, where the life becomes the book and vice versa.

At the very end of his long, path-breaking and resolutely anti-literary paper, Foucault declares that behind its analysis "we could hear little more than the murmur of indifference: 'What matter who is speaking?' "

(138). This now is not a sign of a desire for the anonymous flow of spaced writing quasi-ironically expressed at the beginning of "The Order of Discourse" (or, for that matter, in the 1972 preface to the second edition of *History of Madness in the Classical Age*). Now Foucault is invoking the flood of words that our society produces, some of which are stored in libraries or archives, and declaring that what is worth most attention is the way in which they are classified into texts, genres, oeuvres, canons in order to create particular local socio-political effects. From *this* indifference the work on governmentality proceeds.

GENEALOGY AND THE HISTORIES OF PRESENT PROBLEMS

For Foucault in his archaeological work, analysis is condemned to operate at two interconnected and incompatible levels in the modern epoch: that of the empirical and of the transcendental, of facts and of the theories which organize those facts but cannot ground them, of phenomena and of the unknowable forces which propel those phenomena into existence, of texts and of the interpretations which claim to represent those texts objectively. However, this is the problem of archaeology too, split as it is between organizing its analysis in terms of discourse's "rules of formation" and providing a neutral and true description of statements. How to move beyond the aporia of modern knowledge? First, by avoiding the archaeological assumption that knowledge-as-discourse has internal conditions of possibility, and, second, by attempting to avoid theory – that is to say, by not producing universal axioms, by not offering statements that claim to account for their own articulation. In this spirit, Foucault finds two new names for his work: it is a "genealogy" (or "a history of the present"), and it is a "history of problematizations."

Foucault defined and elaborated his notion of "genealogy" – a word that he borrowed from Nietzsche – in a series of essays and interviews during the first half of the seventies. He takes up the concept to reintroduce memory and purpose into his own work: "Let us give the term genealogy to the union of erudite knowledge and local memories which allows us to establish a historical knowledge of struggles and to make use of this knowledge tactically today" (1980b, 83). Genealogy cannot remain as conceptually simple as this though. Even in this definition certain phrases have a more particular meaning than may meet the eye. Genealogy is an *erudite* knowledge, for instance, not in the sense of "the great warm and tender Freemasonry of useless erudition" (79) but in the sense that erudition is required to release forgotten memories and documents. For genealogy is also an "insurrection of subjugated knowledges" (81). Not only does it retrieve the buried texts of those whom history has silenced (though Foucault is appealing to the "plebs" in us all (138)), it uses *methods* that previous historical procedures ignore. Genealogies are not, like most marx-ist histories, nostalgic or utopian, pointing back or forwards to better eras that have been, or will be, distanced from the present by the veil of vast socio-historical change. Thus, at a more conceptual level, functionalism and systematization are procedures which Foucault especially disowns; for him, institutions and discursive formations cannot be understood in terms of their role in maintaining social stability or permitting cultural or social reproduction. The word "local" takes on its particular resonance in Fou-cault's genealogy too, for it does not attempt systematically to draw particu-lar events into connections with a wider sphere. Genealogy is also defined in opposition to the universalism of the marxist and sociological history in two other ways. First, the place of each individual is not substitutable for the place of any other. Second, it is focused on the body, both on the way in which the body is historically, culturally and socially "imprinted" (by housing, training, diet, manners and so on) and the way in which the constantly shifting distinction between the self and the body is organized at particular historical moments.

What makes a genealogy urgent is a particular need, the sense that a research project written now, here, would reveal weaknesses, and historical connections, that might have a specific political effect; which might, in particular allow the unvoiced to find a voice. Thus, for instance, Foucault claimed that the notion of disciplinary power, which he developed in his genealogical analyzes, came from his experience with the group GIP (Groupe Information sur les Prisons). This groups attempted to provide occasions in which prisoners could articulate and distribute their own *éconcés* in the early 1970s.[3] He was also, though more peripherally, involved in GIS (Groupe Information Santé), a group of medical professionals who worked towards the de-medicalization of the health-care system by attempting to reduce the gap between medical knowledge and hospital practice, to provide care more attuned to the patient's needs and wants, and to place medical questions to the political arena. (See 1972c). Thus, genealogy also circulates knowledge and information. Again one can see that, despite its anti-theoretical bias and its avowedly political impetus, genealogy has affinities with archaeology: it is against totality, it is against the received unities, it does not operate in terms of deep structures, it does not work in terms of essences or origins or finalities. For it, discourse is not produced by a subject "behind" a particular utterance or group of utterances, for it, the past is not "dead" – condemned to an irretrievable otherness. And whereas archaeology aims to be about the ordering of one kind of material thing – the *éconcé*, genealogy aims to be about the ordering of another – the body.

Genealogy also resists that kind of "continuous history" which emerged as the central theme of secular humanism – or, rather, as a "screen memory" covering up the reality of modern state administration (a "screen memory" is a Freudian term for an image which stands in the place of, though it retains traces of, a repressed idea). It is in these terms that, unlike continuous history, genealogy is tuned to the contemporary social world:

> "Evolutive" historicity, as it was then constituted – and so profoundly that it is still self-evident for many today – is bound up with a mode of the functioning of power. No doubt it is as if the "history-remembering" of the chronicles, genealogies, exploits, reigns and deeds had long been linked to a modality of power. With the new techniques of subjection, the "dynamics" of continuous evolutions tend to replace the "dynastics" of solemn events.
>
> (1977b, 160)

So against both "dynastics" and "dynamics," genealogy responds to and attempts to avoid the current "mode of functioning power." Such a programme is enormously attractive, and there can be no doubt that in his history of the birth of the prison (and of madness and sexuality); in his dossiers on forgotten figures of the past – the hermaphrodite Herculine Barbin, the murderer Pierre Rivière – Foucault certainly did help provide room for the articulation and dispersion of what had been silenced or forgotten, as well as to put pressures on institutions and modes of thought that cause misery by failing to hearken to the demands of those who are their subjects.

Yet there remain difficulties. First, as Foucault himself recognized, the offer to give the unvoiced a voice is connected to "that great system of constraint by which the West compelled the everyday to bring itself into discourse" (1979a, 90). Where does this system of constraint end? Where does the positive programme of enabling the "unsayable or unsaid" to speak, begin? To give prisoners, gays, the colonized or the marginal a voice is also to demand of them their "truth," to suppose that they are the originating subjects of a specific, more or less univocal, "voice," and therefore, to some degree at least, to call them into that de-centred centre which constitutes the (post)modern world. Indeed, as we shall see in chapter 8, Foucault will include this possibility, as "pastoral power," in his genealogy of modernity. In short, to what degree is genealogy itself connected to modern power – as, say, Macaulay's histories were to British imperialism or Shakespeare's history cycle to the emergence of early absolutism? Also, it is not always clear what is local and what is not, and, thus, it is often difficult to fix the place towards which genealogical commitment is to be directed. Who decides *that* – and by what criteria? Here the author effect of Foucault's own signature cannot be discounted. His name was used on behalf of prisoners, of those in asylums, the hospitalized, even for those whose sexual preferences are marginalized – but not on behalf of the colonized, or of women. It could well be urged that the signature "Michel Foucault" (leaving aside the formidable talents of the individual himself) should have been used – however indirectly – on *their* behalf. Is it up to Foucault himself to decide this – might not the imperatives of a collective commitment creep back in here? Might not a certain political calculus be required to formulate a hierarchy of need and urgency (and such a calculus would itself have to move from a broad reading of the present situation)? Certainly if such a hierarchy were calculated, it would not be easy for Foucault to ignore questions about the West's relations with the so-called Third World, and the way his own work fails to recognize the effects of this relation. (See Spivak 1988 for a development of this critique.) Furthermore, as Foucault came to realize, the movements to de-institutionalize the asylums and, to a lesser degree, the prisons, for which his histories were harnessed, were not wholly successful. The reason for this – briefly – was that under advanced capitalism, outside of welfarism, there exists little space between, on the one side, the public sphere of the market and the media and, on the other, individuals and their families. So that to "de-institutionalize" inmates is to place them in a vacuum, that is to say, on the street. Thus, and this is perhaps the most telling problem with the genealogical project, the tactical purpose of his most elaborated counter-histories somewhat misfired.

Partly in response to the first and last of these difficulties (he seems to have ignored the second), Foucault began to emphasise a rather different side of his project in later presentations. In one of his last interviews he calls his work a "history of thought," where "thought" is a response to "problems." He had appealed to the notion of the "problematic" as far back as the "Preface" to Binswanger, but, more particularly, these problems re-formulate *The Archaeology*'s "points of incompatibility" in which a particular discursive practice or situation is splintered so as to permit alternative strategies. But these are not theoretical contractions – they are problems simultaneously in discourse and for practice. Where an impasse is reached, where different solutions circulate – life imprisonment or death sentence? adoption or abortion? for the Greeks, marriage or boys? – then, in that impasse, thought and, often, struggle, are generated. Foucault, describing his work in these terms, would enjoin us "to rediscover at the root of these diverse solutions the general form of problematization that has made them possible" (1984b, 389). Although the two later volumes of *The History of Sexuality* are articulated in these terms, it is in his last interviews that hints emerge that these "general forms of problematization" cast very large shadows indeed over our history. They consist, in fact, of two large blocks: the Western implementation of rationality on the social field in order to maximize economic production (which involves selective historical memories), and – against this – the "liberal" attempt to distribute and maintain individual liberty and autonomy. Making a point not unfamiliar to marxism, Foucault often argues that, in practice, liberalism often disguises and, thus, enables, the development of that rationalized and disciplined society to which it is opposed. But still, as he put it in a lecture, liberal claims that "one governs too much," and statist claims that "one governs too little" cannot be reconciled (1989, 111). It is as if all modern historical impasses are connected to this large problematization. We can give as obvious instances imprisonment as a punishment and the debates that incessantly surround it; or (an example Foucault avoids) the relation of non-modern to modern societies. How to disentangle demands for individual liberty from those for social order? Rationality from imperialism? In the penumbra of these large historical and political undecidables, the local disappears. To analyze an event as a problem is to be led out into a "multiplication" of analytic "salients," in what Foucault calls an "increasing polymorphism" (1987b, 105). Thus, for instance, an account of the emergence of the modern penal system leads, more or less inevitably, into an examination of modern schooling. Both are instances of the same large "impasse" or "problematization."

Foucault's theory of problematization revolves around an ambiguity. On the one hand, he suggests that the history that Western societies tell themselves is constituted by events which involve strategy and struggle, and in which incompatible demands and legitimations are repeatedly interrogated. In the last instance, historical continuity exists in the persistence of such difficulties and struggles. This is a very suggestive formulation, which once again historicizes a philosophical conception of Kant's: Kant described as "paralogisms" the problems that thought repeatedly encounters whenever it attempts to analyze consciousness in terms of material objects, or vice versa.[4] On the other hand, the genealogist "makes visible" singularities, "at places where there is a temptation to invoke a historical constant, an immediate anthropological trait or an obviousness that imposes itself uniformly on all" (1987b, 104). Here the historian of the present teases out specific problems that generalizing historicism or "common sense" hide from view. Taking a position at the point where these two lines of Foucauldian thought intersect, one can say that, for Foucault, ours is a "noisy" – a much narrated – history, and one that requires genealogical work because it is formed within the problem of liberty versus governmentality. And it is also, and paradoxically, a noisy history because it has devised such powerful and various, yet still inadequate, means for de-problematizing itself. Of such means, the reduction of a large field of interconnections to singular events, and – inversely – the transformation of particular moments, persons and happenings into placeholders of larger formations or large historical events (such as "modernization") are merely two. Finally, for Foucault, societies have histories to the degree that they produce records that exist both as tools of government and as documents that permit historians to explain and narrate society to itself. At the level of administration, society "deproblematizes"

129

or "reforms" itself by producing information (which makes history noisy). The genealogist can read this information against the grain, not as a tool of reform but as the elaboration of power networks. Nonetheless to understand thought as work on problems is to place intellectuals (for whom, of course, thought is work) in a relation of some impotence and repetition *vis-à-vis* their objects. In Foucault's final formulation, the intellectual's role is to stand as far back from such struggles as possible in the attempt to grasp what conditions them *as* struggles. The work of thought projects its effects on the socio-political field from this distance – which is to move a long, long way from the genealogist or specific intellectual working near the frontline of a micro-political struggle. In these late statements Foucault has moved away from micro-political activism.

THINKING ABOUT POWER

Foucault's later work deals with three intersected topics: power, truth and the formation of selves. Towards the end of his life, when asked yet again, "what is genealogy's task?" he replied:

First, an historical ontology of ourselves in relation to truth through which we constitute ourselves as subjects of knowledge; second, an historical ontology of ourselves in relation to a field of power through which we constitute ourselves as subjects acting on others; third, an historical ontology in relation to ethics through which we constitute ourselves as moral agents.

(1983a, 237)

Here "historical ontology" implies that genealogy is a history of being – the being of actual bodies as against Heidegger's *Dasein* or Being-in-the-world. It is easiest to engage these various "historical ontologies" from the side of power mainly because Foucault's account of it is most extensive and has had most impact on other writers. Yet, despite its success, his view of power again has quite deep-rooted methodological and theoretical difficulties. Of course, his interest in the topic goes back to *Madness and Civilization*, where as we have seen he described strategies of division and exclusion, asking questions such as: how are people who suffer from madness separated from society? What are they required to do? In what kind of building are they put? However, as an analogue to discourse-analysis, the work on power can be broken down into three separate strands. First, Foucault constructs what we can call a new ontology of power: a radical revison of what power *is*. Second, he articulates an "analytics of power," a somewhat sociological classification of the modes in which power has worked since the eighteenth century. And, third, he offers concrete histories of specific "power technologies" – especially a history of "penality" (in *Discipline and Punish*) and, more sketchily, a history of "bio-power" (in the

130

first volume of *The History of Sexuality*). In the 1980s, the theory shifts again. Foucault declares that he is concerned with power given within individual liberty, outside both relations of domination and submission and the larger social technologies which have overwhelmed and formed modernity. This "self-governmentality," as he calls it, entailed some more backtracking, as is clear from another of his last (male-centred) interviews:

> Myself, I am not sure, when I began to interest myself in this problem of power, of having spoken very clearly about it or used the words needed. Now I have a much clearer idea of all that. It seems to me that we must distinguish the relationships of power as strategic games between liberties – strategic games that result in the fact that some people try to determine the conduct of others – and the states of domination, which are what we ordinarily call power. And, between the two, between the games of power and the states of domination, you have governmental technologies – giving this term a very wide meaning for it is also the way in which you govern your wife, your children as well as the way you govern an institution. The analysis of these techniques is necessary, because it is often through this kind of technique that states of domination are established and maintain themselves. In my analysis of power, there are three levels: the strategic relationships, the techniques of government, and the levels of domination.
>
> (1988a, 19)

The levels sketched here – strategical relationships, techniques of government and domination – map quite easily onto the divisions classically drawn between (1) family and self; (2) civil administration; and (3) state politics. It had been the strength of Foucault's description of power hitherto, that he had insisted that the second of these levels (i.e. techniques of government) impinged on the first (strategical relationships) in ways generally ignored, and that the role of the last (domination) had been overrated by historians and sociologists. So as not to lose sight of this, Foucault's earlier and important revisionism, I want to concentrate here on modern power.

Foucault's crucial move is to regard power as a condition for society in general:

> Power relations are rooted deep in the social nexus, not reconstituted "above" society as a supplementary structure whose radical efface-ment one could perhaps dream of. In any case, to live in society is to live in such a way that action upon other actions is possible – and in fact ongoing.
>
> (1983c, 222–3)

In a formulation which owes much to Gilles Deleuze's 1962 monograph on Nietzsche, "power" is the name for the conditions of possibility for "an

131

action upon actions." The concept is transposed from post-Galilean science for which the basic element in the world was "motion," as for instance, in Hobbes's thought. By the nineteenth century, this "motion" becomes itself celebrated as an ontological and social principle against both God and Man:

> This Universe, ah me – what could the wild man know of it; what can we yet know? That it is a Force, and thousandfold Complexity of Forces; a Force which is *not we*. That is all; it is not we, it is altogether different from *us*. Force, Force, everywhere Force; we ourselves a mysterious Force in the centre of that.
>
> (Carlyle 1935, 11)

For Nietszche, force merges into the concept "power" (in the German word *Macht*) and can thus be used to re-narrativize history. Now history becomes intelligible as a series of a-teleological struggles and strategies, in which power/force is everywhere but is not everywhere the same. As Foucault wrote in the first volume of *The History of Sexuality*:

> It seems to me that power must be understood in the first instance as the multiplicity of force relations immanent in the sphere in which they operate and which constitute their own organization; as the process which, through ceaseless struggles and confrontations, transforms, strengthens, or reverses them; as the support which these force relations find in one another, thus forming a chain or a system, or on the contrary, the disjunctions and contradictions which isolate them from one another; and lastly, as the strategies in which they take effect, whose general design or institutional crystallization is embodied in the state apparatus, in the formulation of the law, in the various social hegemonies.
>
> (1980c, 93)

To establish a method upon this ontology of power is, once again, to work against dialectics or any conflict resolution model; against those human sciences (including semiology) which base their analyzes on concepts such as "system," "structure" and, finally, against sociological history which distinguishes social phenomena from economic and cultural phenomena.

More radically still, for Foucault, power as the precondition for an "action upon an action" is relational. Therefore it is not primarily possessed by an agent – though, of course, some people may be able to control acts by others. For instance, any division between work and play areas in a school distributes bodies, and thus constructs subjects, in a particular way, and is a power-effect in Foucault's terms, even if that power belongs to no individual. It follows both that power cannot be analyzed in terms of conscious intentions, and that the dominant themselves are constrained within power networks. This means that these networks are not adequately

132

described in the kind of analysis associated with the Frankfurt school or so-called "critical theory." Critcal theory aims to demonstrate that power in general works to cover up people's real interests by offering them a false view of what those interests are.[5] It implicitly relies on a notion of ideology as the primary instrument of domination, a notion extended and reworked by French marxists – Louis Althusser in particular. For Althusser (to put a complex matter simply), ideology exists as a unified set of beliefs that masquerade as common sense to as to allow existing conditions to be reproduced and to permit individuals to recognize themselves as unities (rather than as beings that live and think at the intersection of social processes and differences). Foucault refused the Althusserian concept of ideology partly because it implies that external criteria exist for telling what is "ideological" as against what is "true" (or "scientific"), and partly because formalist analyzes based on a concept of the ideological presuppose what they dismiss: that is, a "human subject on the lines of the model provided by classical philosophy, endowed with a consciousness which power is then thought to seize on" (1980b, 58). Ideology must appeal to, or be recognized by, such a subject even as it shapes him or her. Finally, ideology-critique also ignores the way in which practices have consequences that differ from the ideas that legitimate them. When prisons replace locks and warders by TV eyes and remote-control electronic "keys," ideology may not change but power-effects do.

Foucault's power, then, is not simply a system of domination: prisons can be redesigned within a rhetoric of humanitarianism that saves lives, yet this redesign can lead to more surveillance, more control of those lives, and so on. The streets can be policed, this leads to a genuine increase of personal safety. But, at the same time, it consolidates social divison by forcing the very poor into a choice: to become a criminal or not to become a criminal? The design of a barrack affects both officers and privates. Also, power-effects can be hidden from view, and they can always misfire in part because they are not simply intentional. This means that it is difficult to judge a particular formation or event in advance: what might appear to be the consequences of setting up a particular institution, for instance, may always turn out quite otherwise. Because, for Foucault, societies do not possess a single "ideology" or a single agency of domination (the bourgeoisie, the state . . .) which work in a single direction, the analysis of power is more effective when it starts "from the bottom up" – from the design of school yards – rather than from the top down – from reports on education to parliament or what Matthew Arnold wrote about culture. Power also flows from the resistance out, from petty acts like that fictional-ized in Oliver's "more" rather than, simply, from the 1834 report on the English Poor Laws. However, these two injunctions: "from the bottom up" and "from the resistance out" are not rules, just because power's path is not unidirectional. Foucault's argument is, rather, that these events at the "bottom," at points of "blockage," are crucial because they have most intensity. They are where power, most of all, touches and shapes the body, the thingness of human life, or what will become in his later work "ethical substance."

Because power has no outside it belongs to what Foucault calls a "productive network." It does not repress. In particular it invites people to speak: to assess and articulate themselves. He describes many protocols for self-assessment: for instance, particular pieces of sexual behaviour begin to be carefully itemized in the Christian confessionals; the penitent is there given a voice, her actions divided into minute categories which may be worked on. And during the nineteenth century, students are encouraged to express themselves in poetry, art and music lessons: these activities being moulded by the very place in which they are performed. Such self-expression, shaped by its context, but not ordered from above, produces new forms of "deep" subjectivity. Where power is self-imposed it is most dispersed – and most effective. From this Foucault draws a quasi-archaeological conclusion: the intelligibility of history is not to be found in its documents. Behind documents exists the non-discursive condition – the power network – which allows the subject to speak (and act). Even in Pierre Rivière's confession of his crime, discourse, action and power are intertwined. Rivière, the peasant parricide, uses murder to express himself, because murder, which so fascinates the media, communicates between the rich and the poor. Yet the question, "how are you able to speak?" has a rather mysterious relation to "why do you say (or do) *this* in particular?" – and Foucault never quite succeeded in drawing these two levels together. Especially in the presence of subdied, forgotten voices, voices which speak without official permission, he tended to respond with a vitalist, if not indeed a neo-classical aesthetic vocabulary, as for instance, in his remarks on Rivière himself, or his celebration of the "beauty" of the "classical style" of long-dead criminals. He wanted to reprint the "lives of infamous men" in order to circulate their "intensity" and communicate the "vibration" he felt on first reading them (1979a, 77).

Foucault, then, is attempting to balance the monism of power against its dispersion into events. Where power is dispersed it still operates against resistance, it works at specific times in specific places on subjects who return its pressure. And, just as in judo one's opponent's resistance is turned to one's advantage (a possibility that permits feints and ruses), the pressure back in power-relations rapidly crosses and re-crosses sides. That there is no power without resistance – as inertia or as liberty, does not simply mean that power liberates, partly because the substance to be liberated, like a child invited to express herself, is already formed within power's network:

let there be no misunderstanding: it is not that a real man, the object

134

of knowledge, philosophical reflection or technical intervention, has been substituted for the soul, the illusion of the theologians. The man described for us, whom we are invited to free, is already in himself the effect of a subjection much more profound than himself. A "soul" inhabits him and brings him to existence, which is itself a factor in the mastery that power exercises over the body. The soul is the effect and instrument of a political anatomy; the soul is the prison of the body.

(1977b, 30)

On the one side, networks of power drive people to speak and inscribe individuals with souls. On the other, the exercise of power, as well as resistances to it, involve pleasure. It is for these reasons that, for Foucault at this stage of his career, the systems in which utterances are considered to be true or false back out onto the splintered and dynamic order of power-relations, bodily events and feelings, not onto nothing or death as in *The Order of Things*. There exist more than one kind of relation between power and truth, however. For nineteenth-century working-class radical-ism, the Baconian adage, "knowledge is power" was a cliché – as it appeared on the masthead of a famous radical journal, *The Poor Man's Guardian*, for instance. This progressivist sense that knowledge enables control over self and others, as well as self-confidence, is not foreign to Foucault. And yet the benign Baconian reading of the relation conceals its darker side: "In the end we are judged, condemned, classified, determined in our undertakings, destined to a certain mode of living or dying, as function of the true discourses which are the bearers of the specific effects of power" (1980b, 94). The desire to know, to find out the truth, can itself entice us into new relations of power. For Foucault, discourse about sexu-ality in the nineteenth century works precisely in this way. Once more, it is not a matter whether discourses are *really* true as it is for ideology critique; the "truth" constrains our "undertakings" whether it can be contested or not. And there are various ways of recognizing truth: either it can be defined, for instance, as that which helps one live a particular kind of life, or as a function of the fit between representations and the world, or as the degree of generality that a set of statements have attained – to take some instances at random. In this later work, Foucault thinks about such variations as types of "truth games." In stategical situations, particular truth games link up, in non-lawlike ways, with specific "relations of power" – power-relations like those between an anthropologist and a local community, an employment bureau and its clients, a wife and a husband, a psychiatrist and a patient, and so on (1988a, 16.) Indeed, the later Foucault can suppose that intellectuals differ from non-intellectuals in that they have enough competence with truth games to protect certain forms of truth from power encroachments.

DISPUTING GENEALOGY

Foucault's problematization of the power-knowledge relation triggered debate amongst both historians and social theorists. By applying – or trying to apply – Foucault's account of modern power to particular instances, historians in many fields have modified it.[6] In the aftermath of such work, one has again to concede that his general method, and his case-studies, have tended to underestimate those areas to which traditional historians have attached importance: particularly, religion, nation, the law and the market. These formations continued to have major effects both on the trajectory of history and on individuals during the period in which modern power emerged – as we shall see in the more historical chapters to follow. But historians, also, made more general objections to Foucault's work – arguing that its account of modernity was too unnuanced. To take one early and often-cited example, Jacques Léonard argued that Foucault "exaggerates the rationalization and normalization of French society in the first half of the nineteenth century" (Léonard 1980, 12). It is clear, however, that in raising this issue, one must be careful not to fall into the danger of believing that particular social formations have a *proper* place in history, being otherwise "survivals" or "emergents." Once one does not think like that, then it is possible to regard certain popular traditions as in fact reinforcing "normalization" – where, for instance, theatrical performances in public houses aided police detection, and law enforcement (fictionalized by Dickens in the "he do the police in different voices" scene of *Our Mutual Friend* and elsewhere); or the gradual transformation of sports into spectacle during the late nineteenth century so as to de-politicize the proletariat. On the other hand, the stamping out of religious carnivals in France during the nineteenth century seems to have been more difficult and provoked more resistance than any totalizing model of carceral society might lead one to expect. And society is, for Foucault (whatever a critic like Léonard might say), constituted precisely by resistances (ultimately grounded on the *body's* resistance – pain). Genealogy attempts to keep memories of such resistance alive *against* historicism and the human sciences; in doing so it uncovers an event – the emergence of modern power – that had previously been ignored. At one level, for Foucault, "rationalization" is less a monolithic force working on the nineteenth century than a feature of the way "normal" history selectively channels memories of those times into our own. The emergence of modern power has been concealed by those traditional and "evolutive" histories which concentrated on topics like religion, nationality, and the law.

The social theorists expressed their reservations about Foucault in related, if more abstract, terms. If local truth regimes cannot be measured against some overarching Truth; if knowledge is produced within power relations; if modern society shelters no subjectivity which lies outside power, then what room is left for freedom, for reflection, for criticism? What remains of the Enlightenment project? Questions and protests of this kind were articulated most forcefully by Charles Taylor, Jürgen Habermas and Peter Dews. Foucault did not remain obdurate in the face of this line of attack: as we shall see in the next chapter he responded in part by arguing that the promise of enlightenment is to be found in its invitation to self-fashioning. And certainly he was capable of anti-Enlightenment gestures. When, for instance, he reviewed André Glucksmann's *Les Maîtres Penseurs*, which argues, along lines established by Karl Popper, that the ideals of the French Revolution led to twentieth-century totalitarian régimes, Foucault suggested that the German Enlightenment was an apocalyptic movement in which revolutionary desire and reason were able, strangely, to legitimate the construction of a totalizing state. Finally, Foucault argues, "Bismarck, social democracy, Hitler and Ulbricht" form a single chain (1978b, 68). Nonetheless, as we shall see, in the early eighties he retreated from such dangerous arguments, and began to distinguish humanism from *Aufklärung* (Enlightenment); the former he still dissociated himself from, with the latter he entered into negotiations. It was this that enabled him to re-affirm the critical task of the intellectual which had been submerged in his own work since "The Order of Discourse."

In "Foucault on Freedom and Truth," a widely read and commented-upon article, Charles Taylor gives notice of a number of disagreements with Foucault. Of these, three – two philosophical arguments and the other a moral rebuke – are of particular interest. Taylor, whose philosophic work is well known within the Anglo-American academy for its application of German idealist and hermeneutic concepts, argues that Foucault's account of power fails to provide the basis for an understanding of history because it does not meet a minimum criterion of intelligibility. For Taylor, "explanations" of history must be related to the "purposeful action of agents in a way that we can understand." This means that Foucault's concept of flows of power, as "strategies without projects" are, in fact, unintelligible (Taylor 1985, 170). Because it focuses on conditions of intelligibility, Taylor's is a transcendental, quasi-Kantian argument, thereby encountering difficulties that Foucault himself rehearses in the "Man and his Doubles" chapter of *The Archaeology of Knowledge*. Taylor concedes that historical "models" need not be reducible to the conscious aims of individual agents. For him, examples of such "purposefulness without purpose" include economic "invisible hands" and unconscious motives (terrorists may be motivated by Dostoyeveskian self-hatred invisible to themselves, for instance). But, Taylor insists, "the text of history, which we are trying to explain, is made up of purposeful human action. Where there are patterns in this action which are not on purpose, we have to explain why action done under one description on purpose also bears this other undesigned description. We have to show how the two descriptions relate" (71). The problem

137

here is the organizing metaphor: history is not a text, especially not *this* kind of text. To suppose that it is, is to assume what Foucault demands we do not assume: that history has an "author" and subject. No, says Foucault, history is better conceived of in terms of struggles or problems, or, as we might add in a Derridaean or Lyotardian spirit, in terms of incommensurabilities. For him, actions are not performed "under description" – indeed action is not a category upon which Foucauldian historiography rests, just because it does indeed imply intentionality. On the one hand, Foucault's actual historical works are directed towards events, which, as events, are neither simply driven by intentions nor simply interpretable as intentional. On the other, his history is directed towards documents; it preserves them, circulates them and places them in new connections with other documents. The metaphor "history is a text" expresses Taylor's humanist bias: history is always already an articulation of the human, it has recoverable meaning and grounds. Indeed, certain remarks aside, Foucault is not trying to "explain" history. Far from asking his readers to look at history in terms of larger purposes, in terms of what we "understand," he presents it as a nexus of tensions and offers a method by which we might break down the constitutive elements of discrete categories such as "penality" or "sexuality." How do aims, institutions and discursive formations which fall under such headings change? What problems and struggles do old documents about prisons and sex address? How do these discourses, struggles, institutions affect lives? And, though they do not suppose a large historical "text" or meaning, such questions do not make history less "intelligible." What, anyway, *is* intelligibility for Taylor? That which we can understand. Once that is said we realize that a doubling, a particular tolerance of tautology, characteristic of modern discourse, remains embedded in Taylor's critique.

Taylor also dismisses Foucault's assertion that power may be a productive force, as well as a limiting one, as meaningless: "Power, in [Foucault's] sense, does not make sense without at least the idea of liberation" (ibid., 175–6; italics Taylor's). Taylor argues that there must be an outside to power if the concept is to signify anything at all. Again, obliquely, this argument attempts to drag Foucault into a humanist frame. Foucault *does* specify an outside to power in his analytic, but finally that outside exists in the substantiality, the inertia and singularity of things and bodies, in the pleasure that power excites and in the local means of struggling against felt restrictions, rather than in an abstract notion like "liberation." Foucault would ask: what kind of "liberation"? For whom? At what cost? And with what unintended effects? Also, Foucault's power-relations are not modelled on a logical structure of opposition or contradiction but on a field of "polymorphous" singularities. We can repeat, Foucauldian power is not a unitary thing, it is constituted in knotted struggles or events each different – if tied – to the other. Certainly no single journey towards the light – or vacuum – of human "freedom" drives such struggles. This is not to say that the socio-political engagements *against* the reduction of movement, of discourse, of action are in some way "impossible" within his theory.

Taylor's own values are most apparent when he describes Foucault's "relativism." After arguing that Foucault's idea of different "truth-regimes" means that "we cannot raise the banner of truth against our own regime," Taylor insists that Foucault "leaves out" that:

> We have become certain things in Western civilisation. Our humani-
> tarianism, our notions of freedom – both personal independence and
> collective self-rule – have helped to define a political identity we
> share; and one which is deeply rooted in our more basic, seemingly
> infra-political understandings; of what it is to be an individual, of
> the person as a being with "inner" depths – all the features which
> seem to us to be rock-bottom, almost biological properties of human
> beings, so long as we refrain from looking outside and experiencing
> the shock of encountering other cultures. . . . Of course, these
> elements of identity are contested; they are not neatly and definitely
> articulated once and for all. . . . But they all count for us. None of
> them can be simply repudiated in the political struggle. We struggle
> over interpretation and weightings, but we cannot shrug them off.
> They *define* humanity, politics for us.
>
> (ibid., 181)

This apologia for "Western civilization" is worth citing at length because it seems to me that it demonstrates less what Foucault "leaves out" than what he rejects. Of course, Foucault works on the side of certain victims of this "we": the mad, gays, "criminals" – and he himself is such a victim too. But his oeuvre, from beginning to end, also attempts to undo the conceptual underpinning of that kind of culturalist transcendentalism for which cultural identity provides the tacit horizon of understanding within which individuals relate to society, and for which the transmission of tradition provides social norms. For Foucault, actual social and ethical practices cannot constitute an abstract "identity." Rather identities granted in terms of, say, "civilized" or "American" ways disseminate modes of self-surveillance. It is this side of Foucault's work: his archaeology, his analysis of truth-regimes, his insistence on the importance of intellectuals as technicians of truth, his ethics, that begins to expose gaps through which the least enabled Others of Western humanism (including those he ignores like the colonized and their heirs) might proceed to their own power-relations and truth-games. Ironically, one of the advantages of reading Charles Taylor's panegyric to his own tradition and cultural identity is to show how Foucault's work remains tied to the specific task of combating the identity granted by the culturalist tradition.

Dews and Habermas also attack Foucault from a fixed position. But not, this time, one for which cultural "identity" – despite rifts and conflicts – is secure. On the contrary, they reaffirm the project of modernity by fixing a mechanism that might non-destructively carry it forward. In their account of Foucault, they use Habermas's own theory of "communicative action" against Foucault's power/knowledge thesis. It is impossible to do justice to Habermas's case here, but its broadest contours can be outlined. Habermas extends the accounts of modernity found both in the early critical theorists and in Max Weber – for whom the modern era is characterized by what Weber calls "disenchantment." In *Dialectic of Enlightenment*, Theodor Adorno and Max Horkheimer argue that the long process of disenchantment began when magic was replaced by mythology. The era of myth, for which "knowledge is power" (they cite Bacon's truism), began when one tribe conquered and colonized another, dissolving the *mana* or aura of the local. In mythology, active cunning and instrumentality overcome passivity and terror in the face of nature and death. At the same time signatures or analogies are replaced by signs as the vehicle of thought. If this last idea sounds familiar (Adorno and Horkheimer's "magic/mythology" distinction echoing Foucault's division between the Renaissance and classical epistemes), that is because both Foucault and the critical theorists write under the spell of Heidegger. With the emergence of capitalism, means-ends or instrumental rationality begins to dominate both thought and social structures: knowledge and institutions are powerful to the degree that they provide efficient (or rational) means for the increased production of commodities. At the same time (and this is a Weberian thesis), society breaks up into a series of differentiated and incommensurable spheres of value: legal, economic, "the humanities" and so on. Finally, Horkheimer and Adorno argue, in modernity, true individuality is extinguished, as persons become, on the one hand, tools in the productive machine, and, on the other, are "sublimated into the transcendental or logical subject" – becoming abstract, deterritorialized and "rational" beings (Horkheimer and Adorno 1972, 29).

Adorno and Horkheimer wish to apply demystifying reason against instrumental reason, their difficulty being that they can locate no social institution that might motivate this project in the contemporary world. Given their suspicion of modern subjectivity and the private sphere, they are antagonistic to attempts to "reconcile" the individual to society or, more metaphysically, to reconcile the particular to the universal. Given their fundamentally evolutionary perspective, they tend to regard appeals for (and trends towards) "de-sublimation" – a return to pleasure, feeling, the body – as "regressive." And for them, such appeals also avoid the question of fundamental political or structural reform. Thus Adorno, at least, regards modernist art as the only way out of modernity, because it is not "regressive," and has no use-value. In modernist art, form "negates" content so that "art's own language" can work against "that language of signification" which cannot avoid instrumentality and abstract subjectivity.[7] These formulations too have a familiar ring: they echo transgressive theory.

To return to Habermas. He offers a less pessimistic diagnosis than Adorno, because he claims to have found a formation that permits (enlightened) reason to work against (instrumental) reason. That formation is communication or "linguistic intersubjectivity." Drawing together "hermeneutic and analytic strains of linguistic theory . . . and a reading of Humboldt," he detects in language a built-in teleological structure (Habermas 1986a, 98–9). For him, a reaching for "mutual understanding" is immanent in language. Language is essentially dialogic, possessing a performative (or, in J. L. Austin's terms, "illocutionary") force that binds speakers to one another. Because speakers are connected in *Verständigung* (a reaching towards understanding), the preconditions for utterance provide internal "validity claims." That is, language constitutively implies the following questions (to formulate them a little crudely): "does a speaker have a right to utter these statements?" "is he or she sincere?" and "are these propositions true?" (Habermas 1984, 307). It follows that, for Habermas, to utter is, implicitly, to have a stake in truth-values, sincerity and social order. This is the position from which he and Dews criticize Foucault. They argue that Foucault's theory of power/knowledge itself belongs to means-end rationality, as, for it too, knowledge can never escape instrumentality. Foucault's work cannot escape the modernity it deplores either: it can provide a basis neither for alternative truth-claims (truth, for it, being merely a "régime"), nor for effective political action as it can bring to bear no "other possible images" or "points of view" to the social and historical processes which order it. Nor can it provide a "normative conception of what reason might be" (Dews 1987, 188–9). One might reply that this is, at least in part, to miss Foucault's point: he is not dealing with abstractions such as "means-end rationality," he is preoccupied with the practices of instrumentality. As he put it, "One isn't assessing things in terms of an absolute against which they could be evaluated as constituting more or less perfect forms of rationality, but rather examining how forms of rationality inscribe themselves in practices or systems of practices, and what role they play within them" (1987b, 107). Yet the strongest riposte to such assertions is to place the ball back in Habermas's court. For it is difficult to see how the formal features that Habermas finds in language, his so-called "universal pragmatics," can ground a socio-political base for action.

History and ethnography point in quite another direction from Habermas's. All societies have language but few articulate "validity claims." We can ask, then, what social conditions are necessary, first, to formally articulate the validity claims that Habermas believes to be immanent in linguistic

141

communication, and, second, to use these validity claims to structure a form of political rationality. After all, as Habermas himself has insisted in his debate with Hans-Georg Gadamer, the German champion of hermeneutics and disciple of Heidegger, "Language is also a medium of domination and social power; it serves to situate relations of organized forces" (Habermas 1977, 360). And, as Foucault asserts in reply to Habermas, "In a given society there is no general type of equilibrium between finalized activities, systems of communication, and power-relations. Rather there are diverse forms, diverse places, diverse circumstances or occasions in which these interrelationships establish themselves according to a specific model" (1983c, 218). Language, as a social technology, may work against free exchange: syntax and dialect may, for instance, mark social and gender difference. One does not have to appeal here to extreme cases such as the secret language of the initiated in many non-modern societies – what about the use of the imperative which fathers may use to children but not vice versa, or that syntax of hesitancy which (as many studies have shown) distinguishes women's speech in conversation with men? Thus, any attempt to *apply* the norms that Habermas believes precondition "linguistic intersubjectivity" would require power – just like the attempt to clear a space for "free" market forces. And this power would enforce the "normativeness" of communication by normalizing. What, for instance, would a Habermasian philosopher-king say, or do, to a Marquis de Sade, or, more to the point, to a transgressive theorist like the young Foucault who believed that language's truest dimensions edge out onto radical solitude, madness and death? Also, in locating hope and rationality in a *formal* "intersubjective linguisticity" rather than in small shifts in institutional and social conditions, Habermas makes it harder to sanction actual political intervention. His theories don't cash out into concrete action. More theoretically, as Seyla Benhabib and others have pointed out, communicative rationality is a formal, before it is an empirical, condition, in that it takes no account of the actual conditions of human existence, neither the kind of bodies we have, nor, to take an example at random, the state of the environment.[8] Like all formal normative systems, from Kant on, it cannot provide values that sufficiently protect differences and given identities. This is a problem precisely because the demand for justice, which is not natural or inevitable, often comes in order to protect difference from universalizing and normalizing forces. Once one accepts that Habermas and Dews have not themselves found a way of escaping the "dialectic of enlightenment," because the gap between universalist principles and social practices must still be sealed by power, then one can accept that Foucault's proposals at least possess the virtue of modesty. Foucault recognizes the ever-present forces of co-option and containment, the limits, dangers and attractions of speaking both for oneself and for others, the difficulty of finding an external position from which one can "reflect" on the modern, and the relative

142

impotence and technicality of modern intellectual work. It was his refusal of grand synthesizing theory that allowed Foucault to work as an activist for social outsiders. Foucault's work does not imply that the oppressed, for whom prayer, sexual preference, style, gender identity are more important than the purposive interchange of discourse, must change their beliefs in order to approach the path to freedom.

Yet Habermas and Dews do highlight important difficulties in Foucault's position. The problem is not so much that Foucault cannot answer the question "what are the norms by which we should direct socio-political action?" because, at the requisite level of concreteness, neither can Habermas. Foucault's work seems particularly inadequate when one wishes to act or think on behalf of institutions or goals which are themselves sanctioned by classically enlightened or humanist ideals. I am thinking of the struggle to maintain the role of the humanities and cultural critique in the universities, a struggle against the populist, right liberal governments which, as I write, administer most Western nations, though, of course, this battle is sharpest where the universities are public rather than private. This is not just one among many issues; we confront it as soon as we attend to the power and effectiveness that theory and, indeed, the humanities, actually have in society. It is worth pausing on, therefore. At first sight, Taylor's and Habermas's positions would seem to be more effective than Foucault's in mounting a defence of the university which insists on academic freedom and right of tenure, say.[9] On the one hand, appeals for an institution in which ideas are freely circulated, which provides a space for reflection, and in which cultural traditions are maintained may seem more likely to gain public support than appeals for institutions which support problematization or transgression. On the other, a Foucauldian insistence that educational institutions train individuals in specific practices, rather than forming an abstract subject with a generalized capacity for critical thought, radically demystifies notions like "reflection" and "academic freedom."

It is in this context that it is tempting merely to repeat the old legitimating discourses of the academic humanities. But recent history, at least in the United Kingdom and Australia, shows that this is more or less futile. The defence of the humanities that is now required must have taken the force of the various critiques of humanism, of which Foucault's is the sharpest. What can they affirm after such critiques? First, that the academic humanities are worth defending just because they still shelter critique, even if such critique need not rest on hallowed notions such as academic freedom, progress or formal rationality. In the humanities, too, discursive experimentation may be encouraged, even if this experimentation does not have particular social ends in view; in them a variety of ways of thinking and living are presented and the archives may be reread in the light of present problems and needs, even if these problems do not have obvious solutions, and the needs are not recognized as legitimate by politicians and, more particularly, by the media. That is to say, humanities in the university can claim that their tasks are not performed under the sign of representation: they can insist that they represent neither a section of the market like the media, nor a sector of the established national will like politicians. It is because they do not belong to an institution legitimized through representation, but are pedagogical, future-directed, and, furthermore, dedicated to training students in skills which are not immediately vocational, that they can focus on theoretical, methodological, practical problems and difficulties, that they can help prevent cultural objects, memories, points of view falling out of sight, that they can draw connections that have no functional or commercial interest to the market or the state, and can work to maintain the voices of those whom history, the market or the will of the people silence. Literature departments conceived of through this kind of post-humanism would not be quite the literature departments we have, of course; they would be more involved in producing and disseminating genealogies of cultural work, especially, genealogies of writing. Central to such a project are histories of the means by which differences between literature, scholarship, criticism and journalism have been articulated, evaluated and used to create power-effects – and I will offer an example of such an analysis in my last chapter. Obviously such a project is profoundly un-Habermasian, at least that Habermas who is interested in developing norms from the formal and unhistorical conditions of linguistic intercommunication. Equally obviously it owes a great deal to Foucault – though not the Foucault who, in the early seventies, dismissed the universities both for being "exclusive," in pursuing knowledge as a mere ideal, and for being an important element in the socialising apparatus.[10] The project would owe more to that Foucault for whom intellectuals use "régimes of truth" *against* "relations of power" and strategies of rationalization. Indeed, in the 1980s, Foucault himself became increasingly worried about the loss of critical activity in the universities, and, in particular, the way in which the marketing of academic books made such activity less likely (Eribon 1989, 312). But, perhaps because of the legacy of his early public anti-academicism, he never brought these anxieties openly to bear on his own most serious projects.

If Habermas, Dews and Taylor, all of whom are connected to the old new left, provide the enlightened humanist attack on Foucault, then Jean Baudrillard mounts the avant-garde attack. Or so it may seem. In fact, Baudrillard sets a standpoint not unlike that of the Foucault who commented on Bataille and Klossowski, against the Foucault who theorizes power. Baudrillard's central charge is that "power is dead" – which he deduces from Foucault's talking so much about it (Baudrillard 1987, 11). If power pervades social relations, how can a place from which it be truthfully commented upon exist? Baudrillard passes quickly over this analytic argument, which is used by both Habermas and Taylor, to assert that the rhetoric and structure of Foucault's own writings on power mimic the fluidity, the entwinements that he finds in his subject. For Baudrillard, Foucault writes so much about power, imagines it so effectively, internalizes it in his style because he *wants* to believe in its reality. That is, he still wants to believe in what Baudrillard calls "irreversibility" – in history as a sequence of events and inscriptions, in productivity and, finally, in the reality of reality itself. It is this that Baudrillard questions. He regards Klossowskian simulacra, the "irreal" to be fundamental to and in (post)-modernity. The irreal world is internally driven not by power but by "seduction," a word which names that "by which everything wants to be exchanged, reversed or abolished in a cycle" (44). At the boundary of seduction awaits the "challenge" directed at the irreal by those who are truly oppressed but with whom the seduced world can have no dialogue and who thus simply demands "an immediate response or death" (56).

So Baudrillard pictures a epochal melodrama, a conflict between seduction and power, between the irreal and the real, between (imaginary) forces of production, resistance and life and (fundamental) drives to death and metamorphosis. Ultimately Baudrillard is writing as a prophet, rather like D. H. Lawrence in his pamphlets or Freud in sections of *Civilization and its Discontents*. Thus to raise logical quibbles against him seems slightly maladroit. What does it matter that Baudrillard's thesis of the "end" of the real, of history, and of power, grants "seduction" with the very analytic force and historical dominance that he supposes it to destroy. Perhaps it is more useful to note that his work in this instance is underdeveloped in comparison to Foucault's. Baudrillard wishes to individuate and describe relations between the primal forces that he believes to be constitutive of the contemporary social field. In order to do this effectively, however, he needs to provide such forces with historical sites: at least Foucault offers concrete examples of how his power operates in his histories of modern punishment and sexuality. But seduction has no social site, no agents – not even the marketing industry. It is a kind of "spirit of the age." Baudrillard's failure either to specify the level of his analysis, or to offer the detailed histories that his analysis requires, is connected to a political difficulty in his dualistic thesis. A world divided between seduction and challenge is a world conceived of in terms of a simple presence/absence opposition. In fact, the so called "First World," that domain of consumption and the media, is constantly challenged by those it marginalizes and de-realizes, some of whom – philosophers and historians, for instance – themselves belong to the First World. In reverse, "outsiders" themselves are habitually "seduced" by the commodities, images and circulation flows of modern production. To be seduced and oppressed are very far from exclusive conditions. Thus exchanges between those inside and outside the First World undo any global thesis of the triumph of irreality. To take a very obvious instance, First World liberal protests against imperialism may be more or less complicit with imperialism, but, at the same time, apartheid is slowly defeated by appealing to "enlightened" values at least somewhat *against* the economic interests of the West. To concede such folds and transactions is to return to a world of localized power struggles, it is to return to power more like Foucault's power, a history more like Foucault's history.

In the following two chapters I turn to Foucault's power and history at a rather more specific level. In chapter 6 I deal with his concept of the docile society, and in chapter 7, with his history of sexuality and ethics.

6

DISCIPLINE

Foucault claimed that his account of power relied on an intricate methodological scaffolding which he called an "analytics of power." This "analytics" classifies the field of power-events according to five criteria. First, it concentrates on "systems of differentiation," namely, classifications and exclusions between groups, even where these are not normally understood in terms of power-relations – an example would be the relation between primary and secondary school teachers or students. Second, it enquires into power's objectives – though it does not assume that the effects of an act of power are identical to the intentions behind it. Third, the analytics of power analyzes power's means – whether arms, words, administrative routines and so on. Fourth, it examines power's mode of institutionalization, that is to say the zones in which a certain operation of, or resistance to, power is played out – whether literal spaces (prisons or barracks, say) or institutional spaces (for instance, the family or the legal system.) Finally, the analytics of power is concerned with power's techniques and degrees of rationalization: the strategies by which its objectives are brought closer to its means in particular situations.[1] Foucault does not use this analytic of power mechanically, and one could certainly read *Discipline and Punish* with little awareness of it. But it did help him make a large historical division between modes of power. He distinguished modern power from sovereign or juridical-discursive power, though, as we shall see, it would be wrong to think that, for him, modern power ever totally replaces sovereign power. And the analytics also helped him break modern power down into closely interconnected kinds: disciplinary power, bio-power, pastoral power. In this chapter I will briefly describe disciplinary power, with particular reference to the British context. In chapter 7, I will describe the other forms of modern power.

Most generally, for Foucault, sovereign power is possessed by a presence at the centre of society and filters downward. This is expressed most fully in the "King's two bodies" thesis by which the King was supposed to have both an actual and a symbolic body, the latter in attendance at state and juridical occasions.[2] Behind the presence of the king stood (as it were)

God himself. The closer a person is to that centre the greater degree of individuality granted to him or her. Furthermore, the network of power exhausts itself to the degree that one moves further from the presence of the sovereign. In particular, those whom E. J. Hobsbawn called "social bandits" (and who were to become what Henry Mayhew called "urban nomads") lived outside the reach of sovereign power.[3] Under sovereignty, legitimate power is a possession, a thing that one has or does not have. Such power is not directed towards the control of individual lives, it is more directed towards specific acts which have a public – indeed, a cosmic – significance. It works within a framework for which individuals were differentiated from one another by external marks of filiatively inherited status, but which, at least most of the time, operated with widespread consent. The sovereign's aura could be disseminated peacefully and seductively into what might be called the social imagination in events such as court masques or festivities associated with the court's "progress" – its movement around the country. In certain events, however, like hanging, drawing and quartering, the effects of sovereign power were displayed in cruel quasi-theatrical spectacles, intelligible as acts of a centralized power. *Discipline and Punish* begins, like Dickens' *A Tale of Two Cities*, by describing the execution of Damien the would-be regicide, and that scene for both Foucault and Dickens stands as an emblem of the ultimate means by which feudal and absolutist society organized itself. Imaging itself in clearly demarcated and ceremonial public spaces, sovereign power has a never too deeply hidden capacity to torture and kill. To take the case of criminal punishment, in the *ancien régime*, "the sentence had to be legible for all" (1977b, 43). At the moment of death, an *amende honorable* was expected – a full and true confession: "those last moments when the guilty man has nothing to lose are won for the full light of truth" as Foucault puts it (ibid.). Here, "punishment is only the law overstepped, irritated, beside itself" as he wrote in his essay on Blanchot (1987a, 35).

Up until the eighteenth century, as Douglas Hay has argued, the law also relied on less open forms of symbolic power: its secrecy and "irrationalities" were part of its mystique (Hay 1975). Perhaps it was most obviously arbitrary in the way that crimes were only selectively recorded, detected and punished, especially in the cities. It is, however, easy to overemphasize the "irrationality" of sovereign power and its reliance on symbolism – as Foucault, I think, does. For instance, *lettres de cachet* were used by the French state as a means of prosecution; they were generally solicited by neighbours or relations who wished to have an "offender" imprisoned. The King, who signed them, was supposed to hold a juridical inquiry into the case before the signing. In the United Kingdom, there was also a long tradition of the rules of equity, which were intended to counteract injustices perpetuated in common or customary law by appealing to "natural justice," and often worked in the interests of women and

148

children. Equity was administered by the sovereign and his representative, the Chancellor (called the Keeper of the Royal Conscience) in the Court of Chancery. In both the French and English cases, sovereign power works outside the glare of the spectacle with a certain dialogicity and rationality.

In more general terms, for sovereignty, the possession of power is regarded as a right, that is what Foucault means when he calls it juridical-discursive. As a right, power takes the form of a law that must be stated and ceases either to express itself in a spectacle or to use secrecy and arbitrariness to produce anxiety and submission. Foucault argues that the notion that the sovereign had rights that subjects were legally obliged to obey masked the brute fact of domination, though it also defined the area of the subjects' freedom. A juridical concept of power, in which legal obligations and sovereign rights were intertwined, legitimized state administration. However, he notes that, during the seventeenth century, the view that power is a sovereign's right was inverted. Sovereign rights were transformed into so-called "natural rights," considered to be derived from a pre-historical, social contract in which subjects gave up their liberties so as to establish social order. Under this dispensation, oppression can be recognized – it exists whenever sovereignty breaks the primordial contract. This contractual notion of power can then be turned against autocracy to argue liberty's case. But, according to Foucault, this classic liberal view has a hidden function: it masks the emerging, non-juridical function of power.[4]

At one level, Foucault's vision of pre-modern power and its relation to modern power is not especially unusual. Dickens, who articulated certain popular beliefs in these matters, anticipates its imagery as does Victor Hugo, a writer whom Foucault himself cites. The warning against reading the fall of absolutism as simply progressive, together with the insistence that modern power is invisible, is also outlined, for instance, in Gramsci's notion of the shift from rule to hegemony, itself an inversion of theses established by anti-Benthamite Victorian political theorists such as Henry Maine, who thought of modernization as a move from status to contract. Gramsci too argues that, in modernity, power is separated from the machinery of the law and politics and is thus less easy to grasp and combat. In fact, Foucault's thesis is most original in its detailed classification of modern power. Yet to say this is to sidestep a crucial ambiguity: in his writing it is not always clear what is supposed to be true of power as such, and what is true of modern power in particular – here again the historico-ontological gap wreaks its effects. This ambiguity is partially concealed because his theory of modern power is constructed less on its own terms than *against* other theories of power. We have already seen how Foucault defines his metaphysical or abstract notion of power by distinguishing it from other such notions, and the same is true of his sociological account of power – despite the classificatory system that he devised to analyze it.

Unlike the marxists, for instance, Foucault does not consider that power primarily supports the economic structure that, in turn, maintains the dominance of a particular class. Foucault's thesis also opposes the most common view of modernity, for which sovereignty was replaced by liberalism. Liberal theorists suppose that modern society can, uniquely, tolerate both economic adventurism and quite marked differences of political points of view. Conflicting interests are contained within a total socio-economic system, kept in order, autonomously and without reference to individual or collective intentions, by, on the one hand, the market as organized by an invisible hand (a self-regulating mechanism of supply and demand) and, on the other, by national, democratic political institutions in which all interests are represented. For liberals, power is what is required to maintain the system, to keep it going. It is not required to change hearts or minds, let alone to demand signs of fealty and protect social hierarchies. For them, it ought to be visible only when the continuity of the socio-political order is threatened in so-called "crises." By contrast, Foucault would regard liberalism as itself a form of modern power. Liberal tolerance, which encourages the other to speak and involves a certain licence, actually extends power. The proliferation of beliefs, feelings and identities under a tolerant regime increases the number of entities that can enter power transactions.

Finally, Foucault's account of modern power is far removed from that aesthetic discourse in which power was declared to be an ontological basis of the world, that is, in meditations on the sublime. The sublime is a category that reaches deep into aesthetic thought especially after Kant and Schiller. The first modern theorist of the sublime, Edmund Burke, writes: "I know of nothing sublime which is not some modification of power. And this branch . . . rises from terror, the common stock of every thing that is sublime" (Burke 1958, 64). Burke links power psychologically to pain and submission, that "terror" which accompanies both the sovereign and God, who is not "an object of the understanding": kings, he reminds us, are often called "dread majesty." For Burke, sublime power is experienced where human finitude and integrity confront the destructive, the infinite. One could read Burke's description of universal power as hinging sovereign to modern power. For instance, one might argue that, at the level of a political unconscious, he is allegorizing the way that the state, reacting to the revolutionary desire, will hollow out sovereign power, placing in its empty shell increasingly extensive forms of surveillance and subjection. In Burke's lifetime the political sublime, the imposition of a huge and unrespresentable state apparatus, is in fact to be found less in the guillotine than in Wellington's spies and the stirrings of what was called "philosophical" reform, such as Howard's crusades on prison conditions. However, to regard Burke's early account of sublime power as a political allegory cannot displace the more conventional view that his work is a moment in a process of secularization for which the sublime becomes an aesthetic problem (how to represent the unrepresentable?) rather than a religious and political prop.

So Foucault argues that marxist, liberal and aesthetic theories of power prevent recognition of the true nature of modern power, which, had it been recognized, would have spread less effectively and rapidly. (This argument must be tempered in Britain where, of course, the "philosophical radicals" were the object of massive resistance, both political and cultural.) For Foucault, only an analytics of power can, as it were, present modern power for display, but what it presents is not a unified force working in one direction – even to the degree that sovereign power is a unified and unidirectional force – but rather a set of interconnected strategies each with its own, not fully controlled, feed-back mechanisms. Of the various classes of modern power, each intertwined with the other in terms of aims and effects, let us treat discipline first because Foucault believes that it was the earliest modality to appear.

Disciplinary power works in quite strictly delimited spaces, though its pathways and mazes spread across the social totality, unlike sovereign power which is centralized and evaporates at the margins. It is deritualized and privatized, working on individuals as individuals rather than either as members of castes or as markers of a wider cosmic or social order. Its object is behaviour and the individual body; its tools are surveillance, examinations, training, and its sites, factories, prisons, schools, hospitals. In general, it is directed towards narrowing the gaps both between discursive practices and techniques of production, and between formal regulations and social practices. Again Foucault provides a little narrative of its emergence, one which owes much to his early work on madness. When forms of control by exclusion (in the classical epoch, applied most prominently to lepers but also to the mad) are merged with those forms of control by surveillance that were applied to plague victims (the collection of data, limitations on travel) – then, from the late seventeenth century on, what emerges is disciplinary power. For him, behind the impulse to discipline lies the "haunting memory of 'contagions' of the plague, of rebellions, crimes, vagabondage, desertions, people who appear and disappear, live and die in disorder" (1977b, 198). Disciplinary power brings the "nomads" and "mobs" into order.

If we depart a little from Foucault's own histories, and think more specifically, and in a little more detail, of the British case, we can say that, in Britain, the first stirrings of this kind of power do not occur in explicit resistance to sovereign power, but rather in order to correct sovereignty's failure to adapt to the conditions of urban life and to enforce the conditions needed for the expansion of a capitalist economy – a failure exacerbated by the fall of the absolutist monarchy in 1688. In the last decade of the seventeenth century, groups such as the "Society for the Reformation of

Manners" set out to control such "immoralities" as adultery (which was no longer being prosecuted), prostitution, gambling, swearing, rowdy public entertainments and drunkenness.[5] These groups established a form of policing: they encouraged informers to come forward and initiated prosecutions themselves. But for sympathisers like Henry Fielding, the "reformation of manners" required an ensemble of tactics – including education, satire and journalism – of which law enforcement was only one. By the late eighteenth century, the voluntary societies had been largely absorbed by the Evangelical movement which established a set of new groups, the most active of which was the "Society for the Suppression of Vice and the Encouragement of Religion and Virtue." Their activities included the prosecution both of radical, Paineite journalism and of literature deemed corrupting, most famously Matthew Lewis's Gothic masterpiece, *The Monk*, as well as attempts to control gambling, drinking, swearing and prostitution. The most important early advocate of organized policing and penal reform, Patrick Colquhoun, who was also a professional magistrate, belonged to this movement. Around 1800, it was Colquhoun who championed what he called the "new science" of policing in Britain, borrowing the notion from the French (Colquhoun 1806, 1). In his *Treatise on the Police of the Metropolis* (1796), he spelled out the central presuppositions of this new science. They were, first, that the state had a continuous peace-time role to play in preventing disorder in civil society; second, that crime could be controlled without the eradication of poverty; third, that policing should be separated from sentencing, and, last, that *all* offences could be punished if an efficient enough policing mechanism were put it place. None of these ideas were uncontentious. They were seen to threaten the fundamental liberties of the "free-born Englishman," both by Radicals like Francis Place and Tories like Robert Southey. But in Colquhoun's writings we find early flickerings of those forms of knowledge and policy-advice that would produce the later disciplinary apparatuses in Britain.

Ultimately, disciplinary power works on bodies, which Foucault (following Nietzsche) primarily thinks of as socially malleable substances, rather than (as Freud did) as partly pre-programmed. Disciplinary power is "centred on the body as a machine; its disciplining, the optimization of its capabilities, the extortion of its forces, the parallel increase of its usefulness and its docility, its integration into systems of efficient and economic controls, all this was ensured by the procedures of power that characterized the *disciplines*: an *anatomo-politics of the human body*" (1980c, 139; italics his).[6] The pun on "disciplines" in that sentence points to the way in which practices on the body combine with the disciplined production of knowledge about the "human" in the human sciences. The various methods and paradigms which order those sciences – norms, conflicts, systems, but especially norms – are developed both on disciplined bodies (the psychiatric patient, the prisoner, the policed, and most important, the pupil of the disciplined mass school systems), and on the population considered as a productive resource. In a loop mechanism, these methods and paradigms produce social norms and stereotypes that strengthen discipline and increase production: "The power of the Norm appears through the disciplines" (1977b, 184). The norm – that which society disciplines people to be – is sheltered beneath the normal – a condition of existence. To take one instance, from the early nineteenth century on statistics provided tools to construct an order in which norms were transformed into the normal: in particular, the "normal curve," which, late in the century, asserts that an average or normal I.Q. is 100, is a mathematical construct that becomes a social reality and an administrative tool, when I.Q. tests begin to be used to create hierarchies of educational and career opportunities late in the century. In general terms, Foucault argues that such binding of power on knowledge "transforms human beings into subjects" (1983c, 208). What is a subject? We can cite Foucault directly in answer. "There are two meanings of the word 'subject': subject to someone else by control and dependence, and tied to one's own identity by a conscience or self-knowledge" (ibid., 212). This division is complicated by the very fact that since the late nineteenth century at least, self-knowledge has been articulated in language moulded by the human sciences – whether in a psychological discursive practice based on notions like "intelligence" or a popular post-psychoanalytic lexicon ("psycho-babble") or a fully fledged sociological knowledge which links selves to "sub-cultures" or class, and conceives of "society" as an autonomous agency. In such discourses, social control cannot be pulled apart from self-identity. And – on a different front – those individuals with most cultural capital are also the most subjected, the most addicted to their own selves.

Although disciplinary power infiltrates and shapes most modern institutions, Foucault developed his account of it in his work on what he called "penality," a word which covers both the development of imprisonment as the prime form of punishment, and modern policing focused on the criminal. Previously the terms "police," "preventative police" or "public police" included any officer of the state whose business it was to manage disorder – whether medical or social. Foucault's analysis is mounted "from below": he cites Hugo's epigram that crime is "a *coup d'état* from below," that is, it is, or can be, a political act (Foucault 1974a, 161). Hugo is rewriting, from the perspective of the transgressor, Hobbes's contention that a crime is directed against the sovereignty of the state. Certainly the distinction that left/liberal historians of social control like E. P. Thompson draw between "victimless" crimes of protest against the state (smuggling, poaching) and "real" crimes, like rape and assault, are of little interest to Foucault. *Discipline and Punish* and related essays and interviews work on a different track: they argue that from the eighteenth century on, laws are directed less at "mass crimes" such as vagrancy and begging than at

153

"marginal crimes" which can be ascribed to professional criminals. Before the early nineteenth century, in England at least, pursuance and persecution of most criminal acts was the responsibility of four separate groups: private individuals; associations like the early Societies for the Reformation of Manners; "police" hired by commercial interests; and, last, more or less professional thief-takers – who were often criminals themselves, and lived on the rewards for giving information about crimes. Up until the establishment of modern policing, the state itself took no responsiblity for prosecution: indeed early state policing owed much to techniques developed by both the thief-takers and the more respectable reforming societies. These new techniques of law enforcement came into existence in ordeal to deal with planned and entrepreneurial crime rather than, for instance, vagrancy and begging. As Foucault notes, from the late seventeenth century on, fraud and property theft become of more legal and penal interest than crimes of "blood" (primarily murder, infanticide and rape).[7]

It is important to note that Foucault neglects the legal system in his account of modern power because it remains an area in which formal rights are clearly demarcated. But the law too becomes increasingly rationalized and secularized over this period. This process is most dramatic in France where a national and written "Civil Code" is produced under Napoleon. In the United Kingdom, "common law" is given great value precisely against both the French example and the Benthamite championing of "positive law." Nonetheless, to take two specific English instances, Chancery Court is rationalized in 1852, and by 1873 – the year of the Judicature Act – the old order, in which different legal traditions (ecclesiastic law, equity and common law) each had their own courts, had disappeared. Second, the law became increasingly independent of the doctrines and institutions of the Established Church: the controversy over the 1857 Matrimonial Causes Act – the Divorce Act – involves this aspect of its passage rather than any other, as it provided no principles for divorce other than those that had been established by private Acts of Parliament for almost two centuries. Lawyers themselves became increasingly powerful and professionalized following the establishment in 1825 of the Law Society, so that the proportion of crimes that came under their jurisdiction – as against that of the old amateur Justices of the Peace – increased (Perkin 1972, 254–5). Again these transformations excited fierce resistances (one thinks of Dickens' magistrate, Mr Fang, in *Oliver Twist*), and, therefore, continuing demand for reform.

As to punishment: Foucault notes that theorists like Cesare Beccaria, and later Patrick Colquhoun and Jeremy Bentham, begin to insist that the gravity of the punishment ought to be proportionate to the crime. Penal reformers like John Howard agitate against punishments which work on the body either as a site of sensation or symbolically (for instance, the cutting out of the tongue for blasphemy) in favour of those which work on the body as the home of that discursive object, the "soul." Also, it began to be argued that punishment should be hidden from the public gaze. As early as 1751, in his *Enquiry into the Causes of the Unfortunate Late Increase of Robbers*, Henry Fielding had argued for the abolition of public executions. For him, punishment was a private affair and a social necessity, rather than the sign of the relation between sovereign and subject. Such arguments were strengthed by the fact that public executions themselves often caused riots against the authorities, the crowd sometimes taking the side of the offender, and, indeed, were occasions for an orgy of pickpocketing. In Britain a sustained campaign was also mounted against the number of offences – well over 200, many of them trivial crimes of property – that were subject to capital punishment.[8] But, as Foucault was the first to point out, most importantly, though most abstractly, punishments were less and less aimed at acts – the crime – and more and more aimed at the subject who commits the act – the criminal. Under these pressures, people who break the law gradually became not so much "sinners," nor, as an often used melodramatic language would have it, "monsters" or "beasts," and even less ordinary people who have committed illegal acts, but essentially pathological, delinquents or *criminals*. In the mid-nineteenth century, the human sciences will develop a sub-branch, criminology (first called "criminal anthropology"), to study this new object and its preconditions. Its topic is the criminal and his/her body, heredity, psychopathology and environment. Criminology's aim is to show how genetic, evolutionary, sociological pathologies and failures produce this being, the criminal, so that crime can be better controlled.

Thus, for Foucault, the history of penal punishment passes through three main stages (which echo the history of madness): punishment as spectacle (death in public places, branding, pillorying and so on), humane punishment, which aimed to recuperate the criminal; and last, normalizing punishment, which accepted the existence of crime in the society, if only under the sign of pathology. Both humane and normalizing punishment characteristically work through a particular and *new* apparatus – the prison or, as it came to be called, the penitentiary. For this is not the old prison of the absolutist monarchies in which families often lived, which were themselves commercial enterprises and were certainly not secure from break-outs in the modern sense. The old prisons remained closely attached to the economy of the outside world, prisoners having to pay for goods and services: the more you paid, the better room and service you received. In them, sentenced criminal offenders (of whom there were relatively few because prison was a rare form of punishment) were restrained by chains rather than bars and walls. The "hulks" which were also used as prisons, and which became chronically overcrowded during the war with America when transportation temporarily ceased, were even more disordered, insecure and infested with contagious disease. And there was another image of the old prison – very different from that depicted in Gay's *The Beggar's Opera*, for instance. One finds it in Sterne's mention of the Bastille in *A Sentimental Journey*, or more forcefully in Piranesi's imaginary designs collected in his book of engravings *Prisons*. In these baroque buildings, whose scale has nothing to do with the individual body, people can rot and die forgotten – the key having been, as prisoners still say, thrown away. During the nineteenth century imprisonment becomes a more focused form of punishment, and, in Britain, by its end it is no longer used for debtors at all. Prisons are gradually removed from private hands; by 1877 the state takes full responsibility for them. A particular kind of architecture is developed for penitentiaries.[9] But, for Foucault, it is Jeremy Bentham's Panopticon (1791) which stands as the type of modern penality. Bentham himself took the idea of the Panopticon from his brother Samuel, who invented it – a circular building with cells built at its circumference – for Catherine the Great. Jeremy thought of it as a machine for increasing productivity and managing moral reform in a variety of contexts, at least at first, attempting to market it like any other entrepeneurial project.

The Panopticon was a building that made no concession to tradition or to its surroundings: its design shares the fascination with circular forms, and the lack of interest in ornamental façades, characteristic of contemporary French architects like Boullée and Ledoux. When it was used as a prison, its unique and revolutionary feature was not that inmates were to be isolated in their cells (all the more opportunity for self-inspection, individuation and remorse); condemned to hard and productive labour (the treadmill is invented as a form of punishment in the 1810s, the same decade that saw the last of the pillory); deprived of their civilian clothing, and subject to a system of rewards for good behaviour, but that they could be viewed at all times by a guard at the centre of the circle whom they could not see – hence *panopticon*. All their acts came under official regulation and inspection. The guard, living with his family, could in turn be inspected by the general public, who now become the ultimate agent of invigilation and judgement, replacing the "dread sovereign" who, present or not, had both stage-managed spectacular punishment, and underwritten access to legal rights. In this structure, everybody is exposed to light and sight; nobody exists outside inspection. Also, nobody can see themselves or anybody of their own status – in that sense, there are no mirrors. Because the viewed cannot see the viewer it is as if the invigilating eye has been disjointed from any bodily eye: the guard "sees" whether he is present or not. And, though Foucault does not explicitly say so, the "invilating" apparatus extends beyond the prison into the public sphere through the media. During the nineteenth century, more and more activity – sexual, commercial, legal – becomes accessible to the press. If the public could not literally inspect the prisons, then the press, as their "representative," could, at least at strictly prescribed times. It would be a mistake to reduce the role of the press to that of a simple adjunct to disciplinary power, yet it is worth noting that where it was most inspectorial it was also most normalizing. Thus, it was Henry Labouchère, the proprietor of the path-breaking, "muck-raking" journal *Truth* – which uncovered a series of commerical scandals during the 1880s – who, as a member of parliament, sponsored the 1885 Bill that outlawed sexual acitivity between men.

Bentham (who was himself no mean journalist and a proponent of the press's power to bring corruption to light) believed that his architectural machine, the model of a new form of power, could be used to organize schools, barracks, factories, reformatories and so on, though, in fact, it was only exploited for prisons proper. He promulgated the Panopticon to most effect against transportation – which was a common form of non-capital punishment until the 1850s, when it was stopped in New South Wales and Van Diemen's Land (Tasmania) partly because of protest from the increasingly "respectable" colonies, partly because it was seen as too lenient a form of punishment and partly because imprisonment had become increasingly more efficient. Bentham's most famous pamphlet on his invention was called *The Panopticon or New South Wales*. To ship offenders to New South Wales, Bentham argued, neither fitted punishment to crime nor offered opportunity for moral reform. Indeed, he believed, it merely reproduced the conditions of militarism, sovereignty and enslavement which were the worst features of an unenlightened age. But few actual panopticons were built, largely because they were expensive – and in none, I think, were prison officials exposed to public inspection. The first penitentiary constructed along reformist lines in England, Pentonville (1842) sparked intense public protest and was considered a failure because of its cost and inhumanity; and as the century went on restrictions on communication between prisoners, work-hours, use of proper names, reading material etc, relaxed. Yet, even though the "humane" penalty that legitimized the Panopticon was itself "reformed," and was gradually replaced by the practices and discourses of "normalization" and "rehabilitation" (which themselves have been continuously contested), imprisonment has remained the principal punishment of serious felonies.

As the prison became the "natural" form of punishment, policing became – to use a non-Foucauldian term – increasingly "bureaucratically rational." In the United Kingdom, for instance, a series of Acts of Parliament during the first half of the nineteenth century set a centralized police force in place alongside the increasingly professional, respectable and powerful lawyers. The 1829 Metropolitan Police Act established, in London, the first police force paid for, and administered, by the state. They were called "Peelers," and were administered by magistrates under Home Office control. Further acts in 1839 and 1856 extend such policing to the counties – against much resistance. The consequences of drawing together the arms of modern penality – policing, imprisonment and a professionalized legal system – have an unexpected consequence: a criminal sub-culture develops with its own economy and lingo ("canting"), centred around the prison system. During the first decades of the nineteenth century, this sub-culture enters the popular imaginary in lurid images of so-called "flash-houses" – labyrinthine, urban dens inhabited by those who live outside the law, weird mirror-images, in fact, of the unreformed prisons. As Foucault points out, transactions between criminals and the professions that deal with them, enables the policing/prison apparatus to reproduce itself in a circle: the apparatuses that "reform" criminals are also the apparatuses that make criminals. Throughout the twentieth century, the prison system becomes increasingly flexible in an attempt to break this circle: it separates first offenders from recidivists, it provides different kinds of prisons, not just for different kinds of delinquents but also for different kinds of "security risk" – risk decreasing as the sentence comes closer to ending; a number of more specialized penal institutions are developed – borstals, so-called "open prisons" – and, from the other side, disciplinary techniques borrowed from the military are used in "short, sharp shock" sentences, especially for young, previously non-institutionalized, offenders. But the increasing flexibility of the system fails to break the circle: recidivism remains high. Indeed the system's capacity to institutionalize its subjects increases by virtue of its capacity to classify them, to cater for a variety of needs and wants. As disciplinary techniques infiltrate orphanages, workhouses, schools, a large young population is prepared for imprisonment. Here the prison "reforms" those who have been moulded into institutionalized subjects by the techniques of penality themselves.

Although the corruption of the "thief-takers" of the era before state police was one of the reasons for the creation of professional police "establishments," in fact the division between police and criminal continued to be problematic. The police, even criminal lawyers, share the delinquent's world. Nonetheless, Foucault argues, in the nineteenth century, a criminal sub-culture acquired an important social role: it helped bourgeoisify the worker. By excluding the criminal from normalcy, by establishing a whole social sector outside the law, the "respectable" working class could be placed, discursively, on the side of the property-owning classes as against that of the "social bandit." Literature is important to this strategy, just as the strategy is important to literature. The novel, in particular, helps consolidate the difference between criminality and non-criminality, while it also took advantage of the difference's residual and circular unsustainability. The novel could play this dual role because, on the one side, it was a moral genre, an instrument of social control, while, on the other, it remained an entertainment, designed for domestic, private amusement and, in principle at least, dissociated from the public sphere in which disciplinary "reform" operated. There was a further complicating factor in the relation between the novel and penality because nineteenth-century prose fiction about crime also inherits a tradition in which law-breaking was represented for quite specific ends, of which we can briefly take note of the three most successful. First, Defoe's *Moll Flanders*, a classic early eighteenth-century representation of criminality. The novel is narrated in the first person: Moll, narrator and character, is not *essentially* criminal; she is merely an example of a failure of class hierarchies; her "illegalities" (as Foucault would say, discriminating between these and the modern "crime" committed by delinquents or "criminals") are signs of an excess of social and entrepreneurial desire, which sometimes she is able to interpret as the work of the devil. She tries hard to excuse her less serious transgressions by applying the casuistry that was published in the advice columns of contemporary journals like John Dunton's *Athenian Mercury*. Against this, second, the eponymous hero of Fielding's *Jonathan Wild* is "naturally" bad, an unchristian and fallen man: Wild being the most notorious thief-taker of his time. But, for Fielding, his career is also an allegory of that of the Prime Minister, Sir Robert Walpole. Finally, illegal acts could be seen as the natural outcome of poverty: in John Gay's *Polly*, for instance, the sequel to *The Beggar's Opera*, a fundamentally "good" woman joins a gallant, criminal band, out of love – and also because she possesses too little, rather than, like Moll, desires too much. This adds something to *The Beggar's Opera*'s message that the difference between law-abiding and outcast "gentlemen" is more illusory than real, and provided an example for any number of novels of the 1780s and 1790s in which idealistic and progressive young men find themselves on the wrong side of the law – Thomas Holcroft's *Hugh Trevor*, discussed in chapter 3, being one. Walpole passed his 1737 Licensing Act to control those theatrical performances which established analogies between the authorities and bandits. However, this Act, which underpinned censorship for over a century, was not effective against the novel, purchased, as it was, in the market and read in private.

After the Napoleonic wars, relations between criminality and literature became more complex – and have yet to be fully attended to by scholarship. Let us say, cursorily enough, that the so-called Newgate novels written in the 1820s and 1830s by writers like Edward Bulwer Lytton and Harrison Ainsworth do, to some degree, repeat plots set in place by Gay and the radicals of the last decades of the eighteenth century and even by liberal texts, sympathetic to bandits, like Schiller's *The Robbers*. Their purposes were very different though. Lytton's early novels, in particular, were consciously writtem as part of the moment for penal reform: they insisted that criminals were not fundamentally "other" and thus were open to rehabilitation by humane punishment. In Lytton's very successful *Paul Clifford* (1830) the hero is a dandy who, in his gallows speech, protests against social injustice, and regards his life outside the law as his best chance for freedom in a restrictive, finite society. But, and this is the important point, novels like this, which asserted the rationality of criminal acts and promulgated penal reform, also constrained the spread of revolutionary desire. They did so by a sustained refusal to write in realist registers, and by constructing romantic, "Byronic" criminal characters, whose poverty and powerlessness had little connection with the lives of the actual poor. More subtly, they did not permit the reader to identify with their characters – the characters' very romanticization prevents readerly identification. So do obvious breaks with verisimilitude – like the "received" idiolect in which the criminal hero (or for that matter Oliver Twist) speaks. In their distance from the social world of the poor these novels were also very remote from – and hence marginalized – the sympathetic and non-respectable narratives and ballads about famous law-breakers (such as the Ned Kelly ballads in Australia) that circulated, more or less informally, around Robin Hood type criminals. Finally, in terms of readerly expectations and writerly techniques established by Walter Scott and Jane Austen, the Newgate novels seem thin, careless – and were attacked as such in journals like the conservative *Fraser's Magazine*. As these novels transformed revolutionary desire into a will to discipline, and came under fire from traditionalist critics, a new cultural domain – the liberal "middlebrow" – began to emerge.

Dickens, who was sometimes linked with Lytton and Ainsworth, and who was certainly fascinated by crime, escapes this thinness, even in an early text like *Oliver Twist* where he is closest to the Newgate novel. He does so because he is unable either to represent any kind of revolutionary will affirmatively, or to imagine any outside to the hegemonic social formations. Unlike Lytton, he creates characters designed to engage the reader's sympathy, but, as in *Olver Twist*, such characters are products of social institutions: they are bounded and limited rather than Byronically "free." The consequences are unexpected: in *Oliver Twist*, as D. A. Miller has shown, Oliver moves fron one institution to another with extraordinary ease – from workhouse, to family, to "flash-house," back to the family and so on; in doing so he becomes an empty signifier who merely demonstrates the proliferation of such institutions (Miller 1988, 5–6). Dickens invests his intense linguistic energy into characters who cannot move through institutions or cultural zones, and thus cannot be "reformed" – like Mr Fang, Bill Sykes, Fagin, even the Artful Dodger. The outpouring of invention on characters who are both static (in this precise sense) and embody institutions, marks the entry of a more advanced stage of disciplinarity – that in which, after the 1850s, "normalizing" punishment begins to replace "humane" punishment.

Other novelists attacked the Newgate novel more directly for its reformist and pseudo-revolutionary bias, Thackeray's *Catherine* (1839), a satire of the genre published in *Fraser's*, being an instance much discussed at the time. Here criminals are, as they had been in Fielding's *Jonathan Wild*, simply greedy and callous, though they lack allegorial significance. After about 1850, however, those who break the law are trapped in their bestiality, even in Lytton's and Ainsworth writings. And late in his career Dickens directly rewrites the Newgate novel: Compeyson in *Great Expectations* (1860–1), for instance, is an inverted Paul Clifford: a gentleman-criminal whose criminality seems a motiveless will to do harm. Compeyson's more sympathetic alter ago, Magwitch, is also unable to "reform," to escape the desire to be different from what he is, which has become for Dickens, as it had been in *Moll Flanders*, the mark of the law-breaker. Non-realist genres, centred on the "villain," enter the market as it becomes impossible to construct characters with whom the reader may identify but whose drives take them beyond the law. Such genres – melodrama and the "sensation novel" (a term first used in the 1860s) – have little cultural value, being scorned by those for whom the novel was primarily an ethical form. But they create difficulties for "serious" writers like George Eliot – because nineteenth-century ethical and psychological novels avoid the sensational *within* progressive plots that require most characters to *fail* to reach full empathy, "humaness" and "normality." This failure is necessary for reformist novels so that they can point to a future more fully achieved than the present. A heroine like Gwendolen in *Daniel Deronda* (1876), who is presented through the full armoury of "realist" techniques and given "deep" subjectivity, is nonetheless driven by hidden, murderous sensationalist impulses. Her criminal aggression is directed towards the social order that constrains her, at the same time as it is the sign of a hidden, "motiveless" taint, that only remorse and solitude – a form of imprisonment – can remove. Thus penality's circularity organizes, at some remove, these deeply disturbing texts: their sensationalism is required for them to produce "better selves" in their readers, just as, in the wider society, the very system designed to rehabilitate offenders, criminalizes them. It is important to remember, too, that the literary critical pedagogy of what I have called the "cultural hygiene" movements came partly to be grounded on these texts, and invested them with immense value. This indicates that such pedagogy contains internal blockages too – a point I shall take up in chapter 8.

Penality also relies on non-literary representations of criminals. At the beginning of modern policing, in the 1740s, Henry Fielding, in his role as advocate for a centralized London police "establishment" and magistrate, repeatedly insisted on the importance of handbills, gazettes and verbal descriptions of criminals in crime control. There is some continuity between these handbills, which provide information and publicity about law-breakers, and later crime literature. After the Newgate novel, literature and journalism helped provide that gallery of "types" – the mad woman who poisons her spouse, the professional criminal à la Bill Sykes, Fagin and so on – that criminologists, backed by the disciplinary apparatus, transformed into objects of biological and quasi-Darwinistic science from the 1860s on. It is this "biologizing" of Colquhoun's "new science," the notion that criminality has a biological basis, which distinguishes the second half of the nineteenth century. Not only does such science destroy any sense that criminals are fighting for their freedom, or sustaining themselves in poverty, it separates "criminality" from universal original sin. In this move too, discursive relations are complex and enfolded. For instance, one of Dickens' aims in *Great Expectations* is to detach the view that boys are born "bad fellows" (as Jaggers conventionally says) from the view that some individuals in particular are born to a life of crime and imprisonment. However, Dickens harbours an ambivalence which prevents him from dissociating a displaced Christian belief that we are all potential criminals – that, like Pip, we share a fundamental, fallible humanness – from his quasi-sensationalism, his flooding of static characters with linguistic energy. What both Dickens' humanitarianism and sensationalism stand against is the closed circuit of the "reformed" penal technology – as is most apparent in his attacks on the model prison, the Panopticon, Pentonville, in *David Copperfield*. Furthermore, this ambivalence by no means forecloses on criminal anthropology: one thinks of the eyes and hands, as well as a certain callousness, that Estella, in *Great Expectations*, inherits, genetically, from her murderess-mother.

From about 1870 on, naturalism attempts to cut through the complex interactions between the novel and penality, to detach itself from the circle of penality. The naturalist novel represents society as a totality by applying discursive techniques, at least in theory, borrowed from the social sciences. For Zola, novel-writing was a form of "experiment" and the novelist was a kind of social scientist who deduced plots from the laws by which lives and actions are determined by heredity and environment. No circuits of shared will or sympathy between characters, readers and narrator are possible. Yet the characters themselves, as unable to move through society as a Dickensian villain, retain traces of sensationalism and melodrama. Like Fagin, they embody external institutions. With an important difference: in naturalism, the old flash-house becomes the "slum." This extension and concretization of the domain of the "other," the transmutation of the sensational into naturalism, is enabled by the increasingly efficient processes of invigilation and information retrieval that lie behind the normalizing apparatuses – all those inspections of, and reports on, the urban poor by health agencies, journalists, charity organizations, photographers, urban planners and so on throughout the nineteenth century. The alliance between normalizing apparatus and the novel is not broken when, for the first time, novels are written from the point of view of the victims of such apparatuses – as in Jules Valles' *L'Enfant* (1885). Such texts are an outcome of "naturalism," and were read as naturalist, because they fulfil a demand for exact information about what lies beyond the repectable. Yet, however much they may protest against social conditions, however much they make it harder to maintain the biologist thesis that delinquency belongs to the body and its limits, they exist as data – especially if they are not written in received idiolects. In a further twist, to the degree that the objects of penality, the delinquents, write their own story as against being romanticized or sensationalized, they too enter the normalizing community, in the sense, at least, that they are knowable for it. In this situation the limits to the normal are increasingly sought from within – through forms of transgression confined to culture and the formal possibilities of the aesthetic. In a broad way, it is to this project that Foucault's early literary theoretical work belongs.

So far this account has omitted an important section of the relation between writing and crime. As Foucault notes, from the late eighteenth century, the bourgeoisie begin to produce their own actual criminal martyrs and heroes (Foucault 1980b, 46). Foucault cites Lacenaire (of *Les Enfants du Paradis* fame) as an example; in Britain, two cases – Dr Dodd and Thomas Wainewright – seem more apposite. The first, Dr Dodd, was presented more as a martyr than as a hero. According to Leon Radzinowicz, he was the first offender to excite bourgeois, as against popular, activism on his behalf. Dodd, a well-known clergyman allied to the "reformation of manners" movement, was convicted of forgery and sentenced to death in 1777. A man who spent more than he earned, Dodd had forged the signature of Philip Stanhope, Lord Chesterfield's illegitimate son and heir. Dr Johnson helped organize the widespread public protest against his sentence: Johnson was especially angry that a clergyman should be *publicly* executed, though, it is perhaps not irrelevant to note that he also had grudges against Chesterfield – who had refused to patronize his dictionary. Johnson wrote the preamble to a public petition which, according to Boswell, 20,000 people signed (Boswell 1980, 830). But what is crucial, once again, is the connection between crime and representation; here a writer takes the side of a criminal against the authorities in a tactic which helps secure the prestige of an intellectual through his ability to speak for others. In a rather tenuous way, Johnson is a figure in Foucault's own genealogy. His campaign for Dr Dodd founds strategies that Foucault was both to elaborate and to work against.

My second British example, Thomas Wainewright, is closer to Lacenaire. Wainewright committed his crimes, and became famous, during the 1820s – a very different moment in the history of delinquency. (His career was, in fact, fictionalized by Bulwer Lytton in *Lucretia*.) He was a poisoner and forger, though, like most poisoners during the nineteenth century, he was never convicted for murder – forensic medicine being insufficiently accurate to detect the crime. The failure of detection, and lack of violence in his case established him as the prototype of the criminal as dandy; for a while his cell became – like Lancenaire's – "a fashionable lounge" as Oscar

Wilde put it (Wilde 1922, 89). Wainewright was an artist and an art critic for *London Magazine*, and in his brilliant essay on him Wilde shows how Wainewright's facility, his simultaneous courtship of, and contempt for, the public, and his invention of that kind of journalism which "by continued reiteration" contrives "to make the public interested in his [the journalist's] own personality," form a piece with his own painting, art collection, "taste" and lack of concern for the lives of others (ibid.). So for him murder can become a fine art – to borrow from the title of an essay by Thomas de Quincey. When reprimanded for his lack of remorse for one of his crimes, Wainewright is said to have excused himself on the grounds that the victim had "thick ankles." Wilde's Wainewright "recognized that Life itself is an art, and has its modes of style no less than the arts that seek to express it" (Wilde 1922, 67), at the same time as he argued that there is no essential moral difference between his career and that of successful business men. In bringing these two points of view together, Wainewright bridges the era of Jonathan Wild (and his "illegalities"), Dr Dodd's ability to attract intellectuals to take his side, and Wilde's own high-cultural aestheticization of the life-world. He seems a very Foucauldian counter-hero. This aestheticization of crime may stand outside the processes by which offenders were criminalized, but it also passes over the life and suffering of crime's victims who were – and are – very often women. As Foucault points out, in detective fiction, which is grafted onto the "murder-as-fine-art" tradition at the point when convicting criminals became more a matter of finding and presenting evidence than of extracting confessions, the reader, the detective and the criminal form a bond sealed by the uncovering of a "mystery," in which, once again, the victim is of no account.

It is in Foucault's continued attempt to develop modes of analysis which avoid dividing victims from non-victims, the aesthetic from the lived, transgressions from convention, that he will develop both his ethics and his account of bio-power – as we shall see in the next chapter.

7

LIFE, SEXUALITY AND ETHICS

Unlike disciplinary power, bio-power is primarily directed at the life of the population. Both "life" and "population" are resonant terms for Foucault. "Population" is a notion which, early in the nineteenth century, begins to contest the more traditional terms of the "people" or the "mob"; while "life," of course, is the category at the foreground of the modern episteme. Bio-power is that aspect of modern power that is aimed at sustaining life throughout society: it organizes society so as to increase production; it cares for, and controls, the social body in the interest of health. It also responds to the generalized problems that followed its own success – that is, rapid population increase and the need for a healthy workforce able to service industrialized factories. The narrative of Chadwick's reforms and the debates over hygiene and death, given in chapter 3, tell part of the story of bio-power's extension. In general, bio-power's technology includes the gathering of social statistics; state investment in, and control over, drainage, burial and quarantine; inoculation; popular education against old folkloric medical beliefs; bureaucratic measures to improve the diet of children, and the medicalization of state administration through the appointment of Public Health Officers. It does not primarily place bodies in a particular spatial pattern as disciplinary power does. Its strategies are less visible. Just as Foucault privileged the prisons as examples of disciplinary power, so, in his account of bio-power, he foregrounds sexuality – on which I will concentrate in the first section of this chapter. The reasons for Foucault's interest in sex are at least as much political as historical: just as he worked on the prisons as part of the movement around GIP in the late sixties, during the seventies he worked on sexuality as part of a more general movement in which heterosexuality's claim to normalcy was being contested.

The concept of the *dispositif*, which, in various forms, had always been important for Foucault, is used again for his work on bio-power and sexuality. *Dispositif*, a common French word (usually translated as "apparatus"), refers to the relations between, and totality of, a heterogeneous ensemble of elements, of which the most important are, discursive practices,

165

institutions, scientific or medical techniques, architectual and other spatial forms in which actions are structured, the valorization of particular tasks, and the living out of stereotypes (the selfless doctor, for instance). For Foucault, the unity of a *dispositif* is strategical but hidden. Bio-power first stirs when, at the end of the eighteenth century a whole series of previously unconnected phenomena come together to ensure a healthy and numerous population, including demography, hospitals, negative images of mastur-bation, changes in breast-feeding practices, new images of midwives and so on. But where sexuality more specifically was concerned, the core or unifying principle of the *dispositif* became marked by a certain opacity – though, paradoxically, one that was often discussed, especially from the middle of the nineteenth century on. As Foucault puts it, "The notion of 'sex' made it possible to group together, in an artificial unity, anatomical elements, biological functions, conducts, sensations, and pleasures, and it enabled one to make use of this fictitious unity as a casual principle, an omnipresent meaning, a secret to be discovered everywhere: sex was thus able to function as a unique signifier and as a universal signified" (1980c, 154). Sexuality's constructed elusiveness constitutes what Foucault calls the "intrinsic latency" of the new formation (66). And, because the logic of sexual behaviour was deemed elusive, and its practices were deemed radically private, a great deal of a population's conditions of existence could be examined and altered to uncover, protect and manage sexuality's workings.

Foucault insists that what distinguishes the *dispositif* of sexuality is that it encourages and requires *talk* about sex, a thesis which, when it first appeared, was regarded as revolutionary. After all, was not sexuality that instinct all human beings possess, and which societies, particularly Victor-ian society, have repressed and channelled? Was it not essentially and naturally connected to private desire? According to Foucault: no, at least not most importantly. He rejects what he famously called the "repressive hypothesis" – the belief that sexual drives exist in opposition to social stability and have been especially stunted throughout Western history. To begin with, the repressive hypothesis forgets a whole other tradition – that of *ars erotica* – in which manuals and techniques for the crafting of, and education into, pleasure are transmitted across generations. And it also forgets the various uses that sexual behaviour served under protestantism and, then, under captialism. For Foucault, modern sexuality begins in a more specific sense when talk about sex is no longer primarily directed at, or uttered by, the clergy in confessions and sermons but becomes the object of doctors, writers of literature, bureaucrats and police. The medicalization of sexual behaviour and, in particular, the attention focused on the physi-ology of sexual response, means that old "truths" are undone, most notori-ously the theory that male and female sex organs are analogous to one another – a typical piece of Renaissance correspondence thinking. It might seem that as sexual activity is increasingly thought about in medical terms – as a bodily function – a space might open for a discourse about sex that is not primarily ethical. But, it is Foucault's argument that science's encounter with sex worked otherwise. For instance, scientists discover – and continually rediscover – children's sexuality throughout the nineteenth century and their concern circulates into the family in the form of increased surveillance. During the century, sexual relations other than heterosexual monogamy are also increasingly closely scrutinized. Sexual practices between individuals of the same gender become "perverse," outside "true sex," as Foucault puts it in his introduction to the hermaphrodite, Herculine Barbin's, memoirs. Within the scientific-governmental *dispositif* of sexuality, acts are replaced by essences. Sodomy becomes something rather different: homosexuality – the word is first used (like "sensationalism") in the 1860s. A homosexual is a particular kind of pathological person, not just somebody who enjoys certain kinds of acts, pleasures and object-choices. Male "homosexuals" especially are proper objects both for the police – homosexual acts between consenting male adults are first made illegal in Britain in 1885. (This construction of the "homosexual" mirrors the production of the criminologists' "criminal.") Within what Foucault calls the "sexual mosaic," the distribution of sexual essences is uneven; homosexuals are more essentially homosexual than heterosexuals are heterosexual; male "homosexuals" are more attached to their sexuality than female "homosexuals." On the other hand, heterosexual women's social identities are more attached to their sex than are heterosexual men's.

Medical, bureaucratic and normative discursive practices interpenetrate in many forms and to many strategical ends. Perhaps most famously, when sexual behaviour becomes linked to bio-power, the status of venereal diseases changes: far from being ills that the flesh is heir to, they become objects of administrative routines such as the Contagious Diseases Acts of the 1860s in which women defined as "prostitutes" were registered and compelled to undergo medical examination. Venereal diseases are also focused on within a discourse for which they threaten national security, as in Meredith's *The Ordeal of Richard Feverel*. Indeed, by the 1880s, though Foucault does not emphasize the point, the sexual *dispositif* (and, particularly, a discourse about syphilis) helped underpin imperialism. Particularly in Britain, the settler-colonies were regarded as places in which an increasingly "degenerate" European stock could exist and reproduce itself healthily – free from congenial syphilis. This discourse was all the stronger in a situation where fears were also being expressed about the slowness of metropolitan population increase – in a complete inversion of the Malthusian discourse earlier in the century. Sexual acts between men were also medicalized and policed all the more thoroughly because, unlike those between women, they could transmit venereal diseases. Within the *dispostif* of bio-power, "homosexuality," as a form of degeneracy, was connected to colonial expansion, as a cure of degeneracy. And yet there was another side to the policing of venereal diseases: protests against the Contagious Diseases Acts were crucial in the developments of political feminism – in a turn that, as we shall see, Foucault comes to regard as characteristic of the sexual apparatus.

To paraphrase and elaborate Foucault's more general argument: it is within bio-politics that the nuclear family is isolated as the central social unit, the institution that underpins social welfare. It forms the basis of the "Malthusian couple," that respectable family unit which the 1834 Poor Law Commissioners, for instance, so rigorously distinguished from what were called "improvident and wretched marriages" (S. G. and E. O. A Checkland (eds) 1974, 351). During the nineteenth cenury, the household as the basis of "alliances" that included kin, servants and peers was gradually reduced to that of the family. An equation between a particular kind of domestic building (the house) and a social unit (the family) is increasingly made to seem natural. It is in the family that a moral life is lived far from the "unsanitary" life of "promiscuous intimacy" of over-crowded and unhealthy "slums" (to use a word that enters the language in this sense during the 1830s). The early nineteenth-century laws that permitted rehousing and redraining in the interests of public hygiene required an image of society as the aggregate of a particular kind of happy and healthy family: husband at work, wife at home, and, increasingly, children at school. Up until the second half of the nineteenth century, the family was legally construed as an institution that provided the basis for the transmission of property across generations. Married women had little right to family property (including any property which they may have brought into the marriage), and, indeed, under the common law principle of "coverture" they were themselves, to all intents and purposes, part of that property. The most graphic instance of this – the wife sale – only ceased in England in the 1860s, though it had always been rare, and, of course, it stands against the kind of family envisaged by the Poor Law Commissioners and other state managers. The *dispositif* of sexuality emerges from within the larger structures of bio-power as the notions of the "citizen" and of the "father" cease to coincide, that is, as relations between the state and its subjects are less and less mediated through the "heads" of families. Under sovereign power, the relation between a father and his wife and children had been like that between the king and his subjects, but on a domestic scale. It was by this logic that, in England until the early nineteenth century, if a wife or a servant murdered the family head, it was regarded as an act of petty treason. Bio-power relations, on the other hand, operate directly between individuals – of whatever age, class or gender – and the government.

Within the sexual apparatus, individuals do not interest the state primarily as owners of property, or as citizens, or even, finally, as productive workers, but as emotionally stable subjects capable of strong interpersonal relations – that is, capable of domestic stability and love. At this point, as we shall see, sexuality begins to split off from classic nineteenth-century bio-power in the process of extending it. Foucault argues that the family becomes the object of state administrative concern in a discourse which anchors affection across two axes: the husband–wife axis and the parent–child axis. This question of "anchoring affection" is vital: ultimately, for instance, it is the connection between sex and interpersonal relationships that lies behind the strong sanctions against masturbation in the nineteenth century. Sex takes up its function as an anchor for love as legal relations between spouses change: as wives gain rights. The 1878 Matrimonial Causes Act, for instance, enabled magistrates to grant separation and maintenance orders on behalf of women (as mothers) who were subject to domestic violence or "Wife Torture," as Francis Power Cobbe called it in an influential pamphlet of the time. With the legal and religious support for the life-long marriage contract weakening during the 1880s and 1890s, conduct books, admittedly by radicals like Karl Pearson, began to advise women not just on how to manage a house but on how to keep a marriage "happy" by improving sexual techniques. As to children: it is where children's health is concerned that experts come to have their least problematic access to the family, especially in the programme of national vaccination – the first British compulsory Vaccination Act being passed in 1853. But the state's right of access into the domestic sphere was fiercely resisted (Wohl 1983, 10–43). By the first decades of this century, "sex education," designed to produce a "healthy" or "natural" attitude to sex in children, had become a site of contestation. Here the state's right to take a pastoral role was not generally accepted. By the late nineteenth century, however, proto-welfarist agencies monitor working-class domestic life to prevent children from becoming prostitutes, and to protect them from incest (though, in Britain, incest only becomes illegal in the first decade of this century). Domestic space becomes not just a sanctuary from the supposedly necessary immoralities of business, or the horrors of alienated labour, or even a site available for women to manage and to keep clean and "respectable," but a defence against outsiders, most vividly conjured up by the image of the "sex criminal" preying on children.[1] And in anti-"perversion" rhetoric, the concept of nature is called upon. Non-heterosexual sexual acts between adults are troped as "unnatural."

So, in sexuality, as in penality, a moral discourse is consolidated and displaced by practices and modes of thought that construct norms and impose them as respectable, natural or normal. Foucault argues that the "medicalization of children's sexuality" is one channel for this event; the "psychiatrisation of perverse pleasure" another. A third, Foucault calls the "hysterisation of the woman's body." He means by this that women's bodies become "saturated with sexuality" (1980c, 104) in the sense that they are regarded as *primarily* biologically (rather than economically) productive. Foucault argues that, as primordially fecund and increasingly removed from the labour force, women's bio-sexual functions (menstruation, pregnancy, menopause) all fall under the care of doctors who increasingly tended to explain women's non-sexual behaviour by reference to the reproductive system and, indeed, their domestic inter-personal relationships. Women cease being men's personal property as they become childbearing and sexual subjects whose welfare is a matter of national security and prosperity. Like so many nineteenth-century formations, this rationalist–sexual discourse reaches its climax during the First World War: thus, for instance, Guillaume Apollinaire, poet and promoter of pre-war avant-gardism, could write in 1916, with a bare trace of irony: "We see too few pregnant women nowadays. Needless to say, it is not on the boulevards or on café terraces that we would fain see them . . . Rather, we would have them appear in the parks and public gardens, in the Bois de Boulogne and the Bois de Vincennes, grave with the grace that makes for the charm of young matrons" (qu. Steegmuller 1963, 261). Around the fundamental and fragile sexuality of women's bodies, new notions, half somatic, half physical, either come into being or gain unprecedented attention – of which, at the end of the nineteenth century, the most important is "hysteria" itself. Women become prone to "nerves" and later "neurosis" – their acts symptoms of a supposed underlying and fundamental tendency of the feminine to border the pathological, because they are more defined by, and supposedly attached to, their bodies than men. In the most influential psychological knowledge of the time, psychoanalysis, "hysteria" and other neuroses are made intelligible in terms of a complex narrative by which the child's erotic relations with its parents form the – shaky – ground for achieving autonomy.

Between "nerves" and "neurosis" lies a fundamental shift however. Around the time of the First World War, sex strengthens its contact with "desire" – most obviously, again, in psychoanalysis. This works in two ways: sex itself becomes what is desirable, in a value system that intensifies the culture's sense of importance of the individual's body. For the new therapies, "neurosis" quickly comes to denote a failure to feel at home in and with sex-as-desire-and-pleasure, a private rather than a social pathology. This permits forms of self-management to develop, aimed at achieving happiness defined primarily in terms of sexual satisfaction. To offer one concrete historical instance of this shift: Jacques Donzelot, in an analysis of sex manuals of the period, had shown that, whereas late nineteenth-century advice books on how parents should deal with their children's sexuality stress surveillance, by the 1920s, frank and honest replies to questions were being recommended (Donzelot 1979b, 205). Indeed, in the twentieth century, the law itself relies increasingly on para-legal regulating agencies. Probation services that keep track of family life, and psychological reports that concentrate on familial/sexual relations, provide much of its knowledge of individuals, and are increasingly extensively used in sentencing. "Honesty" and openness about sex provides the basis for a new set of values, actions, subjections, pleasures, anxieties and administrative routines.

From the eighteenth century on, sexuality also had a function in the reorganization of class relations. First of all, as have begun to see, it helps provide a "proliferation of discourse" within which large and impersonal categories – the "masses," the "citizenry" – could be broken down into gender and age groups for instance, and, thus, more effectively administered. Second, it provided a marker of class difference – and a limit to such differences. Foucault argues that aristocrats had traditionally defined themselves in terms of "blood": their identities were given to them by virtue of descent and their glamour finally rested on their – and their ancestors' – capacity to lead in battle. The bourgeoisie, on the other hand, distinguished themselves by their self-ascribed ability to repress and defer desire as well as the value they gave to health against death and glory. In eighteenth-century literature, this difference is expressed in the character-type of the aristocratic "rake," seducer of middle-class virgins, most fully articulated by Lovelace in Richardson's *Clarissa* who applies a military discourse of "conquering" and "surrender" to the sexual relations of civil society. Sade is also exemplary here: according to Foucault, he works at the border which joins "sanguinity" (the aristocratic "blood line") to "sexuality" by making sex the prime good at the same time as he refuses all Laws, all Norms "except" (as Blanchot writes in his exposition of Foucault), "that which quickens pleasure through the satisfaction of violating Good" so that "blood reabsorbs death" (Blanchot 1987, 97). Sade's heroes retain aristocratic control over the life and death of their subjects, but now on a more or less fantastic register of sexuality and sexual exploitation, in one of the earlier moments in which sexual acts form a discursive field. Later, however, as the element in the field of bio-power that reaches furthest into the personal and psychological, it is the apparatus of sexuality that helps both to de-politicize individuals and to detach them from identities constructed in class terms. It is increasingly assumed that sexual happiness is, potentially, available to all, just as sexual desire derives all. More and more, it determines the choice of marriage partners – even for women. During the later nineteenth century, when desire is singled out as a category to explain what moves individuals, it provides the population with the possibility of pleasure and fulfilment as consumers. The pleasures of purchase and of possession are increasingly attached to those of the sexual body by the advertising and marketing industry. This mode of binding eros onto consumption is not limited to advertising however: Emma Bovary, in whom the desire for romance, sexual intensities and commodities fuse, represents the emergence of this form of governmentality in canonical literature – and, as we have seen, she is a character with whom the "literary" reader enters a complex play of identification and disidentification. Or rather, in Emma, Flaubert produces, perhaps for the first time, a character whom the reader is supposed to desire rather than to identify with, or emulate for moral purposes.

In general, then, sexual preferences and desirability become increasingly important in the construction of subjectivities. They do so as styles and values come to be formed, for instance, by the representation of women's bodies in advertising and the mass media; by professional opinions that marriages or "relationships" are made in bedrooms; by dietetics and fashions which aim at "looking good" rather than, for instance marking cultural identity or social status. Movies in Hollywood's "classical" period are important here too: for them, again, love, marriage and sexual satisfaction form a seamless continuum. This kind of subjectivity has not been easily connected to the older public discursive practices and institutions, however. Defined against the kind of satisfactions available within the continuum of love, sex and domesticity, politics became more and more focused on economic management, interrupted by debates about rights attached to "life" or the "environment" etc. which, as Foucault puts it, "the classical juridical system was utterly incapable of comprehending" (ibid., 145). And sex has not been as quickly aestheticized as crime. As we have seen, all kinds of literature draw on crime, from Agatha Christie to Dostoevesky, from Mrs Henry Wood to Joseph Conrad. But literary discourse has been slow to appropriate sexuality or to create sexual desire. No doubt this has been because sexuality, unlike crime, belongs firmly to the private sphere. But, even more to the point, it is precisely because sexuality is considered so strong, so authentic a motive for forming relationships with others, that desire produced by texts (or images), and experienced in solitude, has been devalued. Indeed, ever since the latter part of the nineteenth century, writing designed to elicit sexual response has been criminalized as "pornography." Thus, in the first decades of this century, avant-garde writers like D. H. Lawrence, James Joyce, Henry Miller and Theodore Dreiser found themselves writing about sexuality in terms which could neither produce readerly desire nor accept the cultural values attached to official "obscenity" rulings. For them sex could be used against the apparatus of normalization and productivity; it could be turned against domesticity. Here sex has a different use: both the aesthetic value of avant-garde writings and their "truth" was directly appealed to in the courts which tried to prosecute them as pornography. Their status as art is officially sanctioned in their fight with censorship aimed at pornography and the protection of family life. These institutional struggles may be taken further: in a writer like Lawrence, sex is ontologized. For him, sexuality is where life forces are revealed in their duality (the lightness and grace of the phallus, the darkness and primitiveness of the anus). True sex escapes all social contracts – including modern marriage. But even in Lawrence sex-as-writing is not aimed at producing desire: there have been few sterner enemies of masturbation than Lawrence. For him, when sex ceases to function as expression of ontological forces, it forms part of a linguistic regeneration. An old language about sex ("fuck," "cunt," even – in the posthumously published *Mr Noon* – "spooning"), having escaped the banality, the commodification, the stylizing of the various forms of literary or official or mass-circulated prose, may be used to revivify the language of literature.

After the first volume of *The History of Sexuality*, Foucault reworked his description of modern power. Now he begins to emphasise those forms of control which fix on individuals as individuals, calling them forms of "pastoral power." Foucault derives the notion of "pastoral power" from those power-relations that had developed between the clergy and their parishioners, and between abbots and monks in Catholic Christendom. In the confessional, using their ability to promise salvation, they had elaborated techniques which connected to, and produced, the individuality of the individual, and encouraged individuals to recognize a certain depth in themselves (1983c, 214). What are the equivalents to this pastoral power in modern society? Sex, again, has a particular role to play. For it is where sexuality is in question that the therapeutic practices which uncover deep selves first appear. And this partly because Foucault defines the workings of pastoral power very much in transactional terms. The particular situations, or what Foucault calls, the "local centres," in which sex and sexual relations are discussed and placed into hierarchies, constitute "matrices of transformation." In these matrices, the weaker subject – the child, the women – may undergo shifts which allow them to enter into a new relation with the stronger subject. Such shifts of relations may have quite dispersed effects. As Foucault put it in an interview, women begin to ask: "Are we sexed by nature? Well then, let us be so but in its singularity, in its irreducible specificity. Let us draw the consequences and reinvent our own type of existence, political, economic and cultural." (1977c, 156). Clearly these remarks gesture towards the feminist separatism of the seventies, but the point is important – and extends beyond the sexual apparatus. Pastoral power frames, classifies and administers by providing selves with deep and "singular" identities, by inviting what we can call "auto-narrations," and by positing selves whose everyday experiences may be worthy of utterance. But it does so only because, at the same time, it develops rules that order when, where and how selves can speak of themselves. The differences and singularities that proliferate within this new – tolerant – power enable new struggles and strategies: women, for instance, find that their singularity only emerges with the utmost difficulty from the tensions between three roles the sexual apparatus allows them: that of independent agent (being like a man), that of mother and that of sexually desirable object. In this spread of singularities one kind of behaviour is of especial importance, as Foucault notes – novel-reading. Novel-reading provides a complex process of identification and disidentification with authors and characters (themselves psychologized after Scott and Austen and increasingly so throughout the nineteenth century); it occurs in times of leisure, usually, silently and privately at home. As novels are read, complex responses are elicited; deep selves can be sensed whose substance everyday life offers little occasion to express, and which seem untouched by the modes of invigilation and productivity through which society is reproducing itself. And, of course, at another level, this sense of deep, unique selves untouched by power-relations only makes those relations work more easily.

Foucault connects pastoral power to a larger *dispositif* which he calls the *dispositif* of "individuation." I wish, again to paraphrase and elaborate his statements on individuation in quite broad terms. As state officials and the professions take over and re-form techniques of pastoral governmentality in the health, welfare and educational apparatuses, they apply a set of categories, thresholds and types that enable them to turn individuals into "cases." Not everyone is equally likely to be a "case," of course. It is those marginalized by the spread of discipline and normalcy who disproportionately provide the social services with their "cases." At the same time, slowly after the First World War and much more quickly after 1945, pastoral power becomes connected to fully fledged welfarism (in Britain, backed by economists such as John Maynard Keynes and William Beveridge). Organized state welfare requires unprecedented amounts of data to be gathered and stored, and this data concerns individuals rather than households represented by the male breadwinner. It is in this context that archival information held in documents like passports, educational records, credit information, tax file or social security numbers and death certificates provide a framework for everyday life; the state, of course, holding this information. If only some individuals become "cases" for the therapeutic or medical professions and bureaucratics, everyone has a file in some state apparatus. The case and the file are both arms of individuation. Although Foucault does not always concede it, it was this process of individuation, in alliance with the apparatus of sexuality, backed up by widespread improvements in health and housing, that pushed class struggle, and indeed, all rhetoric of deep conflict, into the political margins. By the late 1970s, though, Foucault himself tended to enter debates on social management with a view to offering policy and planning advice rather than in radical contestation. In a late interview on "Social Security," for instance, Foucault can repeat new rightist phrases against welfare dependency, except that he believes that economic rationality produces the very "system of dependency" to which, according to the right, it provides the solution (1988b 162ff.). Dependency is reduced when state pastoral procedures lessen the "descisional distance" between expert and individual: that is when decisions made on the individuals' behalf are intelligible, flexible and open to mutual discussion. Here a certain Habermasian strand enters Foucault's thought. Like Habermas, Foucault regards the possibility of dialogue as a safeguard against the machinery by which the state cares for its least provided-for subjects.

More theoretically, the explosion of documentation on individuals under pastoral power is linked to a powerful epistemological shift. From the late eighteenth century on, academics in the humanities begin to deal not just with a-temporal problems ("what is the good?" "how do words connect to things?") but to interrogate the present. In particular, statisticians search and record the social field for signs of historical shifts. They bring to light not transcendental categories but "trends," and help produce those thresholds and types which determine how and where "welfare" is to be applied. But philosophers had posed similar questions in their own terms: according to Foucault, Kant asks "What are we today, now?" philosophically, for the first time in his essay "What is Enlightenment?" This provides the intellectual basis for the human sciences to encroach upon and absorb philosophy – sciences which, of course, relied on dossiers and information often gathered by the state, and which was used also as data for administration of social services. According to Foucault, with Kant, modernity itself becomes a problem, and in this interrogation of modernity, a space outside the disciplinary archipelago, bio-politics, pastoral power and the government of individuation begins to be articulated. This is the domain of what Foucault will call the "ethical."

ETHICS

Foucault believes that rereading Kant's "What is Enlightenment?" allows us to regard modernity not so much as an epoch as an attitude:

> by "attitude" I mean a mode of relating to contemporary reality; a voluntary choice made by certain people; in the end, a way of thinking and feeling; a way, too, of acting and behaving that at one and the same time marks a relation of belonging and presents itself as a task. A bit, no doubt, like what the Greeks called an *ethos*. And consequently, rather than seeking to distinguish the "modern era" from the "premodern" or "postmodern," I think it would be more useful to try to find out how the attitude of modernity, ever since its formation, has found itself struggling with attitudes of "countermodernity."

> (1984d, 39)

Here, implicitly, the subject of modern power, produced in bio-power and the disciplinary archipelago, is *contrasted* to the modern ethical subject who is able to make "voluntary choices" based on self-imposed attitudes and tasks. The modern ethical subject asks, as a matter of choice, "what is the present?" and answers by setting him or herself the task of fashioning "a way of thinking or feeling" appropriate to belonging to "a cultural ensemble characteristic of . . . contemporaneity" – as Foucault puts it in another lecture on Kant (1986c, 89).

Foucault can propose this rather unlikely and radical reading by taking advantage of the fact that Kant is concerned not with "The Enlightenment" (a term popularised by later intellectual historians) but with Enlightenment (a personal, as well as a social, quest), and emphasizing that Kant finds Enlightenment in the transformation of a self-imposed immaturity (*Mündigkeit* – literally "minority") into individual autonomy and modernity. For Kant, however, such autonomy is limited: it exists in a free public "use of one's reason" separated from a private civil obedience. He writes: "on all sides I hear 'Do not argue!' The officer says, 'Do not argue, drill!' The taxman says 'Do not argue, pay!' " (Kant 1983, 142) and, though Kant insists that these disciplinary injunctions must be obeyed, he also argues that there exists a (again rather Habermasian) public sphere in which the individual need obey nobody. So Foucault is returning to Kant when, towards the end of his life, he reconciled himself to the enlightened philosophical enterprise:

> On the critical side – I mean critical in a very broad sense – philosophy is precisely a challenging of all phenomena of domination at whatever level or under whatever form they present themselves – political, economic, sexual, institutional, and so on. This critical function of philosophy, up to a certain point, emerges right from the Socratic imperative "Be concerned with yourself," i.e. ground yourself in liberty through the mastery of self.
>
> (1988a, 20)

But it is not in Kant that one can find authority for an ethical attitude such as "ground yourself in liberty through the mastery of self." (We can leave aside the fact that Nietzsche's friend and colleague Jacob Burckhardt defined the "Renaissance" as that epoch in which each individual's life first became a "work of art.") Kant's critical philosophy is based on the dissemination of writing and ideas in a dialogue carried out amongst those we would call, after an earlier Foucault, "universal intellectuals." Kant is interested less in any "care of self" than in that private self-restraint that he considers necessary for public liberty. And yet the "freedom" Kant envisages is a freedom to imagine the future otherwise: his modernity consists less in the belief that "anything is possible" or "I can make of myself what I wish" than in a recommendation like "let us direct ourselves as a community towards a future whose shape is open to, and malleable by, the ordered exchange of discourse." In fact, what attracts Foucault about Kant's "What is Enlightenment?" is simply that, in it, "reason" is defined by establishing limits to discipline and obedience, that is, in resistance to (the rudiments of) modern power. (It is worth noting that in the early eighties Foucault taught courses on "free speech" very much with Poland and Iran in mind.)

However unlikely it may seem, this account permits Foucault to imply that Kant, the first modernist, is a predecessor of Baudelaire for whom "the high value of the present is indissociable from a desperate eagerness to imagine it, to imagine it otherwise than it is, and to transform it not by destroying it but by grasping it in what it is" (1984d, 41). What Kant and Baudelaire share is not just a problematizing but a herocizing of the present: for both writers time "now" has more energy, more vitality, more aura, than time "then." According to Foucault, in Baudelaire (but, of course, not in Kant) this anti-historical impulsion towards autonomy connects to a private asceticism in which the individual aims to make of "his body, his behaviour, his feelings and passions, his very existence, a work of art" (41–2). The pressures which underlie Foucault's ethical turn now begin to become apparent. In "What is Enlightenment?" Foucault argues that the privileging of imagination and autonomy in enlightened modernity works against that humanism for which an essence, embedded in all, fashions, rather than is fashioned by, human beings. Also, to give value to ethical self-governing is to reject any psychology for which the subject is formed in and by events, structures, psychic elements, inherited or environmental determinants that lie beyond conscious control. At the same time, it rejects the primordiality of the notion of "culture" – for ethical techniques do not work on an individual conceived of as already fundamentally acculturated. We might say that Foucault's earlier, archaeological insistence that discourse has no unconscious is now applied to the self. Lastly, ethical formation is not essentially connected to the Law or Laws: for, in his own words, it can provide "a very strong structure of existence, without any relation with the juridical per se, with an authoritarian system, with a disciplinary structure" (1983a, 235).

Foucault is using the word "ethics," then, in a very specific sense to designate the realm of "self-governmentality" or "self-formation" within the private space, the locus of liberty available to individuals inside modern society. This realm is fundamentally characterized by the possibility of failure (a point Foucault had made as far back as *The Archaeology of Knowledge*). It is because individuals are likely *not* to fulfil their aims, protocols and exercises by which they fashion themselves that such fashioning is "ethical" – having the force of a duty, an "ought." In this the ethical distinguishes itself from the "normal"; normality is a feature of what *is*, it has no moral charge, however much it may be turned into an instrument of control. In fact, as we might expect, Foucault is attracted to the ethical because it stands outside the normal. Yet of course the possibility of transformation and the likelihood of failure in ethical undertakings are not equally distributed across societies or in a particular society. Thus, as Foucault often points out, intense ethical programmes are often embarked upon either by élites, those with most private liberty, or those who, like the early Christians or contemporary gays, already stand furthermore from "normality." And the likelihood of failure also means that ethical texts may tell us little about the actual lives of individuals – and it is the texts, not the lives, which ultimately interest Foucault. Having marked out the domain of the ethical, Foucault applies to it the techniques that he had developed in his archaeology and used again on the work on power. Again, he constructs an "analytics" of the ethical: a classification of its constituent parts, and proceeds to write histories of shifts within these constituents. As we have seen, the point of these histories is to show how *other* ethics are possible, and thus to contest the modern empire of the Same and the Norm (without falling into culturalism and anthropology). *The Order of Things* worked to similar ends – there his account of pre-modern epistemes was also intended to make us less at home in the era of the "modern."

Ethics does not consist of a code of prohibitions but of protocols, divisible into distinct aspects. Certain faculties belonging to ethical agents are felt to have more ethical value than others: these Foucault, following Hegel, calls "ethical substances," they are what ethics works on: they change historically. The discourse in which people conceive of their obligations changes also: for example, one may choose a particular "care of self" either because that is the divine will or because it is "rational." Foucault calls these various legitimations, "modes of subjection." Ethics also contains a teleological impulse: what kind of person is one to become? Masterly, sensitive, stylised? Techniques are constructed to achieve these different ends, and techniques may be more or less law-like, more or less obvious, according to what end is in question (it is harder to draw up a programme for "sensitivity" than for "self-control" for instance). Finally, there exist forms of "ethical work that one performs on oneself" – which he also calls "ascetics" (1985a, 17). Does one use a notebook to record daily transgressions or goals? Does one fast? Lift weights? Obviously this, the technology of self-government, also varies historically. Indeed, ethics, as constituted by these elements, changes when moral codes do not. Morality is more conservative than ethics: the code of prohibitions, in certain areas particularly, has remained remarkably constant since the Greeks. "Don't be unfaithful to your spouse" is an imperative which has been accepted from before the period of the Stoics but the ethics it involves – the why, how, what and when of faithfulness have changed enormously.

It is not my intention to present Foucault's account of the history of ethics in great detail. That history is, in fact, quite sketchy: in developed form it exists only in the case-studies of Greek and early Christian sexual ethics, published as volumes two and three of *The History of Sexuality*. The implicit argument of this history is that we have failed to study and treat ethics as conscious study: it is no longer a valued element of the cultural archive, and we have tended to ignore how texts – including literature – have presented "practices of self." Whereas in the pre-Stoical Greeks especially, ethics was a crucial concern of the citizen, now, or at least until recently, it is only in the avant-garde, in Baudelaire and the dandies, that self-formation has been given due attention. Foucault's over-arching narrative – the story of the retreat of self-fashioning – leads in two directions. It shows where and how ethical imperatives have worked historically even where they have not been recognized, so that it becomes possible to reread Romanticism and Renaissance humanism, in particular, in terms of strategies for the formation of selves either privately or institutionally. It has made us pay more careful attention to relations between conduct books and the early novel. But it also makes the demand that ethics should today be turned against modern power, humanism, the human sciences and the state.

For Greeks before Stoicism self-fashioning was crucial, because it was connected to techniques of self-mastery required by the Greek citizen if he were to master others – that is, his household (and it is a question of *men*). Thus, for instance, it did not matter whether one found sexual pleasure with boys or women but it did matter whether or not one took the passive position, or gave way "immoderately" to desire. For the Greeks, "care of self" was also a matter of perfection, one could enhance the beauty and glory of one's existence. The Stoics, however, insisted that one looked after and ordered oneself not for civic or aesthetic reasons, but because as a human being one was rational. Thus Stoicism universalizes the subject – indeed, it begins to take women into account, though only in Christianty are women provided with full ethical substantiality. And whereas the Greeks of Plato's time had relied on *hypomnemata* (manuals in which one entered truisms etc. to be used for training in the art of living), and had related "moderation" (*sophrosyne*) to health, erotics, the household and the polis, the later Greeks and the Romans broke ethical techniques down more specifically into different fields: medicine, dietetics, mental exercises (in your morning walk, practise not feeling desire for passers-by) and so on. The Christian ethical agent was increasingly passive in the face of an increasingly abstract ethical substance, inspecting and deciphering his or her behaviour (twinges of desire, dreams) for signs of their fundamental fleshliness, their connection with the devil. Although practices for avoiding temptation, for instance, are insisted upon, this already represents a move from the ethical to a certain proto-psychological subjectivity in which what one *is* is given rather than a substance to be shaped. The spiritual self is more or less submissive to the fleshly self. And Christian techniques for self-fashioning involve the re-making of the self not just a making: it is a

179

question of moving past that primordial fallen state in which one lived before awareness of sin.

If Stoicism and Christianity constitute the first two major breaks in the history of ethics, Cartesian rationalism provides the next, and perhaps the most radical of all. Before the seventeenth century, in order to know the truth one had to live or behave in particular ways; it was how the individual lived that enabled access to truth. In other words, truth had not been completely detached from "wisdom." After Descartes, however, the subject of knowledge has direct access to the truth through the application of doubt, truth is not grounded on traditionally validated statements but by taking a certain attitude, applying a method of scepticism to knowledge and the world. Henceforth, ethics (as the formation of a moral agent) exists outside of philosophy and science. Kant inherits this problem in the form of the following question: how to connect moral imperatives – the domain of freedom and autonomy – to questions of truth – the domain of certainty and pure reason. He solves it by turning ethics into a mode of relating to the universal: the Kantian moral subject applies laws which pure reason sanctions and which therefore hold true for all rational and autonomous subjects. Freedom, the keystone of morality, becomes a matter of transcending the world of the senses, of *obeying* moral laws. Although Kant does demand that we work on our intentions, that we act in ways which will allow a free human community to be realized, in fact because the categorical imperative (the universal moral law as we saw above) cannot help us form a self (it is not a great deal of use even in telling us how to act in particular situations) Kant, in fact, sets the ethical subject *against* the moral subject.

Of course the moral Kant is not the Kant who problematizes modernity, and when Foucault at this stage of his career turns to him, he becomes the thinker for whom freedom consists in anticipating a radically more free future – which cannot be imagined but of which there are signs. (See Foucault 1986c, for his development of this reading of Kant's essay.) Yet in more recent times, according to Foucault, a new ethical substance has appeared – Kant's intention has been replaced by feeling. Now, for instance, we consider that sexual promiscuity is acceptable if it does not hurt people's feelings or transmit disease. When intention gives way to feeling and sensibility as the ethical substance, a juridical ethics also begins to be replaced by a "stylistics of living." This substitution of law by style does not mean that "anything goes" but rather that those who are constrained by prohibitions – gays, for instance – ought to be placed in positions where they can modify them (1988b, 294). Indeed Foucault was very distrustful of the "regime of tolerance" which, as he saw, not only expresses a new social alignment of money and power but also a new set of anxieties. In part because the production of anxiety is so strong a form of control, tolerance itself "subjects" individuals (1977d, 24). What

Foucault likes about the aesthetics of self is that its ethical substance is *bios*, the stuff of existence, and not a psychological constituent of existence such as "feeling." A preference like this develops because politics and ethics overlap. Foucault is championing a world in which modes of self-fashioning have priority over political activity, as against one in which the political institutions are considered to be the proper sites for the administration and distribution of liberties. His earlier descriptions of, and injunctions to, a modern ethic are much more concerned with politics than his later ones. We can take for instance his prescriptions for an "art of living counter to all forms of fascism" outlined in the "Preface" to Deleuze and Guattari's *Anti-Oedipus*. There he encourages his readers to take the book as a "manual or guide for everday life" which will enable them to "free political action from "totalizing paranoia"; to "believe that what is productive is not sedentary but nomadic"; to be "happy" rather than "sad" or, as he might have said, resentful; not to place action against thought but to use action to intensify thought; not to become "enamoured of power," and, finally, not to demand "rights" but rather "to de-individualize by means of multiplication and displacement" (1977e, xiii xiv). Such a "de-individualized" and thoughtful life is directed against the political much more directly than the post-Baudelairean aestheticized style or the gay style (which is, anyway, Foucault says, interested more in the recollection and imaging of sexual acts than their performance). Yet, the micropolitical, the aesthetic and the gay ethic do share the impulsion to make "the real unacceptable" by imprinting the imagined on the lived. (For making "the real unacceptable" see Foucault 1988b, 65.)

In his description of ethics today, Foucault hovers between the analytic and the exhortative. As we have seen, he is attempting to re-embrace the enlightenment project, to demonstrate that, within the broad logic of his earlier work, spaces remain in which freedom may be affirmed, and that these spaces are produced by the desire to be modern. What are the limits and difficulties with the ethical? It seems to me that they fall under one general heading: as Kant's essay implies, the counter-ethical is to be found in the determined. For it is by no means clear that the self to be shaped or invented is simply a malleable ethical substance; it seems also to be constrained by solid givens whose force must be conceded and measured. Failures of ethical self-formation certainly cannot be simply dismissed as Kantian "immaturity." This means too, that the historian of the ethical must attempt to separate the order of self-agency from determination of and on selves – which is not at all an easy task, as it is rarely clear what is shaped by us and what is given to us from without and, therefore, hems us in.

So, to finish, three short examples in the story of modern ethics. The most obvious constraint on self-formation is economic: in bald terms the poor have fewer ethical opportunities than the rich – less opportunity to travel, to educate themselves, to be healthy and so on. Thus it is no surprise that the most self-consciously ethical texts of our time have been written by aristocrats:

> Do you see yourself to carve, eat, and drink genteelly, and with ease? Do you take care to walk, sit, stand, and present yourself gracefully? Are you sufficiently upon your guard against awkward attitudes, and illiberal, ill-bred, and disgusting habits; such as scratching yourself, putting your fingers in your mouth, nose, and ears? . . . When you return here, I am apt to think that you will find something better to do, than to run to Mr. Osborne's at Gray's Inn, to pick up scarce books. Buy good books, and read them; the best books are the commonest, and the last editions are always the best, if the editors are not blockheads; for they may profit of the former. But take care not to understand editions and title-pages too well. It always smells of pedantry, and not always of learning.
>
> (Chesterfield 1984, 165)

This is a letter from Lord Chesterfield to Philip Stanhope, his illegitimate son and Dr Dodd's pupil – it was Stanhope's signature that Dodd forged. It was published in a famous, posthumous collection. The instructions are precise, they are directed at both body and mind: or rather at the impression a particular body and mind will have on others. They are written in a world in which financial limits are almost totally non-existent. Which is not to say that, when published, the collection was used primarily as a conduct book. Chesterfield provided an image of an aristocratic life to be desired, as much as imitated, by the middle classes. To live like this was to undergo a "reformation of manners," like that the middle classes and the state were attempting to organize for the poor. But this image of aristocratic life also provides a fantasy of the life of luxury – to use a word highly charged in the eighteenth century. When a reformer like Dr Dodd attempts to live such a life, he must become a forger, a criminal. His fate is not completely different from that of Moll Flanders, say. It is in this context that, as we have seen, new alliances between intellectuals and crime can be set in motion. As an exercise in the government of selves. Chesterfield's book fulfils an important and ultimately counter-revolutionary task, namely the breaking down of a hard and fast difference between the two classes, independently of political activity. Chesterfield's letters are imaginary rather than utopian – and even early journals like the *Tatler* and the *Spectator* have this double function – guides for conduct *and* presentations of an imaginary, reconciled urban scene.

As we have begun to see, ethics stop where work on the self encounters memories, habits, obsessions, compulsions – the whole array of the psychically given and the symptomatic. Thus, in empiricist thought from Hobbes on, the question has not been "how to form selves?" but "what passions or motives have most power in determining behaviour?" It is worth noting two concrete instances in which this division is probed. What kind of entries does Baudelaire himself, the progenitor of the modern alignment between the ethical and the aesthetic, make in his personal journal? Some fit into the old tradition of the *hypomnemata*: "The more one works, the better one works and the more one wants to work" (Baudelaire 1983, 96); others are focused more specifically on hygiene and diet – he records recipes, for instance; and in others he plans repayment of his debts. Others still bind the ethical to the aesthetical: "Always be a poet, even in prose" (98). Yet often a different note is struck, as in the entry: "To achieve a daily madness" (98) or, "We are weighed down, every moment, by the conceptions and sensations of time" (97). In fact, Baudelaire's notebook is agonistic, it records the struggle between the ethical, the psychological, the economic and (to put a name to it) the ontological. To work hard, to increase one's madness, to attend to those fundamental structures of existence which no personal effort can budge – the intensity of Baudelaire's work, the strength of his intimate journals exist in the tensions between these imperatives and drives.

A different intertwining of the ethical and the psychological can be found in contemporary performance art. Since the 1960s, the appeal of the notion "performance" – whether in avant-garde theatre, dance or the art world – had been found in its promise of a coalition between the lived and the presented. We can take a particularly radical branch of this movement, what a critic has called "lifelike art" (Kaprow 1983, 41). Perhaps the richest display of this genre was presented in the New Museum of Contemporary Art in New York in 1986 under the title "Choices: Making an Art of Everyday Life" of which the most arresting contribution was Tehching Hsieh's. His performance document records the following projects:

> 1978–9 Remain in cage for a year.
> 1980–2 Punch time clock every hour on the
> hour, 24 hours a day, for a year.
> 1981–2 Remain outdoors for a year.
> 1983–4 Tie with rope to Linda Montano and do
> not touch for one year.
>
> (Tucker 1986, 46)

Here Tehching Hsieh has – seemingly – radicalized an ascetic care of self for aesthetic ends: the *telos* of this particular self-fashioning is to produce art, as Marcia Tucker, the curator of the show, tirelessly insists. This of course produces its own problems, for the "aesthetic" is a category which changes over time. (No doubt a continuity can be traced between Baudelaire's aestheticized ethics and lifelike art.) In fact criticism and legitimation of lifelike art by established art critics seems to owe something to Foucault's work of the period (see McEvilley 1983). Yet the "decadent" project of turning oneself into a work of art begins from a secure sense of what art is and a rejection of life, while the contemporary school have a secure sense of the lived (they are very comfortable with the category "experience") and a much less secure sense of the aesthetic. (This is worth noting because in his comments on aesthetic self-fashioning Foucault does not allow for these shifts in the signification of "art" or the aesthetic.) More interestingly, despite the fact that Tehching Hsieh's pieces rely on their being *chosen* rather than determined regimes, his work, like that of many artists in the New Museum's exhibition, mimics classic neurotic symptoms. He himself conceives of his projects less as self-technologies than as metaphors for an alienated, industrial society. But it is as if, in his need to critique and distance himself from the everyday by radically ordering his experience, he turns to those who remain outside the ordered and normal – to madness and extreme physical constraint.

The artists in the exhibition tended to hystericize, discipline and imprison themselves in order to insist on the autonomy of their chosen acts. They enter into relation with one disorder in particular – Freud's "compulsion to repeat," an obsessional neurosis by which a (version of) an act or memory is repeated so as to annihilate or undo it. The logic of the compulsion goes: if I choose it now, it did not happen to me then, or: if it did happen to me then, now, by repeating it, it is under my control. Leaving questions of personal obsession aside, many "lifelike art" artists have been priests or nuns (and indeed this is recognized by Tehching Hsieh, who takes some pains to show how his work is not monk-like); in their work it is as if the *history* of techniques of self-government (in which Christian institutions played so large a role) can be experienced in individual lives. Repeating rather than countering the alienation effects that is practitioners find so disturbing, this lifelike art does constitute a problem for the ethical. It demonstrates that where self-formation is insisted upon most strongly it is also most likely to disappear into the merely symptomatic. In sum, the fascination of Tehching Hsieh's work is that it fits neither the categories "ethics" nor "psychology" nor "aesthetics." It is not quite uninterpretable – it just eludes the codes to which interpretation (as a form of cultural processing) appeals.

At this point we can usefully distinguish between various modes of modern aesthetic self-formation: first, the large project of civilizing or "polishing" the bourgeoisie by imposing "aristocratic" techniques of grace; second, as in the Baudelaire invoked by Foucault, for whom life is to be worked on to produce an object of style and beauty; then, as in the anti-bougeois Baudelaire of the Intimate Journal who wills himself to choose the uncontrollable, the determined, to become more mad, to deliver himself to the emptiness of time (and drugs and dreams can – and for Baudelaire do – substitute for madness and time here); fourth, the repetition compulsions of contemporary lifelike art in which psychology takes revenge on ethics and extreme choice becomes extreme bodily restriction. The last category is what we might call the transgressive ethic that Foucault hinted at in his book on Raymond Roussel. Here art and life come together, not because a technology of self-governance is available to the self, but because Roussel's madness, addictions, sexuality, love of mimicry (say) share features, across a divide, with his writing techniques (the "process"). Unlike Baudelaire, Roussel did not nurture madness – he has nothing of *that* private theatricality; and, he differs from the lifelike artists in maintaining the separation of life and art. That is the point of his obsession with technique, with crafting language as a material. In this context, Roussel seems exemplary: his madness is not finally experiential or available to spectacle and imitation – a point Foucault took from him in the early sixties. That is how Roussel helps remind us that art and life cannot always and fully come together under the rubric "self-fashioning." Each life has its own psychological limits and possibilities which are not represented in, but are inscribed on, the work and – importantly – vice versa. A paradox operates here too: the more the structure and materiality of language is permitted to organize the work, the more the work orders the life of the writer. In this interplay between the dedication and drivenness of the life and the formal (non-mimetic) rigour of the text we do not confront ethics but something else – a condition of superficiality and scarcity that the processes of language and of living share.

8

POST-FOUCAULDIAN CRITICISM: GOVERNMENT, DEATH, MIMESIS

Foucault and literature. It seems an obvious enough conjecture – after all nowhere in Foucault's writings do literary texts and examples completely fall out of sight, and for a short period they form its core. In broad terms, one can classify his remarks and essays on literature under four headings: first, the literary theory that underpins *Madness and Civilization*, the book on Roussel and the essays on transgression; second, the literary history that lies embedded in those transgressive essays; third, his description of the uses to which literary realism was put in the production of the docile society, and, last, a not very fully developed description of literary criticism both as a particular manipulation of the author effect and as a mode of modern power. Yet Foucault rarely deals with literature itself as a category or an institution. For good reasons: in both his archaeological and genea-logical work he is sceptical about the continuity, specificity and abstraction implied by a topos like the "institution of literature." In this chapter, I want to comment on two post-Foucauldian books, both of which share – and elaborate on – Foucault's scepticism: they are Ian Hunter's *Culture and Government* (1988) and Stephen Greenblatt's *Shakespearean Negotiations* (1987). Most of all, I want to use Hunter's and Greenblatt's work to begin to show what a genealogy of literature might look like. But I also use it to explore the possibilities, and limits, of a mode of analysis that does not presuppose concepts like "representation" and "mimesis." For, as Fou-cault's career helps demonstrate, if it is becoming harder to accept the value and autonomy of literature today, this is largely a result of its central strut – representation – being so strongly contested not just analytically but politically. This is not to say, however, that representation can be avoided as an analytic category.

LITERATURE AS GOVERNMENT

Of the compartments into which I have divided Foucault's contribution to literary studies, the least explored has been the relation between literary criticism and modern power. But recently Ian Hunter, in his important, if somewhat unrecognized, book has offered a radical revision of the whole academic literary critical project by arguing that it must be viewed as an arm of modern power. *Culture and Government*, then, serves as a convenient starting point for my analysis of the directions that literary studies are taking after Foucault. Hunter's is a revisionist thesis: it is positioned against the cultural studies movement inaugurated by Raymond Williams, which recorded the story of criticism's "social mission." Hunter argues that the history of literary criticism as taught in higher education ought not to be regarded as a chain of ideas and influences leading from Coleridge and Schiller, through Matthew Arnold and I. A. Richards, to Leavis and the American New Critics.[1] He does not tell the story of the emergence of "English" as a sustained bourgeois rejection of the alienations and divisions caused by industrialization and "mass culture," a rejection whose actual effect, so Williams claimed, was to reproduce and legitimate depoliticized cultural values. For Hunter, expanding on a Foucauldian line of analysis, literary education in England first appears in the "governmental apparatus" whose object was the "moral and physical condition of the population," early in the nineteenth century. It does so at a specific moment, one in which relations between various pedagogical institutions were realigned. He argues that it was under the guidance both of the proto-welfarist bureaucrats like James Kay-Shuttleworth, who administered the state's entry into popular education from the 1830s on, and contemporary, professional educationalists like David Stow, especially concerned with establishing the spatial arrangement of schools, that the rather progressive pedagogy previously attached to some Sunday schools came to dominate the educational apparatus. In this move, state education replaced monitorial techniques by procedures that invited pupils to express themselves.

According to Hunter, it was only early in the twentieth century that tertiary literary education entered this history – in order to provide mass education with teachers and inspectors who could function as ethical exemplars and invigilators. At that point so-called "romantic" criticism was called upon to teach the teachers. For Hunter, Friedrich Schiller founds the critical tradition embodied in Britain by Arnold, and is a "romantic." Before the early twentieth century, Hunter believes, advanced critical discourse had not formed part of the transactions between culture and the state at all. And that discourse's entry into pedagogy was made possible because of "romantic" criticism's claim that literary texts cannot be translated into propositions: it produced an aesthetic, closely connected to Kant, for which literature was neither essentially rhetorical nor representational. So reading literature becomes less a matter of acquiring or parroting certain beliefs, or of acquiring techniques of persuasion or expression, than of forming an "aesthetico-ethical" self, that is, a self which is harmonious and reconciled. Literary pedagogy controls by offering the promise of individual fulfilment or completion. Hunter also claims that, as criticism

187

becomes firmly established in the academy, it is contested by literary theory, which, on the face of it, is neither humanist nor ethical. In an account that differs slightly from the one that I sketched in chapter 5, he argues that theory is the arm of the human sciences within advanced literary studies. However, for him, the differences between theory and criticism can be over-valued. The future-directedness of literary theory, the way that theory recovers a textual "unconscious," whether mythic, structural or political, shares literary criticism's drive towards reconciliation. This is true even if theory aims at the fulfilment of a less tangible object – not, like criticism, individual selves grouped together as "man" but, instead, the mythic, structural or political "subject" of writing.

What is refreshing and important about Hunter's account is that it begins to fulfil Foucault's advice to historians to work "from the bottom up" (from the lay-out of schools for instance) so that the marxian cultural studies approach now does indeed appear idealist. Hunter's work also allows us to see that recent literary theory is, in part at least, a moment in a more generalized intellectual framework – even if his appeal to the human sciences seems quite inadequate to deal with Derrida's and Paul de Man's work, arguably at the very centre of current "literary theory." Yet it is his implicit claim to speak from outside history that leads Hunter's account into difficulties – just as it undercuts Foucault's own archaeology. The story that he tells does not include his own project. Hunter cannot quite take account of his own double agenda; his writing, simultaneously, a disenchanted, truth-telling work and a polemical and corrective one. It is corrective in that, for Hunter, Schiller and Arnold were wrong because they thought that they were producing better selves while they were "really," far in the future, going to produce more administrable selves; the cultural studies movement is wrong in that it ignores the governmental genealogy of criticism; literary theorists are wrong in so far as they think that they are accounting for signification and its effects whereas they are in fact bringing to light "unsaid" conditions of possibility that can never be tightly enough connected to what these conditions are designed to explain. On the other hand, a genealogy like Hunter's is truth-telling in that, for it, what there is is just what there is, and what has been said is just what has been said, so that *Culture and Government* supposes no foundational truth to place against Schiller, Leavis, Williams, and so on. Unlike Foucault, Hunter does not strategically ally himself with those who have little access to what power can offer. In fact, Hunter's desire to speak from a place at which the true story of institutionalized literary studies can be told (therefore, a place not inscribed by those studies or their objects), often seems to organize and bend the processes of historical narration, as well as to permit the discounting of crucial theoretical/methodological categories. Of these last the most telling are exchange, resistance and inscription itself – terms around which much current criticism moves. So it is worth enumerating certain historical and theoretical problems and difficulties that follow from Hunter's approach in a little more detail: here the two sides of the Foucauldian aftermath become clearest.

As far as history is concerned, Hunter's account finds a point of origin in the Sunday schools. Like most historians of education, he regards them as precursors of popular education, though, unlike the marxists, he does not believe that they simply imposed an ideology on their students. Rather, they provided the framework for certain disciplinary practices, not at all against the will of the parents and pupils who were their clients. Nonetheless, many early connections between schooling and the state escape Hunter's attention. To begin with, the Sunday schools were, of course, not secular – they taught the Bible (which also legitimated their stress on literacy, "respectability," "cleanliness" etc.) – and they stood against both the older "charity schools" and the monitorial schools. Charity schools were regarded as contaminated by archaic values of patronage and servitude – most notoriously by William Cobbett, but ever since Bernard Mandeville in the early eighteenth century. In their turn, monitorial schools were widely criticized by liberals for their rigidity and lack of individual attention. These divisions within primary education were partly caused by the scarcity of money and teachers. Monitors were the cheapest way to educate pupils *en masse* (Andrew Bell's famous system was developed in India): Sunday schools, relying on volunteers, were somewhat less exposed to economic constraint. Most importantly, the divisions in primary education were organized around debates about class and religion. The Sunday school movement was primarily a Dissenting movement, unlike the older Charity schools which were under Anglican control, and in which places were limited and relatively expensive. As Sunday schools became increasingly popular, they were subject to the complaint that they would educate their pupils "above their station" and cause minor versions of the kind of desire and acts that worked on Dr Dodd, for instance. Such complaints, in fact, helped orchestrate arguments against the state playing any part at all in the population's education. It is generally agreed that the state intervened in education in the late 1840s quite reluctantly, by establishing pupil-teacher training schemes, and by setting minimum standards for staff, equipment and discipline in schools that wanted to receive funds. It did so mainly to prevent crippling struggles between the various denominations as to who was to control education at a time when satisfying proletarian demand for education made good political and administrative sense. This sense, of course, belongs to Foucault's bio-power. An educated workforce was thought to be more productive than an illiterate one. It was also less likely to be riotous or revolutionary.[2]

Thus, as the state began increasingly to encroach upon primary education it confronted the questions: how to move education from under the wing of religion? How to avoid imposing class identities on pupils? The main strategy was to minimize the objectives that each student was to attain. These, Kay-Shuttleworth spelled out as the ability to read a newspaper, to write a correctly spelled letter, to add up a bill, and to follow a sermon (Fraser 1984, 265). But, during the 1850s and 1860s, lobby groups which aimed to provide *every* child with education were formed, and the restricted nature of elementary education became increasingly apparent. It is at this point that an older discursive formation was revitalized – one which gradually filtered into the training manuals for teachers. This older discourse was that of the late eighteenth-century, so-called followers of Rousseau, and in particular Thomas Day (author of *Sandford and Merton* which appeared throughout the 1780s) and Richard and Maria Edgeworth who, in their *Practical Education*, had began to promulgate for a "Rousseauistic" elementary education around the same time.[3] The latter book, in particular, is worth dwelling on, because it clearly indicates the terms in which the expansion of education was to be articulated. It begins with a chapter on toys that emphasises the importance of "play" for learning. The Edgeworths attack those frivolous toys which do not instruct, on the grounds that toys which both please and instruct could provide a bridge across which progressive pedagogy could move out of domestic space into the schoolroom. (The vogue for "useful" toys had a decisive effect on the young Percy Shelley, for instance.) *Practical Education* also contains a careful account of how language and literature ought to be taught – asserting that reading and literature are central to modern self-formation because they develop sympathy and allow moral ideas to be associated with pleasure. For them, literature is important because it manages ideas and actions almost invisibly, consisting as it does of ordered – not "mad" – ideas and imitable representations of acts. It provided the means for a "true" or "natural" self to be expressed – one that appeared to be uncontaminated by doctrinal or class prejudices.

So reading was privileged over rhetoric, criticism or grammar, and the management of children's reading became of acute importance. It is an emphasis that will culminate in the value given to "close reading" in the twentieth century. The Edgeworths insist that children should not be exposed to Gothic horror stories, only to moral texts like *The Robbers* – a pre-Romantic and humanist play by the same Schiller whom Hunter regards as irrelevant to the history of infant pedagogy. They go so far as to include instances of children's written response to poetry – not directly as in I. A. Richards' *Practical Criticism* (to take the most famous later example) – but via the pupil's descriptions of nature after having read a poem. And, like Richards and Arnold in his *Reports on Elementary Schools* over half a century later, who both also print students' writing, they prefer those exercises in which the students have *not* been "habituated to the poetic trade" as they put it (Edgeworth and Edgeworth, 1974: 2: 618). To increase "understanding," careful written expositions of difficult texts may be offered to pupils, but in forming children's minds, the human, invigilating, presence is to be preferred. Writing itself is not a central element of "practical education" because that education aims at forming a way of being rather than a set of techniques of which literacy is merely one. When pupils *do* write, it is to express themselves, a practice that is permitted because, having read morally and psychologically correct books, their self-expression will be both original and imitative – where, of course, "imitative" no longer means the rote copying of the older "scholastic" or monitorial educational programmes.

Ian Hunter neglects the impact of writings like the Edgeworths' on state pedagogy, especially as part of the resistance to the claim that mass education would lead to widespread unsatisfied wants. He also neglects the "cultural hygiene" movement discussed in the section on *Middlemarch* above.[4] Instead, he concentrates on David Stow's discussion of the school playground, seemingly because the state first took responsibility for infant pedagogy in England (in 1833) by providing grants for the building of school-houses. Were he directly to face the importance of both "Rousseauistic" education theory and the "cultural hygiene" movement, then the larger thrust of his work would falter. Because then the classical or "cultural critical" lineage from Schiller and Coleridge, through to Arnold and Leavis, would *not* be wholly removed even from pioneers of state education like Stow. Indeed, Arnold's work on education is itself written in a very practical and immediate spirit against the economistic and *laissez-faire* values expressed in Robert Lowe's "Revised Code" legislation of 1862, which proposed minimal standards for mass education in the interests of the employers, as against that of the population at large. Lowe's legislation prevented schools from receiving state grants except to teach the three Rs: reading, writing and arithmetic, an act that Arnold considered to disadvantage both poor individuals and the national culture as a whole. In the light of all this, we can say, against Hunter, that the "high" and the "low," the theoretical and the practical, become moments of a single historical, if fractured and contested, trajectory shared by the Edgeworths, Stow, even Kay-Shuttleworth, Arnold – and, finally, Leavis. They do so within a larger formation articulated in broad terms by Rousseau, within which the administrative practices of popular education cannot easily be granted causal and narrative priority over the theorists or critics in the story of the unfolding of literary pedagogy.

There is a strong case to think about these matters in larger terms still: since the Renaissance, figures like Bacon, Hobbes, Locke, Mandeville and Hume all write in explicit and tedious rejection of scholasticism and the *trivium*, at the same time as, more or less implicitly, they write outside of religion. The paralogism of modern pedagogy from the seventeenth century is installed in this double gesture: how to teach (and assume secular authority) *against* scholastic and religious authority. How to provide pupils

191

with individual autonomy at the same time as they are being situated within received social norms? How to have them imitate spontaneously that which they are taught? And the problem this large paralogism bequeaths to the sociological historian is: how to judge where continuities, discontinuities, grafts and differences begin and end within it? For historians of the "discipline" of English studies, there can be no absolute choice between the analytic methods of Foucault, and the post-Leavisite cultural studies that Foucault's work is positioned against by a writer like Hunter. It is more a matter of testing the ways in which each invoke the larger problematization of modern pedagogy, and deal with the archival evidence of its detailed and material historical itinerary. What Hunter's work does show, however, is how difficult it is, today, simply to affirm the *progressivist* discourse of Raymond Williams, say.

The second main difficulty with Ian Hunter's application of Foucault is that it discounts the fact that literature entered the pedagogical institutions precisely because it cannot be simply appropriated for the purposes of government. It is especially tempting to neglect the resistance that literature offers to government because, first, however much education leads to docility, by and large the proletariat desired it (which the marxists tend to forget). Throughout the nineteenth century, literature, in particular, was widely studied by working-class, dissenting, and petit-bourgeois adults who had no chance to go to university, in non-certifying institutions such as the Mechanics Institutes, and in informal reading-groups like the widespread "Literary Societies." And the resistance that literature can offer government is also easy to ignore because, later, literary studies, and the "sympathy" and "imagination" that they were supposed to nurture, were deemed appropriate for (semi-)professional careers in civil and imperial administration. Nevertheless, as we have seen, since the early nineteenth century much writing – including journalism – had allied itself with madness, death, drugs, crime, transgression and the signifier, against the more or less officially sanctioned values embodied in literary pedagogy. This has lead to the paradox around which teaching modernist writing has turned, a sharper, if more local, version of the larger problematic involved in teaching autonomy and spontaneity. How to maintain subversion within the academy? How to teach "life" in the classroom? Even today, students who read, for instance, Shelley's "Julian and Maddalo," *Les Fleurs du mal*, "Howl," *Women in Love*, *The Trial*, *Good Morning Midnight*, *The Man Who Loved Children*, *Junky*, *Story of the Eye*, even *Madame Bovary* and *The Wings of the Dove*, may be shaped by these texts in ways that literary critical techniques of reading (including deconstruction) do not touch. To teach English at a tertiary level today, as the Arnoldian heritage declines, may be to manage the transformation of the desire to read literature into the ability to write (the shifting modes of) criticism/theory. Yet it is always too soon to concede that only the second involves a practice on the self. To put it this way is to gesture at a hidden essentialism that it is easy to take from Foucault's later work. For him, of course, selves, constituted by various "ethical substances" are formed, in the modern world, largely by "governmentalities." However useful if may be, such a formulation makes it too easy to assume that there *are* substances to be shaped into unified "selves." But an "ethical substance" simply consists of utterances, actions, thoughts, desires, modes of deportment and so on: it is on *these* that education acts. Not only may thoughts, practices, desires work against each other, but a single individual may be shaped by different discourses, different practices, different objects, each of which can exist in some tension to another internalized, and shaping, object. On occasions, Foucault himself was more than capable of recognizing this: let us emphasize again that for him history is to be written as much from the resistance out as from the bottom up.

Literature, then, is not able to be absorbed into the process of government as easily as Hunter supposes. Literary studies do not simply belong to the apparatuses that have produced the docile society, though they do not stand quite outside them either. This leaves literary studies with the question, how to account for their own relations to modern power? What are the internal properties that enable literature's complex interactions with both social order and individuals? I think that we must begin to consider this question by analyzing a category – representation – which is larger than literature itself. The first reason for this is that literature has long been considered a sub-species of representation. As Derrida puts it: "If, as we have been precisely tempted to think, literature is born/dead of a relatively recent break, it is nonetheless true that the whole history of the interpretation of the arts, of letters has moved and been transformed within the diverse logical possibilities opened up by the concept of *mimesis*" (Derrida 1982a, 187).[5] Traditionally at least, the notion of "representation" legitimates and suffuses that of "literature"; it permits literature to be placed both inside and outside the "real world," to escape the logic of "true discourse."[6] Thus, it allows texts their glamour, which they cast back on the real world, and their ethical potential. Even the "romantic" claim that literature ultimately transcends representational categories like beliefs and ideas, takes its force from the representational paradigm. Its energy is derived from its continual negation of representation. So we can ask what might a writing look like that was thought of neither in terms of the paradigm of representation nor as its negation?

The use of literature for government rests on representation in another sense too. Cultural pedagogy attempted to form individuals within a unified and coherent cultural tradition – a tradition for which each individual was a place-holder, though not quite in the same way as paternity was once a place-holder for sovereignty, for instance. It did so as administrations negotiated with wider social wants and collectivities. Writers like Matthew

Arnold and George Eliot argued that the stability of representative democracy rests on a belief that norms and traditions are shared, and that each individual represents them, and thus, one another. It was those norms and traditions that education was required to produce and reproduce, so as to form individuals who, within a range of variations, represented a single entity – the culture and its values. Individuals invisibly embody and represent the culture; the political sphere represents (groups of) individuals. It is in these terms that one can say that the complex system, within which education, culture (including literature) and politics are interlocked, rests on an acceptance of the efficacy and validity of the notion "representation." Where that system is being contested politically, as it is today, then, of course, that notion too must be interrogated, as Heidegger first realized. Furthermore, as I shall argue, Foucault and other literary theorists have demonstrated, representation and mimesis are essentially unstable or "delirious" categories, having been described as "madness" from the beginning of Western thought. It is partly this very madness that makes representation so powerful a concept, and so difficult to move beyond. And finally, as I shall also argue, representation is so powerful a category, because we use it in our attempts not to let the past die – attempts in which modern governments play their part as they maintain the cultural tradition. To say that it may be difficult to abandon representation as a tool for analyzing culture, however, is not to push aside the kind of non-representational politics and work that Foucault pioneered. Nor is it to return to the old mode of literary studies, aimed at producing sensitive and representative – if not wholly vigilant – citizens.

THE DELIRIUM OF MIMESIS

To work towards a mode of thinking about literature that is not controlled by the concept "mimesis" we must ask: how do mimesis, writing and madness interlock? And to ask that is to return, however briefly, and before defining mimesis in more detail, to Plato's *Phaedrus* where the Western delirium of representation is established. *Phaedrus* posits two kinds of madness: worldly and divine. Worldly madness is uninteresting, worthless; but, as Plato's Socrates declares, divine madness was previously regarded, and should be regarded, as a fine thing. (Plato is already telling Foucault's story of madness's secularization, its split between insanity and *la folie*.) Divine madness is the channel through which the godly is communicated to human beings. Divinely mad people love, express themselves in lyric poetry inspired by the Muses, foretell the future by reading signs and perceive the world as symbolic of the Platonic forms or essences. Against this, writing eradicates the difference between the reality with which divine madness is in closest contact, and mere appearance. To learn from writing is to learn mechanically, to know at second hand. Readers are always

194

passive; like paintings, writings cannot answer questions. The shifts of the argument may seem obscure but it seems that Plato's fear of writing is to be understood in terms of his pedagogy, his personal and, as it were, institutional, need to maintain the force of "protreptic" – the branch of rhetoric designed to persuade an audience that a teacher was fit to teach virtue and truth. "Spoken truths," he has Socrates say, "are to be reckoned a man's legitimate sons, primarily if they originate within himself, but to a secondary degree if what we may call their children and kindred come to birth, as they should, in the minds of others" (Plato 1973, 101). Writing, by removing language from the teacher's mouth, destroys the basis of protreptic, makes of pupils bastards, whereas divine madness, solely the possession of individuals and the absolute warrant of authoritative insight, is unteachable. This leaves the teacher – the dialectician – a tiny margin in which to exercise his skills; his prestige rests on a vanishing point. Of course, Plato's preference for the teacher's bodily presence over the textbook is repeated by the Edgeworths among many others, just as the problem of "spontaneous imitation" or "taught autonomy" is foreshadowed in his attack on writing.

Nowhere in modern thought is the logic which orders these relations more clearly examined than in the first sections of Derrida's essay "Plato's Pharmacy," from which the following remarks derive. For Derrida, platonic *mimesis* may be in question whenever an event is repeated, an object copied, a feeling is expressed or language is considered to hook onto the world. It is also in question whenever a cultural product is interpreted as representing a social formation – in however displaced a fashion: where, for instance, a text is read as a "symptom" of a particular socio-political tension, or as the expression of a particular ideological contradiction.

In general, mimetic objects are either the same as, or different from, their originals. If they are the same, then the very distinction between copy and original disappears. This is to enter the dangerous world of *simulacra*: the negative version of the mimetic relation that Foucault calls "similitude" in *This is Not a Pipe*, his own treatise on mimesis (1982, 44). Yet the closer mimesis comes to representing the presence of an original, the more it reveals of that object's essence; thus truth as unveiling (Heidegger's *aletheia*) has already buried within it a mimetic moment. To unveil is to reveal, mimetically, the external aspect of an inner essence. Here the potential for a mimetic object not to differ from its original is inflected positively, and can found a whole aesthetic theory, as it does with Aristotle's *poesis*. In *This is Not a Pipe* Foucault called this form of repetition "resemblance" (ibid.). On the other hand, if the mimetic object differs from its original, then it is false – though here again a positive inflection is possible. For both neo-classicism and classic realism, art, itself untrue, can reveal the deeper truth of nature or society. In fact, the concept of "representation" is implicitly aimed at controlling both the category of repetition (simulacra), and that of absolute singularity (and the prolifer-ation of otherness), but it does so at the cost of falling into either basket as soon as it is analyzed and conceptualized – then, as we have seen, the forms of "bad mimesis" come to light. And because under the paradigm of mimesis the world is experienced as double – split between reality and its representation – it also becomes harder to affirm the ontological superficiality that Foucault and the transgressive theorists find there.

Despite these complexities and difficulties, mimetic categories seem so "natural" partly because they implicitly appeal to a hierarchical view of representation. An original, standing at the apex of a little hierarchy, acts as a standard of comparison for the image which mirrors it. Yet, as Derrida points out, trust in an originality behind resemblance – trust, that is, in *logos* – can only occur once a threat to the origin has been articulated. *Logos*, the vehicle of what is "true" before or behind representation, is, paradoxically, not older than, but coeval with, mimesis, for the question of "truth" can only arise when there is something to be true about or towards, as well as a subject to be true for. Derrida, repeating Plato, thinks of this necessity in terms of a story about partriarchal reproduction. *Logos* is not simply the "father" – the secure ground of truth-in-discourse – but a "son," displaced from the origin, who has a father next to him and who speaks for the father. This logocentric structure is inhabited both by the possibility that the son *precedes* the father and by the possibility that the relation between son and father is already one of similitude. (So, as rumour has it, Charlie Chaplin can enter a "Charlie Chaplin-look-alike" competi-tion – and come third.) Again we return to the proposition that, to regard a copy as more like the original than the original, is to broach a non-divine madness that cannot be avoided at all times and in all places. The self-present, that to which truth corresponds, turns out, at best, to be an effect of a system of *good* mimesis in which the re-presentation (or mirror image) is simultaneously different from, and the same as, its presentation.

So neither self-presence, nor a structure of good mimesis, nor of bad mimesis, can be drawn out singly from the system of representation. Indeed, bad mimesis is found not just in simulacra or sheer repetition but also where the relations between the representation and its object them-selves break – in the mirage of autonomy. Autonomy, the form of negative mimesis favoured in modernity, can only itself be represented as the conse-quence of a *will* to avoid repetition as one form of bad mimesis. It is here that modern pedagogy is itself entrapped in the fractured logic of mimesis. Autonomy can be represented, ascribed or imagined only by supposing that an original and its image become detached from one another, as if a mirror were to shatter just in reflecting, letting the image become an original in its own right. The force that shatters the mirror is often imaged as dangerous, allied to madness, especially as it pushes towards radical subjectivity. The young Hegel rebukes Fichte in these terms for instance:

196

"we have sometimes heard tell of people who went mad in their efforts to produce the pure act of will and the intellectual intuition" (Hegel 1977b, 157). This rush to autonomy is, of course, not always or necessarily directed towards subjectivity, it can also be traced in the doomed attempt to separate the materiality of language from its referential and reflective force – to disengage the "signifier" from the "signified." Such theory expresses the hope that, if there were such a thing as a signifier apart from a signified, then language would be freed from its mimetic dependence upon the world yet still, somehow, remain *language*.

Though representation as a concept is *necessarily* unstable, the forms of that instability empty out any transcendental possibilities. To put a complex matter very simply: conditions of possibility for mimesis are indescribable because such conditions are always already in a mimetic relation to that which they ground. Reflections on, or theories of, mimesis are, for that reason, flat, trivial. There is no possibility of explaining how effects of representation are produced by a signifying system – though that was the aim of certain earlier movements, most notably structuralism, which attempted to escape the mimetic paradigm. Rather, the challenge is to analyze a history of writing (in particular) *outside* that paradigm – without trying to account for "meanings" non-mimetically.

What, to recapitulate a little, does Foucault, the theorist of practices of the self, of discursive formations, of truth-games and power-relations, have to say to students of mimesis? He attempts to drag Western thought out of the logic of mimesis as far as possible, first, by presenting discourse and other domains of representation as ordered by immanent rules, that is, as not reflecting the world; second, by insisting on their "rarity" – by insisting on the material specificity of particular *énoncés* and their channels of distribution; third, by rigorously refusing to find a given and fixed human essence reflected in cultural products and, fourth, by accepting that "representations" are also events, if events of a particular kind. More "metaphysically," he also argues that discourse enters the paradigm of representation when it attempts to organize what cannot be organized – madness, for instance; or to replace what cannot be replaced – death, an attempt that cannot be avoided. And by rejecting the notion that history consists of large progressive movements sweeping through time and which leave the past behind (such as rationalization or liberation or, even, as the anxiety of influence), he encourages us to work at the level of local relations between events.

To think of Foucault like this certainly leads to different projects than those taken up by literary critics and historians who first turned to his work. They accepted and elaborated his specific accounts of sovereign and modern power and demonstrated how that power was reflected by, or structurally enacted in, particular texts or oeuvres. For instance, the narrative voice of the Victorian realist novel, together with its impossibly neat

197

ending, becomes an agency of panoptical vision; or the carnivalesque aspect of an Elizabethan play is shown not to subvert, but to prop up, the power and glory of the monarch.[7] Useful and perceptive as such work may be, the approach itself knows where it is going from the very beginning and passes too confidently from history to writing. It is especially difficult to account for the specificity not just of texts and genres but of socio-cultural interactions when one starts from a theory of a historical epoch and moves mimetically to examine its products, though some of the strongest new historicist criticism (such as D. A. Miller's *The Novel and the Police* or Catherine Gallagher's essay on *Our Mutual Friend*), focuses on the strategies by which literary texts distance themselves from social power-flows and circuits of exchange, and by those very strategies both belong to, and resist, modern power.[8] Analyses that begin with a theory of society and work outwards, regarding the text as an expression, an allegory or a symptom – in a word, a representation – of the society in which they are written, also leave open the question, why should this matter now? But, perhaps more importantly, most Foucauldian accounts fail fully to explore what is at stake when analysis, buffeted between mimetic and non-mimetic paradigms, tries to work in terms of the latter with all possible rigour and force. It is at this point in particular that Foucault's long career of historical revisionism begins to involve a reformulation of the methods by which literature, in particular, has been studied.

Such a project, then, would examine the technologies in which images and writings (as rare *énoncés*) are produced; the circuits through which they are transmitted; their relation to suffering, pleasure, power, seduction and order; the cultural, social and legal uses of, and constraints on, their circulation; the ever-present possibilities and effects of misfirings and loop mechanisms, and their complex effects on individual lives – which are not simply ethical or imitative. It would do so with some sensitivity to the systems by which populations have been administered and which fall outside the old divisions between the orders of politics, culture and civil society. It would do so with a strong sense of its own social and institutional place and function, and a disposition not to take the side of those whom history has most advantaged and normalized. All this, if at all possible, without falling back on simple distinctions between the other and the same, especially where that other is the past and the same is the present; without assuming, that is, at least too quickly, that "we" share a set of dispositions with "them" – the producers and consumers of past cultures. It seems to me that this kind of genealogy of the literary has been most carefully and subtly embarked upon by Stephen Greenblatt, especially in the essays on Shakespeare published under the title *Shakespearean Negotiations*.[9] And it is in his work that the difficulties of such a project are most openly exposed.

REPRESENTATIONS IN HISTORY

Greenblatt's methodology is presented in the first chapter of *Shakespearean Negotiations*, which remains his most sustained exposition of his aims, pre-suppositions and procedures, and on which, therefore, I concentrate. The essay begins by claiming that literature works most powerfully "in the formal, self-conscious miming of life" (Greenblatt 1987, 1). In such "simul-ations," death's finality may be, to some degree at least, avoided in advance, and "traces" of the past transmitted into the future. Unlike most post-structuralist thought, including Foucault's account of Roussel, here representation is thought of less as death's emissary in life, or absence's structuration of presence, than as life's transcendence of death, presence's incorporation of absence. And unlike post-structuralism (but like an anthropological/sociological tradition that begins with Émile Durkheim and Marcel Mauss), these simulations are the product of a general "social will" (4). In Durkheim's famous phrase, they belong to a "conscience collective." Greenblatt remains in tune with Foucault and post-structural-ism, however, in aiming to analyze representations through non-mimetic categories. He wishes, as he declares, to avoid falling back upon the concept "reflection." Instead, he calls upon transactional notions; in par-ticular, exchange and appropriation: "Mimesis is always accompanied by – and indeed is always produced by – negotiation and exchange" as he puts it (13).[10] Leaving aside exchange for a moment, Greenblatt requires a concept like "negotiation" because for him the circulation of represen-tations may be driven by tensions, differences, conflicts, and these, in turn, are not always to be separated from pleasure and seductions. Thus to take two connected examples from the body of the *Shakespearean Negotiations*: the anxiety that Elizabethan authority produces, and which invokes neither sheer fear of tyranny nor anticipation of mercy, is not so much sublimated as moulded into a moment of pleasure and irony through Shakespeare's theatricalization of it. In return, a certain deferral of resistance and obedi-ence proper to theatrical response may itself enter the apparatus of govern-ment. Second, a Shakespearean prince who is, like real monarchs, already a "collective invention" and a source of awe, may talk to his subjects with a certain empathy and casualness, to the delight of the spectator. This unbending – in the play, half feigned, half not – repeats and consolidates occasions in the larger world where authorities, partly theatrically, partly out of necessity, relax their aura. On these occasions of relatively free exchange they can, however, "record alien voices," and therefore rule all the more effectively and fearsomely. Within a model that can shelter such nuances, social divisions and hierarchies are much less than absolute differences. After all, to take another connected example, where the colonial conquerors' sympathy for the cultures they invade, their willingness to learn new practices, and, indeed, the flow of puzzlement and wonder between the two sides, all help the colonialists turn the colonized to their will, then barriers between different social sectors do not merely shut out or repress, they transform and create.

We confront an immediate and difficult problem in this transactional model however: in Greenblatt's essay notions like exchange and negotiation have a function analogous to that of the "regularities" or rules of Foucault's archaeological work. Both avoid the kind of thought for which events, texts or social formations represent larger, more "real" formations. That, as I have suggested, is their strength. Yet, once Foucault's work is invoked, it is difficult not to ask: to what degree are Greenblatt's cultural transactions themselves ordered? Do they form patterns, that is, are certain kinds of exchanges and negotiations systematically connected to certain times, places and institutions within, say, a more or less well-defined strategy? As we shall see, these are questions that Greenblatt engages in several ways – by describing, in formal terms, the transactions favoured by Shakespeare's theatre, by insisting that theatre's effects and functions are not quite localizable and predictable, by analyzing the relation between the theatre and quite large social formations – atheism and colonialism, for instance. Nonetheless, his work remains focused on specific cases. And he forestalls us asking, why *this* instance? – is it typical of, that is, representative of, some larger social force? – by invoking the quasi-aesthetic fascination of, even the weirdness of, his skilfully chosen instances. Perhaps it does not matter that this tactic forestalls rather than answers tendentious questions about the representativeness of a particular example – for those questions merely draw us back into the delirium of mimesis and interpretation. But his appeal to the wonder or fascination of the individual case and his responsiveness to the political use of such fascination, can interrupt another, less easily deferred, set of connections and continuities – those by which old divisive social forces and formations reproduce themselves, religion and colonialism being good examples of such forces. We can ask, does his fascinating, non-interpretative academic work have, in the present, something like the relation to these divisive formations that Shakespeare's theatre had in the past – in however minor a key? This is an important and disquieting question, which once again relies on mimesis – and can only be answered by breaking the spell both of the theatre and of the wonderful story.

Let us turn to Greenblatt's typology of transactional modes. He figures the barriers, hierarchies and distances, across which transactions move, spatially. For him, cultural differentiation can be understood in terms of various "zones" so that exchange is defined as the shift from one zone to another. It is in these terms that he offers a classification of those kinds of cultural transposition used by the Elizabethan theatre. The modes that he distinguishes are, first, "appropriation" – in which shifts from one zone to another involve no cost, and of which language is the most important instance. Language, after all, costs nothing and circulates quite easily. The second example of cultural exchange is "purchase" – in which objects are exchanged for money. The third, he calls "symbolic acquisition." Here the theatre takes possession of a thing from another zone by signifying or "representing" it. Representation may seem to re-enter Greenblatt's methodology at this point, but he attempts to avoid it by drawing upon classical rhetorical/structuralist distinctions, that is, by returning to non-mimetic categories. He argues that symbolic acquisition takes both a metonymical form (as when the theatre signifies the world by presenting part of a larger whole) and a metaphorical form (as when names of pagan gods are substituted for Christian ones to avoid censorship). But the theatre may also "acquire" happenings from other zones by "simulation" – as when "the actor simulates what is already understood to be a theatrical representation" (10). As the staged repetition of an already staged event, this too is less than a reflection of the world.

What drives these transactions? To answer this, Greenblatt sets out what we might call an "ontology of culture." For him culture moves from, has its being as, "energy." This permits him to define his task as "the analysis of the cultural circulation of social energy" (13). Although Greenblatt insists that this "energy" is closer to the rhetorician's *energia* than to any physicist's notion, it is impossible to dissociate it from Carlyle's earlier "force" or Foucault's "power," happy power, power voided of irredeemable suffering or metaphysical anxiety. Though, for Greenblatt, "everything produced by [Elizabethan] society can circulate," social energy then existed in particular as "power, charisma, sexual excitement, collective dreams, wonder, desire, anxiety, religious awe, free-floating intensities of experience." Of course it can also take the form of money: Greenblatt, unlike Foucault, does not neglect the market. The dynamism of circulatory flow, the sheer currency of things, belongs to proto-capitalism; Shakespeare is an entrepreneur, partner in a joint stock company, able, indeed required, to turn social conflict, anxiety, hierarchies and negotiations into fun, wonder, pleasure, cash and so on. Strangely enough this echoes and inverts the later puritan attacks on the theatre which saw it not just encouraging licentiousness but as making use of the reputation of authorities for show business profits and salaries, as well as encouraging role playing and maintaining the "pagan" in the Christian – or Protestant – world. Thus social energy, itself the expression of an expansionist, mercantile society, circulates into the theatre simultaneously through social (especially economic) and rhetorical channels, which continually displace the intensities through which energy is experienced. There is another potential difficulty in this line of thought however. For it can easily slip into supposing that these intensities, felt as "wonder," "awe," and "anxiety," for instance, are basic human responses, rather than products of the interactions between the analytic method with its desire to modulate into a celebratory and life-affirming tone, and the drives and the objects or moments being described.

Still, it is important to remember that, in *Shakespearean Negotiations*, Greenblatt's method, his "cultural poetics" as he calls it, is directed towards a specific historical moment, a specific institution and even, often, specific texts or groups of texts. Thus it is not absolutely clear to what degree he is setting out a general method at all. Just as Foucault's work on power is positioned ambiguously – is it a theory of power in general or an account of modern power in particular? – so Greenblatt's schema for the "social circulation of energy" makes some claim to be both a general frame for a historical sociology of culture, and a specific description of the relations between Shakespearean society and Shakespearean theatre. Such ambivalence is probably unavoidable. After all, any method of socio-cultural enquiry must borrow its features and its appeal from the context that it is designed to analyze. But the persuasiveness of Greenblatt's project today owes much to its focus on *this* historical era in particular, posed as it is at a threshold of modernity. To speak in large generalizations, we can say that, in Greenblatt's work, the era of the rise of modernity speaks as directly as is possible to the era of its decline. And without pushing this any further, it is important to the persuasiveness of Greenblatt's method that Shakespeare's theatre was an urban phenomenon, not completely complicit with classical or absolutist power, and based on economic institutions like the joint stock company that were to provide a motor for later industrial capitalism. On the other hand, Shakespeare belonged to a society in which a fully-fledged capitalist mode of production had yet to emerge. There were, in particular, no "classes" in Marx's sense. Shakespearean society knew no industrial proletariat, defined as having nothing to sell except a labour power available to be transformed into exchange-value and profit by capital. Nor had literature and criticism, "culture" in one modern sense, been put to the kind of governmental use that Hunter describes. In fact, the universalist narratives of secular enlightenment had yet to be articulated. So, as a hybrid of absolutist and modern formations, Greenblatt's Elizabethan theatre resists the kind of analysis that classical marxism and Foucauldianism provide. The ambiguity between the general and its local applicability of Greenblatt's project, is all the less visible because we can mirror our "post-modernity" in Shakespeare's theatre. There is a sense here, once more, that Greenblatt's work takes its power from a mimetic claim that, on the face of it, it is designed to avoid.

It is possible to draw Greenblatt's work more closely into connection with Foucault's work on literature, by examining it rather more philosophically. We can begin by noting that while his model does rely on a concept of cultural differentiation, Greenblatt makes it clear that, for him, the theatre belongs simultaneously to a particular site (in the case of the *Globe* an immovable one) and to forms of acting that spread through society at large. For Greenblatt, theatre was "non-exclusive" in three senses in Shakespeare's society: a wide variety of situations could be presented on stage, most, if not all, of the population had access to it, and theatrical performance was not limited to a narrow range of places and times – it was not simply institutionalized. Theatre's non-exclusivity, especially in the first and second sense, was connected to its being construed as "non-useful" – that is, formally disconnected from religious rites, productive work or political institutions. And its non-exclusivity also meant that the division between what is theatrical and what is not theatrical, becomes blurred: the distinction was "improvised" as Greenblatt puts it.

Nonetheless the failure of formal markers or barriers to divide the world from the stage did – and does – not quite grant the theatre a mobility, or rather a pattern of mobility and immobility, like that available to language. Greenblatt's typology of cultural exchange recognizes this. For him, the theatre freely "appropriates," rather than "purchases" or "symbolically acquires," language. The fact that language costs nothing, that its mobility is relatively unpoliceable, means that literature is not as easily analyzed in terms of "zones," "exchanges" and "negotiations" as is theatre, for all theatre's constant evacuation and re-creation of its borders. This is not to say that language does not have internal divisions: idiolects mark geographical and class differences as Gadamer notes against Habermas; professions have their own discourses, and print can be censored. Indeed, the significance and mobility of particular natural languages depends, in part, on their relation to other so-called natural languages in hierarchies of cultural value. English was not, in Shakespeare's time, the language of official knowledge at all, nor were relations between literary or written English and spoken English as well defined as they were to become – factors which would seem to have offered Shakespeare more liberty than they caused him anxiety. Further, as Foucault's work makes clear, statements are removed from everyday speech to form discursive unities as a result of techniques of exclusion like ordination, academic examinations and other acts of certification. As Foucault fails to note, statements may also be separated from the *doxa* within a system set in place by inherited, filiative identities and differences. In Shakespeare's time, state power protected many of these filiations and rites of certification: to feign being a nobleman or a cleric, to say or write the words they could say or write, could be a crime. It was part of theatre's non-exclusivity that such prohibitions did not apply there.

The vernacular, then, which moves across the social body so easily, constitutes a background across which exchanges and negotiations move. But once everyday discourse is repeated on the stage, it changes its status. It is no longer casual, free utterance, but chosen, scripted utterance – an effect to which Greenblatt is himself very sensitive. It follows that certain constitutive properties of the vernacular cannot be staged, or, indeed, written. Even improvisation on stage is not everyday language, just because, from the point of view of the spectator, there can never be absolute certainty as to what is, and what is not improvised. The spontaneity of everyday language can only be represented – as we so easily say. It is in the way that everyday language eludes appropriation that we find one limit to Greenblatt's desire to avoid representation as an analytic category. For the transactional terms that he privileges do not quite account for the way in which theatrical language structurally differs from ordinary language. For that, we need concepts like "representation," that point to a more profound break between the theatre and its social setting. And these concepts lead us into the delirium of mimesis. They lead us to believe that it might not just be on stage, or in writing, that events – and words – are scripted. The most "spontaneous" discourse in the everyday world may be, in some sense, determined in advance, organized in what psychoanalysts might call an "other scene."

From the opposite side, to the degree that something is unique, cannot be bought, repeated, transported or gestured to through metaphor or metonymy, then it too, by definition, is unavailable to social circulation as Greenblatt describes it. Do such things exist? It seems that they do, and, furthermore, as I will argue in a little more depth, it is from them too that the paradigm of representation gains its prestige. We can begin making this rather obscure claim clearer by noting the difference between, for instance, kissing, philosophizing, falling in love, undergoing a marriage ceremony, and dying on stage. One can kiss on or off stage: a kiss and, sometimes, its sensations, including pleasure, is merely repeated when it is theatricalized. When one philosophizes on stage, this too may be – to use the language of mimesis – simultaneously feigned and unfeigned: its truth-value is not affected by its staging. One can also fall in love on stage: indeed, acting out love in a space separated from the "real" world may cause real love. Suspicion of the way this muddies the distinction between the authentic and the inauthentic motivates Jane Austen's animus against theatrical representation in *Mansfield Park*, for example. On the other hand, to repeat the marriage ceremony on stage is merely to feign it: one can only be married as oneself – not as a fictional character, just as one can only be a priest, lawyer or nobleman as oneself. Indeed the division between fiction and non-fiction derives some of its force from legal sanctions against pretending to be another in circumstances like the marriage ceremony. But death on stage is something else. Were an actor to die on stage, interactions between the proper and improper, the feigned and the unfeigned, the theatre and the world would take another direction. For at the moment of death, the actor stops acting – as in so-called "snuff movies."

There are other events (such as having an orgasm) in which to repeat on stage is never simply to feign, events in which the body takes over and

204

which do not simply belong to what Foucault would call the "ethical substance" – that aspect of the self under socio-cultural direction. Such examples remind us that what can, and what cannot, be repeated or feigned on stage is under the control of authorities who have used their power to restrict moments when the body takes over, like death or orgasm, being shown on stage, and to enforce the reality of the real and fictionality of fiction. Yet, as I say, the sharpness of the division between repeating and feigning in a case like that of staged death is not simply under social or cultural control, because what dies, in the final instance, is a body rather than a mind. Thus one cannot repeat one's own death: when a person dies then dialogue, exchange and negotiation with that person ceases for ever – in this world at least. It is because bodies die only once and death is not fungible that death can only enter the institution of theatre either as feigned or, otherwise, as an accident. Not even the performance artists mentioned in the last chapter, who were trying as hard as they could to work outside the paradigm of representation, scripted their death into their performances. If they did, in what would be simultaneously their last performance and their last action, the always problematic split between the performing self and the organizing self, that is, the self "behind" the performance who can move from one performance to the next, would at last disappear. It would be the organizing self, the self continuous across performances, whose loss would be mourned, whose corpse would be buried. In the "real" self's absence, she is finally separable from her performance – and, at the same stroke, mimetic categories reassert themselves.

As we have seen, Greenblatt declares his interest in the power of "simulations" to escape death's finality; indeed he begins his book by confessing his "desire to speak with the dead." In his introductory essay, Shakespearean theatre finally matters to him because it has some power to satisfy that desire. We can now note further that his analytics of the social circulation of energy avoids death in another sense. It fails to allow for those social breakdowns in exchange and negotiation of which death is the sharpest instance. This is particularly noticeable because the Elizabethan/Jacobean public theatre – like most other institutions which disseminate what we now call "fictions" – almost obsessively dealt in acts of violence, murder, death as well as madness – all instances in which social negotiation falters or collapses. It is as if that theatre wanted to draw such instances into representation – to keep their finality, or their failure to enter into social interactions, at bay. Two points follow: one formal, the other, ethico-political. First, this relentless staging of death and violence does not simply rely on the modes of social exchange that Greenblatt calls "symbolic acquisition" because staged death, staged violence even, repeats the external face, the public side, of a recognizable event rather than signifying that event metonymically or metaphorically. After all, what tropes can we persuasively provide for the moment of death, which can never be experienced? Paradoxically, it is because death is not, finally, an experience, although it is a radically personal event, that staged death, even more than staged violence, can re-enact or "appropriate" (to use Greenblatt's phrase) every last gasp of the death throe – a fact of which theatre in Shakespeare's time took full advantage. Because a staged death may be simultaneously so real (repeating its outer aspect) and so unreal (not be a bodily death at all), it is all the easier to describe it in mimetic categories – as feigned, simulated. This is the other side of Greenblatt's sense that "simulations" have the capacity to keep the dead alive. Second, it is partly through practices defined through mimetic categories, given value as "fictions," "representations" and so on, that individual lives are ethically formed in modern society – as Foucault reminds us. The way that the realm of fiction represents violence and death with such vigour helps us see that ethically formed individuals are formed against death – in modes of power that conceal and replace state-sanctioned violence, and the state's right to send people out of exchange or negotiation, to destroy the life in their bodies. When a culture is at home with death, directed towards life-after-death like Christian cultures confident of the possibility of individual salvation, then exchange and negotiation never cease, and the power of fictional representation to structure individuals' lives will be of less account.

When Greenblatt classifies the sources of Shakespeare's social energy he does not single out the force that motivates his own work: the desire to speak with the dead. Shakespeare's contemporaries – as we will see in the next chapter – could speak with the dead, at least in a manner. In particular, for them, ghosts still, just, existed. As a secular "shaman," as he engagingly calls himself, Greenblatt has to find more professional and "rational" means to keep in touch with the dead. Yet his desire to construe simulations as the ghosts of our culture, his desire to downgrade mimetic categories – even his emphasis on fascination and wonder – can be understood in terms of his wish to avoid confirming representation's power to discipline lives. It is not a power that is easy to escape. If we ask the questions, why is the theatre so fascinating? why do fictions circulate so widely? the answers are not just to be found in terms, so important to capitalist cultural production, like pleasure, wonder, sexual excitement, intensities of experience, or even in the will to keep the dead alive. The theatre, or better, the theatre-effect, is fascinating because its representations produce what Foucault called a "labyrinth" in which selves are no longer fixed but are "free" to change and be changed – by governments amongst others. And the delirium of mimesis is especially virulent when the living represent the dead. Then, the difference between the true and the false, the real and the feigned may be especially rigorously policed – there were good reasons why, for example, as Greenblatt reminds us, in Shakespeare's time it was always someone else who was an atheist. To think that life after death might be a fiction was a serious transgression. But let us remember that, in the West, representations of death and violence were, for centuries, most widely circulated in passion plays and other images of Christ on the Cross. In these sacred and "true" images, violence, pain, death, the avoidance of death and the promise of conversion, of a new self, merge – as well as, interminably, the possibility of their fictionality. It is one of the rewards of juxtaposing the kind of post-Foucauldian criticism represented by Hunter with that represented by Greenblatt, to be able to see that the most auratic representations in Western society belong to the genealogy of modern government. They do so because, despite their "truth" and sacredness, or rather, because of the very insecurity of that truth and sacredness, they exist at the heart of the labyrinth in which the identities of individuals are not fixed but are open to change. Yet – to make a final point – it is in the living's pain, sickness, poverty and hunger that they are closest to the dead who, in this world, can only be represented. In Greenblatt's "desire to speak to the dead," and in his championing of what we might call the transactional paradigm, he too quickly passes over these marks of oppression, the ways that the life, health and happiness of some can be expropriated, irredeemably, by others. He does so, I suppose, because, like most of us who read and write books like his (and this one too), he finds it hard to speak *as himself* from the position of those whom life offers least, to whom death is, in fact, closest. And to represent such a position has, for some very good reasons, become almost impossible.

In my next chapter, I will offer short analyses of two texts, *Hamlet* and *An American Tragedy* and their interplay with the institutions of literary instruction and transmission in terms that owe a great deal to both Hunter and Greenblatt, and behind them, to Foucault. But I will take more account of the insufficiency of the non-mimetic paradigm, of the advantages gained by marking and analyzing the institutional preconditions of one's own analysis, of the quasi-rule-boundedness of cultural practice, and of literature's transgressive edge. In Dreiser's novels, in particular, the question of how to give voice to, and listen to, those whom life offers least, reappears too.

AFTER READING FOUCAULT: BACK TO THE AUTHOR

HAMLET

Hamlet tells the story of a king's murder. In a monarchy, no act threatens genealogical or "blood" modes of social and political reproduction more deeply than the murder of a king. No act involves less exchange or nego-tiation. The killer has got away with it too – which means that the socially-sanctioned violence which helps secure both the social order and the boundaries between discourses has been eluded. After Claudius' conceal-ment of murder, social order can only be based on lies and pretence. But a fiction may now tell the truth, become a weapon for revealing hidden disorder and discontinuity. In that move, the springs and delirium of mimesis begin to be displayed. For instance, how real is the Ghost?, how true his (?) its (?) claims? It is a question to which others are immediately joined. How "alive" is he? How dead? The possibility of achieving life after death and the possibility that fictions might be true fuse into one another in *Hamlet* as they do so often. In the scene where Hamlet instructs the players to mime his father's death, the play represents the "simulation" – to use Greenblatt's term – of a murder. By having Claudius respond to that scene as if it were real, the play comes as close as drama can to feigning *and* repeating a murder, stretching the limits, and affirming the power, of the representational paradigm. One should note that this simul-ation can have "real" effects because the play within the play exists as writing, a piece of "portable property" endlessly available for revision: Hamlet himself rewrites this piece of theatre before the players play it. With Hamlet an author, *Hamlet* denotes its own institutional space, marked out on one side by its existence as a theatrical event and, on the other, its existence as a script. There exists a gap between the play's performance and its text however. Hamlet's detailed instructions to the players intensi-fies the logic by which it is true that a performance can only reduce a script's range of effects and meanings. As we shall see, moving within this loose and uncertain space, the play unsettles a variety of ethical orders too. More generally still, in exploring the border at which discontinuity and continuity, madness and order, life and death, are joined and separated, in representing the limits of representation – *Hamlet* has served as a classic model for claims that literary texts obey no general laws, that each is unique and that, therefore, "literature" captures reality most finely. For this reason, it has long been a favoured object for close reading, the defining practice of modern criticism. But one can also read, and closely read, to end that kind of criticism – to reflect on it and to re-engage the connections between old texts and current society.

I want to begin to make these remarks more concrete by starting at some distance from the play itself. About 200 years before Shakespeare wrote *Hamlet* (on Sunday 20 June 1389, to be precise) a ghost or "spirit," who had pestered Thomas of Ely and his son for thirteen nights, threw them out of their bed. Annoyed and resentful, they climbed back in. But the ghost, returning, insisted that Thomas go to see St Etheldreda who, appearing from the dead, and praising Thomas as a man who genuinely loved her, told him to tell his confessor to warn certain individuals to pay their tithes and prove their wills. Thomas was also ordered to instruct the Prior and Convent at Ely to hold processions every Wednesday and Friday for five weeks. He objected that as a poor man of no reputation, his visitation by the ghost would not be believed. Upon which the saint caused his legs to curve, told him to stay in bed and promised to cure him on her Saint's day. She kept her word and the miracle gave Thomas's accusations credence. The processions were held, too.

About 150 years after Shakespeare's death, in 1762, spooky noises were heard in a certain Mr Parsons' house at Cock Lane, London. The ghost, who seemed to emanate around Mr Parsons' little girl, Elizabeth, communicated by knocking. It informed the world that it was the spirit of Fanny Lynes, a woman whom Mr Parsons had met at the church where he worked as officiating clerk. (She and her male partner had been looking for lodgings and Mr Parsons had suggested his own house.) The ghost alleged that she, Fanny, had been poisoned by her partner who was unable to marry her because she was his deceased wife's sister. The event excited intense discussion in London and was taken seriously by many, especially the Methodist community. Others were sceptical, and experiments to unmask the ghost were begun. Dr Johnson, who believed in ghosts as signs of life after death, joined a committee set up to enquire into the case. Elizabeth was sequestered to see if the ghost would still manifest itself. At first, she claimed to the committee that Miss Fanny's ghost was crawling under the sheets "like a mouse," but when she was further constrained it failed to appear. Johnson wrote an article for the *Gentleman's Magazine*, publicizing the event as a fraud and finally the Parsons and some of their supporters were brought to court.[1] A clergyman and a tradesman, who had supported Fanny and her ghost, paid the accused man damages. Mr and Mrs Parsons and their servant were all severely punished, Mr Parsons being pilloried three times and then imprisoned for two years. But when, half out of his mind, he was placed in the stocks, the crowd felt sorry for him and took up what the *Annual Register* called a "handsome collection" on his behalf (Anon., 1762, 145). It is worth noting that Fanny was the last ghost to attract wide public support, and she sparked off intense historical and literary activity – including, perhaps, what is generally regarded as the first Gothic novel: Horace Walpole's *The Castle of Otranto*.

Thomas of Ely's story was found in a parson's commonplace book which includes hymns, proverbs and prayers.[2] It is a story to tell a flock, simple enough structurally – the ghost is not even a soul of the dead – but functionally quite complex. The ghost mediates between Thomas and Saint Etheldreda, who herself works as something between what we would now call a prosecutor and a tax-informer. The problem is of course that Thomas will not be believed, at least until a public miracle occurs. Why insert a noisy and violent ghost in the story at all then? Just because the ghost can communicate between the sacred world of the saints and the murky world of everyday life, in which known individuals do not pay tithes. Also because, if miracles hardly ever happen, ghosts were quite common. It is the kind of story that enlightened *philosophes*, Voltaire and Condorcet say, would have delighted in: a priest enshrining his authority to extract money, by inventing tall tales to dazzle and frighten the credulous. Yet, as it speaks for the churchman, it offers a voice to the poor, allowing them to protest against those who fail their social duties. The ghost's very everydayness and humour – throwing its victims out of their bed after being ignored by them for almost two weeks – means that it can mediate between Thomas and St Etheldreda as well as between the parson and his parishioners.

The second story is, as one would expect, both more secular and darker. The ghost is that of an actual person (as in the classical and later literary tradition). The story requires urban anonymity: strangers looking for lodgings, arsenic to be purchased, a public sphere larger than the circle of personal acquaintance through which gossip and news spreads fast and far. Indeed it requires a debate about credulity and the role of reason in sacred and supernatural matters, a debate as to whether the dead continue to inhabit this world. Though this ghost is unmasked as a fraud, it occupies recognizably the same social space as Thomas's "spirit." Again it permits accusations to be made, again it works on and – partly – *for* the poor, again it detects concealed, if in this case, non-existent, crime. This seems to have been why the crowd took Mr Parsons' side at the stocks. Ghosts come into being in social structures without accurate state machinery for the detection of crime (no forensic autopsies to detect the traces of poison, for instance), without a public legal apparatus for bringing a law-breaker to court.[3] How to make an accusation, how to execute a hue and cry, when crimes were secret, untraceable; when, as especially in the case of poisoning, the immediate victim does not live to tell the tale and suspicion so easily overruns evidence? Raising ghosts was one means. Ghosts are hedged about by staginess and fakeness, because, unlike angels who also pass between this world and another, their messages have worldly meanings and uses rather than divine ones. In *Tom Jones*, Partridge, ridiculed for his superstitiousness, declares that he could never murder because his victim's ghost would return to haunt him. Fielding, a founder of modern policing, is intent on constructing more efficient sanctions than that – of which the novel's satire on the supernatural is one.[4] As proto-police detectives, as agents of popular justice, Thomas's and Fanny's ghosts are both awful and sympathetic. As both worldly and other worldly, they are slightly ridiculous, turning the unimaginable into the merely weird; as both immaterial and material they are irredeemably clumsy, clanking; coming into existence where secular authorities fail or seem to fail, they necessarily, and often pleasurably, excite scepticism; as inviting scepticism they can be supported by those – like the Methodists – who wish intuitive faith to triumph; in making accusations which are neither quite private nor quite public, they can be used to figure and consolidate the force of conscience. Greenblatt's literary desire to speak to the dead presupposes the death of ghosts like these – that is to say, the end of this kind of non-literary cultural practice whose function was, in part at least, replaced by literature itself.

Hamlet's father's apparition has a very serious accusation to make against a very powerful person indeed. Whence this ghost's authority? In the first instance, it is grounded on the apparition's physical similarity to the older Hamlet, a likeness easier to achieve on stage than in life. As we have seen, murder can never be wholly appropriated by theatre but, from the points of view of both literary criticism and modern policing, "real" ghosts are always feigned, untrue. Yet the ghost's appearance is not enough to ground his claims – appearances, after all, can be made up. Thus the ghost's right to accuse is also based on its ability to communicate its difference – its experiences in the other world:

> I am thy father's spirit,
> Doomed for a certain term to walk the night,
> And for the day confined to fast in fires,
> Till the foul crimes done in my days of nature
> Are burnt and purged away. But that I am forbid
> To tell the secrets of my prison-house,
> I could a tale unfold whose lightest word
> Would harrow up thy soul, freeze thy young blood,
> Make thy two eyes like stars start from their spheres,
> Thy knotty and combined locks to part,
> And each particular hair to stand on end,
> Like quills upon the fretful porcupine.
>
> (I, v, 9–20)

To describe the experience of this world beyond the grave requires a subtle variation of the old rhetorical device of *occupatio*, or paralepsis, by which a topic is introduced in the pretence of omitting it: "I could a tale unfold . . ." The tale *is* unfolded but only in the form of a description of the effects that telling the tale would have on the bodies of its auditors. The ghost's staginess becomes apparent in its attempt to educate the audience into proper ghost-response behaviour; it is saying less "I am ghastly, I have had inexpressibly awful experiences" than "make your eyes stare and – so – feel horror! feel terror!" The image of a body in terror will be invoked by thousands of horror stories in the centuries to come; in fact, the social placement of the genre is already inscribed in this linguistic device, which demands that the stagy invitation, issued in the conditional voice, be read as an imperative. Who in authority need let "each particular hair" "stand on end" "like quills upon the fretful porcupine" any more than the great critic Dr Johnson could be convinced by the thing "like a mouse" that crawled over Elizabeth Parsons' body? The invitation to imprint one's body by such extravagant commands is issued largely to the powerless, and, as we have seen, is driven out of the schoolroom (in the ban on Gothic horrors) by authorities such as the Edgeworths, more interested in their pupils expressing themselves than in their being emotionally worked on or manipulated. This kind of discourse becomes mere *doxa* – not true knowledge – when it is deemed unsuitable for pedagogy and examination. Yet when police, lawyers and doctors come to manage crime under the aegis of the rationalized state, the presence of ghosts will continue to maintain the hope that evaders of the law may face their punishment if not in this world then in the next. That, for instance, is still the role of the ghost in Ann Radcliffe's massively influential *The Mysteries of Udolpho* – even though her ghosts are explained away at the end. The energy of her plot inverts that of the whodunit: instead of a private eye ferreting out clues of the identity of a criminal Radcliffe's spirits arouse the right suspicion against the right person, the mystery lying in the rationalist question: what is the *ghost's* natural rather than supernatural identity?

Not that the extravagance and staginess of its discourse need disqualify the Hamlet's father's ghost – what else can an apparition say once it must *talk* itself into credibility? Its drive to exceed language's finitude, to transform language into sensation – constitutive of modern discourse according to Foucault – is actually part of its unfulfillable effort to establish its authority and reality. Ghosts, even as ur-police, exist at the centre of discursive – and ethical – struggles and problems. The dead king's spirit, in particular, walks out of night into a religious debate that marks a challenge to available modes of subjectivity and self-formation. Is he of the devil's camp or not? Under such ambiguity, seeing a ghost can produce, and be a sign of, madness rather than terror. These are familiar points in Shakespearean scholarship: it is well known that, for instance, *Hamlet* is

212

written in a period when madness was a topic attracting much interest. No doubt the reason for this in general is, as Foucault suggested, that madness itself was becoming secularized, entering its modern alliance with writing and subjectivity. To take a case often discussed in regard to *Hamlet*, in a Protestant work like Lavater's *Of Ghosts and Spirits Walking by Night* (1572), apparitions are viewed not merely in terms of religious doctrine but as hallucinations, symptoms of madness. Indeed, according to the logic of mimesis, the more that the ghost's speech repeats traditional teaching, the greater the threat to Hamlet if he – Hamlet – *is* mad. That the sober and sensible Horatio also sees the ghost intensifies, rather than settles, the question. In late medieval popular knowledge, "Denmark" was a drunken country through which strange spirits roamed. The dead king's reappearance turns it into a country of psychic and governmental disorder in which the borders between the most fundamental zones of all – between life and death – can be crossed and re-crossed.

Seeing the ghost triggers an immediate crisis of self-government in the younger Hamlet:

> Remember thee?
> Ay, thou poor ghost, whiles memory holds a seat
> In this distracted globe. Remember thee?
> Yea, from the table of my memory
> I'll wipe away all trivial fond records,
> All saws of books, all forms, all pressures past
> That youth and observation copied there,
> And thy commandment all alone shall live
> Within the book and volume of my brain,
> Unmix'd with baser matter. Yes, by Heaven!
> O most pernicious woman!
> O villain, villain, smiling damned villain!
> My tables. Meet it is I set it down
> That one may smile, and smile, and be a villain –
> At least I am sure it may be so in Denmark [*Writes*]
> So uncle, there you are. Now to my word.
> It is "Adieu, adieu, remember me."
> I have sworn't.

(I, v, 97–112)

In extreme distress, but against all verisimilitude, Hamlet records what he has learned in writing. Of course the use of such "notebooks" goes all the way back to those *hypomnetata* of the Greeks, in which individuals noted down apothegms encountered at random to aid memory and help proper action. They were, in fact, one of Plato's objects in his attack on writing in *Phaedrus*. Hamlet is writing simultaneously on the table and on "the book and volume of his brain," so that the relation between "book" and

213

"brain" becomes more an identity than a metaphor. The message that Hamlet inscribes is not like any other. Indeed, it is difficult to be certain as to precisely what he sets down – is it one saying or two? And which? "Adieu, adieu. Remember me" or the "saw," perhaps trivial – "one may smile and smile and be a villain"? This ambiguity is, amongst other things, an effect of the privacy of writing, a feature that is foregrounded on stage. To write requires physical movement but, because one cannot tell what one writes from the movement itself, it remains less than a readable public gesture. More crucially, these messages, learnt when the dead can be spoken to, warn that mimesis as feigning is everywhere – at work at the very seat of authority. Both messages break with those previously noted on his table/brain. The earlier precepts were "observations" that moved directly from the world to his mind, but the difference between appearance and reality is precisely what one cannot observe. To know *that* requires an authority, not here the authority of reason and deduction, but one that is merely persuasive. The problem with persuasion, however, is established by Locke's attack on it, quoted in my second chapter, which repeats rather than settles Hamlet's predicament. Thus Locke: "if the light of persuasion be the light that must guide us, I ask how shall anyone distinguish between the delusions of Satan and the inspiration of the Holy Ghost?" (Locke 1975, 703–4) The *appearance* of a persuasive authority might differ from its reality too. As soon as this possibility is articulated, it unfolds at a deeper level still: who now is the "me" that Hamlet commands himself, and is commanded to, remember? What identity remains when the view that writing is the firm structure of the world and all its parts (including brains), is replaced by the view that individuals possess an inner core that may be betrayed by a false appearance, that feigning is uncontainable, and when, at the same time, an ancient mode of self-government falls apart?

Here, ethical and epistemic orders are not quite separable. As far as the second is concerned, "that one may smile and smile and be a villain" is a general proposition which, privileging a form of dangerous mimesis, contradicts "maxims" like "Whatever is, is," dear to scholasticism, that Locke will also attack almost a century later as false principles of science.[5] Locke will aim to replace such maxims which he thinks of as less than ideas (as "trivial," "containing no instruction in them," mere "marks") by a philosophy based on the immediate apprehension of particular *ideas* and their connections, a philosophy which, as we have seen, can ultimately legitimate a pedagogy that demands its subjects be simultaneously imitative and original. However, Hamlet's proposition, which generalizes out into, "Whatever is, may not be," finds (again) a difference between essence and appearance, and thus undoes in advance Locke's attempt to replace scholastic maxims and reasoning by an individual's personal ideas. (Hamlet's first conversation with Rosencrantz and Guildenstern provides a brilliant

214

but already archaic parody of scholastic reasoning in which an original maxim is played with and examined according to the rules of Aristotelian logic.) Of course, "ideas" remains open to Shakespearean/Cartesian interrogation: "Are you real?" "Do you belong to me or to the world?" They require a linguistic or grammatical subject who *has* them but is not fully constituted by them. To note that mental representation cannot logically account for the subject whose mind they are supposed to form, has been a move by which idealism classically disengaged itself from empiricism. In terms of Foucault's archaeological epistemes, we can see that Hamlet is doubly stranded – he belongs neither to the prose of the world, nor to a (Lockean and mimetic) grid of representations.

This is to speak as if the prose of the world were itself a stable formation. In the "tables" speech, writing repeats itself across different kinds of physical objects (tables and brains) from which it can be expunged. Despite its wider analogies, writing does not attach to the permanent forms of nature, it needs to be "on" something. Thus old messages, which like Hamlet hitherto "knew not 'seems' " can be wiped out for the sake of the new ones, which themselves therefore cannot guarantee their own permanence, their own power consistently to aid or replace memory. Admittedly, the act of erasure requires an imperative not just an "observation." This involves a paradox: the ghost *orders* Hamlet to remember because memory is, in a circle, what has become problematic, just because it is stored as writing which, in turn, is material and expungeable. Although the message, which explicitly tells of the cleft between appearance and reality, is regarded by Hamlet as causing a radical and shocking break in the world, in fact, that world used to be what it seemed to be only because it existed as a particular kind of material thing, one which was the locus of a radically impermanent rhythm of erasure and origination. That the appearance of the world is its truth when it takes the form of a book, of writing, is not wholly separable from the opposite view, that the world is not a book and its appearance is not its truth. To record this new message is dangerous. Hamlet's apothegm enters two language games at once, description and prescription. He himself will smile and smile and be a villain, when he takes on an "antic disposition," and, crazily jesting, destroys Polonius, that old man of old maxims. This determination of self by precepts that function uncontrollably as both description *and* prescription, threatens the hypomnematic technology of self that, at least in this form, Hamlet is one of the last to have had access to.[6] Where words have effects that cannot be controlled, where they are imitated or enacted independently of the agent's will, then they explicitly point to the wound, the uncontrollable effects of mimesis. At this very point, as Hamlet will note – in Platonic terms – the "body of contraction" ("contraction" equals the "contract" that binds words to things) has its "soul plucked from it" to appear a "rhapsody of words" (III, iv, 321). Mere words (with their own power) because *not* mere (controllable and knowable) ideas.

This victory of soullessness, of sheer language, in an era opening out into an epistemology of representation and an ethic of spontaneous imitation, also belongs to the long process in which writing lost its sacred and ethical force. For the Church, to possess, and to master, writings was to be in possession of an authority based, finally, on the divine authority expressed in the Holy Book. As we have seen, it is language's capacity to ground such authority that *Hamlet*, in particular, questions – not least in the (Protestant) authority it doubtfully invests in a ghost. When Shakespeare's works become available on the market in folio form soon after his death, they have no clerical aura attached to them. They show few traces even of classical, humanist scholarship. They are not "literature." These books function, rather, as valuable reminders and mementos of much-praised plays and moving performances, as necessary aids for staging the plays, and, most of all, as private substitutes for performances in a socio-legal order within which public theatre-going was increasingly under threat. Obviously, such books have a very different function from the ethical notebooks too. When one used the old hypnomnetata, writing and reading had been intimately connected: one read what one wrote, one noted what one read. Writing was an individual skill, intimately connected to reading, that helped maintain a well-ordered life. As market-circulated print, however, writing increasingly becomes a commodity to be read by unknown others in unknown ways. It disseminates the ethical and epistemological difficulties that follow the appearance of Hamlet's father's ghost; in the print-market, one might almost say, such difficulties become epidemic.

In Shakespeare's era, writing also becomes much more extensively used as an administrative tool – nowhere more obviously than in the legal system. The Marian statutes of the 1550s, which reformed medieval trial procedure, "established the legal necessity to collect all the facts about a particular incident and present them in the form of a written dossier" (Weisser 1979, 96). This legislation squeezed the social space in which ghosts had a role. And the use that the state makes of writing is almost obsessively dramatized in the play. For instance, Polonius, who is ridiculed because he delivers a series of worn ethical maxims to Laertes, also sends a spy to record his son's behaviour. This makes of his fuddy-duddiness itself a disguise and a ploy – by virtue of it, his undercover agent is less likely to be revealed. Polonius uses incompetence, as Claudius mimes tolerance, to leave room for those transgressions that will sanction his prying as much as to mask his secret and absolutist manoeuvres. These manoeuvres, in turn, rely on writing, just as does Claudius's attempt to have the English king kill Hamlet on deliverance of the sealed letter that Hamlet carries with him. Perhaps only unwritten and unrepresentable

216

selves promise control of, or escape from, this scene of systematic betrayal. As writing penetrates the market and increasingly becomes a tool of state, a radical solitude beckons – as if "beneath" the self who reads and writes, a still more solitary self may be harboured: a private reader not formed by what he or she reads. Here, subjectivity (re-)embarks on its long course of radical autonomy, itself defined, as we have seen, as a form of bad mimesis traditionally regarded as closely allied to madness. But Hamlet also attempts to escape the trammels of writing in another way – by embracing Providence, as when he challenges Laertes. The Providential order is scripted without being communicated: it remains a secret known only to God. Not even ghosts know it. In delivering himself to it Hamlet merely broaches another kind of madness. In letting go of his subjectivity, in attempting to escape the logic of mimesis and the traps of writing, he leaps into the unknown. This is the structure through which the other characters interpret Hamlet's jump into Ophelia's grave and his cry, "This is I, Hamlet the Dane" as continuous with his previous "madness." This "I" is, if anything, less fixed, less knowable, than those other "I's" to which Hamlet has been attached.[7]

MIMESIS IN HISTORY

In this brief reading, *Hamlet*, on a threshold of modernity, shows how an analytic and an ethic of inscription (or what Foucault would call a "signature") is unravelled by an analytic and ethic of representation. More than that, it presents a storehouse of the forms by which unstable mimesis and subjectivity shore up – and threaten – authority. And it begins to demonstrate how the "uninterpretability" or "madness" of Hamlet the character may be used to seal the literariness and uniqueness of *Hamlet* the play – or text. This is to work within a Foucauldian approach particularly appropriate to works produced before the era of the "literary." Once the play begins to belong to a historical canon, this "uninterpretability" can be used by the state to produce individuals who are both imitative and autonomous. But this madness or uninterpretability has other functions too. Because *Hamlet* presents an extraordinarily wide range of modes of identity-construction, it can be read as belonging to a range of discursive and socio-political formations. For instance, when its affirmation of bloodlines, war and self-negation are emphasized, it can become Nazified (the remarks on the Third Reich performance of *Hamlet* in the film of Klaus Mann's novel *Mephisto* offer an accessible example of such a reading); when it is recognized that Hamlet's giving up of subjectivity and self-deliverance to Providence still contains a moment of self-reflection, it can be "deconstructed" in a de Manian sense; when it is noted how the realm of interiority is opened up by Hamlet's flight from codes, it can be thought a "psychological" masterpiece and reworked through paradigms such as

217

the Oedipus complex, most famously by Ernest Jones; and in the epoch of criminology (or "criminal anthropology"), Henry Irving could even stage it as a case-study of "criminal" mentality.[8] In each of these instances, the play mirrors needs and discourses that belong to a time which is not its own. It enters the "madness" of mimesis at this level too.

So, when the presence of Shakespeare's aura is required in an epoch for which he is dead, Shakespeare as "author-function," enters the logic of mimesis. He does so, however, only in complex relation to the Shakespearean text. On the one hand, Shakespeare becomes the effect, as against the originator, of his texts, a great deal of institutional power being invested in maintaining this distinction. On the other, strategies are devised for bringing Shakespeare the man back from the dead, to keep him alive in the culture – generally in a different cultural zone from criticism proper. Why? I would argue that Shakespeare's personal presence is required in order to keep the past alive in an era for which the past is destroyed by the triumph of inevitable and progressive historical change. Of course, this kind of modernist history is hard to affirm today, in part because it relies on a certain blindness to the mimetic logic that organizes it. The workings of such a logic are apparent from even the briefest excursion into the history of the Shakespearean author-function – as we shall now see.

Many before Stephen Greenblatt have translated the demand for Shakespeare's presence into the desire to talk with him in his grave. The naive have sometimes claimed success – including a Mr Hugh Junor Browne, a Melburnian, who chatted to Shakespeare's ghost via a medium in 1898, and published the results in a book unconvincingly entitled *The Grand Reality*. James Boswell, Dr Johnson's biographer, also wished for Shakespeare's personal presence:

> How delighted should we have been, if thus introduced into the company of Shakespeare and of Dryden, of whom we know scarcely any thing but their admirable writings! What pleasure would it have given us, to have known their petty habits, their characteristick manners, their modes of composition, and their genuine opinion of preceding writers and of their contemporaries! All these are now irrecoverably lost. – Considering how many of the strongest and most brilliant effusions of exalted intellect must have perished, how much is it to be regretted that all men of distinguished wisdom and wit have not been attended by friends of taste enough to relish, and abilities enough to register, their conversation!

(Boswell 1924, 442)

For Boswell, the playwright, of whom so few records remain, represents a lost opportunity for his own skills. As a biographer, he wished to bring the past alive, re-present it, so as to transcend the graveyard into which secular modernity consigns the epochs it succeeds. Boswell wishes to attach the plays to a "personality," a face, a series of anecdotes. This is the moment in which, to a similar end and for the first time, a portrait of an author – Sir Joshua Reynolds' of Laurence Sterne – is displayed in a public exhibition with the name of the sitter attached – an innovation which belongs more to the history of canonicity and publicity than to that of a Habermasian "public sphere." Boswell's Shakespeare is a person of "wisdom and wit," a conversationalist given to "brilliant effusions of exalted intellect" – a man with all the spark of his dramatic dialogues. Of course, this reminds us of Boswell's Johnson himself – and, indeed, Sterne. That Boswell's Shakespeare duplicates Johnson is not just a further example of the Other being recognized as the Same. The relay through the Bard also allows the eighteenth century to find an image for itself.

In the Revolutionary period, the era of finitude, such relations could not be expressed so simply. Friedrich Schiller, for instance, who, as we have seen, can be considered to "found" the Arnoldian tradition, wanted literature to be a force for freedom, progress, morality and the glory of the Human Race – in effect, to replace religion. At this moment, Shakespeare divides in two: there begins to exist a popular, indeed a radical, Shakespeare (as constructed by William Hazlitt, for instance) and a Shakespeare who lives on as the presiding genius of the high cultural tradition.[9] Schiller attempts to avoid this division by constructing a quasi-sacred Shakespeare, whose life and work cannot be read merely in terms of social struggles or continuities. The trouble was that the young Schiller found Shakespeare profoundly unsympathetic:

> When at a very early age I first made [his] acquaintance, I was incensed by his coldness, the insensitivity which permitted him to jest in the middle of the highest pathos, to interrupt the heartrending scenes in *Hamlet*, in *King Lear*, in *Macbeth* and so on with a Fool.
>
> (Schiller 1966, 106–7)

With maturity, however, Schiller came to recognize precisely how Shakespeare, as a naive poet, was less like a man than like a god.

> Like divinity behind the world's structure he stands behind his work; *he* is the work, and the work is *he*; to ask only for *him* is not to be worthy of it, inadequate to it, or sated with it.
>
> (ibid., 106)

Only in more self-conscious or more "sentimental" times. Schiller argued, have readers demanded to get a sense of, to *grasp* the author in the works. But he believed that this was a vulgar error, for literature had now so crucial a cultural role that its mere authors (and, by implication, mere readers) were of little account. It has its own autonomous presence. Yet it is strange that the features which the young Schiller noted in Shakespeare – "coldness," "insensitivity" – as well as the "objectivity" that the mature

219

Schiller found in him, were characteristics remarked upon in his own great friend and contemporary, Goethe. For his contemporaries, Goethe, more than anyone, possessed the essential characteristics of an author. He too was detached in private, often unscrupulous, did not obey the dominant sexual codes, and did not use literature to express his personality. His authorial authority relied on the way his writings reflected neither the public sphere of politics and journalism, nor the private world of domesticity and sexuality. It was as if the great author existed as a site where the distance between these is maximized. Certainly, as Schiller puts it, Goethe could not simply be "layed hold of" in his work. If Boswell's Shakespeare has more than a little of Dr Johnson, then Schiller's has more than a little of his hero – and *his* historical moment and its needs.

After Schiller, it became a truism that Shakespeare is sublime precisely because the man is absent from the work. But the nineteenth century found less rarefied, less abstract ways of coming into contact with the Founding Genius of English – or Aryan – Literature. In 1847, after a public subscription and after much speechifying by politicians, actors and writers, a cottage at Stratford-upon-Avon was acquired as Shakespeare's "Birthplace." A "National Shakespeare Fund" was established and other properties in Stratford-upon-Avon with more or less legendary associations with Shakespeare's life were purchased.[10] For a time Stratford had a rival. London also had its supporters as the world's Shakespeare capital, but when, during his tercentenary in 1864, London failed in its plans to erect a monumental statue in Shakespeare's honour, Stratford – as the Birthplace – became Shakespeare's home in the modern world. Shakespeare becomes first and foremost the Bard of Avon, a provincial *Wunderkind*, rather than, for instance, the poet of the bustling, entrepreneurial imperialist capital that London has been for the past 400 years.

Getting in touch with Shakespeare became a business – tourism. This did not happen smoothly. After all, how could Shakespeare be a classic just because the man is absent from the work – which remains true for high literary culture in the nineteenth century – *and* the (mythical) traces, the petty objects of his life, become a tourist shrine? One rather obscure individual lived this tension out. Joseph Skipsey, from Newcastle on Tyne and a poet of North Country mining life was given the job of curator and guide to the Birthplace in the 1880s. As a struggling writer he anticipated that it would be a perfect position for him. He was to be disappointed. Henry James, who heard Skipsey's name in a dinner party anecdote, recorded his story in a notebook because he recognized it as material to be transformed into a magazine tale: a saleable and "artistic" narrative. In his story, "The Birthplace," Gedge (as James there calls Skipsey), taking humanist literary criticism to its extremes, deifies Shakespeare so that, for him, tourism becomes a "blasphemy": "They've killed Him. . . . They kill Him everyday" he moans (James 1964, 11, 440). Despite the blasphemy he utters daily, Gedge, as a poor man, cannot afford to quit his job. So he devises a ploy. He consciously constructs a Shakespeare – a birthplace – myth. As he guides the public around the cottage, he gives them exactly what they want, but with an almost imperceptible excessive edge:

> It's not often that in the early home of genius and renown the whole tenor of existence is laid so bare, not often that we are able to retrace, from point to point and from step to step, its connection with objects, with influences – to build it round again with the little solid facts out of which it sprang. This, therefore, I need scarcely remind you, is what makes the small space between these walls – so modest to measurement, so insignificant of aspect – unique on the earth. *There is nothing like it*, there is nothing like it anywhere in the world. Where shall you find a presence equally diffused, uncontested and undisturbed? Where in particular shall you find, on the part of the abiding spirit, an equally towering eminence. You may find elsewhere eminence of a considerable order, but where shall you find *with it*, don't you see, changes, after all so few, and the contemporary element caught so, as it were, in the very fact.

(451)

Not surprisingly this torrent of discourse bewilders the tourists, who, though uneasy, do not know why. Gedge becomes an enormous success as a guide despite the fact that his tone – the extravagant, superior, cynical, theatrical tone of Henry James as a writer and as a private individual – subtly ironises the Shakespeare business. There are still two Shakespeares – the Shakespeare of the tours (who has replaced the radical Shakespeare of the revolutionary era) and the absent genius who exists only in his works: popular culture Shakespeare and the divine, literary Shakespeare of the private study. Outside the two (where James's tale stands) there is only irony – and a dwindling number of readers. Again, it is as if Shakespeare acquires cultural value to the degree that his texts are distanced from the material traces of his life.

In more theoretical terms, then, we can say that each historical moment cannot simply find its own image in Shakespeare. That would be to take the self-identity and authority both of the texts and of the present for granted. The logic of mimesis, which organizes the history of the name and author-function "Shakespeare," does not work as simply as all that. Criticism is in a bind. In "interpreting" Shakespeare, it can strategically separate the biography from the works in order to allow the latter to avoid death and obsolescence. But it has the opportunity to re-present Shakespeare's texts only because the man who wrote them, and the society in which they were written, have disappeared. His texts stand in the place of things and events of which they are the material and unchanging trace.

But they do so only at the cost of gesturing to a loss to which they, as immutable objects, are themselves immune. It is these strange relations that organize the transmission of Shakespeare's writings. Furthermore, criticism both distinguishes itself from other disciplines, and guarantees its currency, by repeating current *énoncés* and fulfilling current demands with reference to a great name of the past. No doubt, as soon as Shakespeare, for instance, acquires a *history* of interpretation any contemporary description of him lacks full authority (it becomes one of many interpretations) and then Shakespeare becomes, for criticism, a mirror of the times. Yet this works the other way too. For if Shakespeare was Goethe, Goethe was also, a bit, Shakespeare too. Within this logic, the tradition lifts itself out of the mass of print by its bootstraps, so to say. In the process, Shakespeare begins to regain his autonomy and the present becomes, a little, the past. It becomes other to itself. University literature departments retain their (diminishing) authority partly by knowing about, reproducing and inscribing on the tables of their pupils' minds the literary tradition of which Shakespeare is an ornament. That this knowledge – and, therefore, this aura – is organized by the logic of mimesis both threatens academic literary studies: criticism is nothing but a displaced reflection of its own moment, and buttresses it: literary study is valuable precisely because it presents the dead – the text, the past – in itself. Yet where, as today, literary studies are less and less absorbed into the programme of mass education and acculturation, less able to present practices that may form selves and styles, then the unstable logic of mimesis freezes into sheer opposition and self-reflection, that is, into the polarities of Foucault's modern episteme. In particular, reader response studies turn the text into the history of its reception, while routinized "deconstruction" finds in each work a specific organization of unreadability.

When "literature" emerges as a distinct category, new relations between text, author and society appear. What relations? We can begin to catch sight of them by noting that while Greenblatt's modernist desire to speak with the dead was shared by Boswell and Schiller for whom Shakespeare also exists as a lack, today Shakespeare is not dead in quite the way that Dr Johnson is dead. That is because Johnson and Goethe both wrote inside a culture centred around print. Shakespeare has no Boswell to keep records of his life. Nor is Shakespeare dead as Goethe is dead. Shakespeare published no autobiography, no Eckermann published his conversations, no newspapers reported on any crazes his works may have started such as *Werther*'s incitement to suicide among the youth of Goethe's time. The lack that Shakespeare now signals is partly a result of his having written outside that archival empire of print which emerged in England after 1688, and whose reign may now, in the age of the visual and electronic media, be closing. (This may be why so few writers have directed an "anxiety of influence" at the Bard.) Modern literature – literature *as* literature – is a

222

particular fold within this archive: it belongs to what Foucault called the "Library" in his essay on Flaubert. It exists in writing's relation to itself, as writing drives out the ghosts of the past, literally, in *Tom Jones*. Writing that will be read in the future against journalism which will not; writing to be voiced against writing to be silently consumed; writing which records and administers versus writing which entertains and instructs; writing which enters the market versus writing which remains in the files of various institutions or is preserved privately; writing which has "authors" versus writing which is anonymous; writing as act against writing as reflection; writing which signifies the cultural heritage versus writing deemed merely topical – relations like these demarcate literature in the era of the literary.

But Foucault, even more than Greenblatt, helps to remind us that print is also a domain of repetition and incorporation, broken into various zones by ever-shifting patterns and modulations of power, pleasure and violence. Propositions move from text to text; in and out of high literature; from governmental and legal archives to journals and fictions and back again, often undergoing transformations as they pass barriers, some of which are guarded by powers that can kill, maim or exhaust. They become commodities because they flesh out readers' fantasies, excite and amaze, cause confusions in which loss and pain are not to be distinguished from gain and pleasure. Where barriers between zones become less rigid then, as Lennard Davis has very usefully pointed out, "fact and fiction" may merge into one another (Davis 1983, 42–71). We are now familiar with the idea that traditional literary criticism which concentrated on mimesis and its limits on the one hand, and a canon of discrete works on the other, has found it difficult adequately to account for this circulation of discourse. Certain of criticism's key tenets – the perfection, untranslatability and finality of the finished work, even the gap between writing and authorial intention – are designed to promote subtle models of representation, and to blind us both to the effects and presence of sanctioned violence and pain and to the market value of print. Nonetheless when encountering the formation of modern literature one must be careful not to dismiss the canon too easily. Ever since Shakespeare, but especially since the emergence of literature as a category, some authors (Alexander Pope, Henry James, or George Eliot, for instance) *consciously* form a great tradition, a means of keeping the past alive. In an era in which ghosts, and other forms of non-textual life-after-death, were themselves dying, they make a bid for death-less fame, inviting biography and close reading through complex strategies of imitation and deviation. Canon construction is not simply an élitist move by literary critics, it is a particular mode of textual production. Not even the most subversive scholarship, not even modes of reading most antagonistic to the values expressed in the canonising drive, can dispel the power of the "classic." Certainly no articulation of a "political unconscious," or the searching out of invisible and exclusionary ideological programmes, can dethrone it.

A very brief example: at the beginning of *Middlemarch*, Dorothea's secular story is seen to be a repetition of that of her favourite writer, St Theresa of Avila – Bernini's Theresa. This is, at least in part, a self-monumentalizing move by Eliot: she grafts her novel onto a classic of devotional and mystic literature. Even more than Theresa, Dorothea as a woman, "foundress of nothing," will find it difficult to fulfil her ambitions, to reconcile herself to her secondariness; like Theresa's her energies are both imitative of, and competitive with, those of the men around her. The men around Theresa? Her brothers were Spanish mercantile conquistadors in the New World. While they crossed the world, Theresa stayed at home, founded a nunnery, had mystic visions, and wrote. It is difficult not to consider her unique combination of administrative pragmatism and ambition, her ability to experience religious ecstasy, and her self-inspection as a version of the breadth of vision, organizational skill and savagery of her brothers – and vice versa. *Middlemarch*, that sheltered story of "provincial life" in England in the early 1830s, is articulated within the imperialist mission through its effort to bind itself to the tradition of widely-recognized great works – though some scholarly delving is required to find the connection. Such scholarship can never be especially damaging to the text's reputation however: after Pope's *Dunciad* say (the epic of print-capitalism), confident, glory-seeking and able writers have known that academic critical and scholarly notes and editions, whatever false trails they may lay or follow, whatever immediacy they may destroy, whatever prejudice they may detect, will also perpetuate the aesthetic and ethical ambitions expressed in the writings themselves.

DREISER: TOWARDS A GENEALOGY OF WRITING

Within the narrative sweep and purpose of this book, the crucial questions set by considering literature as a fold in the empire of print remain: how are its practices related to other discursive practices?, how is the writer bound to the work in a project of self-invention?, how do literary texts connect to the networks of modern governmentalities?, and how do they adhere to, or depart from, the logic of mimesis? In an effort to think about the way in which such questions might be answered, let us finally consider – again very briefly – the case of Theodore Dreiser. He writes, I think, at a particularly revealing moment of literary history – the moment at which criticism becomes professionalized so that literature, and its claim to power and life after death, are backed by bureaucratic institutions. This means that the always problematic borders between literary and non-literary writing become particularly highly charged. While modernist writers could experiment with radical techniques of auto-canonization that seemed to demand professional, or at least very specialised and dedicated readers, writers aiming for larger audiences had to devise other strategies to secure their work's seriousness and transcendence of the topical.

We can begin by examining Dreiser's work by thinking about its *énoncés* materially as print. Indeed, for Dreiser words were material at least as much as mimetic – not in the "modernist" sense which (supposedly) privileges the signifier over the signified, but because they exist as "copy" – on the space of the page, space with commercial value. (The word "copy," which can mean either original prose or its duplication, encompasses the logic of mimesis in its usage, though its force is actually to make it harder to think of language in mimetic terms.) For Dreiser, writing was, before anything else, a form of cutting and pasting. Its finer details were often carried out by his secretaries and editors – he could not "write" at all in the sense of producing a sequence of grammatical, accurately spelled, "elegant" sentences – that is, in the literary sense. Preparing draft after draft of his works ("Dreiser's manuscripts were never finished," F. O. Mathiessen noted (Mathiessen 1951, 150)), material collected for one novel could find its way into another. He preserved piles of newspaper clippings – especially of murder trials – upon which to base his books and often laboriously researched and copied court records and relevent newspaper office files. His private life was not immune from this system of discursive cannibilization: whole segments of his private correspondence were absorbed into *The Genius*, for instance, almost without alteration. He plundered other "creative" writers too, being repeatedly accused of plagiarism.

He was also able to quote, or cut and paste, himself as he moved from one kind of public writing to another – to odd effect. He was, for instance, very successful as the editor of a women's magazine, *The Delineator*, owned by a firm that sold sewing patterns. At the time, that was a business under intense threat by the entry of the ready-to-wear clothing industry and its rapid gains in market-share. Dreiser's prose, which filled the space between advertisements, was required to praise and maintain the values of domestic production and child-rearing that sanctioned home-sewing against the ready-to-wear industry:

> *The Delineator* message is human betterment. Its appeal is to the one great humanizing force of humanity – womanhood. To sustain it, to broaden it, to refine it, to inspire it, is our aim. Our theme is one that a woman may carry into her home, her church and her social affairs – the theme of the ready smile, the theme of the ungrudged helping hand.
>
> This, then, is *The Delineator*'s broadened purpose – to help every woman in this land to live better by teaching her practical homecraft . . . by strengthening her in her moral fight for righteousness in the world.[11]

This is copy precariously balanced between advertising and journalism. The connection between unpaid female work as "practical home-craft" and a future-directed humanism can rarely have been more baldly stated. And he can repeat *The Delineator*'s discourse almost word for word in his novels: *Sister Carrie*'s narrator, for instance, declares, "A lovely home atmosphere is one of the flowers of the world than which there is nothing more tender, nothing more delicate" (Dreiser 1985, 81). But, in *Sister Carrie*, praise of family-values seems inconsistent, a case of discursive circulation out of control. For it, and Dreiser's novels in general, explore the valorization of domesticity from the other side. Their central protagonists find the private, domestic sphere, monogamy and "good works," imprisoning, impossible, a view that Dreiser himself lived out. He was a compulsive womaniser, who deserted his wife and went out of his way to avoid having children. As commentators have noted, Dreiser is a novelist of the effects of consumer desire as it begins to propel the economy as a whole, and as advertising itself becomes a powerful form of writing.[12] But this consumer desire is called into being within a deeply competitive, highly segmented market, one that, thus, dismantles older discursive linkages. It may, in one sector, attach itself to a celebration of sexuality which implicitly works against the family, at the same time, as, in a competitive sector, it appeals to family values in copy directed (paradoxically) against the market. Dreiser finds himself writing in both discourses, sometimes within a single text. Indeed his narratives fail to end "happily," and often end at the point at which they begin (with a child, for instance, bound to repeat a parent's career), because these discourses cannot be reconciled, though they have, in one sense, the same function.

It is important to resist judging Dreiser as insincere, as alienated from a commodified language or as self-contradictory. Such judgements merely assume the connection between an expressive, unified human subject and a sincerity and aura supposed to belong specifically to literature. When we begin to work outside that assumption, then, as we have seen, we require different methods and principles. Those that seem more suitable for an analysis of Dreiser can be classified under three heads – which ought to be sketched before continuing with our brief account of his work and career. First, the rules and conditions which distinguish one kind of textual production (here "copy") from another ("creative writing") within a discursive field need to be examined – where "rules" can be construed much more loosely than in *The Archaeology of Knowledge* for example. These rules need not be explicitly stated of course, it is analysis's task to uncover them. And discursive fields are open-ended enough for new rules to be devised or "improvised" by an individual, while being rigid enough for it to be *difficult* to invent or improvise new rules, the relation between flexibility and rigidity varying from one form of textual production to another. Rules can always be broken too, intentionally or not. Post-Foucauldian analysis's second task is to describe texts' channels of distribution and the interaction between the various zones and technologies in which they are produced and read. Finally, it must attempt to relate the ordered patterns of textual production both to these networks of distribution and to texts' wider social effects, a task which is always uncertain and interpretative. It leaves room for both analytic and academic "creativity" and, therefore, exclusivity. Of course, a method based on these principles no longer falls wholly within the paradigm of representation.

An American Tragedy, Dreiser's most famous novel, was based on a celebrated crime and recycled the journalism that surrounded the crime. In 1906, Chester Gillette, whose parents had been connected with a religious mission, and whose uncle had employed him in his stocking factory as a supervisor, murdered Grace (Billy) Brown. Billy also worked in the stocking factory, she had become Chester's lover and at the time of her death was pregnant. Chester took her for a row in a hired boat on a remote lake and there drowned her – or so the prosecution successfully alleged, arguing that he was motivated by his social ambition, and, more specifically, his desire to marry a richer woman. He (and his mother) protested his innocence to the end.[13] In *An American Tragedy*, Chester Gillette becomes Clyde Griffiths; Grace (Billy) Brown becomes Roberta (Bert) Alden; the stocking factory, a shirt collar factory; Cortland, NY, Lycargus, Illinois and so on. As a supervisor, Clyde/Chester is a member of what Harry Braverman called the "new middle class" that formed a "buffer zone" between the employers and labour as a "transmission agent for the exercise of control and the collection of information, so that management need not confront unaided a hostile or indifferent mass" (Braverman 1974, 407). We could even say that Clyde occupies the equivalent position in early twentieth-century America to the spy that Polonius sends to Paris (both provide information for their bosses) – if not indeed to Thomas of Ely's ghost who mediates in its own way between authority and the "indifferent mass." But in *An American Tragedy*, the "transmission agent" – working in the clothing industry in competition with *The Delineator* – has become Clyde, a novel's hero. Clyde is an avatar of Dr Dodd: his main means of self-formation, and of moving from one social sphere to another, is a "spontaneous imitation" of the rich; the importance of clothes being that they so easily permit imitation of the rich. He is formed by imitation as against the apparatuses of individuating pastoral power or by inherited status – a distinction around which the novel pivots. Indeed, to enforce a sense that there are other modes of self-formation than mimetic ones, the narrative proliferates repetition. It insists that to be like another is to have failed to achieve one's own singularity. So Clyde uncannily resembles his cousin (his rich uncle's son). It is as a better-looking, more stylish and sympathetic, if poorer and duller, double of his cousin that he appeals to rich young women and can concretely imagine and begin his upwardly mobile journey.

His being a more attractive version of his rich cousin also allows him to turn the "indifferent mass" of workers into a set of non-hostile individuals. His sexual charm makes him an effective manager. At a narratological level, it also helps provide him with a degree of singularity – enough, at least, to be "hero," a centre of narrative interest. He is the same as his richer peers, only less well educated; but he is also sexier, and therein lies the germ of Dreiser's, if not Chester's "real life," story.

Let us turn to the system of discursive circulation in which Dreiser worked – which is not to suppose that this system can be thought of *merely* in terms of discourse. At its very heart lies a distinction between journalism and fiction. This distinction was not one of "truth" versus "fiction" in the classic sense though, because "truth" was a word of extraordinary currency when Dreiser was writing. He lived at a moment when there was a strong market for "human documents" – a phrase used in a letter written to him by Joseph Coates (an editor of *Era* magazine) which also notes, "I do not believe there has ever been a greater desire for truth than there is today" (qu. Dowell 1983, xxxxviii). Here "desire for truth" is measured by the market value of a certain kind of copy, fictional or otherwise. Such copy could circulate facts about poverty as "otherness" to a middle-class readership: in America, Jacob Riis, a photographer and journalist, was perhaps the most successful producer of this "truth." His *How the Other Half Lives* (1890) had immense political effects. It is barely an exaggeration to say that writings in this genre formed the life-blood of the left – especially the Popular Front – during the interwar period. "Truth" could also be circulated in the form of sensational and romantic personal narratives, quasi-confessions of sexual desires and acts, which readers could simultaneously identify with and separate themselves from – as in the extraordinarily successful and often imitated tabloids of the time, *True Stories* and *True Confessions*. Here truth is distributed within a new market, consisting of those with a minimal formal education but with money enough to spend on magazines and the commodities advertised in them. "Truth" could also be revealed and commodified in the uncovering of economic and political scandals, as in Henry Labouchère's also much imitated British magazine – succinctly named, *Truth*. Fictional and market-circulated "truth" could gain its material from sociology as well: in Britain, for instance, Sidney and Beatrice Webb, who spent a lifetime amassing facts and figures about social conditions, invited H. G. Wells to fictionalize their data so as to increase its popularity and impact. Similarly, Grant Allen, an important popular writer and scientific popularizer, first wrote fiction in 1880 in order to convince the public of the "scientific truth" that no-one would be able to recognize a ghost even if they believed that they had seen one – a problem of some longevity.[14]

It was because truth as exposé, as confession, as demystification and as contact with social suffering and sexuality was so highly valued and sale-

228

able, that Dreiser could uphold the novel's traditional claims to verisimilitude and creativity by processing and transforming reportage. Reportage becomes fiction through a whole series of quite specific discursive operations – of which I will list some of the more obvious and important. Actual proper names are replaced by invented ones. Generalizing discourse – especially the editorializing, knowledgeable "narrative voice" – is incorporated and interwoven with reported speech. Character-traits are spread across a whole range of characters in a series of subtle variations in order to create internal effects of signification. Literary narratives obey less rigid laws of unity and economy than journalism does: it may be that in a successful literary text nothing is extraneous to a total effect or "meaning," but it requires more readerly effort to work out the relation than in a journalistic "story." And figurative devices unavailable to journalism are used in literature, through what Greenblatt would call "symbolic acquisition": for instance, the turning of a stocking factory into a collar factory in *An American Tragedy* is motivated symbolically – the white collar being a metaphor of Braverman's "new middle-class." Novel writing also differs from journalism by the degree to which creative prose may invest its characters with subjectivity, that is, by its use of point of view, the free indirect style, and more experimental modes. This subjectivity can become the source of narrative progression, a move which allows both the flow of narrated events to merge with psychological description, and narrative to proliferate. Novels may also pay attention to what is never news: the "unchangeability" of nature and Being. Finally, in Dreiser's time, novels may focus more directly and in more detail on sexual desire and acts to explain their characters; here the discourse of sexuality functions as a marker between two kinds of writing.[15]

Such distinctions between reportage and creative writing also require, and permit, a set of economic, ethical and legal distinctions. In the broadest possible sense, copy involved a different author function than creative writing. To begin with, fiction, which has a greater freedom to explore and recycle facts and hypotheses than journalism, may be copyrighted – unlike journalism. By not repeating actual names and places, fiction is also both of less use to the police and politicians, and less likely to be the object of libel suits. On the other hand, fiction is more vulnerable to charges of plagiarism than journalism is, and is the object of a much greater degree of evaluation in reviews. And, as Dreiser's career often bore witness, creative writing aimed at "truth" was often threatened by censorship; appeals to the artistic and creative qualities of writing being most insisted upon, and widely broadcast, in the face of this threat.

In Dreiser's time, novelists also lived differently from journalists both economically and in relation to their experience, though, of course, many, like Dreiser, worked at the join between the two orders. To be a successful literary novelist was considered to require "genius" – a Goethean person-

ality rich and unique enough to undersign the truth of the text's verisimilitude and experimentalism while remaining simple enough to retain a
capacity for wonder, curiosity (a "thirst for life") and defamiliarization.
Genius required a zero-degree of consciousness that permitted the world
to imprint itself on the novelist's imagination (to use a slight oxymoron)
– as in this characteristic sentence, "To the child, the genius with imagination, or the wholly untravelled, the approach to a great city for the first
time is a wonderful thing" (Dreiser 1985, 10). This imagination, which
was also a thirst for life and a zero-degree of consciousness, could not be
contained by social conventions and other artifices – some of which were
enforced by censorship. The way in which novelists were ascribed a genius
lacking in journalists had an economic aspect too: novelists, who wrote in
domestic space and who owned copyright, sold their writing not their
labour, unlike most journalists, who sold their labour. It is as if working
in a private space allowed novelists to remain simultaneously simple,
curious and individuated enough to process the actual into the probable.
Yet it was as private individuals that novelists, interested in "truth" and
for all their "genius," drew on journalism for their material: they simply
did not have the resources to find their true "stories" elsewhere.

So, to process reportage – to turn copy into creativity – involved a
lived triple tension. That is to say, literary novelists had to be especially
individualized, even though they were experts in mimesis which enacted
another's point of view, and even though much of their material was
derived from journalistic reports or social science. A particular mode of
self-fashioning binds these various requirements together: novelists must
be able to live out their material while journalists "merely" report it. In
Dreiser's case, the internal tensions of this ethic are especially clear. For
instance, he himself went through experiences of unemployment and severe
poverty similar to those of his characters Carrie and Hurstwood in *Sister
Carrie* – but only after he had finished the novel and, indeed, mainly
because he found it hard to make a living as a literary writer. He recorded
these experiences non-fictionally in a manuscript published posthumously
under the title *An Amateur Labourer* – where they take the form of a series
of rather sentimental magazine articles. Dreiser writes the experience up
then lives it out – only to write it up again at a greater remove from the
conventions of naturalism. The empiricist hierarchy by which the experience comes first, and the representation of it second, is inverted. His ability
to experience the life of the down and out is a moment in his self-formation
as a writer of "genius," urged upon him by the need to be able to
experience what he is writing about. A joke in the *San Francisco Examiner*
made the point like this: "Mr Dreiser: who was that lady I saw you
walking down the street with? That was no lady, that was material" (see
Swanberg 1965, 340). If Dreiser wrote "copy" and used "material," he
did so as a "genius" whose fictional works might be canonized, and drew

230

from an intensely lived life. It was as if the novelist turned to life – a little as Hamlet abandoned himself to Providence – because the "rules" of textual production that distinguished reportage from fiction were both so flexible and so difficult to invent. He did so in order to find copy that had not yet been written, and "rules" for writing scripts that had not yet been established – mainly unsuccessfully in Dreiser's case. And one reason for that lack of success was that, outside of the techniques and institutions of individuation, large tracts of "life" were still determined by the classical forces of gender, race, class and education while others were organized through social apparatuses (such as bio-power) that produced a shared everyday existence. To find a life that was one's own and only one's own was not easy – especially for those without formal education.

Strange loop-back effects could occur in this situation: when researching *An American Tragedy*, Dreiser rowed with his lover Helen Richardson on the lake where his character Roberta (named after a mistress of his) was to drown. Helen believed for a moment that Dreiser would, hypnotically, re-enact the scene and she would die (Helen Dreiser 1951, 85). The fear was realistic enough as their relationship was violent, punctuated by fights over Dreiser's womanizing – itself a character trait often given to his heroes but also an index of that *lived* capacity for experience, detachment and admiration considered proper to the early twentieth-century male writer, both "creative" and journalistic. The fear also repeats a moment in the real lives of Grace Brown and Chester Gillette. So Dreiser's actions veer towards a repetition of his character's actions – a character who was also an actual individual. As Dreiser's life and writing merge and his experiences are subject to the pressures of his work, his neurotic symptoms – folding and refolding his handkerchief; his obsessive desire to walk round and round in circles – mime the circularity of his narrative's structures. Life itself becomes material. And these symptoms, in turn, are derived from his sense that society is an empty circulatory system, driven by flows that belong, at once, to consumerism and sexuality. In fact, from our own point of view, they mime the non-teleological movement of discourse from one zone to another, a little like Tehching Hsieh's performances, though, of course, non-intentionally. In Dreiser, madness has lost its relation to Being too: it has even lost its medical status. He was scornful of the doctors who, helplessly, tried to help him. His pathology, like Roussel's, is a version of the work and its demands.

This is to consider Dreiser's work as a specific print formation which shapes his life. What happens when we begin to analyze it alongside other *non*-print textual formations? One message that we must take from the relative failure of Foucault's archaeological project is that each discursive practice must be considered in terms of its exchanges with other such practices. If Dreiser writes in a publishing industry for which "truth" is both the object of commercial demand, and the index of political progressiveness, then that industry is producing a specialised commodity, one differentiated against, and interacting with, the mainstream cinema industry – to take the most important example during the first half of this century. His work must be read not just in terms of its claims to canonicity, or its strategies of auto-canonization, or as the expression of a particular ideology and social structure, or even as providing various "subject positions," but in relation to other, especially other dominant, representational techniques. Some gestures towards such relations can be made here: Hollywood's output was organized according to popular genres: the western, melodrama, the musical, comedy and so on. It was not legitimized by its claim to product "truth," despite the fact that it often reworked journalistic stories, including those from magazines in the true confession mode. This is not to say that Dreiser's novelized reportage has no relation to Hollywood's "genres": like many films, *An American Tragedy* derives from the melodramatic side of George Eliot's *Daniel Deronda*, and has a close connection to later "hard-boiled" fiction such as that by James M. Cain, and hence to *film noir*. On the other hand, Hollywood did produce films that can be measured on a spectrum from realism to non-realism, a spectrum with Warner Brothers'' early 1930s social conscience films at one end and animation or the musical at the other. But there is no Hollywood analogy for the recycling of a conflation of personal experience and journalistic discourse that is characteristic of Dreiser's work. Nor is there any equivalent to his particular use of the omniscient narrative voice or the indirect free style – his capacity to structure a narrative through the rhythms by which he alternated, and fused an editorializing voice with a character's "internal" voice. To cite an appropriate example, Eisenstein, in his script of *An American Tragedy* (written for Paramount), transforms Clyde's consciousness into the expression of larger social agencies without using a narrator. This is most obvious in the scene where, after reading a newspaper story about a drowning, Clyde first considers murdering Roberta. In Eisenstein's treatment, visual and sound special effects (including back projection) present the idea as mad. Its madness is caused by the way newspapers destroy any "real union" between individual and society: "The action begins to work along the line of the thoughts of a distracted man . . . departing from sane logic, distorting the real union between things and sounds; all on the background of the insistent and infinite repetition of scraps of the description in the newspaper" (Eisenstein 1969, 286). Later, other back-projected scenes provide the social and "discordant" background for Clyde's individual actions. In the novel, however, Clyde's thought of murdering Roberta is psychologized: as it hovers between consciousness and unconsciousness, he tries to repress it. And the description of his consciousness is focused through a narrative voice, some of whose judgements and discursive traits Clyde repeats – against verisimilitude. The difference between Eistenstein and Dreiser is as much a technical as a discursive difference in the Foucauldian sense. Film, even when it is divided between sound and image, cannot present the play between Clyde's partially conscious moral sense and his desire. Leaving the question of intertitles aside, film must have a visual concomitant for every utterance on the sound-track (even a blank screen does not avoid this requirement) and each utterance must have an identifiable voice, even if it is that of the voice-over: these structural conditions mean that sub-conscious mental states and internal mental struggles can only be presented filmically in highly conventionalized and displaced terms. Literature, in turn, cannot provide an equivalent for two planes of dramatic action which, while sharing a single frame, are connected by their very discordancy. But the larger point of this brief reading of Dreiser against film is that the difference between literary fiction and film propels literature towards representations of deep subjectivity in the age of the image. This, of course, helped literature become a prime source of the pedagogical institutions' pastoral power – an event which, from a certain distance, organizes *An American Tragedy*.

What, then, about Dreiser's relations with power networks? For Dreiser, power works in interactions between the media, the professions and the individual. Few filmic set-ups could be more in Dreiser's spirit than one in which newspapers are back-projected onto a plane in front of which an individual flounders. Dreiser, who was not formed in any advanced educational institution, who called upon no cultural or religious roots, and whose class background provided him with no identity he could value, who wrote to make money, possessed only a self-ascribed "genius" that he could express as a technician of the interplay between mimetic and non-mimetic writing modes, and by intermittently placing himself, and finding himself placed, on social margins and at the psychological edge. Driven by sexual and consumerist desires, as well as by desire for knowledge, mastery and status, Dreiser's success as an author allowed him to move across social barriers, from one class to another. His character Clyde, and presumably Chester Gillette too, share Dreiser's impulsions, but can only follow suit by murder. Clyde/Chester suffers the ultimate penalty for not obeying the rules, for trying to move "up" at another's expense. When he is arrested and becomes an object for naked state power, a number of administrative agencies immediately attend to him. First, the lawyers and police – both with an eye to the media, and hence to the political opportunities of the crime and its successful prosecution; second, the press, of course; third, briefly, medicine – is Clyde mad?; then prison officials; and finally the Church. Each profession or institution marks itself (and the discourse proper to it) from the others and protects its power and identity, over Clyde's imprisoned, and soon to be executed, body. These professions are situated in a cluster of alliances and rivalries around the threat represented by Clyde who, like Christ before him, becomes a victim of society's ability to send citizens to a realm outside exchange. Their interest in his case is all the stronger because he never confesses: he carries his story into the grave. Various groups ask: is he guilty or not? Large problematizations (deeply embedded in the technologies and discourses by which the docile society was produced) loom at once. Is his crime the particular expression of a generalized and necessary social motive force – one which underpins, for instance, consumption, "upward mobility" and progress. Or is it rather a matter of individual pathology? Questions like these are all the more urgent because Clyde, as uneducated, as pure imitation himself, seems to have no autonomous self.

Ultimately, *An American Tragedy*'s "truth" is found in the way that it records the interconnections and tensions between various professions, and the way each makes use of Clyde's crime and its preconditions. Yet, the novel itself profits from the uninterpretability and inimitability of Clyde's case, its break in the large networks of social negotiation and exchange. Most immediately, the novel's publisher attempted to upstage the courts and sell the book with a marketing gimmick. A national competition was organized in which readers could win a prize by guessing whether Clyde was innocent or guilty. More profoundly, the novel profits from Clyde/ Chester by reaching deeply into its character's "consciousness" and "sub-consciousness" and implying that no profession has the power to judge, control or "save" him. For Dreiser, the case can only honestly and truth-fully be circulated in print by himself as a "genius" who accepts and represents its undecidability, who presents it as a tale of irrepressible male sexual, social and consumer desire and, finally, as an allegory of ontological emptiness. By doing so he can transform it into literature – and live it. This marks his ultimate victory over journalism, as well as over the lawyers, politicians, doctors and clergy. This is still too simple though: for it leaves out of account the complexity of Dreiser's relations with the literary and pedagogical institutions – which are marked by an irreducible doubleness. On the one side, an absence of post-compulsory education provides the condition of possibility both for Dreiser's writing and Clyde/ Chester's career. Because, in their world, to be educated in the humanities is to gain the capacity both for sanctioned social mobility and for individu-ated, unimitated selfhood, Clyde's crime would have been much less likely had he been so educated. But, when post-compulsory education does reach far enough into society to cover the Dreisers/Chesters/Clydes of the world then Dreiser's particular mode of writing and its subject-matter will no longer be produced. Dreiser's writing techniques do not survive either the criteria of "criticism," or the way that the academic humanities fashion selves. Oddly enough, this is anticipated in the enormous value that his texts give to reading and knowledge: Carrie's perusal of *Père Goriot* makes her previous cultural consumption, in which she is formed as a person, "silly and worthless" for instance (Dreiser 1985, 495). Of course, here

234

Dreiser's is not a literary judgement in the Arnoldian sense. It rests on the belief that whereas most reading (outside of pedagogy and "literature") exists simply to fulfil its readers' fantasies and desires, "realism" and autodidactic genius circulate truth as it crosses and re-crosses the division between fiction and reportage. On the other side, literature, and literary education, is itself effectively demystified in Dreiser. *An American Tragedy* can attack journalism's use of crime for political and commercial purposes, it can transform the case-records by making them signifiers of an ontological lack and by saturating them in subjectivity, but as cut and pasted "copy," the novel still undoes the aura of the well-written, individuated and unified masterpiece. Thus it was that his ambitious writing failed to appeal to professional critics who were reforming the canon during his lifetime with high modernism to guide them. When such institutions do take him up, then it is a sign that literature's power-effects are not quite those of the Schillerian epoch, that literature's relation with other social and discursive zones is shifting, and indeed, that the other kinds of lives are being lived.

CONCLUSION

The brief account of Dreiser's life and writings that ends this book seems to belong to a different intellectual world than the analysis of Foucault's early psychological work, influenced by Heidegger and the post-Heideggereans, with which it began. The young Foucault searched for principles, embedded in human existence, through which modernity could be countered, and found them in art's transactions with what cannot be managed or controlled. I have argued that he moved away from his existential and phenomenological base by embarking on careful historical studies of the social apparatuses that organize everyday existence in modern society, and by drawing attention to the connections between those apparatuses and the lives of the "infamous" – those without power, "normalcy" or respectability. He wrote his genealogies to serve the needs of these people, which were also, somewhat, his own. He departs from phenomonology, too, in his conviction that official knowledge, through which individual lives are partly shaped, is differentiated and made coherent by discursive rules and institutional conventions that research can recover, but which reflect or express nothing fundamental. Indeed, throughout his career, Foucault's work is enabled by his "transgressive" sense that "Being" is empty, that the deep and fundamental condition which seems to order our relations with the world, death, has no fixed meaning, is unknowable – and, therefore, provides no "depth" or final meaning to existence at all. This belief also allowed him to recognize that the promise of avoiding death, of staving off pain and sickness, of increasing production, have underpinned the most far-reaching forms of modern power. Nonetheless, as I have argued further, death's relation to life provides a ground for the seduction – and ineluctability – of the representational paradigm that Foucault wished to escape.

These may seem grand claims, suited to the kind of universal intellectual that Foucault hoped not to be. Perhaps we ought to concede that, despite everything, Foucault remained just such an intellectual. But the theses he formulated and re-formulated throughout his life do finally orient us towards local projects. After Foucault, the big, big terms – "being," "reason," "history," "humanity" and so on – can no longer easily thread our thoughts together. And when, having absorbed Foucault and his successor's work, we return to literature then one finds and examines a different literariness than that proposed by traditional literary studies. It helps form no sensibility, no set of appreciative and evaluative responses to culture, no individuals who may serve as exemplars to the young and who may be reproduced by them. It fails to cover the world with an aesthetic sheen of fundamentally insightful representations, or to project sublimities – which, in general, would seem to have been Lionel Trilling's objection to Dreiser in his famous essay "Reality in America." This is why Dreiser, for instance, continues to constitute a challenge to literary studies. As we have seen, Dreiser, mainly despite himself, represents and enacts the nihilism, the consumerism, the passivity and continual re-patternings of society that statist literary pedagogy had been established to control. Yet, the methods and orientations outlined in my brief analysis of Dreiser belong to current literary studies too. And, we can ask, in concluding: where, after Foucault, are they headed?

Most startlingly, given the power of the "intentional fallacy," signalled in Schiller's separation of Shakespeare the man from Shapespeare the works, the author comes back into focus. Biography is no longer utterly separable from textuality: the life is ordered by the work, just as the work is ordered by the life. Both share a condition in which what is scripted cannot be disentangled from what is not scripted as we have seen at three key moments of this study – in the analyzes of Raymond Roussel, of the contemporary performance artists and, finally, of Dreiser. There is no longer any need to accept professional literary criticism's hidden claim that its identity is based on its refusal to accept transactions between texts and lives as proper knowledge. Now we can admit that readers' interest in literature consists of interest in those relations too. Indeed, they help form texts' conditions of intelligibility – to the degree that such conditions exist. After Foucault (amongst others), it is impossible to remain satisfied with knowledge produced either by those techniques of "close reading" that rest on a series of arbitrary and professionally motivated assumptions about texts' autonomy and cultural value, or by those forms of political criticism that see texts as expressions of complex, abstracted social relations.

Leaving the weave of texts and authorial lives aside, the history of writing may now most rewardingly be treated within the history of various overlapping industries and technologies (literature, journalism, advertising and film, for example), each with its own distribution network, some of which transmit texts across generations in a sustained and organized manner. Within each technology, textual production is patterned by certain regularities, as are the displacements through which the "same" material is transposed from one technology into another. Different reading practices appear at different sites along the channels of distribution, and these

237

differences have a certain regularity and order too: one that is, in broad terms, connected to the power-flows within which everyday life is lived. The difficult question, however, asks, what makes texts worth reading? Criticism gains sufficient energy and legitimations to transmit texts across generations by producing convincing, or perhaps better, moving, answers to this question. As we have seen, the old answer: to make better people, will not do; nor will the quasi-religious one: to keep the dead alive; nor the traditional political ones: to help us read society more effectively, outside of ideological entanglement, or to maintain the utopian spirit. Foucault's work helps us to face this difficult question by insisting that one cannot always – or simply – historicize. After Foucault, literary history comes to mean not just an attention to past contexts or to the story of reception and circulation, but the connection of old books to the problematizations or "undecidabilities" in which they were both written and continue to be read. Many of these problems, as we have seen, have long histories. Today the texts that are most worth reading, encouraging others to read and most worth writing about are those that produce active engagement in these problems, a conscious sense of involvement in them – for, in this context, reflection and engagement are far from exclusive conditions. Dreiser's novel, for instance, demands engagement with a quite local issue, capital punishment; but the question of punishment extends into a problem with much greater, and more disturbing, reach and power – the question of who is to control the practices that produce deep subjectivity, how to manage the apparatuses through which individuals are, and might be, given the power to express and know themselves and to master social networks. In the novel, the question takes force through the intensified subjectivity that it produces in its readers, the fear, wonder, identification and relief with which we read about a man who murders and whom the state, in turn, will kill – a man subject to a social apparatus somewhat like that which exists today. Once the work of analysis is done, critics are called upon, first, to articulate and analyze these enfolded relations, of which their own passions form a part, and, more problematically, to begin to think about "re-forming" them. Yet because critics are not quite universal intellectuals, the "formations and problematizations" that intensify texts for them, must refer to the concerns of the academic humanities and *their* institutions, and in particular to the means by which effective criticism can circulate beyond and through the education system's internal and external borders. We can end by merely remarking that the work that follows Foucault's begins to require new forms of organization within the pedagogical humanities and, if at all possible, new relations to the outside world, as well as means of engaging the forms in which that world represents the academic humanities. This requirement, of course, may involve loss and struggle, as well as gain.

NOTES

INTRODUCTION

1 It is worth noting that until he was 24 Foucault was a paid-up member of the then Stalinist French Communist Party.

2 For further commentary on this see Donzelot 1979a, Pasquino 1978, and Rajchman 1985.

3 Foucault's name is introduced to the Anglo-American literary audience by Susan Sontag in her 1963 essay on Nathalie Sarraute. See Sontag 1966, 104.

4 See, for instance, Fekete 1978.

5 See Dreyfus and Rabinow (1983).

6 See Foucault 1984e for a development of this idea.

7 See Bourdieu and Passeron 1967, 162–211 and Eribon 1989, 151.

8 See Foucault 1988b, 153.

9 See Pocock 1975.

10 For a good discussion of the topic in general see Soper 1986.

11 For a wider discussion of Foucault's relation with Sartre see Poster 1984, 1–43.

12 The most influential document in the philosophic resistance to humanism remains Heidegger's *Letter on Humanism*, published in 1947 as a protest against the Sartrean reading of his early masterpiece *Being and Time*. See Megill 1985 for further discussion of Nietzsche's influence on European thought from Heidegger to Foucault.

13 See Derrida 1984a for a good account of *Dasein*.

14 See Foucault 1980a, 53.

15 The classic statement of this aspect of Heidegger's later thought is to be found in his essay "The Age of the World Picture."

1 MADNESS

1 For Hyppolite on humanism and historicism, see Roth 1988 "Part One."

2 Macherey 1986 gives a full description of these important revisions.

2 MEDICINE, DEATH, REALISM

1 *The Birth of the Clinic* was reissued in 1972. For this revised version, Foucault erased most of the "structuralist" language of the first edition. The English translation, which I have used in this chapter, is of the first edition.

2 See Michael Fried's account of Thomas Eakins' painting of an operation, *The Gross Clinic*, for the ways in which sadism (in the Freudian sense) and medical penetration can overlap (Fried 1987, 59ff.).

3 Canguilhem 1988, 57.

4 *The Times*, 5 March 1845, 23.

5 The hope for a time when, after a "life spent almost without sickness," death takes the form of "peaceful euthanasia" is actually expressed by one of Chadwick's inspectors. But he wholeheartedly endorses it.

6 The figure of the doctor, with which my readings are closely concerned, begins to shift markedly in a novel like Scott Fitzgerald's *Tender is the Night*, which is, amongst other things, a rewriting of *The Wings of the Dove*, and which no longer simply assumes the authority of medicine.

3 LITERATURE AND LITERARY THEORY

1 For "living eye" see Rousseau 1960, 474.

2 Some of my following commentary is based on Foucault's review essay of Philippe Sollers' *L'intermédiaire*, Marcelin Pleynet's *Paysage en deux* and Jean-Louis Baudry's *Les images* published in *Critique* under the title "Distance, aspect, origine." I have also used two discussions between Foucault, Sollers, Baudry, Pleynet, Claude Ollier, Jean-Paul Faye, Jean Thibaudeau and others, published in *Tel Quel*, one on prose, the other on poetry – see Foucault 1964d and 1964e.

4 KNOWLEDGE

1 To say that Foucault mounts a critique of the "modern" era is not to say that he is a post-modernist – that is a term he shied away from. For Foucault on post-modernity see Foucault 1983b.

2 Megill 1985 is the critic who sees the book as a parody – of Descartes' *Discourse on Method*.

3 This is the point of Kant's description of reason's "conflict with itself," a section of the First Critique to which Foucault turns in a series of veiled references in "The Empirical and the Transcendental" section of the "Man and his Doubles" chapter of *The Order of Things*. See Foucault 1970a, 318ff. and Kant 1961, 443ff.

4 Presumably the title was changed in translation because Ernest Gellner had already used it (and W. V. Quine had his *Word and Object*).

5 Heidegger's notion of *Subjektitat* (subjectness or subjectity) refers to the mode in which Being manifests itself in respect to what is as a subject. The ego is merely one form of subjectness.

6 Canguilhem 1988, 84.

5 GENEALOGY, AUTHORSHIP, POWER

1 See 1978a, 24.

2 The most widely available translation – placed at the back of the American edition of *The Archaeology of Knowledge* – is not at all reliable.

3 See Foucault 1980b, 184; and for a good description of Foucault's relation to GIP, Deleuze 1986b.

4 In "The Order of Discourse," Foucault notes that what he finds inspiring about Jean Hippolyte's work is its sense of the paralogic. Hippolyte, as Foucault puts it, "transformed the Hegelian theme of the completion of self-consciousness into one of repetitive interrogation" (1971a, 76). This, however, is to jump over Marx, who insisted that contradictions such as those Kant and Hegel formulated were, from the perspective of materialism, conflicts between different interests – and "interest" is a category which problematization theory ignores.

5 See Hoy 1986 for an excellent account of sociologists' various definitions of power.
6 It is impossible to offer anything like a complete list of the historical scholarship that engages with Foucault's research: let me just note two of the more general and accessible works in the most important areas: Michael Ignatieff's work on the penitentiary in Britain (Ignatieff 1978), Jeffrey Weekes on British sexuality (Weekes, 1986).
7 See Adorno 1984, 203.
8 Benhabib 1986, 197–236.
9 See Habermas 1987.
10 See Foucault 1971b. I offer a more detailed account of the history of literary pedagogy in chapter 8.

6 DISCIPLINE

1 This description of an analytics of power is based on Foucault 1983c.
2 The King's two bodies thesis has been most famously discussed in Kantorowicz 1959.
3 See Hobsbawm 1959, 13–29 and Henry Mayhew 1968, 1:2.
4 See Foucault 1980b, 78–108.
5 See Radzinowicz 1957–68, 2: 1–25.
6 In his previous work Foucault had not been much concerned with the body: his sense of its importance seems to have been stimulated by his rereading of Nietzsche under the influence of Deleuze's interpretation. In "Nietzsche, Genealogy, History" the body begins to exist as a "volume" which is both sensitive and inscribable. "The body is the inscribed surface of events (traced by language and dissolved by ideas), the locus of a dissociated Self (adopting the illusion of a substantial unity), and a volume in perpetual disintegration" (1977a, 148).
7 This shift has been quantified by more recent English studies: see Beattie 1986, 77–192.
8 This number had increased over the eighteenth century, particularly after the notorious Waltham Black Act (1722), though courts – and juries – often went out of their way to circumvent the death sentence.
9 See Evans 1982 for a full account of the development of prison architecture.

7 LIFE, SEXUALITY AND ETHICS

1 For Foucault's work on the use of anti-pedophile sentiment and legislation see 1988b, 271ff.

8 POST-FOUCAULDIAN CRITICISM

1 The kind of historiography that Hunter's work is directed against is represented at its best by Baldick (1983) and Mulhern (1979).
2 See for instance the chapter on education in Fraser 1984.
3 We should note that the Edgeworths' personal opinion of Rousseau as an individual is ambivalent, and that Rousseau himself believed pedagogy ought to be based in the home.
4 The debates on "liberal" versus "professional" (including teachers' training) education in Oxbridge from about the 1860s until about the First World War are also absent from Hunter's account. Consideration of this material would

make much more difficult his claim that English as it enters Oxbridge before Richards is a dead end, as well as his belief that "romantic criticism" is grafted onto the governmental apparatus in modern criticism.

5 Paul de Man repeats this remark with a slightly different stress: "It is imposs- ible to conceive of a phenomenal experience that would not be mimetic, as it is impossible to conceive of an aesthetic judgement that would not be dependent on imitation as a constitutive category, also and especially when the judgement, as is the case in Kant, is interiorized as the consciousness of a subject" (de Man 1986, 67).

6 This is to pass over the extraordinarily virulent history of attacks on non- representational, or "non-reflective" modes of thoughts in Western thought – attacks which from about the seventeenth century begin to demonize, in particu- lar, women and non-Europeans as being incapable of representational thought.

7 Amongst the best of such works I would mention Arac 1979, Goldberg 1983 and Bender 1987.

8 See Miller (1988) and Gallagher (1989).

9 This is not to say that Foucault alone lies behind Greenblatt's work which is also marked by a reading of modern ethnography and ethnographical theory.

10 It is worth noting that it is in the work of Marcel Mauss, in particular, influenced by Bronislaw Malinowski, that "exchange" becomes a crucial ana- lytic notion.

9 READING AFTER FOUCAULT

1 Boswell includes the article in his *Life of Johnson* (Boswell 1980, 288). The fullest modern account of the affair is to be found in Grant 1965.

2 See Blakiston 1923 for a transcription and discussion of the manuscript.

3 For a very good discussion of ghosts see Thomas 1973, 701–35 (my account owes much to it). For changes in processes for prosecution and trial in the eighteenth century see Beattie 1986; a useful introductory guide to Elizabethan justice is available in Weisser 1979. A post-structuralist approach to the ques- tion of Shakespeare's ghosts is to be found in Garber 1987.

4 See Fielding 1966, 410, for the most famous instance of his satirizing of ghosts.

5 See Locke 1975, 591–608.

6 Thus Barker argues that *Hamlet* is not marked by a psychological depth but by the doubling of a surface in which to "seem" and to "be" though distinct, are both open to the gaze, knowable. No area of essential and private opacity has yet been carved out. Hamlet, who alone in the play possesses an interior, has one merely in his refusal to submit to the available codes. He remains "gestural," empty, thus enigmatic. For Barker, only in Pepys's moment will the refusal of the pre-modern codes become something more – the modern self.

7 The relation between providential order and the loss of self through writing and action is discussed in much French theoretical writing of the period between the 1930s and 1950s. See Sartre's *Transcendence of the Ego*, as well as the first two essays in Blanchot 1981, and "Ludwig Binswanger and the Sublimation of Self" in de Man 1983.

8 For Irving, see Mazer 1986.

9 See Levine 1988 for an account of the popular Shakespeare, and Bate 1989 for an account of the radical Shakespeare.

10 See Foulkes 1986 for a fuller account of Shakespeare's Victorian reputation.

11 Quoted in Swanberg 1965, 119–20.

12 See, for instance, Bowlby 1985 and Michaels 1987, 3–28.

13 See Moers 1970, 199–201.

14 See Lepenies 1988, 146ff. for discussion of the relations between Wells and the Webbs. See Donaldson 1980 for material on Allen.
15 This focus on erotic desire also separates the novel from Taylorite management manuals which could not mention the use of sexuality as an administrative tool – or executive reward.

BIBLIOGRAPHY

PRIMARY SOURCES

Foucault, Michel. (1954a) *Maladie mentale et personnalité*, Paris: Presses Universitaires de France.
—(1954b) "Preface", in Ludwig Binswanger *Le rêve et l'existence*, trans. from German to French by Jacques Verdeaux, Paris: Desclée de Brouwer, 9–128.
—(1961) *Folie et déraison: Histoire de la folie à l'âge classique*, Paris: Plon.
—(1962a) "Introduction", *Rousseau juge de Jean-Jacques: Dialogues*, Paris: Librairie Armand Colin, vii-xxiv.
—(1962b) "Un si cruel savoir", *Critique* 182: 1159–60.
—(1963a) "Distance, aspect, origine", *Critique* 198: 931–45.
—(1963b) *Naissance de la clinique: une archéologie du régard medical*, Paris: Presses Universitaires de France.
—(1964a) "La folie, l'absence d'oeuvre", *La table ronde* 11–21.
—(1964b) "Le Mallarmé de J.-P. Richard", *Annales* 19, 5: 996–1004.
—(1964c) "La prose d'Actéon", *La Nouvelle Revue française* 135: 444–59.
—(1964d) "Débat sur le roman", *Tel Quel* 17: 12–54.
—(1964e) "Débat sur la poésie", *Tel Quel* 17: 69–82.
—(1965) *Madness and Civilization: A History of Insanity in the Age of Reason*, trans. Richard Howard, New York: Random House. (This is a translation of an abridged version of 1961 with some additional material.)
—(1966) *Les mots et les choses: une archéologie des sciences humaines*, Paris: Gallimard.
—(1969a) "Jean Hyppolite", *Revue de metaphysique et morale* 74: 131–5.
—(1969b) *L'Archéologie du savoir*, Paris: Gallimard.
—(1970) *The Order of Things: An Archaeology of the Human Sciences*, unidentified collective translation, London: Tavistock Publications.
—(1971a) *L'Ordre du discours*, Paris: Gallimard.
—(1971b) "A Conversation with Michel Foucault", *Partisan Review* 38: 192–201.
—(1972a) *Histoire de la folie à l'âge classique*, Paris: Gallimard (2nd revised edn of 1961a).
—(1972b) *The Archaeology of Knowledge and the Discourse on Language*, trans. A. M. Sheridan Smith, New York: Pantheon Books (first published in Paris, 1969).
—(1972c) "Médicine et la lutte de classes", *La Nef* 29, 67–73.
—(1973a) *The Birth of the Clinic: An Archaeology of Medical Perception*, trans. A. M. Sheridan Smith, London: Tavistock Publications (first published in Paris, 1963).
—(ed.) (1973b) *Moi, Pierre, ayant égorgé ma mère, ma soeur et mon frère*, Paris: Gallimard.
—(1974) "Michel Foucault on Attica", *Telos* 19: 154–61.

BIBLIOGRAPHY

—(1975a) "Entretien avec Michel Foucault", *Nouvelles littéraires* 2477 (March 17–23): 3.

—(1975b) *Surveiller et punir: Naissance de la prison*, Paris: Gallimard.

—(1976a) *Mental Illness and Psychology*, trans. Alan Sheridan, New York: Harper (translation of a revised version of 1954a, first published in French 1962).

—(1976b) *Histoire de la sexualité: La volonté de savoir*, Paris: Gallimard.

—(1977a) *Language, Counter-Memory, Practice: Selected Essays and Interviews by Michel Foucault*, ed. with intro. Donald F. Bouchard; trans. Donald F. Bouchard and Sherry Simon, Ithaca, New York: Cornell University Press.

—(1977b) *Discipline and Punish: The Birth of the Prison*, trans. Alan Sheridan, Harmondsworth: Penguin.

—(1977c) "Power and Sex: An Interview with Michel Foucault", trans. David Parent, *Telos* 32: 152–61.

—(1977d) "Les matins gris de la tolérance", *Le Monde* 9998: 24.

—(1977e) "Preface", in Gilles Deleuze and Felix Guattari, *Anti-Oedipus: Capitalism and Schizophrenia*, trans. Robert Hurley, Mark Seem and Helen Lane, New York: Viking.

—(1978a) "Politics and the Study of Discourse", *Ideology and Consciousness* 3: 7–26.

—(1978b) "Le grand colère des faits", in *Faut-il brûler les nouveaux philosophes?*, ed. Sylvia Bucasse and Denis Bourgeois, Paris: Nouvelles Éditions Oswald.

—(1979) "The Lives of Infamous Men", in *Michel Foucault: Power, Truth, Strategy*, ed. Meaghan Morris and Paul Patton; trans. Paul Foss and Meaghan Morris, Sydney: Feral Publications.

—(1980a) "Georges Canguilhem: Philosopher of Error", *Ideology and Consciousness* 7: 51–61.

—(1980b) *Power/Knowledge: Selected Interviews and Other Writings 1972–1977*, ed. Colin Gordon, Brighton: Harvester Press.

—(1980c) *The History of Sexuality, Volume 1: An Introduction*, trans. Robert Hurley, New York: Vintage Books.

—(1980d) "Introduction", in *Herculine Barbin: Being the Recently Discovered Memoirs of a Nineteenth-Century French Hermaphrodite*, trans. Richard McDougall, New York: Pantheon Books.

—(1982) *This is Not a Pipe. With Illustrations and Letters by René Magritte*, trans. and ed. James Harkness, Berkeley: University of California Press.

—(1983a) "On the Genealogy of Morals: An Overview of Work in Progress", in Hubert L. Dreyfus and Paul Rabinow *Michel Foucault: Beyond Structuralism and Hermeneutics Second Edition. With an Afterword by and an Interview with Michel Foucault*, Chicago: The University of Chicago Press.

—(1983b) "Structuralism and Post-Structuralism: An Interview with Michel Foucault", *Telos* 55: 195–211.

—(1983c) "The Subject and Power", in Hubert L. Dreyfus and Paul Rabinow *Michel Foucault: Beyond Structuralism and Hermeneutics*, Chicago: The University of Chicago Press.

—(1984a) "Le souci de la vérité (propos recueillis par François Ewald)", *Magazine littéraire* 207, May 1984, 18–24.

—(1984b) "Polemics, Politics, and Problemizations: an Interview with Michel Foucault", trans. Lydia Davis, in Paul Rabinow (ed.) *The Foucault Reader*, New York: Pantheon Books: 381–90.

—(1984c) "Space, Knowledge and Power", trans. Christian Hubert, in Paul Rabinow (ed.) *The Foucault Reader*, New York: Pantheon Books: 239–56.

—(1984d) "What is Enlightenment?", trans. Catherine Porter, in *The Foucault Reader*, ed. Paul Rabinow, New York: Pantheon Books: 32–50.

— (1984e) "Qu'appelle-t-on punir? Entretien avec Michel Foucault", *Revue de l'Université Bruxelles* 113: 35–46.

— (1984f) *Histoire de la sexualité: Le souci de soi*, Paris: Gallimard.

— (1985a) *The Use of Pleasure: The History of Sexuality, Volume Two*, trans. Robert Hurley, New York: Vintage Books.

— (1986a) "Dream, Imagination, Existence", trans. Forrest Williams and Jacob Needleman, *Review of Existential Psychology and Psychiatry* 19, 1: 29–78.

— (1986b) *Death and the Labyrinth: the World of Raymond Roussel*, trans. Charles Ruas, intro. John Ashbery, New York: Doubleday & Co.

— (1986c) "Kant on Enlightenment and Revolution", trans. Colin Gordon, *Economy and Society* 15/1: 88–96.

— (1986d) "Nietzsche, Freud, Marx", *Critical Texts* 3/2: 1–5.

— (1987a) "Maurice Blanchot: the Thought from Outside", in *Foucault/Blanchot*, trans. Brian Massumi, New York: Zone Books.

— (1987b) "Questions of Method: An Interview with Michel Foucault", in Kenneth Baynes, James Bohman and Thomas McCarthy (eds) *After Philosophy: End of Transformation?*, Cambridge, Mass.: The MIT Press.

— (1988a) "The Ethic of Care for the Self as a Practice of Freedom", trans. J. D. Gauthier, in *The Final Foucault*, Cambridge, Mass: MIT Press.

— (1988b) *Politics, Philosophy, Culture: Interviews and Other Writings 1977–1984*, ed. with intro. Lawrence D. Kritzman, London: Routledge.

— (1988c) *Technologies of the Self: A Seminar with Michel Foucault*, eds Luther H. Martin, Huck Gutman and Patrick H. Hutton, Amherst: University of Massachusetts Press.

— (1988d) "The Prose of Acteon", in Pierre Klossowski, *The Baphomet*, trans. Sophie Hawkes and Stephen Sartarelli, New York: The Eridanos Library.

— (1988e) *The Care of Self: The History of Sexuality, Volume 3*, trans. Robert Hurley, New York: Pantheon.

— (1989a) *Résumé des Cours: 1970–1982*, Paris: Julliard.

Literary Texts

Baudelaire, Charles. (1983) *Intimate Journals*, trans. Christopher Isherwood, San Francisco: City Lights Books.

Burton, Robert. (1932) *The Anatomy of Melancholy*, ed. Holbrook Jackson, London: J. M. Dent & Sons.

Dreiser, Theodore. (1981) *An American Tragedy*, New York: New American Library.

— (1983) *American Diaries, 1902–1926*, ed. Thomas P. Riggio, Philadelphia: University of Pennsylvania Press.

— (1985) *Sister Carrie*, ed. Neda M. Westlake, Harmondsworth: Penguin.

Eliot, George. (1965) *Middlemarch*, ed. with intro. W. J. Harvey, Harmondsworth: Penguin.

— (1967) *Daniel Deronda*, ed. with intro. Barbara Hardy, Harmondsworth: Penguin.

Fielding, Henry. (1966) *Tom Jones*, ed. R. P. C. Mutter, Harmondsworth: Penguin.

Flaubert, Gustave. (1965) *Madame Bovary*, ed. with substantially new trans. by Paul de Man, New York: Norton.

— (1971) *Madame Bovary*, ed. Claudine Gothot-Mersch, Paris: Garnier.

Holcroft, Thomas. (1978) *The Adventures of Hugh Trevor*, ed. with intro. Seamus Deane, Oxford: Oxford University Press: 289–90.

James, Henry. (1947a) *The Art of the Novel: Critical Prefaces*, intro. and ed. Richard P. Blackmur, London: Charles Scribner's Sons.

— (1947b) *The Notebooks of Henry James*, eds F. O. Matthiessen and Kenneth B. Murdock, New York: Oxford University Press.

—(1964) *The Complete Tales of Henry James*, 12 vols, London: Rupert Hart Davis.

—(1965) *The Wings of the Dove*, Harmondsworth: Penguin.

—(1987) *The Complete Notebooks of Henry James: The Authoritative and Definitive Edition*, eds Leon Edel and Lyall H. Powers, Oxford: Oxford University Press.

Lawrence, D. H. (1974) *Women in Love*, Harmondsworth: Penguin.

Montaigne, Michel de. (1958) *Essays*, trans. J. M. Cohen, Harmondsworth: Penguin.

Pope, Alexander. (1963) *The Poems of Alexander Pope: A One Volume Edition of the Twickenham Pope*, ed. John Butt, London: Methuen.

Rousseau, J.-J. (1960) *Julie ou la nouvelle Héloïse*, ed. René Pomeau, Paris: Garnier.

Roussel, Raymond. (1966) *Impressions of Africa*, trans. Lindy Foord and Rayner Heppenstall, London: John Calder.

Shakespeare, William. (1987) *Hamlet*, ed. G. R. Hibbard, Oxford: Oxford University Press.

SECONDARY SOURCES

Adorno, Theodor. (1984) *Aesthetic Theory*, trans. C. Lenhardt, ed. Gretel Adorno and Rolf Tiedemann, London: Routledge & Kegan Paul.

Anon. (1762) "Report", *Annual Register* 53: 142–46.

Arac, Jonathan. (1979) *Commissioned Spirits: The Shaping of Social Motion in Dickens, Carlyle, Melville, and Hawthorne*, New Brunswick N.J.: Rutgers University Press.

Armstrong, Nancy. (1987) *Desire and Domestic Fiction*, New York: Oxford University Press.

Arnold, David. (1988) "Touching the Body: Perspectives on the Indian Plague", in *Selected Subaltern Studies*, eds Ranajit Guha and Gayatri Chakravorty Spivak, New York: Oxford University Press, 391–426.

Baldick, Chris. (1983) *The Social Mission of England*, Cambridge: Cambridge University Press.

Barker, Francis. (1984) *The Tremulous Private Body: Essays on Subjection*, London and New York: Methuen.

Barthes, Roland. (1981) *Le grain de la voix: entretiens 1962–1980*, Paris: Seuil.

Bataille, Georges. (1985) *Visions of Excess: Selected Writings, 1927–1939*, ed. and intro. Allan Stoekl, trans. Allan Stoekl with Carl R. Lovitt and Donald M. Leslie, Jr, Minneapolis: University of Minnesota Press.

—(1988) *Inner Experience*, trans. and intro. Leslie Anne Boldt, Albany: State University of New York Press.

Bate, Jonathan. (1989) *Shakespearean Constitutions: Politics, Theatre, Criticism, 1730–1830*, Clarendon Press: Oxford.

Baudrillard, Jean. (1987) *Forget Foucault*, trans. Nicole Defresne, New York: Semiotext(e).

Beattie, J. M. (1986) *Crime and the Courts in England: 1660–1800*, Princeton: Princeton University Press.

Beer, Gillian. (1983) *Darwin's Plots: Evolutionary Narrative in Darwin, George Eliot and Nineteenth-century Fiction*, London: Routledge & Kegan Paul.

Belsey, Catherine. (1985) *The Subject of Tragedy: Identity and Difference in Renaissance Drama*, London and New York: Methuen.

Bender, John. (1987) *Imagining the Penitentiary: Fiction and the Architecture of Mind in Eighteenth-Century England*, Chicago: University of Chicago Press.

Benhabib, Seyla. (1986) *Critique, Norm, and Utopia*, New York and Oxford: Oxford University Press.

Binswanger, Ludwig. (1963) *Selected Papers of Ludwig Binswanger: Being in the World*, trans. and intro. Jacob Needleman, New York: Basic Books.

Blakiston, H. E. D. (1923) "Two More Medieval Ghost Stories", *English Historical Review* 38: 85–7.

Blanchot, Maurice. (1981) *The Gaze of Orpheus and Other Literary Essays*, trans. Lydia Davis, New York: Station Hill.

—(1983) *The Space of Literature*, trans. with intro., Ann Smock, Lincoln: University of Nebraska Press.

—(1987) "Michel Foucault as I Imagine Him", in *Foucault/Blanchot*, trans. Brian Massumi, New York: Zone Books: 61–105.

Blyth, A. Wynter. (1884) "The Disposal of the Dead", *Transactions of the Conference on Domestic Sanitation in Urban and Rural Diseases*, London: William Clowes & Sons: 262–73.

Boswell, James (1924) "The Journal of a Tour to the Hebrides", in *Johnson's Journey to the Western Islands of Scotland and Boswell's Journal of a Tour to the Hebrides with Samuel Johnson LL.D*, ed. R. W. Chapman, London: Oxford University Press: 151–443.

—(1980) *Life of Johnson*, ed. R. W. Chapman and J. D. Fleeman, intro. Pat Rogers, Oxford: Oxford University Press.

Bourdieu, Pierre and Passeron, Jean-Claude. (1967) "Sociology and Philosophy in France since 1945: Death and Resurrection of a Philosophy without a Subject", *Social Research* 34: 162–211.

Bowlby, Rachel. (1985) *Just Looking: Consumer Culture in Dreiser, Gissing, and Zola*, London: Routledge.

Braverman, Harry. (1974) *Labour and Monopoly Capital: the Degradation of Work in the Twentieth Century*, New York: The Monthly Review Press.

Bürger, Peter. (1984) *Theory of the Avant Garde*, trans. Michael Shaw, foreword Jochen Schulte-Sasse, Minneapolis: University of Minnesota Press.

Burke, Edmund. (1958) *A Philosophical Enquiry into the Origin of our Ideas of the Sublime and the Beautiful*, ed. with intro. J. T. Boulton, London: Routledge & Kegan Paul.

Caburnet, Bernard. (1968) *Langage, imaginations et monde chez Raymond Roussel*, Paris: Éditions Pierre Seghers.

Canguilhem, Georges. (1988) *Ideology and Rationality in the History of the Life Sciences*, trans. Arthur Goldhammer, Cambridge, Mass.: MIT Press.

Carlyle, Thomas. (1935) *On Heroes, Hero-Worship and the Heroic in History*, London: Oxford University Press.

Chadwick, Edwin. (1830) "Preventative Police", *London Review* 1: 253–307.

—(1965) *Report on the Sanitary Condition of the Labouring Population of Great Britain*, ed. with intro. M. W. Flinn. Edinburgh: Edinburgh University Press.

Checkland, S. G. and Checkland, E. O. A. (eds) (1974) *The Poor Law Report of 1834*, Harmondsworth: Penguin.

Chesterfield, Lord. (1984) *Letters to His Son and Others*, London: Dent.

Cocteau, Jean. (1957) *Opium: The Diary of a Cure*, trans. Margaret Crosland and Sinclair Road, London: Peter Owen.

Cohen, Stanley and Scull, Andrew (eds) (1983) *Social Control and the State: Historical and Comparative Essays*, Oxford: Basil Blackwell.

Cohen-Solal, Annie. (1988) *Sartre: A Life*, London: Heinemann.

Colquhoun, Patrick. (1796) *Treatise on the Police of the Metropolis*, London: C. Dilly.

Cousins, Mark and Hussain, Athar. (1984) *Michel Foucault*, London: Macmillan.

Cullen, M. J. (1975) *The Statistical Movement in Early Victorian Britain*, Brighton: Harvester Press.

Davis, Lennard J. (1983) *Factual Fictions: the Origins of the English Novel*, New York: Columbia University Press.

Deleuze, Gilles. (1986a) *Foucault*, Paris: Editions de Minuit.

—(1986b) "Foucault and the Prison: An interview with Gilles Deleuze, conducted by Paul Rabinow with Keith Gandal", *History of the Present*, 1–2 and 20–21.

De Man, Paul. (1983) *Blindness and Insight: Essays in the Rhetoric of Contemporary Criticism (New Edition)*, Minneapolis: University of Minnesota Press.

—(1986) *The Resistance to Theory*, Minneapolis: University of Minnesota Press.

Derrida, Jacques. (1978) *Writing and Difference*, trans. Alan Bass, Chicago: University of Chicago Press.

—(1982a) *Dissemination*, trans. Barbara Johnson, Chicago: University of Chicago Press.

—(1982b) "Sending: On Representation", *Social Research*, 49, 2: 294–327. This is an abridged translation of 1987a.

—(1982c) *Margins of Philosophy*, trans. Alan Bass, Chicago: University of Chicago Press.

—(1984a) "My Chances/*Mes Chances*: A Rendevous with some Epicurean Stereophonies", in Joseph H. Smith and William Kerrigan (eds) *Taking Chances: Derrida, Psychoanalysis and Literature*, Baltimore and London: Johns Hopkins University Press.

—(1987a) "Envoi", in *Psyché*, Paris: Galilée.

Dews, Peter. (1987) *Logics of Disintegration: Post-Structuralist Thought and the Claims of Critical Theory*, London: Verso.

Donaldson, Norman. (1980) "Introduction", in Grant Allen, *An African Millionaire*, New York: Dover Publications.

Donnelly, Michael. (1983) *Managing the Mind: A Study of Medical Psychology in Early Nineteenth-Century Britain*, London: Tavistock Publications.

Donzelot, Jacques. (1979a) "The Poverty of Political Culture", *Ideology and Consciousness* 5: 73–86.

—(1979b) *The Policing of Families*, New York: Random House.

Dowell, Richard W. (1983) "Introduction", in Theodore Dreiser, *An Amateur Labourer*, Philadelphia: University of Pennsylvania Press, xi-xlix.

Dreiser, Helen. (1951) *My Life with Dreiser*, Cleveland and New York: World Publishers.

Dreyfus, Hubert L. and Rabinow, Paul. (1983) *Michel Foucault: Beyond Structuralism and Hermeneutics Second Edition, With an Afterword by and an Interview with Michel Foucault*, Chicago: The University of Chicago Press.

Edgeworth, Maria and Edgeworth, Richard Lovell. (1974) *Practical Education*, 2 vols, New York and London: Garland Publishing.

Eisenstein, Sergei. (1969) "The Scenario of *An American Tragedy*", in Ivor Montague, *With Eisenstein in Hollywood*, New York: International Publishers.

Elliot, Gregory. (1987) *Althusser: the Detour of Theory*, London: Verso.

Eribon, Didier. (1989) *Michel Foucault (1926–1984)*, Paris: Flammarion.

Evans, Robin. (1982) *The Fabrication of Virtue: English Prison Architecture 1750–1840*, Cambridge: Cambridge University Press.

Fekete, John. (1978) *The Critical Twilight: Explorations in the Ideology of Anglo-American Literary Theory*, London: Routledge & Kegan Paul.

Felman, Shoshana. (1985) *Writing and Madness (Literature/Philosophy/Psychoanalysis)*, trans. by the author and Martha Noel Evans with the assistance of Brian Massumi, Ithaca, N.Y.: Cornell University Press.

Ferry, Luc and Renaut, Alain. (1990) *French Philosophy of the Sixties: An Essay on Antihumanism*, trans. Mary H. S. Cattani, Amherst: University of Massachusetts Press. First published in Paris 1985.

Foulkes, Richard. (1986) "Introduction", in Richard Foulkes (ed.) *Shakespeare and the Victorian Stage*, Cambridge: Cambridge University Press.

Fraser, Derek. (1984) *The Evolution of the British Welfare State*, London: Macmillan.

Fried, Michael. (1987) *Realism, Writing, Disfiguration: on Thomas Eakins and Stephen Crane*, Chicago and London: University of Chicago Press.

Gallagher, Catherine. (1989) "The Bio-Economics of *Our Mutual Friend*", in Michel Feher (ed.) *Fragments for the History of the Human Body*, 3 vols, Cambridge, Mass.: MIT Press: 3: 127–48.

Garber, Marjorie. (1987) *Shakespeare's Ghost Writers: Literature as Uncanny Causality*, London and New York: Methuen.

Goldberg, Jonathan. (1983) *James I and the Politics of Literature: Jonson, Shakespeare, Donne and their Contemporaries*, Baltimore: John Hopkins Press.

Grant, Douglas. (1965) *The Cock Lane Ghost*, London: Macmillan.

Greenblatt, Stephen. (1987) *Shakespearean Negotiations: The Circulation of Social Energy in Renaissance England*, Berkeley and Los Angeles: University of California Press.

Habermas, Jürgen. (1977) "A Review of Gadamer's *Truth and Method*", in Fred Dallymar and Thomas McCarthy (eds) *Understanding and Social Inquiry*, South Bend, Ind.: Notre Dame University Press.

—(1984) *The Theory of Communicative Action: Volume One, Reason and the Rationalization of Society*, trans. Thomas McCarthy, Boston: Beacon Press.

—(1986a) *Autonomy and Solidarity: Interviews*, ed. and intro. Peter Dews, London: Verso.

—(1986b) "Taking Aim at the Heart of the Present", in David Couzens Hoy (ed.) *Foucault: A Critical Reader*, Oxford: Basil Blackwell.

—(1987) "The Idea of the University", *New German Critique* 41, 3–22.

Hay, Douglas. (1975) "Property, Authority and the Criminal Law", in D. Hay, P. Linebaugh and E. P. Thompson (eds) *Albion's Fatal Tree: Crime and Society in Eighteenth-Century England*, London: Allen Lane.

Hay, D., Linebaugh, P. and Thompson, E. P. (eds) (1975) *Albion's Fatal Tree: Crime and Society in Eighteenth-Century England*, London: Allen Lane.

Hegel, G. W. F. (1977a) *Phenomenology of Spirit*, trans. A. V. Miller, Oxford: Oxford University Press.

—(1977b) *Faith and Knowledge*, trans. W. Cerf and H. S. Harris, Albany: State University of New York Press.

Heidegger, Martin. (1962). *Being and Time*, trans. John Macquarrie and Edward Robinson, Oxford: Basil Blackwell.

—(1977) "The Age of the World Picture", in *The Question Concerning Technology and Other Essays*, trans. and intro. William Lovitt, New York: Harper & Row.

—(1982) *Nietzsche Vol. IV: Nihilism*, trans. Frank A. Capuzzi; ed. David Farrel Knell, San Francisco: Harper & Row.

Herder, J. G. (1966) "Essay on the Original of Language", in Jean-Jacques Rousseau and Johann Gottfried Herder, *Two Essays on the Origin of Language*, trans. John H. Moran and Alexander Gode, Chicago: University of Chicago Press.

Hobsbawm, E. J. (1959) *Primitive Rebels*, Manchester: Manchester University Press.

Holland, P. H. (1873) "Burial or Cremation?", *The Contemporary Review* 23: 476–84.

Horkheimer, Max and Adorno, Theodor W. (1972) *Dialectic of Enlightenment*, trans. John Cumming, New York; Seabury Press.

Hoy, David Couzens. (1986) "Power, Repression, Progress: Foucault, Lukes and the Frankfurt School", in David Couzens Hoy (ed.) *Foucault: A Critical Reader*, Oxford: Basil Blackwell.

Hunter, Ian (1988). *Culture and Government: The Emergence of Literary Education*, London: Macmillan.

Ignatieff, Michael. (1978) *A Just Measure of Pain: the Penitentiary in the Industrial Revolution, 1750–1850*, London: Macmillan.

Ingleby, David. (1983) "Mental Health and Social Order", in Cohen and Scull (1983): 141–90.

Janet, Pierre. (1987) "The Psychological Characteristics of Ecstasy", in Alastair Brotchie, Malcolm Green and Antony Melville (eds) *Raymond Roussel: Life, Death and Works Essays and Stories by Various Hands*, London: Atlas Press.

Kant, Immanuel. (1961) *Critique of Pure Reason*, trans. Norman Kemp Smith, London: Macmillan.

— (1983) "An Answer to the Question: What is Enlightenment?", in *Perpetual Peace and Other Essays*, trans. Ted Humphrey, Indianapolis: Hackett Publishing Company.

Kantorowicz, Ernst. (1959) *The King's Two Bodies: A Study in Mediaeval Political Theology*, Princeton, N.J.: Princeton University Press.

Kaprow, Allan. (1983) "The Real Experiment", *Artforum* 22/4: 37–43.

Krauss, Rosalind E. (1985) *The Originality of the Avant-Garde and other Modernist Myths*, Cambridge, Mass. and London: MIT Press.

Leavis, F. R. (1972) *Nor Shall My Sword: Discourses on Pluralism, Compassion and Social Hope*, London: Chatto & Windus.

Léonard, Jacques. (1980) "L'Historien et le philosophe: A propos de *Surveiller et punir: naissance de la prison*", in Michelle Perrot (ed.) *L'Impossible Prison: recherches sur le système pénitentiaire au XIX^esiècle*, Paris: Éditions du Seuil.

Lepenies, Wolf. (1988) *Between Literature and Science: the Rise of Sociology*, trans. R. J. Hollingdale, Cambridge: Cambridge University Press.

Lewis, R. A. (1952) *Edwin Chadwick and the Public Health Movement: 1832–1854*, London: Longmans.

Levine, Lawrence W. (1988) *Highbrow/Lowbrow: the Emergence of Cultural Hierarchy in America*, Cambridge, Mass.: Harvard University Press.

Linebaugh, Peter. (1975) "The Tyburn Plot against the Surgeons", in Douglas Hay, Peter Linebaugh and E. P. Thompson (eds) *Albion's Fatal Tree: Crime and Society in Eighteenth-Century England*, London: Allen Lane: 65–118.

Locke, J. (1975) *An Essay Concerning Human Understanding*, ed. Peter H. Nidditch, Oxford: Clarendon Press.

Macherey, Pierre. (1986) "Aux sources de l'*Histoire de la folie*: une rectification et ses limites", *Critique* 42: 753–75.

McEvilley, Thomas. (1983) "Diogenes of Sinope (*c.* 410-*c.* 320 BC): Selected Performance Pieces", *Artforum* 31, 7: 412–24.

Mathiessen, F. O. (1951) *Theodore Dreiser*, New York: Sloane.

Mayhew, Henry. (1968) *London Labour and the London Poor*, intro. John D. Rosenberg, 4 vols, New York: Grove Press.

Mazer, Cary M. (1986) "The Criminal as Actor: H. B. Irving as Criminologist and Shakespearean", in *Shakespeare and the Victorian Stage*, ed. Richard Foulkes, Cambridge: Cambridge University Press.

Megill, Allan. (1985) *Prophets of Extremity: Nietzsche, Heidegger, Foucault, Derrida*, Los Angeles: University of California Press.

Michaels, Walter Benn. (1987) *The Gold Standard and the Logic of Naturalism: American Literature at the Turn of the Century*, Berkeley: University of California Press.

Miller, D. A. (1988) *The Novel and the Police*, Berkeley: University of California Press.

Moers, Ellen. (1970) *Two Dreisers: the Man and the Novelist*, London: Thames & Hudson.

Mulhern, Francis. (1979) *The Moment of Scrutiny*, London: New Left Books.

Pasquino, Pasquale. (1978) "Theatrum Politicum: The Genealogy of Capital: Police and the State of Prosperity", *Ideology and Consciousness* 4: 41–54.

Perkin, Harold. (1972) *Origins of Modern English Society*, London: Routledge & Kegan Paul.

Philips, David. (1983) " 'A Just Measure of Crime, Authority, Hunters and Blue Locusts': the Revisionist Social History of Crime and the Law in Britain, 1780–1850", in Cohen and Scull (1983).

Plato. (1973) *Phaedrus and the Seventh and Eighth Letters*, trans. with intro. Walter Hamilton: Harmondsworth: Penguin.

Pocock, J. G. A. (1975) *The Machiavellian Moment: Florentine Political Thought and the Atlantic Republic Tradition*, Princeton N.J.: University of Princeton Press.

Pope, Maurice, (1975) *The Story of Decipherment: from Egyptian Hieroglyphic to Linear B*, London: Thames & Hudson.

Poster, Mark. (1984) *Foucault, Marxism and History: Mode of Production versus Mode of Information*, Oxford: Polity Press.

Prendergast, Christopher. (1986) *The Order of Mimesis: Balzac, Stendhal, Nerval, Flaubert*, Cambridge: Cambridge University Press.

Proust, Marcel. (1988) *Against Sainte-Beuve and Other Essays*, trans. John Sturrock, Harmondsworth: Penguin.

Radzinowicz, Leon. (1957–1968) *A History of English Criminal Law*, 4 vols, London: Stevens & Sons.

Rajchman, John. (1985) *Michel Foucault: the Freedom of Philosophy*, New York: Columbia University Press.

Richard, Jean-Pierre. (1961) *L'Univers imaginaire de Mallarmé*, Paris: Seuil.

Robbe-Grillet, Alain (1965) *Snapshots and Towards a New Novel*, trans. Barbara Wright, London: Calder & Boyars.

Roth, Michael S. (1988) *Knowing and History: Appropriations of Hegel in Twentieth-Century France*, Ithaca and London: Cornell University Press.

Rousseau, J.-J. (1973) *The Social Contract and the Discourses*, trans. G. D. H. Cole; revised and agumented by J. H. Brumfitt and John C. Hall, London: Dent.

Said, Edward. (1984) "Michel Foucault, 1927–1984", *Raritan: A Quarterly Review* (4/2): 1–11.

Schiller, Friedrich von. (1966) "Naive and Sentimental Poetry", in *Naive and Sentimental Poetry and On the Sublime*, trans. and intro. Julius A. Elias, New York: Frederick Ungar.

Sciascia, Leonardo. (1987) "Acts Relative to the Death of Raymond Roussel", *Atlas Anthology* 4: 124–9.

Scull, Andrew. (1979) *Museums of Madness: The Social Organization of Insanity in Nineteenth-Century England*, London: Allen Lane.

Sheridan, Alan. (1980) *Michel Foucault: The Will to Truth*, New York: Tavistock Publications.

Simon, Sir John. (1890) *English Sanitary Institutions: Reviewed in their Course of Development in Some of their Political and Social Relations*, London: Cassell & Co.

Skinner, Quentin. (1978) *The Foundations of Modern Political Thought*, 2 vols, Cambridge: Cambridge University Press.

Smith, Roger (1981) *Trial by Medicine: Insanity and Responsibility in Victorian Trials*, Edinburgh: Edinburgh University Press.

Smith, Southwood Thomas. (1824) "The Uses of the Dead to the Living", *The Westminster Review* 2: 59–97.

—(1825) "Contagion and Sanitary Laws: Part II", *The Westminster Review* 3: 134–67.

—(1829) "Anatomy", *The Westminster Review* 10: 116–32.

Sontag, Susan. (1966) "Nathalie Sarraute and the Novel", in *Against Interpretation*, London: Eyre & Spottiswood.

Soper, Kate. (1986) *Humanism and Anti-Humanism*, London: Hutchinson.

Spivak, Gayatri Chakravorty. (1988) "Can the Subaltern Speak?", in Cary Nelson and Lawrence Grossberg (eds) *Marxism and the Interpretation of Culture*, Urbana, Ill.: University of Illinois Press: 271–313.

Starobinski, Jean. (1961) *L'Oeil Vivant: Essais sur Corneille, Racine, Rousseau, Stendhal*, Paris: Gallimard.

—(1971) *Jean-Jacques Rousseau: La Transparence et l'Obstacle*, revised edn, 1st edn 1957, Paris: Gallimard.

Steegmuller, Francis. (1963) *Apollinaire: Poet among Painters*, Harmondsworth, Penguin.

Swanberg, W. A. (1965) *Dreiser*, New York: Charles Scribner's Sons.

Taylor, Charles (1985) "Foucault on Freedom and Truth", in *Philosophy and the Human Sciences: Philosophical Papers 2*, Cambridge: Cambridge University Press: 152–84.

Thomas, Keith. (1973) *Religion and the Decline of Magic: Studies in Popular Beliefs in Sixteenth-and Seventeenth-Century England*, Harmondsworth: Penguin.

Thompson, Sir Henry. (1873) "The Treatment of the Body After Death", *The Contemporary Review* 23: 319–28.

Tucker, Marcia. (1986) *Choices: Making an Art of Everyday Life*, New York: New Museum of Contemporary Art.

Weekes, Jeffrey. (1986) *Sexuality*, London: Methuen.

Weisser, Michael, R. (1979) *Crime and Punishment in Early Modern Europe*, Brighton: Harvester Press.

Wilde, Oscar. (1922) "Pen, Pencil, and Poison", in Robert Ross (ed.) *The Complete Works of Oscar Wilde*, 4 vols, New York: Bigelow, Brown & Co: 4: 61–99.

Wohl, Anthony S. (1983) *Endangered Lives: Public Health in Victorian Britain*, London: Methuen.

INDEX

254